DISCARDED

THE SECOND PAYCHECK
A Socioeconomic Analysis of Earnings

THE SECOND PAYCHECK
A Socioeconomic Analysis
of Earnings

Alice Nakamura
University of Alberta
Edmonton, Alberta
Canada

Masao Nakamura
University of Alberta
Edmonton, Alberta
Canada

1985

ACADEMIC PRESS, INC.
(Harcourt Brace Jovanovich, Publishers)
Orlando San Diego New York London
Toronto Montreal Sydney Tokyo

COPYRIGHT © 1985, BY ACADEMIC PRESS, INC.
ALL RIGHTS RESERVED.
NO PART OF THIS PUBLICATION MAY BE REPRODUCED OR
TRANSMITTED IN ANY FORM OR BY ANY MEANS, ELECTRONIC
OR MECHANICAL, INCLUDING PHOTOCOPY, RECORDING, OR
ANY INFORMATION STORAGE AND RETRIEVAL SYSTEM, WITHOUT
PERMISSION IN WRITING FROM THE PUBLISHER.

ACADEMIC PRESS, INC.
Orlando, Florida 32887

United Kingdom Edition published by
ACADEMIC PRESS INC. (LONDON) LTD.
24-28 Oval Road, London NW1 7DX

LIBRARY OF CONGRESS CATALOGING IN PUBLICATION DATA

Nakamura, Alice.
  The second paycheck.

  (Studies in labor economics)
  Bibliography: p.
  Includes index.
  1. Wives—Employment—United States. 2. Women—
Employment—United States. 3. Wages—Women—United
States. 4. Wages—United States. I. Nakamura,
Masao, Ph. D. II. Title. III. Series.
HD6095.N15 1985   331.4'3'0973   84-24231
ISBN 0-12-513820-2 (alk. paper)

PRINTED IN THE UNITED STATES OF AMERICA

85 86 87 88   9 8 7 6 5 4 3 2 1

To our parents
Fumi and Taro Nakamura, Geil and Guy Orcutt,
and our children, Emi and Ken

CONTENTS

Foreword by James J. Heckman		*xi*
Preface		*xiii*

1.	**Introduction**		1
	1.1	Economists and Working Women	2
	1.2	Our Behavioral Focus	4
	1.3	Viewing the Work Behavior of Married Women in a Broader Context	5
	1.4	Our Econometric Approach	6
	1.5	A Microanalytic Simulation Approach to Behavioral Research and Forecasting	8
	1.6	An Overview of the Chapters of This Book	10
		Footnotes to Chapter 1	11
2.	**Methodology and Data**		
	2.1	An Inertia Model of Work Behavior	14
	2.2	The Inertia Model *versus* Traditional and Evolutionary Schools of Thought	17
	2.3	A Formal Statement of the Inertia Model and Estimation of This Model	24
	2.4	Variable Definitions	28
	2.5	Biases, Biases, Biases	30
	2.6	Standard Errors and Significance Tests	40
	2.7	Our Data Base, and the Characteristics of the Women and Men Whose Data Have Been Used in This Study	42
		Footnotes to Chapter 2	59
		Addendum to Chapter 2. A Standard Model and a First Difference Version of This Model	69
		Footnotes to Addendum	81

3. Estimation Results for Our Inertia Model   83

    3.1   Hypothetical Women and the Calculation of Their Probabilities
           of Work, Wage Rates, and Hours of Work   88
    3.2   Marital Status Variables   91
    3.3   Age   101
    3.4   Race   115
    3.5   Education   124
    3.6   Special Circumstances Affecting Young Women   133
    3.7   Child Status Variables   141
    3.8   Other Income Variables   152
    3.9   Macroeconomic Variables   158
    3.10 Lagged Hours of Work and Wage Rate Variables   164
    3.11 Selection Bias   173
    3.12 Current Wage Rate   180
    Footnotes To Chapter 3   190

4. Comparisons of Our Inertia Model with Various Simpler Models   197

    4.1   How Are Our Empirical Results Affected by the Incorporation
           of Information Concerning Work Behavior in the Previous Year?   199
    4.2   Simulation Comparisons for Our Standard, Dummy, Split,
           and Inertia Models   210
    4.3   Sensitivity of Results to Inclusion of Lagged Dependent Variable
           in Hours Equation, Correction for Selection Bias, and Log-Linear
           Specification of the Wage Equation   224
           4.3.1. Dummy for married in previous year   225
           4.3.2. Age   229
           4.3.3. Race   234
           4.3.4. Education   237
           4.3.5. Child status variables   237
           4.3.6. Other income variables   243
           4.3.7. Macroeconomic variables   243
    4.4   Simulation Comparisons of Inertia Model With Models A, B, and C   244
    4.5   How Well Can Our Alternative Models Capture the Impacts of Key
           Explanatory Variables?   253
    4.6   Out-of Sample Simulation Results   269
    4.7   Sensitivity of Our Simulation Results to Our Treatment
           of Extreme Wage Estimates   272
    Footnotes to Chapter 4   274

5. Previous Work Experience   278

    Footnotes to Chapter 5   291

6. Sensitivity of Our Simulation Results for Wives to Changes in Their Circumstances   294

    Footnotes to Chapter 6   312

Contents ix

7. Unemployment 313

    7.1   Generalizing a Heckman-Type Model of Work Behavior to Include Unemployment 315
    7.2   The Data Base for Our Analysis of Unemployment 321
    7.3   Determinants of the Probability and Duration of Unemployment 337
    Footnotes to Chapter 7 358

8. Conclusions 360

    8.1   Behavioral Results 360
    8.2   Modeling Contributions 361
    8.3   Inference 364
    8.4   A Conjecture Loosely Related to Our Behavioral Results 368
    8.5   Implications for Further Research 374
    8.6   Implications for Further Data Collection 377
    Footnotes to Chapter 8 379

Appendix A.   Year by Year Average Simulation Results for the Standard, Dummy, Split, and Inertia Models 382

Appendix B.   Distributional Comparisons for Our Simulation Results for the Standard, Dummy, Split, and Inertia Models 396

Appendix C.   Distributional Comparisons for Our Simulation Results for the Inertia Model and Models A, B, and C 418

Appendix D.   Actual and Simulated Distributions for Years of Work Out of 7 and Individual Income Cumulated Over 7 Years for Various Partitions of Our Simulation Population 440

Appendix E.   Out-of-Sample Simulation Results for All Models 473

Appendix F.   Simulation Populations for Models with Log-Linear Wage Equations, and Results Using $20 Wage Cutoff 477

References 489
Author Index 497
Subject Index 499

FOREWORD

The Second Paycheck by Alice and Masao Nakamura is a gold mine of empirical evidence on the dynamic labor supply behavior of men and women. It is the most comprehensive study of this topic. The book presents a variety of new findings that are bound to influence and stimulate further research on the topic.

The major conclusion of this work is that dynamic models of labor supply are required to understand labor supply. Among the major findings of this book are that (a) properly specified dynamic labor supply equations for men and women are very similar (so that observed sex differences in cross section behavior can be attributed to the estimation of misspecified dynamic models), (b) children have little impact on the dynamic labor supply of men and women, (c) changes in marital status strongly affect female labor supply, (d) in a dynamic framework black women are less likely to work than white women (controlling for previous work), (e) sample selection bias is important in estimating labor supply functions for men and women, and (f) only recent labor market history is important in forecasting current labor market activity. Their finding that labor force attachment behavior differs greatly between career women and those who enter the work force to smooth family income, suggests that static approaches to the estimation of female labor supply equations overlook an essential feature of the female labor supply story. Successful prediction models must now account for such heterogeneity in behavior.

This book demonstrates the value of longitudinal data. Without such data it would not have been possible to uncover the dynamic empirical relationships presented in this book. Because only recent labor market history matters in determining current labor supply, the authors demonstrate that short panels (with only two waves) will suffice to estimate well-specified dynamic models of labor supply. Thus, from this work it appears that it is not necessary to maintain long panel studies to recover the empirically relevant components of labor force dynamics.

This book advocates and implements a novel approach to model verification. The approach pursued in many recent studies of labor supply has been to arrive at final, empirical specifications for a single demographic group by means of a battery of "t" and "F" tests on the coefficients of candidate variables. The problem of pretest bias is conveniently ignored. Only rarely as in the work of Mincer (1962) and Cain (1966) do analysts ask how well fitted micro relationships explain other aspects of labor supply such as the aggregate time series movement. Focusing on one demographic group in isolation, these studies present a bewildering array of findings that have thus far eluded synthesis.

This book does not adopt the conventional "t" ratio methodology. The authors estimate the same models for a variety of age, marital status, and sex groups and look for commonalities in findings across groups. They look for consistency in the impact of explanatory variables on different dimensions of labor supply. Models are simulated both within samples and out of samples. The final models that are presented to the reader survive all of these simulation, consistency, and comparability checks. The simulation format has the additional feature of spelling out the implications of complex models that are not obvious from reported coefficient estimates. The rigorous body of tests proposed and implemented by the authors of this book is much more convincing than the usual procedure followed in labor supply studies and sets a new, high standard that will be followed by all serious scholars of the subject.

The book departs from a more recent "structural" tradition in labor economics that formulates and estimates very explicitly derived theoretical models of labor supply. That work has proved successful in the analysis of cross section labor supply, but it is important to note that second generation structural models were built on an earlier generation of more eclectic, less structured, analysis by Mincer (1962), Cain (1966), Bowen and Finegan (1969), and others.

This book is frankly eclectic in its use of theory. It is used as a guide for inclusion of variables into models but not as a sharp source of explicitly parameterized hypotheses. Given the lack of basic knowledge about empirical regularities of labor force dynamics, the approach taken by the authors appears the most scientifically promising one. No doubt this book will spawn its own second generation of more structured dynamic models. In the future no serious scholar can build formal dynamic models of labor supply that neglect the empirical regularities presented in this book.

JAMES J. HECKMAN
UNIVERSITY OF CHICAGO
AND YALE UNIVERSITY

PREFACE

Economists have drawn a picture of the work behavior of married women that is at odds with the "new woman" featured in recent advertisements and women's magazines: the career woman who is also a wife and mother. According to most of the models economists have proposed, the labor supply of married women is sharply responsive to child status and the incomes of their husbands. According to these models, working women who have a new baby are likely to quit work or to drastically reduce their hours of work. Women whose husbands are promoted are also more likely to quit or to work less. Surely it would be unsettling to employers investing in training women for important or highly specialized jobs to think that even fulltime, apparently committed women workers might quit at any time because of becoming pregnant or because of increases in the incomes of their husbands. Fertility behavior is also difficult to forecast. If the work behavior of women is highly responsive to child status, forecasters will not be able to make good predictions of the work behavior of women unless they can also accurately forecast the number and timing of their children.

Another conclusion that emerges from the labor economics literature is that married women who work tend to increase their hours of work in response to a wage increase, while men tend to show no response or to decrease their hours of work if they are paid more per hour. If this is true, then raising female wages at the expense of male wages would lead everyone to work more!

In this book we reexamine these and other conclusions that economists have drawn about the employment behavior, wage rates, hours of work, earnings, and unemployment behavior of married women. We broaden the usual scope of investigation to include comparative results on all of these aspects of work behavior for unmarried women and men. We examine some of the basic econometric and statistical problems associated with research on the work behavior of individuals, including the issue of selection bias, heterogeneity, and the use of panel data. Since this examination is verbal in nature, econometrically unsophisticated readers should be able to gain an intuitive understanding of the nature of these problems. Also, in addition to the usual tables of coefficient estimates, our main results are presented in easy-to-understand tables of distributions of years of work and earnings over periods of years for various types of individuals, and in tables of predictions of the probabilities of work, annual hours of work and wage rates for women of various types.

The work behavior of women is of general interest because it represents one aspect of a major social revolution, affecting everything from how children are raised to consumer buying behavior. It is of interest to those concerned with forecasting the size of the labor force and unemployment rates because historically women have been the most volatile segment of the labor force. It is also of interest to those concerned with income distribution and poverty problems. For example, women who have not worked while married are less likely to work if they become divorced or widowed, and will tend to earn substantially less if they do work, than women who have combined work and marriage. Thus these women and their children will be more likely to be in poverty, and more likely to need long-term public assistance, if they become divorced or widowed. The accumulation of future benefits under the Social Security and other old age security programs also results primarily from employment over the prime ages, when most women are married. The research reported in this book has led to the development of a new labor force module for a microanalytic simulation model of the U.S. household sector. This model will be used to examine the effects of various possible changes in the Social Security program on the income situation of older Americans.

This book is for labor economists, students of labor economics, and those from all backgrounds who are interested in understanding or forecasting the employment and earnings behavior of women. It is also for economists and sociologists concerned with problems of heterogeneity in modeling individual behavior and for those interested in the basic econometric issues of bias and inference in a micro data setting. Some of the results in this book may be of special interest to researchers and forecasters residing outside the United States. Most of the more recent models of individual work behavior that have appeared in the economics literature require panel data. Unfortunately, the United States is one of the few countries in the world where good quality panel data exist. The models presented in this book can be estimated with data that can be collected in a cross-sectional survey such as a population census. In order to accommodate the diversity of backgrounds of potential readers, technical material and material concerned with issues of model selection have been concentrated in portions of the book that can be skipped, if desired, without loss of continuity. Nevertheless, some background in labor economics and econometrics will aid a reader in understanding the material in this book more fully.

Our intellectual debt to James Heckman is evident throughout this book. Our work has also been influenced by discussions over the years with Guy Orcutt on inference and on his work with microanalytic simulation models. We benefitted from extensive written comments on an earlier version of this manuscript from Charles Beach, Steven Caldwell, Claude Felteau, F. Thomas Juster, Mark Killingsworth, Shmuel Sharir, Hiroki Tsurumi, and Arnold Zellner. Helpful comments were also received from Marianne Ferber, Morley Gunderson, and John Ham.

This work has been in part supported by the University of Alberta and also in part funded by Grant Number 61A-8001, "The Analysis of Retirement Security Issues

Using Simulation Models," from the U.S. Department of Health and Human Services to the Survey Research Center, Institute for Social Research, The University of Michigan. Finally, we are grateful to Carolyn Lauder who struggled with our word processing system to produce the original manuscript and our many revisions of it. Portions of the book were also typed by Elaine Sykes. All remaining errors, omissions, and misinterpretations are, of course, our responsibility.

CHAPTER 1

INTRODUCTION

Discussions of the work behavior of married women are often fraught with controversy, innuendo, and allusions to the biological and efficiency origins of women as homemakers and men as breadwinners, as well as concern about the welfare of children and families. For instance, Victor Fuchs (1983, p. 158) writes:

> It appears that children are central to the question of ... inequality in the labor market ... [To] the extent that women become less interested in bearing children or less concerned about their welfare after birth, the future of the family and of society looks bleak ...

And Simone de Beavoir writes in her manifesto of the liberated woman, The Second Sex, that "The advantage man enjoys ... is that his vocation as a human being in no way runs counter to his destiny as a male." (p. 641) She goes on to argue:

> The independent woman ... does not want to feel that her husband is deprived of advantages he would have obtained if he had married a "true woman" .... Thus the independent woman of today is torn between her professional interests and the problems of her sexual life. (pp. 653-656)

Even the terminology associated with this topic is filled with social meaning. For instance, economists routinely classify wives as part of the secondary work force, regardless of variations among individual wives in work experience or job commitment. Furthermore, politicians and others often raise the issue of secondary family workers (meaning wives) in discussions of unemployment insurance regulations and of the meaning of current unemployment levels. Questions about the extent to which families with one or more unemployed members can rely on other sources of nonlabor income or on accumulated equity in owned housing could also be raised in such discussions. But only the issue of working wives is usually mentioned.

Despite the social and personal trauma as well as the institutional and other barriers to be overcome, the representation of U.S. wives in the labor force has increased dramatically since the early years of this century. In 1900 only 5.6 percent of married women in the United States participated in the labor force. By 1980, this figure had climbed to 51.0 percent, and all indications are that it is still climbing.[1] This change has affected everything from how children are raised to markets for insurance policies and has been accompanied by growing special interest pressure for legislative and legal changes that would create more favorable labor market conditions for women. Young women have been flooding into previously male-dominated training programs in areas ranging from medicine to business administration. It is clear why housewives, educational leaders, executives for financial institutions, marketing experts, union leaders, politicians and government policy makers are interested in these dramatic changes. But why have economists been so interested of late in these changes? One could easily point out a dozen important economic questions -- from a social or political perspective -- in which economists have little or no interest, at least as evidenced by publications in the major academic journals of the profession.

In this introduction we briefly consider several reasons why the labor force behavior of married women has become an important topic in the mainstream of the economics literature. We indicate the scope of our analysis. We next summarize some of the key behavioral questions that we address in this study. We consider the importance of embedding our analysis of the work behavior of married women in the larger context of the work behavior of unmarried and married women, and of men as well. We consider how our work fits into efforts to understand and forecast aggregate and distributional aspects of the work behavior of women. Finally we conclude this introductory chapter with an overview of the chapters in this book.

1.1. Economists and Working Women

James P. Smith (1980, p. ix) writes in the Preface to his book titled <u>Female Labor Supply: Theory and Estimation</u>:

> Labor economics has undergone (at least) two revolutions in the last two decades. First, there was the explicit recognition that human skills are both malleable and durable. This led to much work

1   Introduction

on 'investments in human capital.' Second, labor
economists discovered women!

The social relevance of this topic area has not hindered its
growth. It is easier, for instance, to raise research funds
for socially relevant topics. An essential element for a topic
to attract substantial interest in mainstream economics
journals, however, is that it must present interesting
confirmations of or challenges to as well as yield
opportunities to extend accepted economic theory. It is an
additional plus if a topic area lends itself to the practice
and development of innovative and intellectually challenging
mathematical modeling and econometric skills.

Gary Becker, Jacob Mincer and Theodore Schultz deserve
much of the credit for having established the modern links
between the topic of the labor force behavior of individuals,
including married women, and received economic theory.
Theodore Schultz and Becker developed the analytical concept
of human capital. Becker also introduced and popularized the
concepts of consumption time and the household production
function. Mincer depicted married women as having both market
and home wage rates, thus encouraging innovative applications
of the marginal calculus of neoclassical price theory. He
called attention to the special circumstances of married women
which may facilitate the measurement of income and
substitution effects. Mincer also applied Milton Friedman's
concept of permanent and transitory income effects on
consumption to the labor supply decisions of so-called
secondary earners in a family, with wives being the main
example.[2]

Following these seminal contributions by Becker, Mincer,
and Theodore Schultz, a rich array of issues that fall in the
interface between model specification and econometric
methodology have come to prominence in the literature. For
instance, Glen Cain, T. Paul Schultz and others suggested that
many of the explanatory variables being treated as exogenous
in studies of the work behavior of women should really be
treated as endogenous.[3] H. Gregg Lewis (1969), Harvey Rosen
(1976), John Cogan (1981), and others argued that fixed or
semi-fixed costs of employment should be considered. And
Takeshi Amemiya (1973), Reuben Gronau (1974), Lewis (1974),
James Heckman (1976, 1979), and Arthur Goldberger (1981) have
made us aware of the selection bias problems associated with
the estimation of models of the labor force behavior of
married women. It is this vast flowering of new opportunities
to test and extend economic theory, and to develop and apply
sophisticated econometric techniques, that have made the labor
force behavior of married women a major topic in economics.

In our present study, we are concerned primarily with
understanding and predicting the employment and earnings

behavior of married women, rather than with testing propositions related to the central core of economic theory. In particular, we are interested in isolating factors that lead to breaks in the continuity of the work behavior of women over time. Nor do we treat directly important feminist issues, such as sex discrimination in employment, or draw on the literature associated with these issues, although some of the findings in this book may have implications for further work on these issues. Nevertheless, in carrying out this study, we have tried to take advantage of some of the important behavioral insights, behavioral modeling and econometric accomplishments contained in the large literature that has evolved on the labor force behavior of married women.

1.2. Our Behavioral Focus

Considered on an individual basis over time, the employment and earnings behavior of most women, and particularly of most women who get married and stay married to the same spouse, is characterized by continuity rather than by dramatic change.[4] That is, viewed over time periods of, say, 3, 7 or 10 years, most women either work continuously or never work; and those who do work tend to continue on from one year to the next with much the same level of work activity and earnings.[5] Our key objective in this study is to discover what observable factors affect the work behavior of married women after controlling for, or taking account of, their work behavior in the previous year.

T. Paul Schultz (e.g, 1978, 1980) and others have long argued that observed child status, a woman's educational level, various characteristics of a woman's husband such as his income and educational level, and a woman's work behavior may all, to some unknown extent, be manifestations of a woman's long-standing preferences for a particular lifestyle. This line of reasoning led us to speculate on whether the usual explanatory variables that have been included in micro studies of the work behavior of married women would have any detectable effect on current work behavior after controlling for a woman's work behavior in the previous year. For instance, would the birth of a child be likely to cause a woman who worked last year to quit work? These are the type of behavioral questions addressed in this study.

A related type of question focuses on possible differences in the factors, or the impacts of factors, that affect starting and continuing work behavior. For instance, a person's educational level might be a major screening factor in determining initial eligibility for various sorts of jobs with various ranges of wage rates (see Thurow, 1972, 1975; Gintis, 1971; and Taubman and Wales, 1975) but might have much less effect on year-to-year changes in the person's wage rate if the person continues working over some period of years.[6]

1.3. Viewing the Work Behavior of Married Women in a Broader Context

In an essay on the extinction of dinosaurs in *Discover* magazine, Stephen Jay Gould (1984, pp. 67-68) writes:

> There is no separate problem of the extinction of dinosaurs. Too often we divorce specific events from their wider contexts and systems of cause and effect. The fundamental fact of dinosaur extinction is that it coincided with the demise of many other groups across a wide range of habitats, from terrestrial to marine .... We need a coordinated explanation for a system of events that includes the extinction of dinosaurs as one component.

Likewise the labor force behavior of married women should not be treated in isolation. Although married women have been the most volatile component of the labor force in recent years, there have also been considerable changes in the labor force behavior of the young, the old and even of prime-aged men (see Kreps and Clark, 1975, Table 2.2 and Figure 2.3). At the same time, major changes have also been taking place in the nature of the family and marital unions (see, for instance, Glick and Norton, 1973).

All this does not necessarily mean that we can analyze the current labor force or work behavior of wives only within a complete model of family behavior that encompasses and treats all aspects of family formation and dissolution as well as the work behavior of all family members as endogenous over the life cycle. Surely there is a place for partial analyses of complex phenomena within the limitations of the a priori behavioral knowledge on which we must draw in specifying our models and the data available to us. Gould (1984, p.67) also writes that "science works with testable hypotheses." We do feel, however, that there should be a return to the earlier practice of showing results for married women together with comparable results for unmarried women and for men.[7] Some recent and technically sophisticated studies show results for only a single sample of white wives.

Noticing which results are replicated for both men and women, which are specific to women, which are only observed

for married women, and which exhibit some pattern over age
groups is a necessary step toward gaining the behavioral
understanding necessary to specify more comprehensive models
of the labor force behavior of married women in a family and
life-cycle context. Comparative results of this sort provide a
check on our intuitive and theoretical reasoning concerning
why we observe the results we do. They also make it more
likely that we will spot spurious results due to
misspecifications of our models, anomalies in the performance
of our estimation procedures, or peculiarities or errors in
the coding or handling of our data samples. In many ways
modern micro data sets, with their thousands of observations,
provide a much more comprehensive basis for our behavioral
conclusions than the national or regional aggregate data
sources on which earlier studies of labor force behavior were
based. However, the preprocessing required to use many of the
modern micro data sources can require computer programs that
are hundreds, or even thousands, of lines long. Even the
simpler of the estimation procedures applied to these data
sets, such as those on which this study is based, also involve
numerous intermediate steps between the application of
packaged computer programs. These intermediate steps are
frequently carried out in an interactive mode on the computer
with the intermediate results being displayed on the screen of
a computer terminal. Thus, the researcher may not even retain
a hard copy of these intermediate steps and results. More
complex maximum likelihood estimation procedures are often
programmed entirely by the researcher or an assistant. We,
ourselves, have carried out all the preprocessing of our data,
all the estimation, and all the simulation for which results
are presented and have entered and checked every number in the
tables of this book. Thus, we have more reason than many to
feel confident that the results presented in this book are not
due to errors in the handling of our data or the transcription
of our results. Nevertheless, we are awed by the potential for
making such errors. The role of replication in catching errors
of this nature may be almost as important in studies like this
as the role of replication as a basic scientific method for
uncovering behavioral regularities.

1.4. Our Econometric Approach

The most up-to-date econometric procedures for estimating
models of the labor force behavior of married women require
data on the same individuals over many time periods. Data of
this sort are called panel data. The United States is one of
the few countries in the world where high quality panel data,

based on a national sample and spanning a reasonable number of years, are available to the general research community. It is difficult to publish research that is not technically up-to-date; and advisors of Ph.D. students, untenured faculty members, and even senior faculty members must all be concerned with publication for reasons of self-interest. Besides, publication is the principal means by which research results are disseminated. Thus, in a country like Canada, studies of the labor force behavior of married women are increasingly being carried out using U.S. panel data. However, there are important differences in industrial structure, institutional factors, customs and historical circumstance between the Canadian and U.S. labor markets.[8] The differences between the U.S. labor market and the labor markets of countries like Japan are obviously greater. Thus, other countries should not adopt uncritically the results of studies based on U.S. data as appropriate to the domestic situation.

Those of us living and working outside the United States must strive to find better ways to make use of the data that are available in our countries of residence or that might reasonably become available in the foreseeable future. In this study, we show what can be done with cross-sectional data augmented by a limited amount of information that could be collected on a recall basis for a single previous year. We believe that the results obtained provide hope that high quality research on the work behavior of married women can be carried out in the near future in countries like Canada. The results obtained provide direction for further data collection efforts. We also present substantive results with respect to the work behavior of U.S. wives. Certainly these results provide bench marks against which the advantages of estimation methods which are more demanding in terms of their computational and data requirements can be judged.

We depart from common practice in this study in the way in which we seek to establish our behavioral results. In estimating the model on which most of the empirical results presented in this book are based, we have attempted to correct (or partially correct) for particular bias problems that a priori reasoning suggests might vitiate our behavioral findings. Nevertheless, it seems unlikely that our estimators of the parameters of our model are unbiased or consistent, as these terms are used in the literature, under any reasonable set of assumptions. Nor does it seem likely that our estimators of the relevant standard errors are unbiased or consistent. Thus, we make little use of traditional tests of significance in this study. Rather, we seek to establish our behavioral findings through the replication of results. Also, we use stochastic simulation methods with in-sample as well as out-of-sample data to check for major differences in the distribution of the dependent variables implied by our

estimated model from the observed distribution for these
variables and to establish confidence in the predictions of
our model. Major differences between the simulated and
observed distributions of the dependent variables would
suggest model specification or estimation problems. One might
think of our concentration on the accuracy of the predictions
of our model as a "bottom line" approach. Arnold Zellner
(1983, p.3) writes, for instance: "I always like to learn
about new ideas and approaches but the bottom line is how well
they work." Throughout this book we try to present our results
so that they can be understood by those who are interested in
and have some background in labor economics but who may or may
not be up-to-date on the sophisticated econometric techniques
that have come to be applied to the analysis of the labor
force behavior of married women.

1.5. A Microanalytic Simulation Approach to Behavioral Research and Forecasting

A microanalytic research strategy involves the
formulation and estimation of relationships concerning the
behavior of individuals, the testing of these relationships at
the individual level, and the comparison of various
distributional and aggregate implications of these estimated
relationships with observed behavior. It has long been
recognized that conceptual modeling is easier at the micro
level.[9] We can think intuitively about factors that might
affect the work behavior of an individual woman. Also, Guy
Orcutt and others (e.g., Orcutt and Edwards, 1969; Orcutt,
Watts and Edwards, 1968) have made us aware that there are a
variety of econometric advantages to carrying out our
estimation of behavioral relationships at the micro level.

Given an estimated set of behavioral relationships for,
say, the probability of work, the wage rates and the hours of
work of individual women, and given an appropriate data set,
we can use the estimated relationships to simulate the work
behavior of the women for whom we have data. We can then make
various sorts of distributional and aggregate comparisons
between the simulated and the actual work behavior of these
women. These comparisons can be made at many different levels
of aggregation, where the aggregation is carried out over
individuals or over time periods or both, so long as the
information on which the comparisons are based was not fully
used in the estimation of the model. These comparisons are, of
course, conditional on the nature of the particular data set
used in carrying out the simulation comparisons and the
specified distributions for generated random terms used in the

1 Introduction

simulation. On the other hand, they are not conditional on a whole set of generally untestable assumptions about the specification of a model and the distribution of the unobservable true disturbance terms of the model as are most traditional tests of significance and specification error tests. Thus, the microanalytic approach to research adds a new dimension to the testing of estimated relationships.[10]

The motivation for the microanalytic simulation approach to forecasting that has been developed by Orcutt and his associates is also compelling. While it may be advantageous to carry out model formulation and estimation at the level of individuals, inferences or predictions about changes in distributions or aggregates are required to answer many policy questions. A microanalytic simulation model of the household sector of a country consists of an initial population of individuals and sets of behavioral relationships sometimes called operating characteristics. These behavioral relationships are grouped into modules by the aspect of behavior with which they are concerned. Thus, a microanalytic simulation model may contain modules of relationships concerning fertility, family formation and dissolution, death, labor force behavior and so forth. These behavioral relationships are used to sequentially update the characteristics of the individuals in the simulation population in each year of the simulation period.[11]

One of the potential uses of microanalytic simulation models is in conjunction with auxiliary models that calculate the expected financial flows into and out of government transfer programs, such as the U.S. Social Security program.[12] The calculation of benefits and replacement rates for government programs like the U.S. Social Security program requires good individual earnings histories. It is not sufficient for the year-by-year distributions of earnings for various age-sex groups to be correct. Rather, the observed continuity of the employment and earnings behavior of individuals over time must be properly captured (see James H. Schulz et al., 1980, p. 132). In a microanalytic simulation model, information about an individual's behavior or circumstances in the previous year, or in previous years, can easily be retained for use in the current simulation period. For instance, relationships relating the work behavior of individuals in the current year to their work behavior in the previous year can easily be incorporated into a microanalytic simulation model. However, there are limits, due to computational costs and the problems of storing information, on the amounts of information about past behavior that can be carried forward for individuals in a microanalytic simulation model. The research on which our results are based was originally undertaken in an effort to produce a new labor force module for a major microanalytic simulation model of the

U.S. household sector.[13] Our objective was to produce a module that would properly capture the observed continuity in the employment and earnings behavior of individuals while utilizing only limited amounts of information from previous time periods.

1.6. An Overview of the Chapters

In Chapter 2 we present the behavioral model used in this study, we describe our data base and explain how the parameters of our model were estimated, and we relate our model and the manner in which our model is estimated to the literature. We also explain our approach to establishing that an observed relationship is stronger than might be expected by chance and our approach to the problems of coefficient bias and inconsistency. In Chapter 3 we present the behavioral results for our model. In addition to coefficient estimates, we show the probabilities of work, expected wage rates and expected hours of work implied by our estimated relationships for various sorts of hypothetical women. In Chapter 4 we compare the behavioral results of our model with behavioral results for several other related models. We also present both in-sample and out-of-sample simulation comparisons for these model variants. (Chapter 4 may be skipped without loss of continuity by readers who are less interested in questions of model specification.)

In Chapter 5 we examine how our estimation results presented in Chapter 3 would differ if we had included in our model information about the number of years a woman has worked since turning 18 years of age. In Chapter 6 we use simulation methods to demonstrate the sensitivity of the model for which estimation results are presented in Chapter 3 to various experimental changes in the child status and other characteristics of the women in our simulation population. In Chapter 7 we consider how unemployment can be conceptualized within the sort of theoretical framework that underlies the rest of this study. We also present empirical results for the probability that an individual will be unemployed during a year and for the number of weeks of unemployment for those who are unemployed during the year. As in Chapter 3, comparable empirical results are presented for married women, unmarried women and men. In Chapter 8 we present a summary of our conclusions and findings. Finally, in the Appendices to this book we provide details of the simulation results reported in Chapter 4, as well as a great deal of descriptive information (under the "Actual" headings in our tables) about the work behavior of women.

1 Introduction

FOOTNOTES TO CHAPTER 1

1. See Long (1958, Tables A-2 and A-6) for participation rates for all married women at least 16 years of age and for participation rates for various other demographic groups for 1900, 1910, 1920, 1930, 1940 and 1950. These figures are reproduced in Bowen and Finegan (1969, p.561, Table 1-C) along with participation rates for these same years for women and men 25-64 years of age, as well as with figures for 1960. In the footnote to this table, Bowen and Finegan also summarize some of the important adjustments Long has made in calculating the figures he presents. The source for our 1980 figure for the participation rate for married women in the United States is the U.S. Department of Commerce (1983, Table 639).

2. For early contributions on human capital, see, for example, Theodore Schultz (1961,1962) and Becker (1964,1975). See Becker (1965) for the analysis of the household production function and Mincer (1962) for his original modeling of the labor force behavior of married women.

3. See, for example, Cain (1966) and T. Paul Schultz (1978,1980). It has been suggested, in fact, that we should look at the economics of the family as a whole, including the fertility, marriage and divorce decisions of families. See T. Paul Schultz (1974), Becker, Landes and Michael (1977) and Becker (1981).

4. An important exchange of views on the nature of the continuity over time of the work behavior of married women is found in Mincer and Ofek (1979) and Heckman and Willis (1979).

5. Based on panel data for 1971-1973 for continuously married white women, Heckman (1981, p.105) writes:

> A noteworthy feature of the data is that roughly 80 percent of the women in the sample of older women either work all of the time or do not work at all .... The corresponding figure for younger women is 75 percent .... Both samples are roughly evenly divided between full-time workers and full-time nonworkers. There is little evidence of frequent turnover in these data, nor is there much evidence of turnover in the full seven years of data.

Using panel data for the 10-year period of 1969-1978, Nakamura and Nakamura (1983a, Table 3) find that 27 percent of the continuously married women 21-64 years of age in their data sample never worked over this period, while 38 percent worked all 10 years. Thus, 65 percent of these wives are found to either work all of the time or never work over a 10-year period. Nakamuro and Nakamura (1983a) also present evidence on the continuity of the hours of work and earnings of individual wives over this 10-year period.

6. Within the context of the signalling hypothesis, a similar view regarding how the wage rate offered by the employer converges to a market rate is found in Spence (1974).

7. For instance, Bowen and Finegan (1969) present results for prime-aged males, married women, prime-aged single women, younger persons and older persons. They give some of their results for whites, blacks, and other nonwhites. Hall (1973) presents results for white and black males and white and black females, married and single, in several different age groups. Cain (1966) and T. Paul Schultz (1980) present results for both white and black wives. Heckman (1981) presents results for two age groups of wives. And Johnson and Pencavel (1984) consider wives, unmarried women and husbands.

8. From Table 1 in Nakamura and Nakamura (1981, p.452) we see that in the 1969-1970 period employment rates were substantially lower for Canadian wives than for their U.S. counterparts, and Canadian wives who worked did so for fewer hours and earned less on the whole than their U.S. counterparts. From Table V in this same paper (pp. 462-463) we see that the U.S. wives whose data were used in that study had more years of formal education, married younger, lived in families where the combined income of the husband and family asset income were higher, had different patterns of fertility, and lived in regions with lower unemployment rates and more job opportunities for women per potential member of the female labor force than their Canadian counterparts. In Nakamura and Nakamura (1981), attention is also paid to institutional differences in the U.S. and Canadian tax laws that might have special effects on the labor force behavior of wives.

9. Cain (1966, p.25) writes, for instance:

Price theory of economics is based on the individual -- person, household, or spending unit -- as the unit of analysis. Our a priori predictions made about aggregations ... are usually derived from what we expect numbers of individuals (as individuals) to do .... [The] use of disaggregated data ... allows us to apply more directly our theoretical models.

10. For applications of this approach to testing estimated relationships see Heckman (1981), Heckman and Willis (1977), Nakamura, Nakamura, Cullen, Grant and Orcutt (1979), Nakamura, Nakamura and Cullen (1979, section VI), and Nakamura and Nakamura (1981, p.468; 1983, pp.249-251; 1983a; 1983b; 1984).

11. What is widely acknowledged to be the first

microanalytic simulation model is presented in Orcutt, Greenberger, Korbel and Rivlin (1961). A more elaborate microanalytic simulation model of the U.S. household sector, which also embeds a small macroeconomic model, is presented in Orcutt, Caldwell and Wertheimer (1976). This model, called DYNASIM, has been used extensively for policy analyses. It has also formed the starting point for the development of a number of closely related microanalytic simulation models of the U.S. household sector such as MICROSIM (see Social Security Administration, 1980). Other references on this topic include Orcutt (1957,1960), U.S. Department of Health, Education and Welfare (1973), Sadowsky (1977), Eliasson (1978), Nakamura and Nakamura (1978), Caldwell (1979,1983), and Orcutt and Glazer (1980).

12. See Social Security Administration (1980) for a description of the MODASS model. MODASS uses historical information from the longitudinal Social Security earnings exact match file and individual earnings histories for subsequent years generated by MICROSIM to calculate quarters of coverage in each year under the Social Security program as well as Social Security earnings for those who work, and Social Security benefits for those found to be eligible for benefits. See also Zedlewski (1974).

13. This microanalytic simulation model, which is an extension of DYNASIM (see footnote 11), was developed by Orcutt and his associates and is described in section 3 of Orcutt and Glazer (1980). It is currently being maintained and extended at the Survey Research Center of the Institute for Social Research at the University of Michigan under the direction of James D. Smith in collaboration with Orcutt and others.

CHAPTER 2

METHODOLOGY AND DATA

As indicated in Chapter 1, we seek to establish confidence in our empirical results primarily by showing that the simulated outputs of our model properly reproduce key features of the observed joint distribution of the dependent variables of the model. Nevertheless, we believe it is important for the reader to understand why we have adopted the behavioral model on which most of the estimation and simulation results presented in this book are based and how this model relates to various lines of thought represented in the literature. An understanding of the nature of our model is also crucial in interpreting the estimation results presented in Chapter 3 and elsewhere in the book and in relating our empirical results to those of other researchers. Thus, in section 2.1 we give a verbal description of our model. In section 2.2 we discuss the motivation for using such a model and how this model relates to various schools of thought represented in the literature. In section 2.3 we present our model in equation form and describe how we have estimated the parameters of these equations. In section 2.4 we give the definitions of the variables used in this study. The nature of these variables and of our model raises the issues of parameter bias and inconsistency. In section 2.5 we discuss our treatment of these problems. In section 2.6 we discuss our approach to determining when an observed relationship is stronger than what we might expect by chance and our approach to specification error testing. Finally, in section 2.7 we describe our data base and give the average characteristics of the married and unmarried women and of the men whose data have been used in this study.

2.1. An Inertia Model of Work Behavior

A casual examination of data such as that collected in the Michigan Panel Study of Income Dynamics suggests that most

2 Methodology and Data

individuals, including most women, make relatively few major changes in their year-to-year work behavior over the course of their adult lives. Moreover, the data suggest that an individual is more likely to continue working, or not working, in any given year the stronger the individual's attachment to the state of work, or nonwork, respectively, in the previous year. This attachment can be measured, for instance, by the hours of work and the wage rate for those found to be working, or by proxies, such as the proportion of adult years spent working or current age for those not working. These empirical observations seem compatible with the view that most individuals display essentially the same work behavior from one year to the next unless their circumstances have changed. These changes may be in factors such as child status, health status, or the individual's wage rate, on which data are typically collected in surveys. Or these changes may be in factors such as technology, local labor market conditions, the needs of children and relatives and so forth, on which we rarely have data linked up with the other micro characteristics necessary to carry out studies of work behavior. Whether these changes are in observable or unobservable factors, however, casual empirical observation suggests that a larger change will typically be required to cause an individual to switch from working to not working, or vice versa, the more committed the individual is to the present work state. In other words, the work behavior of individuals seems to be characterized by considerable inertia; hence, we call the model on which most of the empirical results presented in this book are based the Inertia Model.

In our Inertia Model the probability of work in the current year for an individual who worked in the previous year is specified as a function of the number of hours worked in the previous year, the hourly wage in the previous year, variables describing changes that may have occurred in the individual's circumstances, and other variables, such as age, that might be related in a proxy sense to changes in the circumstances of an individual. The probability of work in the current year for an individual who did not work in the previous year is specified as a function of variables describing changes that may have occurred in the individual's circumstances, as well as variables that might be related in a proxy sense to unobservable factors, including the strength of the individual's commitment to the state of nonwork.

Many of those found to work in the current year who also worked in the previous year may be continuing on in the same job situations. Thus, we model the hours of work and wage rates of these individuals as functions of their hours of work and wage rates, respectively, in the previous year as well as of variables that describe or might be related, in a proxy sense, to changes in the circumstances of these individuals that might result in changes in their hours of work or wage rates. In the wage rate function, we also include the hours of work in the previous year, since those who work more hours gain more on-the-job experience and are more likely to be in jobs where there are more substantial productivity returns from on-the-job training, more opportunity for employer-supplied training, more opportunities for upward mobility in terms of job classification, and a greater likelihood of being unionized or protected by other types of collective or contractual agreements. All of these factors might be expected to result in larger wage gains from one year to the next for those working more hours. In the function for annual hours of work, we have included a variable for the current wage rate since it is frequently hypothesized that individuals are sensitive to what they are paid per hour in "choosing" their hours of work. It is often argued that women tend to work more when they are paid more per hour, while prime-aged men tend to work somewhat less.

For those found to work in the current year who have never worked or who have been out of the work force for a year or more, we model their wage rates as a function of personal and macroeconomic characteristics; and we model their hours of work as a function of the wage rate and other personal characteristics. We do not impose or test theoretical restrictions relating parameters in our hours of work and wage functions for those who did not work versus those who did work in the previous year, because we suspect that, on the whole, those who are entering the work force after an absence of a year or more face higher search costs, have less relevant information about labor market conditions, and may face suspicion on the part of potential employers concerning both the extent of their commitment to work and the depreciation of their job skills. Hence, we suspect that the variables included in our wage and hours equations will systematically pick up different combinations of unobservable factors, in a proxy sense, for those who did not versus those who did work in the previous year. Nor do we attempt to combine our functions for the probability of work and for the hours of work in a Tobit-type specification, since we feel certain that there are a variety of costs of work, such as transportation and clothing expenses, that are loosely related or completely unrelated to the number of hours worked. These unobservables will thus have different impacts on the probability of work and on the determination of hours of work for those who do work, with some of these differing impacts being picked up by variables included in our functions in a proxy sense. We also include what has come to be called a selection bias term, following the methodology of Heckman (see Heckman, 1976, 1979, 1980; see also Addendum to this Chapter), in our hours of work and wage equations for both those who did and those who did

2 Methodology and Data

not work in the previous year. This term is included in an attempt to allow for possible correlations between unobservable factors affecting the probability of work and unobservables affecting the determination of hours of work and the wage rate, respectively.

In section 2.3 we present a description of our Inertia Model in equation form, along with a discussion of our estimation of this model; and the variables that we have included in our model are defined in section 2.4. Before proceeding with this more explicit statement of our model, however, in section 2.2 we consider how our Inertia Model relates to the literature, what the implications of our model formulation are for the interpretation of coefficients of the model, and what sort of research questions might be addressed using this model.

2.2. The Inertia Model Versus Traditional and Evolutionary Schools of Thought

Our Inertia Model is closely related to a first difference version presented in Nakamura and Nakamura (1983a) of an important class of models of individual work behavior developed by Heckman.[1] We begin this section with a brief summary of the key premises of the Heckman model. We will refer to this model, implemented as it was originally proposed without allowing for fixed or persistent person-specific unobservables, as the Standard Model.

For each individual there is some wage rate (or distribution of wage rates) at which the individual could work, and there is also some minimum wage at which the individual would desire to work. The wage rate at which the individual could work is called the offered wage, and the minimum wage rate at which the person would desire to work is called the asking wage. The offered wage (or offered wage distribution) summarizes both the constraints an individual faces in the labor market and the productivity of the individual as perceived by potential employers. To say that a person has no wage offers and cannot work at any wage is to say that the offered wage distribution of this individual is degenerate and that the most that potential employers would be willing to pay this individual for an hour's labor is nothing. The asking wage summarizes a person's tastes and preferences concerning work, the personal or family constraints that make it costly or difficult for a person to work, and the individual's financial situation. To say that an individual would never consider working is to say that the asking wage of this individual lies above any wage this individual could ever command in the labor market. One of the most obvious costs of working is that the individual's time for all other activities is reduced by the amount of time spent working. Thus, the asking wage is taken to be an increasing function of the number of hours the individual works in a given time period, such as a year. It is hypothesized, furthermore, that an indvdual will work during the given time period if the individual's offered wage exceeds his asking wage at zero hours of work, and that those individuals who do work will choose their hours of work so as to equate their offered and asking wage rates.

Direct estimation of the Standard Model becomes mechanically difficult and demanding in terms of data requirements when this model is modified to allow for fixed or persistent person-specific unobservable factors.[2] Using simulation methods, Heckman has demonstrated that without some such modification, the model cannot account for the observed continuity over time in the employment behavior (years of work and nonwork) of married women (Heckman, 1978,1981). We have replicated this result for wives, and have shown the extent to which the Standard Model is unable to capture the observed continuity in the hours of work and earnings of wives as well (Nakamura and Nakamura, 1983a). This has been a discouraging development for those of us living in countries where panel data of the sort required to estimate most of the alternatives that have been proposed to the Standard Model are not generally available for reseach purposes. The difference version of the Standard Model modified to allow for fixed or persistent person-specific unobservables that we have proposed can be estimated using standard probit and regression programs, however, and requires only cross-sectional data augmented by a limited amount of information from the previous year that could be easily collected on a recall basis in cross-sectional surveys. For the convenience of the reader, the derivation of this difference model from the Standard Model is presented in the Addendum to this chapter. In this derivation, an expression is derived for the strength of the attachment to the workforce in the previous year for an individual who worked in that year. This expression, which is a linear combination of hours of work and wage variables for the individual evaluated in the previous year, is shown to embed the hypothesized person-specific fixed and persistent unobservable effects included in the undifferenced form of the model.

The Inertia Model borrows from the difference version of the Standard Model the proposition that any fixed or persistent person-specific effects will be embedded in the lagged hours of work variable and the lagged wage variable for those who worked in the previous year. However, in the Inertia Model the hours of work and wage equations for those who

2 Methodology and Data

worked in the previous year are not in first difference form. Rather the lagged dependent variable has been moved for each of these equations to the right-hand side. Also, whereas some of the variables included in our Inertia Model, such as a dummy variable for the presence of a new baby, are included to capture observed changes from the previous year in the circumstances of the individual; most of the explanatory variables are not in first difference form.

Ideally, we would like to include a great deal of direct information in our Inertia Model about changes in an individual's characteristics or circumstances from the previous to the current year that might lead to changes in the work behavior of the individual. Unfortunately, however, of the variables available to us, those such as education and race do not change at all from one year to the next for most adults, while variables like age change by a constant amount each year. Measures of macroeconomic activity that we can add to our micro data base, like the unemployment rate, do change from year to year. However, each of these variables takes on the same value for all individuals in any given year when measured at the national level as in this study.[3] Since we have observations for many individuals but over relatively few years in our panel data base, problems of multicollinearity with the constant terms for the relationships of our Inertia Model arise in trying to obtain estimates of the coefficients of these macroeconomic variables. We have found these problems to be particularly severe for coefficients of first differences of variables like the national unemployment rate.

We do not account for any changes from one year to the next in the rates at which earnings are taxed. To do so would be computationally difficult. Also, taxes on the earnings of husbands, wives and others are computed in the microanalytic simulation model in which our equations will be used <u>after</u> the determination of these income quantities. On the basis of previous research (Nakamura and Nakamura, 1981), we believe that this is not a serious drawback. We are not trying to make comparisons in this study among countries with different tax treatments of the earnings of spouses, and in our previous work we found that the correlations between our before- and after-tax wage rates for wives in a given country (the United States or Canada) were always in excess of .97.

Many of the unobservable changes of interest to us in an individual's characteristics and circumstances may be correlated, however, with observable current characteristics of the individual and current macroeconomic conditions. For instance, those with more education may be more likely to receive on-the-job training, increasing the likelihood of wage increases; and many older workers may suffer some deterioration in their productivity from one year to the next leading to a negative relationship between age and the wage rate for older workers. Thus, we include undifferenced variables, like education and age, in our Inertia Model in an attempt to account, in a proxy sense, for unobservable changes from year to year in the characteristics and circumstances of individuals. Also, we do not include a lagged or differenced instrumental wage variable in the hours equation, since for most adults, the only variables in the wage equation for our Inertia Model that change from one year to the next are our national macroeconomic variables, age which changes by the same constant for everyone, and the selection bias term.

Another respect in which our Inertia Model departs from the difference version of the Standard Model presented in the Addendum is that in the wage and hours equations of the Inertia Model, we do not impose the restriction, which clearly follows from the difference version of the Standard Model, that the coefficients of the lagged wage variable in the wage equation and of the lagged hours variable in the hours equation equal unity (see equations 2.54 and 2.64 in the Addendum to this Chapter). Despite these differences in specification, though, the Inertia Model can be thought of as closely related to models of the work behavior of individuals of the sort developed by Heckman.

Unlike the models of Heckman, however, the Inertia Model focuses attention on factors that lead individuals who have been working to stop working and that lead individuals who have not been working to start working.[4] In fact, the coefficient of each of the explanatory variables in the Inertia Model, with the exception of the lagged endogenous variables, is properly interpreted as measuring impacts of the variable, and of any unobservables associated with the variable in a proxy sense, after controlling for work behavior in the previous year. The model does not tell us unconditionally why individuals displayed the work behavior observed for them in the previous year. But conditional on this lagged behavior, the model may tell us something about whether the individual's work behavior in the current year is likely to differ from what we observed in the previous year.

In this light our Inertia Model might be viewed as being in a vein similar to evolutionary theories of firm behavior. In promoting evolutionary theories of firm behavior, Richard Nelson and Sidney Winter (1973, p. 22) argue that "the basic empirical questions should be posed in terms of 'what will the firm do next' rather than in terms of what would be an equilibrium position for the firm." They go on to argue that:

> Many of the empirical phenomena often cited as correct predictions of the neoclassical theory can be explained by, and would be predicted from, a theory that assumes some search over production alternatives (rather than a large choice set),

satisficing men and firms (rather than maximizing ones) and some selectivity on the part of the environment (rather than competitive equilibrium). (p. 28)

Analogously, we might view individuals as conducting infrequent and limited searches for employment opportunities; as continuing not to work or as continuing from one year to the next working for the same employer so long as this seems "satisfactory"; and as being subject to selectivity on the part of the environment, including facing rejections by potential employers, demotions, being passed over for promotion or raises, layoffs or being fired.

Clearly it would be possible to frame an evolutionary theory of individual work behavior in such a way that observable price variables, such as the hourly wage rate, are hypothesized to play a major role in determining labor supply, as is the case in more traditional models. The history of price variables in traditional models of work behavior is not illustrious, however. After vast expenditures of research effort and funds it is not even clear that economists have managed to determine whether various demographic groups of workers will increase or decrease their hours of work, on the average, in response to an exogenous wage change.

Nor is the concept of the marginal wage rate, which is the wage rate of interest in traditional models, well defined in an empirical sense. Neither the wage function in the Standard Model nor the wage function in our Inertia Model as specified in this study contains hours of work as an explanatory variable.[5] This is partly because it is not clear whether, or how, wage rates vary with hours of work. To show that wages and hours of work are positively related for some particular sample of workers is not the same as showing that the individuals in this sample would receive higher wage rates, on the average, if the hours they worked were exogenously increased. Full-time workers are more likely to be unionized than part-time workers, and unionized workers may receive higher wages on the average than nonunionized workers. Full-time workers are more likely to continue working over a number of years than part-time workers and thus may receive higher wage rates because they have more seniority or work experience. But none of these factors suggest that an individual could expect to receive a higher current wage rate by deciding to work more hours in the current time period. Nor do workers who lose large numbers of hours of work in a particular year due to illness, layoff or changing jobs necessarily expect to receive lower hourly wage rates because of this. When wage rates are *not* taken to be a function of hours of work, the offered wage, which is assumed in models such as the Standard Model to be equated to the asking wage evaluated at the actual hours of work for those who work, can be thought of as both a marginal offered wage for the last hour of work and as an average wage for the number of hours actually worked. This is theoretically convenient, but may also be an inadequate representation of reality.

Suppose it could be established within certain firms or occupational settings that the hourly wage an individual receives is a well-defined function of the number of hours the individual works within some time period, after controlling for work experience, seniority, union membership and other related characteristics. The expected offered wage rates of individual workers would still not be well-defined functions of hours of work, since workers in these particular firms or occupational settings would still have potential wage offers from outside these workplaces or might even hold second jobs outside these sectors. In most work settings it is difficult to conceive of how one would operationally define a marginal wage rate. Suppose a worker has both a main job and a second job with different basic wage rates. Suppose the basic wage rate for the second job is lower than for the main job. Suppose also that when he or she works overtime on the main job at the employer's request, an overtime rate applies; but when he or she works overtime or brings work home "by choice" to make a good impression on the employer, or to avoid making a bad impression by failing to complete assigned tasks, then the rate of pay per hour is zero dollars. If we were to collect annual data from this worker, how would we define the marginal wage rate? Also, how do we decide which is this worker's last, or marginal, hour of work in the year? Is it the last hour of work in the year, the last hour of work on the second job, the last overtime hour of work, the last hour worked on the longest day of work during the year, or some other hour? If there is no good answer to this question, then perhaps it is more reasonable to view workers as deciding how much to work based on the associated average or total earnings from different possible job packages. Viewing observed wage rates as average earnings per hour of work, as is actually the case for most data bases, presents no obvious problems in an evolutionary sort of model of work behavior.

Also, in a traditional model, such as the Standard Model, the determination of hours of work treats hours of work as an instantaneously adjustable choice variable, conditional, of course, on the offered wage and predetermined factors. While it is possible to justify this treatment of hours of work by noting that individuals can "choose" their hours of work by their choice of the type of job or by combining multiple jobs, the justification seems shaky -- particularly in the short-run. No such justifications are required in an evolutionary framework.

The nature of the data available to us also makes

application of a traditional modeling approach seem somewhat unsatisfying. Angus Deaton and John Muellbauer (1980, p.3) write:

> Consumer behavior is frequently presented in terms of preferences, on the one hand, and possibilities on the other. The emphasis in the discussion is commonly placed on on <u>preferences</u> .... The specification of which choices are actually available is given a secondary place and, frequently, only very simple possibilities are considered .... We begin, however, with the <u>limits</u> <u>to</u> <u>choice</u> rather than with the choices themselves.

In our case, however, we unfortunately begin with data on explanatory variables, such as a woman's educational level, the number and ages of her children, and the income of her husband if she has one, where it is difficult or perhaps impossible to tell to what extent these variables are serving as proxies for tastes for work outside the home versus limits to choice. We add to this information about the characteristics of the individual a few characteristics about the macroeconomic environment in which the individual is embedded, where these characteristics also may alter preferences as well as serving as limits to choice. Deaton and Muellbauer (1980, p.3) go on to write: "Unlike preferences, the opportunities for choice are often directly observable." In our data base, however, we observe neither preferences nor limits to choice directly, but rather the work choices themselves and the outcomes of a variety of other choices concerning educational attainment, family status and so forth that may all reflect the underlying preferences and some of the limits to choice of the individual. In an evolutionary approach, there is more freedom to specify a model that makes the best possible use of the data that exist.

The focus in this study on factors that lead individuals to alter their work behavior from year to year is more narrow, in some respects, than the usual scope of behavioral studies of work behavior. We are uncertain about whether such an approach can lead to an understanding of fundamental questions, such as why married women in countries like the United States and Canada have increased their labor supply so much since World War II. We feel certain, however, that there is value in asking more limited questions about the work behavior of wives as an alternative or complement to simultaneous life cycle approaches, just as it has been found fruitful to ask more limited questions in other branches of science. K.C. Cole (1984, p. 62) writes, for instance:

> As long as people asked grand fundamental questions

about the nature of the universe (What is life? What is matter?) they did not get very far. As soon as they began to ask more focused questions (How does blood flow? How do the planets move?) they were rewarded with more general answers.

Cole goes on to argue:

Newton's understanding of gravity was no less valuable because it was incomplete. As he answered the critics ... "To understand the motions of the planets under the influence of gravity without knowing the cause of gravity is as good a progress ... as to understand the frame of a clock, and the dependence of the wheels upon one another, without knowing the cause of gravity of the weight which moves the machine.

We believe it would be important if researchers could identify what observable factors, if any, increase the likelihood that individuals will alter their work behavior from what it has been in the immediate past, even if we are not able to fully understand or explain this past behavior. The models, research methodology, and empirical results presented in this book hopefully represent a step toward achieving this goal. One might also wish to analyze individuals' present work behavior given their work behavior observed, not just in the immediate past (say, last year), but over the last several years. We have found, however, that most relevant information for our analysis seems to lie in the behavior observed in the immediate past (see Chapter 5).

2.3. A Formal Statement of the Inertia Model and Estimation of This Model

For the Inertia Model, the log of the offered hourly wage of the ith individual, denoted by $\ln w$, is specified to be given by

$$\ln w = \alpha_0 + \alpha_1 w_{-1} + \alpha_2 h_{-1} + Z\alpha_3 + E\alpha_4 + u, \qquad (2.3.1)$$

where the α's are parameters to be estimated, Z and E are vectors of personal and regional characteristics, respectively, and u is a disturbance term. The lagged annual hours variable, h_{-1}, appears in equation (2.3.1) to reflect unobservable factors, such as the institutional

2 Methodology and Data

reality that those who have been working longer numbers of hours are more likely to be covered by collective bargaining agreements and are more likely to have greater seniority rights and power within their organizations than new entrants or those working part-time. Longer hours of work mean more hours of accumulated experience on the job as well. Thus, one might expect the current log wage to be positively related to hours of work in the previous year, after controlling for other relevant factors, due to human capital effects. Other unobservable person-specific fixed or persistent effects are expected to be embedded in the lagged wage rate, w_{-1}, for those who worked in the previous year. For instance, this lagged wage term should help to capture the institutional reality that those who continue in the same job from one year to the next often continue at essentially the real wage rate received in the previous year. Moreover, when looking for a new job, job seekers who have had recent job experience can be expected to try to find a job with a wage rate as good or better than the wage rate for their most recent job, and potential employers frequently request information about a job applicant's rate of pay on his most recent job and use this information as one element in deciding on a wage offer.

The asking wage equation for the ith individual is specified as

$$\ln w^* = \beta_0 + \beta_1 h_{-1} + Z^*\beta_2 + I\beta_3 + \beta_4 \ln w + \beta_5 h + u^* \quad (2.3.2a)$$

when h is positive and as

$$\ln w^* = \beta_0 + \beta_1 h_{-1} + Z^*\beta_2 + I\beta_3 + u^* \quad (2.3.2b)$$

when h is 0, where $\ln w^*$ denotes the log of the asking wage, the β's are parameters to be estimated, Z^* is a vector of constraints arising from previous choices about marriage, family formation and so forth, I is a vector of variables describing the other income available to the individual in the current or previous year or changes from the previous year in other income, and u^* is an error term. It is assumed that person-specific tastes and preferences for work, whether innate or acquired through working, will be reflected in the number of hours the individual worked in the previous year, along with any other unobserved person-specific persistent effects. We would expect the log of the asking wage to be negatively related to the number of hours worked in the previous year. That is, we would expect those with a history of working to have lower asking wages on the average, other factors being equal, due to unobservable factors, such as tastes for work, embedded in the lagged hours variable.

2.3 A Formal Statement of the Inertia Model

Suppose an individual will work in a given time period if w exceeds w*. If it is the case that the disturbance terms u in (2.3.1) and u* in (2.3.2a) and (2.3.2b) are each identically and independently normally distributed with mean 0 in the uncensored population of all individuals, then the probability that an individual will work in the current year is given by

$$P(h > 0) = F(\phi^*) \qquad (2.3.3)$$

where F denotes the cumulative standard normal density function and

$$\phi^* = \delta_0 + Z^*\delta_1 + I\delta_2 + Z\delta_3 + E\delta_4 + \delta_5 w_{-1} + \delta_6 h_{-1} . \qquad (2.3.4)$$

The coefficients of the index given by (2.3.4) must be estimated separately for those who did and for those who did not work in the previous year, since for those who did not work in the previous year we do not observe values for the lagged wage rate and hours of work variables, w_{-1} and h_{-1}. For those who did not work in the previous year we treat the coefficients of these lagged variables as being 0.[6]

For those found to work in the current year, the log wage equation to be estimated is given by

$$\ln w = \alpha_0 + \alpha_1 w_{-1} + \alpha_2 h_{-1} + Z\alpha_3 + E\alpha_4 + \alpha_5 \lambda + u \qquad (2.3.5)$$

and the hours of work equation to be estimated is given by

$$h = b_0 + b_1 h_{-1} + b_2 \ln w_D + Z^* b_3 + I b_4 + b_5 \lambda + u^* \qquad (2.3.6)$$

where we see from (2.3.5) that the deterministic portion of the log wage is given by

$$\ln w_D = \alpha_0 + \alpha_1 w_{-1} + \alpha_2 h_{-1} + Z\alpha_3 + E\alpha_4 + \alpha_5 \lambda \qquad (2.3.7)$$

and the selection bias term is given by

$$\lambda = f(\phi^*) / F(\phi^*) \qquad (2.3.8)$$

with ϕ^* given by (2.3.4). The coefficients of equations (2.3.5) and (2.3.6) must also be estimated separately for those who did and those who did not work in the previous year, since we do not observe values for w_{-1} and h_{-1} for those who did not work in the previous year. Thus, we treat α_1 and α_2 in (2.3.5) and b_1 in (2.3.6) as being 0 for those who did not work in the previous year.

2 Methodology and Data

The condition for an individual to work and the hours equation in the Inertia Model may be viewed as the result of individual maximizing behavior in the tradition of the Standard Model (see the Addendum to this Chapter), or they may be viewed simply as decision rules in the tradition of evolutionary modeling. In estimating this model, it is not necessary to choose between these two ways of viewing these relationships.

For individuals who are found to work in the current year but who did not work in the previous year, any unobserved person-specific effects will be in the error terms of our relationships and may lead to bias problems. Also, it is possible to argue that the response coefficients for some of our explanatory variables may differ for other systematic reasons for those who did versus those who did not work in the previous year. For instance, the impact of education on the offered wage may differ for new job entrants versus those who have established records of on-the-job performance. It should be noted, therefore, that in estimating the coefficients of (2.3.4), (2.3.5) and (2.3.6) separately for those who did and for those who did not work in the previous year, we are also allowing for the possibility that the coefficients of these relationships may differ for those who did versus those who did not work in the previous year. That is, we are allowing for the possibility that the determinants of entering versus continuing work behavior may be different.[7]

The coefficients of the index given by (2.3.4) are estimated separately for those who did and for those who did not work in the previous year using standard probit analysis. These estimation results are used in calculating estimated values of the probit index, ϕ^*, and then of the selection bias term, λ, for all those found to work in the current year. For those found to work in the current year, the parameters of (2.3.5) are then estimated separately for those who did and for those who did not work in the previous year, using ordinary least squares regression. These regression results are used in calculating the predicted values for $\ln w_D$ for all those found to work in the current year. Then we estimate the coefficients of (2.3.6) separately for those who did and those who did not work in the previous year, with predicted values substituted for $\ln w_D$, using ordinary least squares regression analysis.[8] The model given by equations (2.3.3) through (2.3.8) and estimated in the manner described is our Inertia Model, which was introduced in section 2.1.

2.4. Variable Definitions

The dependent variable h is defined to be annual hours of work.[9] The wage rate, w, is measured as the individual's reported earned income for the given calendar year divided by h and then converted to 1967 dollars using the Consumer Price Index.[10] It can be seen from the way in which values of w are computed that erroneously high values for h will lead to erroneously low values for w and vice versa.[11] This errors-in-variables problem is a reason, in addition to the suspected correlation between the true error terms for the wage and hours equations, for replacing the log of the wage rate by an instrument, or predictor for this variable, in the hours equation. The hope is that the measurement errors in the values of the log wage rate that are due to measurement errors for h will not be picked up by this instrument.[12] In this study our instrument for the log wage rate is our estimated relationship for the log wage rate for the given demographic group. The dependent variable for the probit model for the probability of work in the year, given by (2.3.3), is set equal to 1 if both w and h are found to be positive in the current year, and is set equal to 0 otherwise.

The variables included for each individual in the Z vector in the probit index for the probability of work and in the wage equation are the person's current age measured in years, a race dummy set equal to 1 if the person is black and set equal to 0 otherwise, and an education variable measured as years of formal schooling. The variables included in the E vector of macroeconomic conditions for each individual are the national unemployment rate and a national wage index.[13]

Three child status variables are included in the Z^* vector for each individual, where Z^* appears in the probit index for the probability of work and in the hours equation. The first is a baby dummy set equal to 1 if there is a new baby in the family, and set equal to 0 otherwise.[14] The second is a young child dummy set equal to 1 if the youngest child in the family is less than 6 years of age but is not classified as a new baby and set equal to 0 otherwise.[15] The third is a continuous variable for the number of children younger than 18 living at home.[16] The age and race dummy variables[17] have been included in Z^* as well as in Z. For older men we have also included in the Z^* vector a dummy set equal to 1 if the person is 60 to 62 years of age and set equal to 0 otherwise, a dummy set equal to 1 if the person is 63 to 64 years of age and set equal to 0 otherwise, and a dummy set equal to 1 if the person is 65 to 66 years of age and set equal to 0 otherwise. We refer to these dummies as retirement age dummies since they have been introduced to capture retirement regulations and customs that seem to affect men predominantly. For men we have also included in the Z^* vector a dummy variable set equal to 1 if the man reported a disability that limits work[18] and set equal to 0 otherwise. For young women and men 14 to 20 years of age we have included in the Z^* vector a dummy variable for student status in the previous year that is set equal to 1 if years of education increased from the previous to the current year[19] and is set equal to 0 otherwise. For those 14 to 20 years of age, we have also included in the Z^* vector a dummy set equal to 1 if the person is living with one or both of their parents[20] and set equal to 0 otherwise. Finally, for various groups of individuals, we have included in the Z^* vector one or more of the following marital status variables: a dummy variable set equal to 1 if the person is currently married[21] and set equal to 0 otherwise, a dummy set equal to 1 if the person was married in the previous year and set equal to 0 otherwise, a dummy set equal to 1 if the person is currently widowed and set equal to 0 otherwise, and a dummy set equal to 1 if the person is currently divorced or separated and set equal to 0 otherwise.

For different groups of women, we have included various combinations of the following other income variables in the I vector appearing in the probit index for the probability of work and in the hours equation: the husband's earned income measured in thousands of 1967 dollars (husband's income), the difference between the husband's earned income in the current and previous years measured in thousands of 1967 dollars (change in husband's income); a variable set equal to the difference between the earned income of the husband in the current and previous years measured in thousands of 1967 dollars if this change is negative and set equal to 0 otherwise (negative change in husband's income), a dummy set equal to 1 if the family received Aid to Families with Dependent Children (AFDC) benefits in the previous year[22] and set equal to 0 otherwise, and a dummy set equal to 1 if the family received Social Security benefits in the previous year[23] and set equal to 0 otherwise.[24] For men we have included in the I vector a variable set equal to the labor income of the wife in the previous year measured in thousands of 1967 dollars if a wife was present in the previous year[25] and set equal to 0 otherwise.

Mean values for these variables are given in section 2.7. These variables are also listed again, together with some summary remarks concerning our estimation results for these variables, at the beginning of Chapter 3.

2.5. Biases, Biases, Biases

The definition of an unbiased estimator of a parameter is that the expected value of the estimator equals the true value of the population parameter. Thus, if we repeatedly evaluate an unbiased estimator using different data samples drawn from the same underlying population, the sample mean for all these sample estimates should be approximately equal to the true value of the parameter of interest. In a well-defined stochastic setting, it is possible to consider many properties of estimators besides whether or not they are unbiased. For instance, we might consider the trade-offs between bias and variance for alternative estimators of the same parameter using a mean square error criterion. Econometricians are sometimes able to prove analytically, or to use Monte Carlo experiments to show, that one estimator is better than various other estimators for a particular parameter, based on the consideration of a number of desirable properties that an estimator might possess and the trade-offs among these properties.

Trade-offs among various possible desirable properties of estimators are probably more difficult to consider in most applied settings, however. In an applied setting, even when the model to be estimated is precisely specified, in reality the researcher may be uncertain about the appropriateness of the specified functional form, the variables included, and the specified form of the distribution of the error term for the behavioral relationship of interest. Perhaps this is why concern about the properties of estimators in many applied studies is limited to concern about potential bias problems. Bias problems may also be of special interest to applied researchers because they are often closely associated with questions of behavioral modeling and empirical observation.

It is typical in an empirical study for the researcher to claim that the parameter estimates presented are unbiased or consistent under a specified set of assumptions concerning the model estimated.[26] There is sometimes some discussion of the reasonableness of the assumptions stated. Some of these assumptions may be subjected to statistical tests, conditional on the validity of the remaining assumptions. In econometrically oriented applied studies, elaborate mathematical and statistical arguments are often presented as well, concerning how the estimation procedure that has been used overcomes certain bias problems alleged to be present in earlier studies on the same topic. Before preceding to a consideration of particular bias or inconsistency problems that may be present in this study, we first consider more formally the basic meaning of problems of parameter bias or

2 Methodology and Data

inconsistency. The concepts developed in the following discussion are of greatest relevance in a micro data setting, where distributions of variables can be observed.

For simplicity, let X denote a set of exogenously determined variables, which we will refer to as explanatory variables; let y denote the variable of our interest, which will be referred to as the dependent variable, and let β denote a vector of parameters. Suppose that we specify the relationship

$$y = X\beta + \varepsilon \qquad (2.5.1)$$

together with a complete parametric description of the distribution of the error term ε, and suppose that we assert that b is an unbiased estimator of β. (We will ignore the distinctions between unbiasedness and consistency in this section since the following discussion of the meaning of unbiasedness would apply with minor changes to the concept of consistency also.) By this assertion of unbiasedness we mean the following:

1. The distribution of y is completely described by (2.5.1) together with the given parametric description of the distribution of ε.
2. On the average, the values that we obtain for b using many different samples of data will approximately equal β.[27]
3. If we had the matrix of observations for X and unbiased estimates of the parameters of the distribution of ε and β, except for the sampling errors inherent in our estimates of these parameters, we would be able to recreate the distribution of the variable y.

Suppose along with (2.5.1) we also specify that this is a <u>structural</u> relationship. In this case, in addition to statements 1-3 above, by our assertion that b is an unbiased estimator of β we also mean:

4. If the value of any one of the variables in X were exogenously increased by one unit, holding the values of all of the other variables in X constant, from the value of the parameter in β corresponding to this variable, we would be able to determine the amount by which the mean of the dependent variable y would be observed to change, even under <u>changed circumstances.</u> The meaning of changed circumstances should become clear from examples given below.

Basically, we are referring here to so-called structural change.[28]

5. From every element in b, we can determine the amount by which we would expect the mean of y to change if the value of the variable in X corresponding to this element of b were exogenously increased by one unit, even under changed circumstances.

Note that condition 4 is a property of the model that generally follows from logical arguments, including appeals to established economic theory. Condition 5, on the other hand, results from 4 and the properties of the estimator b, where the properties of the estimator b are usually established by econometric and statistical proofs conditional on 4 and the assumed nature of the distribution of the error term ε.

When the term unbiased is being used in the sense that it implies conditions 1-3 above, but not 4-5, we will refer to it, for convenience, as unbiasedness in the reduced form sense or reduced form unbiasedness. When the term unbiased implies 1-5 above, we will refer to this as unbiasedness in the structural sense or structural unbiasedness.[29] In the context of this discussion, the crucial difference between unbiasedness in the reduced form and structural senses has to do with the nature of the implications to be drawn from an estimated relationship. Suppose we estimate a wage equation that includes an education variable. If we wish to use this equation to forecast individual wage rates, where all aspects of the circumstances in the forecast setting are similar to the original setting for the estimated equation, then it would be desirable for the estimator for the parameter of the education variable in the wage equation to be unbiased in a reduced form sense. Structural unbiasedness is not required, however, since no changes are contemplated that would alter the distribution of values for the education variable or the relationship of this variable to the dependent variable of interest. Such an estimated relationship might also be useful for identifying the educational characteristics of individuals with various levels for the expected wage rate, after controlling for other observable characteristics of these individuals. Structural unbiasedness might not be required in this case either.

But suppose, on the other hand, we would like to use the estimated equation to forecast what would happen to the wage rates for some group of individuals if a new government program were instituted to raise their educational levels. If the education variable in the wage equation is picking up not only the direct, current effects of education on the wage rates of individuals, but also acting as a proxy for intelligence, motivation to work as well as to invest in education, the way in which employers select employees for different jobs, and so forth, then the coefficient of the education variable in the estimated wage equation will probably not properly reflect the wage response to the proposed new educational program.

Or suppose the government proposes to change the cost of education by giving a tax credit for education expenditures. To answer the question of how this program might affect the wage rates of some group of individuals, we might first need an auxiliary equation to predict how individuals would change their patterns of investing in education in response to the new tax credit. Then, we would again need to be able to untangle the direct effects of education on the wage rates of individuals from the effects of intelligence, motivation to work and to invest in education, and so forth for which the education variable in our estimated wage equation is serving as a proxy. An estimator of the coefficient of the education variable that is unbiased in the structural sense, in the broadest sense of this term, would give us a proper estimate of the wage response of an individual to a change in the individual level of education brought about in this or any other manner. Thus, certain policy questions or behavioral questions suggested by economic theory may compel a researcher to consider unbiasedness in a structural sense.

The analytic proofs of reduced form or structural unbiasedness found in the literature are all conditional on certain aspects of the correctness of the specification of the model to be estimated. The specification of the model usually includes a functional form relating a dependent variable to a vector of explanatory variables and a disturbance term, assumptions concerning the relationships between the disturbance term and the explanatory variables, and parametric assumptions about the distribution of the disturbance term. None of the available specification error tests allows us to simultaneously test the appropriateness of all these aspects of our model specification. Thus, analytic proofs of unbiasedness, even accompanied by elaborate specification error testing, can do no more than establish that unbiasedness in the reduced form or structural sense is possible if certain assumptions concerning model specification are correct.[30] Analytic demonstrations that a bias problem exists, on the other hand, do not necessarily provide us with a basis for judging the seriousness of the bias problem in a numerical sense. Nor do they necessarily lead to ways of comparing the costs associated with the demonstrated bias problem versus the costs associated with various possible remedies for the bias problem.[31]

An alternative, or complementary, means of demonstrating

the existence of, or assessing the seriousness of, bias problems is through simulation. Monte Carlo simulation experiments have long been used to demonstrate the lack of bias, or extent of bias, for estimators for which it has proved difficult or impossible to establish unbiasedness by analytic means. In these Monte Carlo experiments, however, the specification of the true model is known to the investigator, just as the mathematician or statistician takes the properties of an assumed model to be known or given in working through an analytic proof of unbiasedness. What we are suggesting here is a more general use of simulation for detecting or assessing the seriousness of bias problems in situations where there is no way of knowing a priori whether the model specification is, in fact, correct.

If the parameter estimates of our model, including the parameter estimates for the distribution of the error term, are unbiased in either the reduced form or the structural sense, then except for sampling variability, the distribution of the predicted values of the dependent variable, calculated using actual values for the explanatory variables and using the estimated parameters, should approximate the actual distribution of the dependent variable in all essential features. This is the reasoning that underlies the extensive simulation checks on our estimated model of work behavior that are presented in Chapter 4. Simulation checks of this sort cannot establish conclusively that a set of parameter estimates are unbiased in either a reduced form or structural sense. They can aid us, however, in assessing the nature and seriousness of bias problems that a priori knowledge suggests may exist. Also, these simulation checks allow us to reject estimated models that produce distributions of predicted values for the dependent variable or variables of interest that appear unmistakably different from the corresponding actual distributions.

Predictive checks as a criterion of model evaluation have long been emphasized by macroeconomic model builders, of course. In a macro setting these checks must usually be conducted out-of-sample, since virtually all of the in-sample information is used in the estimation of the model. In fact, for models estimated using aggregate time series that are highly autocorrelated and collinear, even the out-of-sample movements of the dependent variables of interest may be largely a reflection of in-sample information used in the estimation of the model. In contrast, in estimating our relationships for the work behavior of individuals, we have used only a fraction of the information in even our in-sample data base. For instance, we have used lagged information about work behavior for only one previous year. Thus, in the estimation of our behavioral relationships, we have used only a portion of the information concerning the employment, hours of work, and earnings histories of each individual over the in-sample period of 1971 through 1978. The remaining in-sample information can thus be used for in-sample simulation checks, as a supplement to out-of-sample simulation checks. Generally, too, in a macro setting it is only possible to make simulation comparisons involving the predicted expected values for the macro dependent variables of interest. In a micro setting, however, we can make a variety of distributional comparisons, and comparisons can be made for various subgroups or at various levels of aggregation. Thus, in a micro setting the scope for predictive simulation checks will generally be broader than in the macro setting, where this tool of model evaluation has already proved its worth.

To say that an estimator for the coefficient of one of the explanatory variables in our models is biased in a structural sense is often a way of stating that the variable that we measure is more complex, or multidimensional, than the variable that we would like to have available to us.[32] Thus, an education variable measured as years of schooling stands not only for the training received by the individual in the given years of schooling, but also for the socioeconomic background, tastes and preferences, and intelligence that caused or permitted the person to attend school for the observed number of years. In certain applications, the education variable may also reflect the fact that the level of education is sometimes used by employers as a low-cost screening device for sorting potential employees into different career streams. Suppose that what we would like is to measure how the increase in training, or human capital, gained through an additional year of schooling would affect some output of interest,[33] such as the productivity of the individual over time. We could make such a measurement if we were able to alter experimentally the educational levels of individuals independently of their socioeconomic backgrounds, intelligence levels and so forth[34] <u>and</u> if we were able to measure the contributions of the experimental increase in human capital to productivity, as opposed to measuring, say, some combination of changes in productivity due to the experimental changes in human capital as well as to differences in opportunities for on-the-job training for those with different levels of human capital and differences in the physical capital with which workers at different educational levels work. It is difficult to conceive of how we might structure such an experiment, however.

In a nonexperimental setting, factors, such as intelligence and socioeconomic background, associated with observed levels of education all vary together. If the covariation of these factors has always been the same, there will be no way of separating out one component of this variation, such as the component due to education-related increases in human capital, from the other components. If the historical covariation of these factors has not been perfect, we may be able to achieve such a separation by (1) introducing additional explanatory variables into the analysis to pick up the effects of other factors associated with variations in the level of education, or (2) finding an instrument for the education variable that is highly correlated with the human capital component of the education variable but that is uncorrelated with all other factors associated with the measured levels of education. Thus, if we introduce intelligence test scores into a model, along with an education variable, or if we introduce a Heckman-style selection bias term into an equation to account for education-related sample selection effects, we are adopting the first of these two approaches to coping with parameter bias in the structural sense. One major difference between these two approaches is that in the first approach, the portion of the variability of the dependent variable accounted for by the estimated equation is generally increased, and never reduced; while in the second approach, the portion of variability in the dependent variable accounted for by the estimated equation may be substantially reduced.[35] Even so, if the second approach is successful, although the variability of estimates of the conditional expected value of the dependent variable may be increased, the estimated equation, together with the estimates for the parameters of the assumed distribution for the equation error term, should still allow us to reproduce approximately the distribution of the dependent variables for the model, given the values of all explanatory variables. This implies that if the estimated model <u>cannot</u> reproduce key aspects of the distribution of the dependent variables, the coefficients of the estimated model are probably not unbiased in any sense of the term.[36] At any rate, whatever the formal statistical properties of the estimated model might be, one would be reluctant to use it for predictive or other policy-related purposes.

    In this study we make three corrections in an effort to mitigate suspected bias problems. First we attempt to separate out the current effects of our explanatory variables from effects due to associated, person-specific factors that are fixed or that persist over many time periods. We do this by introducing into our behavioral relationships variables describing the person's work behavior in the previous time period that embed the fixed or persistent person-specific effects. Since we want to obtain an appropriate estimated model that predicts well, this correction is important from a number of perspectives. For instance, without making such a correction, we may overestimate the labor force responsiveness of women to changes in current child status. In a policy context, this in turn might lead us to overestimate the amount by which women would increase their labor supply in response to government provision of free or subsidized childcare. In a forecasting context, failure to make this correction might cause us to overestimate the extent to which individual women leave and enter the workforce. Hence, the distributions of the cumulative earnings of individual women over several time periods would be distorted. This correction can be viewed as a bias correction of the first type discussed above, although undoubtedly we do not succeed in entirely eliminating biases resulting from fixed or persistent person-specific unobservables.

Second, we attempt to separate out the direct impacts of our explanatory variables on the wage rates and hours of work of individuals from the indirect impacts these explanatory variables may exert through their impacts on the determination of who works. We do this by introducing selection bias terms, as suggested by Heckman, into our wage rate and hours of work equations.[37] A key assumption on which this particular correction for selection bias is based is that the covariances between the unobservables that affect the determination of who works and the unobservables that affect the distributions of the wage rates and hours of work, respectively, for individuals in the uncensored population are constant parameters for all individuals for whom the estimated relationships are assumed to hold. The introduction of a selection bias term into our wage and hours equations brings into these equations all of the variables included in the relevant probit index for the determination of who works, even though some of these variables may be hypothesized to have no direct effects on wage rates or hours of work. Thus, in our Inertia Model, the education variable enters our wage equation both directly through its inclusion in Z and indirectly though its inclusion in the probit index used in the calculation of the value of the selection bias term for each individual who works in each year. On the other hand, the child status variables are not included in Z or E, and they enter our wage equation only indirectly through their inclusion in the probit index. This Heckman-type selection bias correction is also a bias correction of the first type.

Finally, we attempt to purge the wage variable in our hours equation of errors of observation believed to be correlated with errors in the observed values of our hours of work variable. We do this by substituting for the original wage variable in our hours equation the predicted values for this variable obtained from our estimated offered wage equation. We argue that this instrumental procedure should also purge the wage variable of components, other than those due to the errors-in-the-variables problem, that are correlated with the true disturbance of the hours equation. The errors-in-the-variables problem arises because erroneously high wage observations will be paired, because of the way in which they are created, with erroneously low observations for hours of work and vice versa. There is a potential efficiency cost attached to making this correction, since whatever variability in the observed values for hours of work is explainable in a proxy sense, or in any other sense, by the residual portion of the wage variable will be left in the disturbance term for our instrumental hours equation. This bias correction is, thus, of the second type.

We have argued that many bias corrections are an implicit recognition of the fact that the variables available to us for inclusion in socioeconomic studies are composite variables. An education variable not only picks up the effects of the human capital an individual has acquired in the formal education process, but may also pick up the effects of human capital acquired at home, the ability and desire to learn, the impacts of the use of education as a screening device by employers, and so forth. Child status variables reflect not only the time and money demands of caring for children, but also may reflect general attitudes toward home-oriented versus market-oriented activities. A race dummy reflects everything that is different about the way a model fits for the racial group in question versus the majority population.

Bias corrections and a variety of other aspects of model formulation are also an assertion of a belief, based on econometric arguments, that it is sometimes possible to alter, or exert some limited degree of control over, which factors will be picked up, among all those that might be picked up, by a specific composite variable in a particular applied setting. This alteration or degree of control is supposedly achieved through a combination of the choice of other variables entered into a model and the choice of the estimation method, which may include the specification and estimation of auxiliary behavioral or instrumental relationships. There are those who would argue that in a properly designed empirical study, this process can, and should, succeed to the point that the estimated model can be used to predict the impacts on the distributions of the dependent variables in the model of any exogenous changes in the values of the explanatory variables, however these changes may be achieved. This is the essense of an unconditional claim that all the parameter estimates of a model are unbiased, or consistent, in a structural sense. There are also those who would argue that failure to achieve this goal implies that the resulting estimated model will be of little or no use for policy analysis. According to this position, such a model might at best be useful for forecasting with unchanged circumstances.

2 Methodology and Data

A more modest claim, which has become a trademark in better-quality econometric work, is that the parameter estimates for the model are unbiased or consistent provided that a carefully spelled out list of assumptions are all precisely satisfied.[38] These assumptions usually include the specified functional forms and the specified variables included in all structural relationships, as well as a complete characterization of the distributions for all disturbance terms included in the model. This is equivalent to assuming that conditions 1 and 4 are satisfied for the simple relationship (2.5.1). In other words, this is a claim that if everything we have specified a priori about the world in constructing our model and formulating the assumptions that accompany this model is true, and if all that is left to be learned is the values of the parameters of our model, then our parameter estimates can be considered to be unbiased or consistent.[39] Such a careful statement of the conditions under which the parameter estimates of a model will be unbiased or consistent may be helpful to potential users in identifying and thinking about particular circumstances under which the estimated model would <u>not</u> properly reflect the changes in the distributions of the dependent variables of the model that would result from certain types of exogenous changes in the explanatory variables of the model. Careful thinking of this sort, for instance, was what led to the realization that the estimated coefficient of an education variable in an earnings function probably would not properly reflect the change in earnings that would result for a particular group, such as blacks, if the educational level of this group were exogenously raised through specially funded government programs.[40]

The working out of a precise set of conditions under which the estimates of the parameters of a model would be unbiased or consistent can be a demanding and time consuming task, however, even for individuals who have extensive econometric and statistical training. Thus, whatever understanding is gained through this exercise is not without its costs. The costs may also include the unwillingness of analysts to do even exploratory empirical work concerning problems or extensions of problems where no one has been able to find a set of conditions under which the estimates for the parameters of relevant models could be considered to be unbiased or consistent in a structural sense, or the out-of-hand dismissal of such studies by the profession at large when they are carried out.

In this study we argue that bias corrections should only be carried out for suspected bias problems of special relevance in the given applied setting. We carry out three such corrections, as has been indicated above. We do not go on to lay out a set of conditions under which the resulting parameter estimates could be considered to be unbiased or consistent in a structural sense.[41] We think it is likely that such conditions, if they exist, are highly restrictive for several of the model variants for which empirical results are presented in this study. Thus, we feel certain that the parameter estimates presented in this study do not exactly reflect the expected changes that would occur in the distributions of the dependent variables in our study for all possible exogenous changes in the included explanatory variables. This admission is not, perhaps, qualitatively different from the more customary statement that the parameter estimates presented are unbiased or consistent under a set of precisely specified conditions, which are probably not precisely satisfied in the situation at hand. Of course, such an admission does not provide the reader with any basis for thinking about the potential seriousness and direction of parameter biases and inconsistencies of special relevance for various applications. What we offer, instead, are simulation results showing the goodness-of-fit of various aspects of the predicted joint distribution of the dependent variables of our model to the actual observed distribution for these variables.[42] These simulation results leave many questions unanswered. As Arnold Zellner has pointed out to us, however, emphasis on the quality of the predictions of models is pervasive in science. It should be recalled, too, that a statement of the conditions under which parameter estimates are unbiased or consistent is also just a start toward understanding what bias or inconsistency problems actually exist in a given applied situation where some or all of the assumptions of a model may not be precisely satisfied.

2.6. Standard Errors and Significance Tests

The basic purpose that underlies most of our significance tests is to establish that an observed sample relationship is stronger than might be expected by chance. Until at least this can be established, further discussion and investigation of the sign and strength of a hypothesized relationship are not meaningful.

The most common tests of significance for the slope parameters of an estimated model involve forming test statistics using the coefficient estimates for the slope parameters and estimates of the standard errors for these coefficient estimates. These test statistics have been shown to obey known distributions, provided that the coefficient estimates for the slope parameters and the associated estimates for the standard errors are unbiased or consistent.

In addition to the problems noted in the previous section in claiming that the estimates of the coefficients of the explanatory variables of a model are unbiased or consistent, there are some additional problems concerning the question of the unbiasedness or consistency of the estimates of the standard errors. For instance, the usual estimators for the standard errors of the slope coefficients in a regression model involving sample selection have been shown to be biased except under the null hypothesis of no sample selection.[43] Heteroscedastic or autocorrelated disturbance terms, which might be expected in panel data bases, will lead to biased estimates of the relevant standard errors if these properties of the disturbance terms are not taken into account. For each of these specific bias problems, considered in isolation, we may be able to derive and implement a suitable econometric remedy. However, there are also many models and estimation methods that have a variety of attractive properties, but unbiased or consistent estimators of the relevant standard errors have not yet been derived for them.[44]

It strikes us as unlikely that we would be able to remedy all of the bias or inconsistency problems that must exist with respect to the computation of estimated standard errors for the slope parameters of models of the sort for which empirical results are presented in this study. Thus, we are not able to rely on traditional tests of significance. Also on a more philisophical level, we note that for many practical purposes, it may not matter much if a coefficient is only slightly different from zero. Confidence intervals for coefficients might be more meaningful, with the emphasis on the signs and approximate magnitudes of the response coefficients. Without appropriate estimators for the standard errors of our model, we cannot construct confidence intervals either, however. Nevertheless, for descriptive purposes in the tables of estimated coefficients presented in this book, we use two stars or one star, respectively, to denote coefficients that are at least 1.960 or 1.282 times as large in magnitude as the usual probit or least squares regression estimates of the associated standard errors. For samples that are large, which is generally the case for our samples, two stars could be thought of as indicating a two-tailed level of significance of at least 95 percent and one star could be thought of as indicating an 80 percent two-tailed significance level, if there are not problems of bias or inconsistency or of model specification. For the reasons we have indicated above, however, we pay little or no attention to these stars in our discussions of the significance of the slope coefficients of the estimated relationships. Rather, we attempt to establish the significance of relationships by showing that they can be replicated for more than one demographic group -- or that we can identify related effects of a variable that we would expect to observe on theoretical grounds in different behavioral relationships of the specified model. This mode of attempting to establish the significance of observed empirical relationships does not have the same appearance of rigor as the more conventional statistical tests of significance. In taking this approach, however, we are following a long and, we believe, respectable tradition. For instance, Glen Cain (1966, p. 4) writes in the Introduction to his book on the labor force behavior of married women:

> The economic model of labor force participation of married women used in this book is tested ... with cross-sectional data of two statistical types (aggregated and disaggregated), for two color groups, and from different time periods over a span of 20 years (1940 to 1960). The evaluation of these tests ... involves the following three three issues: (a) Do the coefficients of the explanatory variables agree with the theoretical expectations, and are they consistent among the different statistical studies? (b) Are the results for white and nonwhite wives compatible? (c) Do these cross-sectional results conform with those from time series?

We also feel that the approach adopted is true to the basic tenants of hypothesis testing and the scientific method in the sense that it does not make our conclusions appear more rigorous or conclusive than they really are.[45]

2.7. Our Data Base, and the Characteristics of the Women and Men Whose Data Have Been Used in This Study

The data used in all portions of this study, except section 4.6, are for individuals who were included in the 1970 through 1979 waves of the Michigan Panel Study of Income Dynamics (PSID). We chose to use data from the PSID because in addition to offering us panel data over a substantial number of years, the PSID is a national study, and it offers us data collected using essentially the same definitions and over the same period of years for all of the demographic groups of our interest.[46] Information for certain variables such as earned income is collected in the PSID for the calendar year preceding the survey year (see section 2.4). Thus, we obtain the current values of these variables for each individual from the next year's record for this individual. Also, we obtain

2 Methodology and Data

the values of certain lagged variables from the previous year's record for each individual, and data on certain variables are not available for the earliest years of the PSID (see section 2.4). Thus, the data used in this study, except where explicitly stated otherwise, are for 1971 through 1978.

An annual **cross-sectional** data set for some group of individuals consists of observations for these individuals for a given year. An annual **panel** data set for some group of individuals consists of observations for these individuals over a period of years. Data from the PSID is of the latter sort. When panel data are used without regard for the sequence of observations over years for each individual, we sometimes refer to the data as **pooled** data. When using the panel nature of a data set, it is usually necessary to drop all observations for individuals with missing data for one or more years. This is not necessary when using the data in pooled form.

Our Inertia Model requires only pooled data, where the record for each individual in each year has been augmented by some information from the waves of the PSID for the previous and subsequent years. Thus, in order to estimate our model, we would not have to drop all observations for individuals with missing data for some years. In fact, however, we have only included in our data base information on individuals who were in the PSID continuously from 1970 through 1979, who were at least 14 years of age in 1971, and for whom observations are available for all of these years on all appropriate variables. This is because we cannot include individuals in our simulation population for whom data are missing for some of the years in our simulation period and because we want to use the same data both to estimate the parameters of relationships and to carry out certain simulation checks on these estimated relationships. We do not want to confound failures in prediction due to the failure of our estimated relationships to properly reflect the behavior of the individuals whose data were used in estimation with failures in prediction due to differences in behavior between the group of individuals whose data were used in the estimation of our relationships and the group of individuals whose data were used in our simulation checks on these estimated relationships. That is, before going to out-of-sample simulation checks on our estimated relationships, we would like to make sure that they properly reflect the behavior of the individuals whose data were used in estimation by performing in-sample simulation checks.

There are some costs involved in using the PSID data in this manner. The first is that we have fewer observations to use in the estimation of our relationships than would otherwise be the case. A second is that we can no longer use directly the weights provided with the PSID data.[47] In order to use the PSID weights, we would have to correct them to reflect the censoring of the data due to our data selection rules. We decided not to attempt this because of the apparent difficulty of the task and because the use of weights would complicate some of our computational procedures. If the unobserved characteristics of the individuals whose data are used in the estimation of our relationships are truly uncorrelated, or only slightly correlated, with all of the explanatory variables in these relationships, the failure to weight the observations might have little effect on the nature of the estimated relationships. If this is not the case, the applicability of the relationships estimated in this study may be limited to analyses of the work behavior of groups of individuals similar in composition to the group whose data are used in estimating these relationships. Limitations of this sort on the applicability of our estimated relationships can be explored through out-of-sample simulation, including simulations using an initial population that is representative of the U.S. population in the specified base year. Limitations of this sort may also be discovered by the examination of in-sample simulation results for subgroups of the in-sample data that differ from the subgroups used in estimating the behavioral relationships. We are not aware of any empirical studies of labor force behavior using micro data that are entirely free of potential limitations of this sort.

The out-of-sample simulation results that we present in this study are for a different (and much shorter) time period than the time period for our in-sample simulations. We could also have split our data base for our in-sample period and reserved part of it for model validation through out-of-sample simulation.[48] Doing so would have further reduced the size of the samples to be used in the estimation of the parameters of our behavioral relationships, however. This would have posed a problem in estimating relationships for numerically small groups such as currently working wives 47-64 years of age who did not work in the previous year.

For estimation purposes we pooled all observations on all individuals in our data base for the years of 1971 through 1978. We then divided the observations in the pooled data base into the following ten demographic categories: (1) women 14-20 years of age, (2) wives 21-46 years of age, (3) unmarried women 21-46 years of age, (4) wives 47-64 years of age, (5) unmarried women 47-64 years of age, (6) women 65 or more years of age, (7) men 14-20 years of age, (8) men 21-46 years of age, (9) men 47-64 years of age, and (10) men 65 or more years of age. Thus, for a man 44 years of age in 1971, we would place his observations for the years of 1971 through 1973 in group 8 and the rest of his observations in group 9. Or for a woman who was 22 and unmarried in 1971 and who then married in 1972, we would place her first observation in group 3 and the rest of her observations in group 2. For estimation purposes

2 Methodology and Data

we have also further subdivided the observations in all six of our demographic groups for women and in group 7 for men, depending on whether or not the individual worked in the previous year. The variables for which mean values are shown in the remainder of this section are the variables that are defined in section 2.4.

In Table 2.7.1 we show point estimates of the probability of work in the current year for women who did not work in the previous year (t-1). In Table 2.7.2 we show the same point estimates for women who did work in the previous year. In Table 2.7.3 we show these point estimates for men. The number in parentheses below each of the point estimates in these tables is the number of observations in the pooled data sample used in computing the point estimate. From these tables we see that for both women and men, the probability of work first rises and then falls with age. We see that unmarried women have higher probabilities of work than married women; and men consistently have higher probabilities of work than women in the corresponding age groups, except for unmarried women 47-64 and women 65 or more years of age who worked in the previous year. Finally, we see that the differences in the probability of work, depending on whether or not a woman or young man worked in the previous year, are very large. The differences for the different age and marital status groups for the probabilities shown in Table 2.7.1 for women who did not work in the previous year versus the probabilities shown in Table 2.7.2 for women who did work in the previous years are much larger than the differences commonly reported, for instance, for the employment rates of all women versus all men. Comparing the figures shown in Tables 2.7.2 and 2.7.3, we also find that the probabilities of work for women who worked last year are only slightly lower than those for men in the corresponding age groups, except for the oldest age group where the female probability is much higher. One possible implication of the results in these three tables is that if we were permitted to partition our data according to only one variable rather than several, we might seriously consider partitioning according to work status in the previous year, rather than by the sex of the individual.

Of course, women who worked in the previous year may be different from women who did not work in the previous year in terms of their observable characteristics.

The mean values of our marital status dummies are shown in Tables 2.7.4 and 2.7.5. In Table 2.7.4 and all similar tables for women that follow in this section, the top figure in each group of three numbers is for all women, the next is for women who did not work in the previous year, and the bottom figure is for women who worked in the previous year. Except for the youngest age group, we see from Table 2.7.4 that the proportions of women married in the current or

TABLE 2.7.1
POINT ESTIMATES OF THE PROBABILITY OF WORK:
WOMEN WHO DID NOT WORK IN t-1

Marital status	Age 14-20	21-46	47-64	65+
Married		.21 (1391)	.09 (608)	
	.30 (717)			.06 (594)
Unmarried		.38 (683)	.13 (466)	

TABLE 2.7.2
POINT ESTIMATES OF THE PROBABILITY OF WORK:
WOMEN WHO WORKED IN t-1

Marital status	Age 14-20	21-46	47-64	65+
Married		.85 (2166)	.86 (632)	
	.76 (495)			.74 (164)
Unmarried		.92 (1397)	.92 (796)	

TABLE 2.7.3
POINT ESTIMATES OF THE PROBABILITY OF WORK: MEN

Work status in t-1	Age 14-20	21-46	47-64	65+
Did not work	.35 (546)			
		.95 (6259)	.90 (2961)	.44 (776)
Worked	.85 (602)			

TABLE 2.7.4
MEAN VALUES FOR MARITAL STATUS VARIABLES FOR ALL WOMEN, WOMEN WHO DID NOT WORK IN THE PREVIOUS YEAR, AND WOMEN WHO WORKED IN THE PREVIOUS YEAR

Group	Dummy for currently married	Dummy for married in t-1	Dummy for currently widowed	Dummy for currently divorced
Women 14-20	.14	.08		
	.09	.07		
	.23	.10		
Wives 21-46		.95		
		.98		
		.93		
Unmarried women 21-46		.04		
		.13		
		.00		
Wives 47-64		.99		
		.99		
		.98		
Unmarried women 47-64		.02	.42	.46
		.04	.44	.45
		.00	.41	.47
Women 65+	.24	.25	.56	.05
	.27	.28	.56	.04
	.12	.12	.59	.10

previous year are consistently lower for women who worked in the previous year than for women who did not work in the previous year. Also, the proportions of currently divorced women are higher for women who worked in the previous year than for women who did not. Comparing the figures in Tables 2.7.4 and 2.7.5, we see that a higher proportion of the young women are currently married compared with the young men, but that a much lower proportion of women than men in the

TABLE 2.7.5
MEAN VALUES FOR DUMMY VARIABLE FOR
CURRENTLY MARRIED FOR MEN

Work status in t-1	Age			
	14-20	21-46	47-64	65+
Did not work	.00	.79	.93	.88
Worked	.17			

65-and-over age group are currently married.

In Tables 2.7.6 and 2.7.7, we show mean values for our age, race dummy and education variables for women and men, while in Table 2.7.8 we show mean values for our disability and retirement age dummies for men. From Table 2.7.6 we find no clear age pattern depending on whether or not a woman worked in the previous year for women 21-46 years of age. However, those women in the 14-20 age group who worked in the previous year are older, on the average, than those who did not work in the previous year, and in the 47-64 and 65-and-over age groups those women who worked in the previous year are younger, on the average, than those who did not. From Table 2.7.7 we find that the age pattern for young women depending on work status in the previous year is duplicated for men 14-20 years of age.

The mean values for our race dummy are the sample proportions of individuals in our various groups who are black. We notice first of all from Table 2.7.6 that black women make up 42 to 68 percent of our various subsamples of unmarried women 21-46 and 47-64 years of age, but only 12 to 21 percent of our various subsamples of married women for these age categories. Within the unmarried categories, we see that the proportion of blacks is higher among those women who did not work in the previous year than among those who did work in the previous year. This is also the case for women 14-20 years of age and for women 65 and over. From Table 2.7.7 we see that this racial composition pattern with respect to work status in the previous year is also duplicated for men 14-20 years of age. From Table 2.7.6 we see, however, that this pattern is reversed for married women 21-46 and 47-64 years of age.

From Table 2.7.6 we see that the mean values for our education variable are consistently higher for women who worked in the previous year than for those who did not.

2 Methodology and Data

TABLE 2.7.6
MEAN VALUES FOR AGE, RACE DUMMY AND EDUCATION
VARIABLES FOR ALL WOMEN, WOMEN WHO DID NOT WORK
IN THE PREVIOUS YEAR, AND WOMEN WHO WORKED
IN THE PREVIOUS YEAR

Group	Age	Race dummy	Education
Women 14-20	17.8	.44	11.3
	17.4	.52	11.1
	18.5	.32	11.6
Wives 21-46	32.9	.20	12.1
	33.0	.18	11.8
	32.9	.21	12.2
Unmarried women 21-46	32.2	.58	11.7
	31.8	.68	11.1
	32.4	.53	11.9
Wives 47-64	53.2	.12	11.5
	54.3	.10	11.2
	52.0	.13	11.7
Unmarried women 47-64	55.0	.49	10.7
	55.4	.61	9.7
	54.8	.42	11.3
Women 65+	71.7	.13	10.3
	72.5	.15	10.0
	68.5	.09	11.7

However, comparing the figures in Tables 2.7.6 and 2.7.7, we see that even the mean values for the education variable for women who worked in the previous year are consistently lower than the mean values for men in the corresponding age groups, except for men 14-20 and men 65 or more years of age. Thus, women who worked last year tend to be better educated than women who did not work last year, but not quite as well educated as the men in our data base, except in the youngest

TABLE 2.7.7
MEAN VALUES FOR AGE, RACE DUMMY AND EDUCATION
VARIABLES FOR MEN

Group	Age	Race dummy	Education
Men 14-20 who did not work in t-1	17.3	.54	10.7
Men 14-20 who worked in t-1	18.4	.31	11.4
Men 21-46	33.6	.23	12.5
Men 47-64	54.0	.19	11.8
Men 65+	70.8	.11	11.3

TABLE 2.7.8
MEAN VALUES FOR DISABILITY AND RETIREMENT
AGE DUMMIES FOR MEN

Group	Disability dummy	Dummy for 60-62 years of age	Dummy for 63-64 years of age	Dummy for 65-66 years of age
Men 21-46	.10			
Men 47-64	.21	.11	.07	
Men 65+	.34			.22

and oldest age groups.

From Table 2.7.8 we see that disabilities limiting work become quite prevalent for men in the oldest age group and are clearly of numerical importance even in the younger age groups. Unfortunately, this information is not available in the PSID data for married women for some years over our 1971-1978 time period.

In Tables 2.7.9 and 2.7.10, we show mean values for our

TABLE 2.7.9
MEAN VALUES FOR DUMMY VARIABLE FOR STUDENT IN
PREVIOUS YEAR AND FOR DUMMY VARIABLE FOR LIVING
WITH PARENTS FOR ALL WOMEN 14-20, WOMEN 14-20
WHO DID NOT WORK IN THE PREVIOUS YEAR, AND
WOMEN 14-20 WHO WORKED IN THE PREVIOUS YEAR

Dummy for student in t-1	Dummy for living with parents
.08	.74
.08	.82
.07	.63

TABLE 2.7.10
MEAN VALUES FOR DUMMY VARIABLE FOR STUDENT IN PREVIOUS YEAR
AND FOR DUMMY VARIABLE FOR LIVING WITH PARENTS FOR MEN 14-20

Group	Dummy for student in t-1	Dummy for living with parents
Men 14-20 who did not work in t-1	.07	.95
Men 14-20 who worked in t-1	.06	.72

dummy variables for student status in the previous year and for whether the individual is living with a parent or parents. For both young women and men, we find that those who worked in the previous year are slightly less likely to have been a student in the previous year and considerably less likely to be living with parents in the current year.

In Tables 2.7.11 and 2.7.12, we show mean values for each of our three child status variables for those groups of women and men for which each of these variables is included in our behavioral relationships. We find that the mean values for our child status variables are, in fact, consistently lower for women who did than for those who did not work in the previous year, except for wives 47-64 years of age for the variable for the number of children living at home who are younger than 18. Thus, on the whole, women who worked last year have fewer children to care for than women who did not work last year.

TABLE 2.7.11
MEAN VALUES FOR CHILD STATUS VARIABLES
FOR ALL WOMEN, WOMEN WHO DID NOT WORK
IN THE PREVIOUS YEAR, AND WOMEN WHO
WORKED IN THE PREVIOUS YEAR

Group	Baby dummy	Young child dummy	Number of children younger than 18
Women 14-20	.06	.23	2.51
	.06	.23	2.82
	.04	.22	2.06
Wives 21-46	.08	.35	2.06
	.09	.46	2.43
	.07	.28	1.82
Unmarried women 21-46	.04	.23	1.75
	.06	.33	2.44
	.02	.19	1.42
Wives 47-64			.59
			.54
			.64
Unmarried women 47-64			.64
			.88
			.50
Women 65+			.10
			.11
			.07

TABLE 2.7.12
MEAN VALUES FOR VARIABLE FOR NUMBER OF
CHILDREN YOUNGER THAN 18 FOR MEN

Men 21-46	Men 47-64
1.87	1.03

TABLE 2.7.13

MEAN VALUES FOR OTHER INCOME VARIABLES FOR ALL
WOMEN, WOMEN WHO DID NOT WORK IN THE
PREVIOUS YEAR, AND WOMEN WHO WORKED
IN THE PREVIOUS YEAR

Group	Husband's income	Change in husband's income	Negative change in husband's income	Dummy for AFDC in t-1	Dummy for Social Security in t-1
Women 21-46	.7	.02			
	.4	.02			
	1.2	.02			
Wives 21-46	8.6	.13		.01	
	9.6	.07		.01	
	7.9	.16		.01	
Unmarried women 21-46				.10	
				.18	
				.06	
Wives 47-64	7.5		-1.0		.03
	6.9		-1.2		.04
	8.0		-.9		.02
Unmarried women 47-64					.07
					.13
					.03
Women 65+	.2		-.1		.17
	.2		-.1		.18
	.2		-.1		.13

In Tables 2.7.13 and 2.7.14, we show mean values for our other income variables for the groups in which each of these variables has been included in our behavioral relationships. We see that women who worked in the previous year are less likely to have received AFDC or Social Security benefits in the previous year than women who did not work in the previous

TABLE 2.7.14
MEAN VALUES FOR OTHER INCOME VARIABLES FOR MEN

Group	Wife's income in t-1	Dummy for AFDC in t-1	Dummy for Social Security in t-1
Men 14-20 who did not work in t-1	.0	.01	
Men 14-20 who worked in t-1	.1	.01	
Men 21-46	1.3	.01	
Men 47-64	1.6		.02
Men 65+	.6		.17

year. We see also that the same proportions of women and men 65 or more years of age were in families that received Social Security benefits, but women 47-64 were considerably more likely than men in this age bracket to live in a family receiving Social Security benefits.

The mean values for our macroeconomic variables are shown in Tables 2.7.15 and 2.7.16. Ignoring the youngest age group, from Table 2.7.15 we find that women who worked in the previous year sometimes have slightly lower average rates for the national unemployment rate variable. Also, we find that the averages for the national wage index are slightly lower for unmarried women 21-46 and 47-64 years of age, as well as for women 65 and over who worked in the previous year compared with women in each of these groups who did not work in the previous year; but this pattern is reversed for wives 21-46 and 47-64 years of age. From Tables 2.7.15 and 2.7.16, we see that for the youngest age group for both women and men, those who worked in the previous year have higher average values for both the national unemployment rate and the national wage index variables. We note also that the substantial differences for both women and men in the mean values for the youngest and

TABLE 2.7.15
MEAN VALUES FOR MACROECONOMIC VARIABLES FOR ALL
WOMEN, WOMEN WHO DID NOT WORK IN THE PREVIOUS YEAR,
AND WOMEN WHO WORKED IN THE PREVIOUS YEAR

Group	National unemployment rate	National wage index
Women 14-20	6.3	80.2
	6.2	79.0
	6.5	82.0
Wives 21-46	6.4	90.9
	6.4	89.4
	6.4	91.9
Unmarried women 21-46	6.4	91.0
	6.4	91.1
	6.4	90.9
Wives 47-64	6.5	93.3
	6.5	93.2
	6.4	93.3
Unmarried women 47-64	6.4	91.1
	6.4	91.9
	6.4	90.6
Women 65+	6.5	95.1
	6.5	95.7
	6.4	92.9

oldest age groups compared with the other age groups are due to the fact that the numbers of observations in the youngest groups for women and men are tending toward 0 over the 1971 through 1978 period, due to the way in which our data samples are defined, while the numbers of observations in the 65 and over age group for women and men are increasing over this time period.

It is not just the probabilities of work in the current year and the mean values for some of our explanatory variables

TABLE 2.7.16
MEAN VALUES FOR MACROECONOMIC VARIABLES FOR MEN

Group	National unemployment rate	National wage index
Men 14-20 who did not work in t-1	6.0	77.2
Men 14-20 who worked in t-1	6.4	82.4
Men 21-46	6.4	90.5
Men 47-64	6.4	92.6
Men 65+	6.5	95.0

that differ consistently for women who did versus women who did not work in the previous year. In Tables 2.7.17 and 2.7.18, we show mean hourly wage rates for working women who did not and for working women who did work in the previous year. Comparing the figures in these two tables for women in our various age and marital status categories, we find that wage rates for working women who did not work in the previous year (starting wage rates) are consistently and substantially lower, on the average, than wage rates for working women who did work in the previous year (continuing wage rates). Comparing the mean continuing wage rates shown for women in Table 2.7.18 with the mean wage rates shown for men in Table 2.7.19, however, we find that the male wage rates are still consistently and substantially higher for all age groups.

In Tables 2.7.20 and 2.7.21, we show mean annual hours of work for working women who did not and for working women who did work in the previous year. Comparing the figures in these two tables, we find that annual hours of work for women who did not work in the previous year (starting hours of work) are consistently and substantially lower, on the average, for all age and marital-status categories of women than are the annual hours of work for working women who worked in the previous year (continuing hours of work). However, comparing the

TABLE 2.7.17
SAMPLE MEANS FOR HOURLY WAGE RATES:
WORKING WOMEN WHO DID NOT WORK IN t-1

Marital status	Age			
	14-20	21-46	47-64	65+
Married		$2.24 (293)	$1.67 (53)	
	$1.78 (376)			$.38 (35)
Unmarried		1.89 (261)	2.25 (59)	

TABLE 2.7.18
SAMPLE MEANS FOR HOURLY WAGE RATES:
WORKING WOMEN WHO WORKED IN t-1

Marital status	Age			
	14-20	21-46	47-64	65+
Married		$2.54 (1844)	$2.69 (543)	
	$1.98 (376)			$2.04 (122)
Unmarried		2.65 (1280)	2.46 (736)	

TABLE 2.7.19
SAMPLE MEANS FOR HOURLY WAGE RATES: WORKING MEN

Work status in t-1	Age			
	14-20	21-46	47-64	65+
Did not work	$2.02 (192)			
		$3.95 (5968)	$4.52 (2653)	$3.25 (346)
Worked	2.13 (514)			

TABLE 2.7.20
SAMPLE MEANS FOR ANNUAL HOURS OF WORK:
WORKING WOMEN WHO DID NOT WORK IN t-1

Marital status	Age 14-20	Age 21-46	Age 47-64	Age 65+
Married		671 (293)	734 (53)	
	614 (219)			96 (35)
Unmarried		993 (261)	737 (59)	

TABLE 2.7.21
SAMPLE MEANS FOR ANNUAL HOURS OF WORK:
WORKING WOMEN WHO WORKED IN t-1

Marital status	Age 14-20	Age 21-46	Age 47-64	Age 65+
Married		1359 (1844)	1378 (543)	
	1112 (376)			1070 (122)
Unmarried		1676 (1280)	1711 (736)	

TABLE 2.7.22
SAMPLE MEANS FOR ANNUAL HOURS OF WORK: WORKING MEN

Work status in t-1	Age 14-20	Age 21-46	Age 47-64	Age 65+
Did not work	823 (192)			
		2198 (5968)	2130 (2653)	1120 (346)
Worked	1301 (514)			

figures in Tables 2.7.21 and 2.7.22 we find that the continuing hours of work for women still fall short, on the average, of the hours of work for men in each age group.

The women and men whose characteristics are described in the tables in this section are the women and men for whom estimation and simulation results are shown in the following chapters, except where we explicitly indicate that other data samples are being used.

FOOTNOTES TO CHAPTER 2

1. See Heckman (1974, 1976, 1979, 1980). (See also Amemiya (1984) for a summary of Heckman's and other related estimation methods.) The empirical results presented in these studies by Heckman are all for married women and are based on cross-sectional data. A number of other researchers have carried out cross-sectional studies of the employment and earnings behavior of married women, building on the model and estimation procedure developed in the references cited for Heckman. Nakamura et al. (1979) apply Heckman's modeling approach and econometric methodology in a cross-sectional study of the work behavior of Canadian wives, and results for Canadian wives are also presented in Nakamura, Nakamura and Cullen (1979). An extension of this model to the case where households must pay federal and state or provincial income taxes is presented in Nakamura and Nakamura (1981), together with empirical results for both the United States and Canada. In Nakamura and Nakamura (1983), Heckman's behavioral model and estimation method are extended to allow for the possibility that the responses to certain explanatory variables may differ over the range of variation for the annual hours of work of individuals. For instance, the change in hours of work in response to a change in the log wage rate might be different for women who work part-time than for those who work full-time. H. Rosen (1976) extends Heckman's model to allow for the possibility that the offered wage depends on the number of hours an individual works in a year; and Dooley (1982) treats both the labor supply and fertility of married women.

2. There are two formats for introducing person-specific, time invariant effects into a model. In random effects models, the person-specific effects are assumed to be distributed over individuals in accordance with some probability distribution that is specified a priori. In this case, it is possible to write down a likelihood function to be maximized (see, for example, Heckman, 1981b, p. 184, (4.6) or (4.7)). In this case also, consistent parameter estimates may be obtained as n goes

to infinity for fixed T, where n is the number of individuals in the panel and T is the number of time periods over which data are available on these individuals (see Heckman, 1981a, p. 147 and 1981b, pp. 183-184). However, as Heckman (1981b, p. 184) points out, maximizing such a likelihood function is computationally forbidding.

In so-called fixed effects models, on the other hand, the person-specific effects are simply given parameters. These fixed effects can potentially be estimated along with the other parameters of interest in a model. Within the multivariate probit framework often adopted in studies of the labor force behavior of married women, fixed effects models are generally computationally more tractable than random effects models. There are problems, however. For the estimation methods that have been proposed in the literature for fixed effects multivariate probit models, consistency is typically proved for T approaching infinity and it is necessary to limit the sample used in estimation to wives who have changed their employment status at least once during the period over which the panel data were collected (see Heckman 1981a, pp. 133-134 and 1981b, pp. 186-187). For all existing panel data sets, n is large but T is small. Moreover, we may never have good quality panel data over long periods of time since attrition biases become more and more severe as the length of a panel increases. Dropping out data for women who do not change their employment state over the duration of a panel study may, of course, result in selection biases.

Further estimation problems arise if there are persistent (autocorrelated) as well as fixed person-specific unobservables.

3. In many of our other studies, we have included variables for macroeconomic activity measured at the state level. (See, for instance, Nakamura and Nakamura 1983a). When these variables are measured at the state level, it does appear possible to obtain reasonable coefficient estimates for the first differences of these variables, although in Nakamura and Nakamura (1983a) the results are found to be sensitive to whether the levels state unemployment variable is included along with the first difference form of this variable. In the present study, we use only macroeconomic variables measured at the national level because the microanalytic simulation model into which one or more of the sets of estimated labor force behavioral relationships presented in this book is to be incorporated does not keep track of an individual's state of residence over time.

4. Long and Jones (1980) emphasis the importance of this perspective.

5. H. Rosen (1976) presents a model in which wage rates are assumed to depend on the hours of work.

6. We have included the lagged wage rate, rather than the

2 Methodology and Data

log of the lagged wage rate, in (2.3.1), (2.3.2a) and (2.3.4) solely for convenience. This decision seems to make little difference in terms of the signs or estimated impacts of our variables.

See Kalachek, Raines and Larson (1979) and Johnson and Pencavel (1984) for other related studies including lagged hours of work as an explanatory variable, but where the continuing and entering aspects of work behavior are not emphasized.

7. Entering work behavior refers to the probabilities of work, wage rates and hours of work of those who did not work in the previous year. Continuing work behavior refers to the probabilities of work, wage rates and hours of work of those who did work in the previous year. There are potential costs of entering the labor force for the first time, or after a period of a year or more of not working. These include the costs of searching for a job, the costs of searching for childcare arrangements for a woman with young children, the costs of any training or retraining needed for entry or reentry into the labor force, and so forth. (Note that these costs are distinct from the variable costs of working, such as the costs of paying for childcare or transportation on a week-by-week or month-by-month basis.) Thus, the impacts of observable variables like child status, as well as the impacts of unobservable fixed costs (see, for instance, Cogan, 1980, 1981, and Hausman, 1980), may differ systematically for those who did versus those who did not work in the previous year. Differences may also result from the tendency of employers to "screen" or track potential employees on the basis of characteristics like education, race, child status in the case of women, and so forth (see, for instance, Thurow, 1972, 1975; Gintis; 1971, and Fraker, 1984).

8. See the Addendum to Chapter 2 for further details concerning the need to use an instrument for the log of the offered wage.

9. This is the Hours Worked for Money by Individual variable, also referred to as Annual Hours Worked, in the PSID data base (see Institute for Social Research, 1980, p. 287, Variable 6826 and p. 496).

10. For heads and wives we use the average hourly earnings variables available in the PSID data. For details for these variables, see Institute for Social Research (1980, p. 267). We then deflate these average hourly earnings variables as stated in the text.

11. See Hall (1973), for instance, for a discussion of some of the problems associated with various measures of the wage rate.

12. See Nakamura and Nakamura (1983) for the use of an unconventional rank instrument proposed by Durbin for the wage variable in that study, and for further discussion concerning

the problems with the use of an instrumental wage variable in an equation for annual hours of work.

13. The national unemployment rate variable is the global unemployment rate, which is defined as 100 times the number unemployed divided by the total of the numbers employed and unemployed and which is given, for instance, in Table B30 of the 1982 Economic Report of the President. The national wage index is an index (1977=100) of compensation per manhour in the business nonfarm sector. Values for this index can be found in Table B40 of the 1982 Economic Report of the President. This wage index is not in real terms. These macroeconomic variables, particularly the national wage index, are not ideal choices for this study for a variety of reasons. We used them because they are outputs of the macroeconomic model with which there is a plan to interact the microanalytic simulation model in which our equations for the labor force behavior of individuals will be used (see Research Seminar in Quantitative Economics, 1982, for a description of this macroeconomic model). Our national unemployment rate variable and our national wage index are the variables RUG and JCMH, respectively, in this macroeconomic model.

14. The baby dummy is set equal to 1 if the number of children in the family unit aged 0 to 17 has increased by 1 since the previous year, and if there is a child 23 months of age or under in the family unit. See Institute for Social Research (1980, p. 146).

15. This dummy is set equal to 1 if the youngest child in the family unit is less than 6 years of age and if the baby dummy equals 0. See Institute for Social Research (1980, p. 146). Thus, in a given year if there is a 5-year-old child in a family but there is also a new baby, then the young child dummy will be set equal to 0 for this family in the given year. With the baby dummy and the young child dummy considered together, we are able to distinguish among women who have a new baby, women who have a preschool child but no new baby, and women who have no preschool children and no new baby. Information on the actual number of children in various age brackets is not available in the PSID data prior to the 1975 wave (see Institute for Social Research, 1980, pp. 489-490). Thus, we were not able to consider including in our study more detailed information about the ages of young children in family units.

16. This variable is the number of children in the family unit 0 to 17 years of age. See Institute for Social Research (1980, p. 146).

17. Because PSID interviews are now designed so they can be carried out by telephone, the race of the respondent, which used to be assigned by interviewer observation, has not been obtained since the 1972 wave. Since then, respondents have been assigned race based on 1972 data. See Institute for

Social Research (1980, p. 82).

18. This information is only available for family heads over the entire period covered by our study.

19. We used the student status of the individual in the previous year to avoid the obvious problem of simultaneous causation for schooling and work decisions within the same year.

20. Young people living with parents may often receive both direct financial assistance and income in kind, such as free room and board, from their parents.

21. A person is defined as married in the PSID data if that person is either married or permanently cohabitating. Those who are separated are not counted as currently married. See Institute for Social Research (1980, pp. 83 and p. 275).

22. This dummy variable is created using the PSID variable for the Amount of ADC/AFDC for Head and Wife in the previous year (see Institute for Social Research, 1980, p. 133). We have lagged this variable by one year because the institutional reality is that receipt of these benefits in the current year is, in part, a function of work effort and earnings in the current year. Also, in the microanalytic simulation model in which our labor force behavioral relationships will be used, work behavior is determined for each individual prior to the determination of AFDC benefits for the family for the current year.

23. This dummy variable is created using the PSID variable for the Amount of Supplemental Security Income of Head and Wife in the previous year (see Institute for Social Research, 1980, p. 133). As in the case of our AFDC variable, we have lagged this variable by one year because of the institutional reality that the receipt of Social Security benefits in the current year is, in part, a function of work effort and earnings in the current year, and because Social Security benefits are generated after the determination of employment and earnings in the microanalytic simulation model in which our labor force behavioral relationships will be used. We note that data on Social Security benefits are not available prior to the 1970 wave of the PSID.

24. We have not included additional other income variables for welfare, asset income, and so forth largely because these variables are absent or because of doubts about the way in which certain of these other income components are generated in the microanalytic simulation environment in which our labor force behavioral relationships will be used. The effects of these other variables are left, therefore, in the disturbance terms of our relationships.

25. See Institute for Social Research (1980. p. 128). This variable, like the other personal income and wage variables in this study, has been deflated using the Consumer Price Index. We have lagged this variable assuming that it is

the wife's potential earnings, for which her earnings in the previous year may be a reasonable proxy, that might affect her husband's decision about how much to work in the current year. Within the microanalytic simulation model in which our labor force behavioral relationships will be used, the employment and earnings behavior of the husband in a given year is determined prior to the employment and earnings behavior of his wife in that year.

26. Thorough researchers will, of course, perform many diagnostic checks on their models before claiming too much for their results.

27. This is the property emphasized in textbooks. For instance, Kmenta (1971, p. 11) writes: "Perhaps the best-known desirable property of an estimator is that of _unbiasedness_. An unbiased estimator is one that has a sampling distribution with a mean equal to the parameter to be estimated." If current or lagged endogenous variables are included in X, then we may be able to establish the property of consistency for b, but b will not be unbiased. See, for instance, Johnston (1972, pp. 278-281).

28. Carl Christ (1966, p. 247) writes, for instance:

> Each structural equation is supposed to apply to some particular fundamental relationship in the economy .... [Structural] change ... is likely to stem from a change in one or a few of these structural relationships, and to leave other structural relationships unaltered. But _all_ the reduced-form relationships are likely to be altered .... We describe this situation by saying that structural relationships have a high degree _autonomy_ ... and the reduced-form equations have only a low degree of autonomy .... This means that it is relatively easy to discover directly what a structural change does to the old structural parameters ... but relatively difficult to discover what it does to the reduced-form parameters.

29. Obviously, there are intermediate cases where some, but not all, of the elements of the vector of parameters can be thought of as structural parameters. For convenience, however, we will ignore these intermediate cases.

30. Malinvaud (1966, p. 71) notes, for instance:

> Actually, since certain of the assumptions of the model, and in particular those relating to the random errors, are not exactly verifiable, the real properties of the estimators or the tests can differ to a greater or lesser extent from the "theoretical" properties.

31. For instance, in introducing the ordinary least squares bias problem, Durbin (1954, p. 27) writes: "Since the use of an instrumental variable involves a certain loss of efficiency one should feel rather cautious about using it until the extent of the bias of the ordinary least squares estimator has been investigated." Malinvaud (1961) also suggests that ordinary least squares should not be rejected simply because of the existence of bias or inconsistency, since biased coefficients do not necessarily lead to biased predictions of the dependent variable and methods such as instrumental variables that produce consistency often lead to regression coefficients with larger small sample dispersion than the inconsistent ordinary least squares estimates. For an application of this view, see, for instance, the study by Fama and Babiak (1968) of the dividend behavior of firms. Although Bayesian estimators are consistent under appropriate assumptions, this property is not relied on in small sample situations. Rather, the expected loss is the relevant criterion for choosing an estimator in a Bayesian context. If the expected loss is measured as the mean square error, the variance and the bias squared are given equal weight in this criterion (see Zellner, 1971, 1979).

32. See Griliches (1977) for an elaboration of the complexity of an education or schooling variable and the importance of this complexity for behavioral research on the returns to schooling.

33. Griliches (1977, p. 3) writes, for instance:

> Since one views schooling and other forms of training as production processes for human capital, one would like to have independent output measures of such processes. But nobody believes that we can get close to it by having an elaborate examination and summarizing the results by one final grand test score. We are stuck therefore, with input measures of schooling, measures of the time spent in institutions that are called "educational." We should keep this discrepancy between desires and reality in mind when we come later on to interpret the results of our analyses.

34. Or we might use the data from "natural" experiments. Ashenfelter (1978) obtains interesting results using data on individuals in four trainee and comparison groups broken down by race and sex. The data used in his study were obtained by matching program records for all classroom trainees who started training under the Manpower Development and Training Act in the first three months of 1964 with Social Security

records on earnings.

35. Griliches (1977, p. 13) also points out potential problems with the first approach, noting that sometimes "the more variables we put into the equation which are related to the systematic components of schooling, and the better we 'protect' ourselves against various possible biases, the worse we make the errors of measurement problem." Of course, an increase in the proportion of the variability of the dependent variable accounted for by an estimated equation, due to the addition of variables, does not necessarily mean the equation has been "improved."

36. In private correspondence Zellner notes that what we are essentially proposing here is "a predictive test of models which makes sense."

37. For a comprehensive treatment of the selection bias problem and of Heckman's approach to dealing with this problem, see Heckman (1976,1979), and see J.P. Smith (1980, Introduction) for a readable introductory summary of the selection bias problem.

38. Cain (1982, p. 14) writes, for example: "Estimating the conventional model may be described as a search for 'structural' or 'pure' wage and income parameters, which, when obtained, are applied with or without apology to the policy context."

39. In Malinvaud's (1966, p. 614) words: "The model condenses all the a priori information, which, together with the analyzed data, makes statistical inference possible. This information is generally vague and badly formulated. It often appears fairly subjective."

40. Arguments about possible parameter bias are the essence also of the current controversy about reverse regression and salary discrimination. See, for instance, Roberts (1980), Conway and Roberts (1983), Kamalich, Fand, and Polachek (1982), and Goldberger (1984,1984a).

41. We have tried in this study to pay serious attention to Cain's (1982, p. 26) comment:

> Indeed, I would go further and deny that the term 'structural model' has any useful meaning, other than self-flattery, unless the user has carefully explained the purpose for the estimates and has explained how the sample is appropriate for these purposes.

42. Although the approach and motivation are somewhat different, some of the ideas presented in this section were inspired by arguments and concepts developed in Orcutt (1982).

43. For clarification of this point and the derivation of corrected standard errors for various sorts of models including a selection bias term see Heckman (1979), Greene

(1981) and Nakamura and Nakamura (1983, Appendix).

44. Lin and Kmenta (1982, p. 493) note, for instance, that since the sampling distribution of the ordinary ridge regression (ORR) estimator is not known, "the ORR procedure is not suited for testing hypotheses. This makes ORR uninteresting for many econometric problems. It would seem, though, that ORR may well become a powerful tool in forecasting." A variety of specification error tests have been developed for detecting correlation between an included explanatory variable and the equation disturbance term. (Several of these tests are described and related in Nakamura and Nakamura (1981a).) As Nakamura and Nakamura (1983c) and others have pointed out, however, there are problems with the use of these specification error tests. An alternative to making the choice, often implicit in the use of these tests, between ordinary least squares estimation and some alternative estimation method, such as instrumental variables, is to use a combined estimator. For various combined estimators, see Nagar, 1959; Sawa, 1973, 1973a; Feldstein, 1974; Fuller, 1977; Morimune, 1978; Zellner, 1978, 1980; Zellner and Park, 1979; Park, 1982; and Reynolds, 1982. One of the reasons why these combined estimators have been used so little, though, is probably that it is not, in general, possible to carry out standard tests of significance using these estimators because formulas are not available for their standard errors. Zellner (1979, p. 635) notes: "Also, when the system is dynamic ... only approximate large-sample test procedures are available. The quality of the approximation and finite-sample power functions for widely used large-sample approximate tests are relatively unexplored topics in econometric research." Zellner also points out: "Another topic that has received very little attention ... is the effects of pretests on the properties of subsequent tests .... That pretesting can vitally affect properties of estimators is evident from consideration of simple cases." McDonald and Robinson (1984) note problems with the computation of appropriate standard errors that arise because of the fact that we usually drop some number of the observations in a cross-sectional or panel data set due to missing or bad data problems. As a final example, we quote a recent paper by Heckman and Singer (1984, p. 300):

> The preceding analyses have established the existence of a consistent maximum likelihood estimator for a general class of duration models. They are silent on the derivation of the sampling distribution of the estimators. The derivation of these sampling distributions is a nontrivial task left for future work.

45. Kuznets (1965, p. 6) reminds us: "We may avoid

walking off in the wrong direction if we are not required to give explicit answers where no adequate basis for them exists." Also, in a section titled, "Is Economics a Science?", Leonard Silk (1978, p. 26), an economic columnist for The New York Times, suggests:

> The weakness of economics as a science isn't entirely the fault of the economists .... [Their] seemingly hard and precise numbers are soft, synthetic inaccurate reflections of underlying events and moods and tendencies. One worthwhile reform of economic statistics might be to outlaw the decimal point.

46. For a description of the Michigan Panel Study of Income Dynamics carried out by James Morgan, Greg Duncan and their associates, see, for instance, Institute for Social Research (1980). Panel data for the United States on the employment and earnings behavior of women and their personal and family characteristics are also available from the National Longitudinal Survey of Work Experience, which is described in Parnes, Shea, Spitz and Zeller (1970). However, in the case of the National Longitudinal Survey data, information for different types of individuals, such as mature women, has been collected over different time periods.

47. The PSID was reweighted in 1978. See Institute for Social Research (1979, p. 6) for further details concerning these weights.

48. We have done this, for instance, in Nakamura and Nakamura (1983a). In that study, the out-of-sample and in-sample simulation results are found to be very similar.

ADDENDUM TO CHAPTER 2

A Standard Model and a First
Difference Version of This Model

Suppose the individual's tastes and preferences are given by a twice-differentiable quasi-concave conditional utility function such as

$$U(x, \ell; Z^*) \tag{2.1}$$

where ℓ denotes nonmarket time (all time not devoted to work for pay or profit), x is a Hicksian composite good representing the consumption of all goods other than nonmarket time, and Z^* is a vector of constraints arising from previous choices about marriage, family formation and so forth. The individual is assumed to consume those amounts of x and ℓ that maximize the utility function given in (2.1), subject to the income and time constraints given by

$$px = I + wh \tag{2.2}$$

and

$$T = \ell + h, \tag{2.3}$$

where p is the unit price of the Hicksian composite good, I denotes all sources of income available to the individual other than income from working, w is the offered wage rate, h is the hours of work for pay or profit, and T denotes the total number of hours in the given time period. Clearly, it must be the case that h is greater than or equal to 0 and strictly less than T.

In order to solve for the conditions under which (2.1) will be maximized, subject to (2.2) and (2.3), we form the Lagrangean

$$L = U(x, T-h; Z^*) + \xi_1 h + \xi_2(I + wh - px) \tag{2.4}$$

where ξ_1 and ξ_2 denote Lagrange multipliers. The Kuhn-Tucker conditions for this maximization problem[1] are given by conditions (2.2) and (2.3) above, the condition that ξ_1 must be greater than or equal to 0, by

$$U_x - \xi_2 p = 0 , \qquad (2.5)$$

$$-U_\ell + \xi_1 + \xi_2 w = 0 , \qquad (2.6)$$

and by

$$\xi_1 h = 0 \qquad (2.7)$$

where U_x denotes the partial derivative of the utility function given in (2.1) with respect to x, and U_ℓ denotes the partial derivative of this utility function with respect to ℓ. Rearranging conditions (2.2) and (2.5) we get

$$x = (I + wh) / p \qquad (2.8)$$

and

$$\xi_2 = U_x / p . \qquad (2.9)$$

From (2.8) and (2.9) it can be seen that, given any offered wage, w, the equilibrium value of ξ_2 is a function of h, p, I, wh and Z^*. From (2.6) we also see that in equilibrium,

$$\xi_2 = (U_\ell - \xi_1) / w . \qquad (2.10)$$

Solving (2.10) for the offered wage, we obtain

$$w = w^* - (\xi_1/\xi_2) \qquad (2.11)$$

where w^*, defined by

$$w^* = U_\ell / \xi_2 , \qquad (2.12)$$

is the asking wage, or shadow price of the individual's nonmarket time, evaluated at $h = T - \ell$ hours of work. It can be seen that w^* depends on h, p, I, wh and Z^* when h is positive and on p, I and Z^* when h is 0.

From (2.9) we see that ξ_2 must be positive since both U_x and p must be positive. Moreover, (2.7) implies that ξ_1 must equal 0 if h is positive, and must be greater than or equal to 0 if h is 0. Thus, from (2.11) we see that the individual will not work (that is, h will be 0) when w is less than or equal to w^* evaluated at 0 hours of work. On the other hand, when w is greater than w^* evaluated at 0

2 Methodology and Data

hours of work, h will be positive and the value of h will be the value that equates w and w* evaluated at the actual hours of work.

If we redefine $I \equiv I/p$, $w \equiv w/p$ and $w^* \equiv w^*/p$, and if we take the natural log of both sides of (2.12) and linearize the resulting expressions around Z^*, I, ln w and h (with I and w now defined in real terms), for the ith individual we obtain

$$\ln w^* = \beta_0 + Z^*\beta_1 + I\beta_2 + \beta_3 \ln w + \beta_4 h + u^* \qquad (2.13a)$$

when h is positive and

$$\ln w^* = \beta_0 + Z^*\beta_1 + I\beta_2 + u^* \qquad (2.13b)$$

when h is 0 and hence the individual's earnings, given by wh, are also 0.[2] In (2.13a) and (2.13b) the term u* can be interpreted as denoting errors of approximation. Suppose the log of the offered wage of the ith individual is given by

$$\ln w = \alpha_0 + Z\alpha_1 + E\alpha_2 + u \qquad (2.14)$$

where Z and E are vectors of personal and regional characteristics, respectively, and u is a random term. In the context of the specified model, an individual will work if w exceeds w* evaluated at 0 hours of work, or hence if

$$\ln w > \ln w^* \qquad (2.15)$$

where ln w* is evaluated at 0 hours of work.

Suppose that the error terms u* and u are normally distributed. Then the probability that an individual will work is given in this model by

$$P(h > 0) = P(\ln w - \ln w^* > 0) = F(\phi), \qquad (2.16)$$

where w* is evaluated at 0 hours of work, F denotes the cumulative standard normal density function and

$$\phi = (1/\sigma)[(\alpha_0 - \beta_0) + Z\alpha_1 - Z^*\beta_1 - I\beta_2 + E\alpha_2] \qquad (2.17)$$

with the variance of $(u^* - u)$ denoted by σ^2. The parameters $((\alpha_0 - \beta_0)/\sigma)$, (α_1/σ), (β_1/σ), (β_2/σ) and (α_2/σ) of (2.17) can be estimated using standard probit analysis.

Even if the error term of equation (2.14) has a 0 mean in the whole population, this error term will not have a 0 mean in the censored sample of those individuals for whom condition (2.15) is satisfied. It can be shown that for the censored sample of individuals who work, we have

$$E(u|h > 0) = (\sigma_{12}/\sigma)\lambda \qquad (2.18)$$

where σ_{12} is the covariance of u with $(u^* - u)$, σ^2 is the variance of $(u^* - u)$, and

$$\lambda = f(\phi)/F(\phi) \qquad (2.19)$$

with the standard normal density and cumulative density functions denoted by f and F, respectively. Using this result, we can rewrite the error term for equation (2.14) as

$$u = (\sigma_{12}/\sigma)\lambda + V \qquad (2.20)$$

where V has a 0 mean in the censored sample of individuals who work. Thus, we can rewrite equation (2.14) as

$$\ln w = \alpha_0 + Z\alpha_1 + E\alpha_2 + (\sigma_{12}/\sigma)\lambda + V. \qquad (2.21)$$

An estimated value of λ can be computed for each individual using probit estimation results for (2.17) to estimate ϕ in (2.19). The parameters of equation (2.21) can then be estimated using ordinary or generalized least squares regression analysis.[3]

We cannot estimate equations for the log of the asking wage, since the only asking wage rates that we observe are values for individuals who work. The equilibrium condition for individuals who work can be stated as

$$\ln w = \ln w^* \qquad (2.22)$$

where w^* is evaluated at the equilibrium hours of work. Thus, equating $\ln w$ with the right-hand side of (2.13a) and solving for h, we find that the equilibrium hours of work for the ith working individual are given by

$$h = (1/\beta_4)[(1-\beta_3)\ln w - \beta_0 - Z^*\beta_1 - I\beta_2 - u^*]. \qquad (2.23)$$

It is commonly argued (see, for instance, Heckman, 1974) that the error term of $\ln w$ in (2.23) is correlated with u^*. Thus, we rewrite (2.23) as

$$h = (1/\beta_4)[(1-\beta_3)\ln w_D - \beta_0 - Z^*\beta_1 - I\beta_2 + (1-\beta_3)u - u^*] \qquad (2.24)$$

where

$$\ln w_D = \alpha_0 + Z\alpha_1 + E\alpha_2 \qquad (2.25)$$

is the deterministic portion of $\ln w$.

It can also be shown that even if the error term

2 Methodology and Data

$U = (1/\beta_4)[(1-\beta_3)u-u^*]$ has a 0 mean in the population of all individuals, for the censored sample of those who work we have

$$E(U|h > 0) = (\sigma_{13}/\sigma)\lambda \qquad (2.26)$$

where σ_{13} is the covariance of U with (u^*-u), σ^2 is again the variance of (u^*-u) which is the random term in (2.16), and λ is defined as in (2.19). Thus, we have

$$U = (\sigma_{13}/\sigma)\lambda + V^* \qquad (2.27)$$

where V^* has a 0 mean in the censored sample of those who work, and we can rewrite equation (2.24) as

$$h = (1/\beta_4)[(1-\beta_3)\ln w_D - \beta_0 - Z^*\beta_1 - I\beta_2] + (\sigma_{13}/\sigma)\lambda + V^*. \qquad (2.28)$$

The parameters of (2.28) can be estimated by substituting into (2.28) predicted values for $\ln w_D$ from equation (2.21) and then applying ordinary or generalized least squares regression.[4]

Since this sort of model has been used extensively in the empirical literature following its presentation by Heckman, we refer to this model (including the distributional assumptions about the error terms of the model) as the <u>Standard Model</u>.

It has been shown that the Standard Model does not adequately capture the continuity over time in the work behavior of individuals.[5] Heckman and others have suggested that this is because the error terms associated with (2.16), (2.21) and (2.28) contain person-specific fixed or persistent components that are not taken into account in the specification and estimation of the Standard Model (see, for instance, Heckman, 1981, 1981a; Heckman and Macurdy, 1979).

In formal terms, what is being suggested might lead us to rewrite (2.13a) and (2.13b) as

$$\ln w^* = \beta_{0i} + Z^*\beta_1 + I\beta_2 + \beta_3 \ln w + \beta_4 h + u^* \qquad (2.29a)$$

when h is positive and as

$$\ln w^* = \beta_{0i} + Z^*\beta_1 + I\beta_2 + u^* \qquad (2.29b)$$

when h is 0, and to rewrite (2.14) as

$$\ln w = \alpha_{0i} + Z\alpha_1 + E\alpha_2 + u \qquad (2.30)$$

where the subscript i denotes the ith individual. In (2.29a), (2.29b) and (2.30), β_{0i} and α_{0i} stand for unobserved factors, including tastes and preferences and future expectations that do not change over the relevant time period and that are specific to each individual; and u* and u are assumed to obey autoregressive processes such as

$$u^* = \rho^* u^*_{-1} + \varepsilon^* \qquad (2.31a)$$

and

$$u = \rho u_{-1} + \varepsilon \qquad (2.31b)$$

where the subscript 1 denotes a one-period lag, ρ^* and ρ are autoregressive parameters with values in the interval of -1 to 1, and ε^* and ε are normally distributed with 0 means over individuals and over time. Consistent estimation of the parameters of this modified model is a difficult econometric problem.[6] It has been shown (see Nakamura and Nakamura, 1983a), however, that consistent parameter estimates can be obtained for this model using standard packaged probit and regression programs for the special case where both ρ^* and ρ equal 1.[7]

Simple first difference, or Cochrane-Orcutt-type, autoregressive transformations are not possible, in general, in a model embedding an inequality decision rule like (2.15) that states that a person will work if the log of his offered wage exceeds the log of his asking wage evaluated at 0 hours of work.[8] Notice that the difference expression

$$\ln w - \ln w_{-1} > \ln w^* - \ln w^*_{-1} \qquad (2.32)$$

is *not* equivalent to (2.15). An equivalent expression can be obtained, however, by subtracting $\ln w_{-1}$ from both sides of (2.15) and then adding and subtracting $\ln w^*_{-1}$ evaluated at 0 hours of work on the right-hand side of (2.15). Rearranging terms on the right-hand side, we obtain

$$\ln w - \ln w_{-1} > (\ln w^* - \ln w^*_{-1}) - (\ln w_{-1} - \ln w^*_{-1}) , \qquad (2.33)$$

where $\ln w^*$ and $\ln w^*_{-1}$ are both evaluated at 0 hours of work. Notice that no special assumptions are used in obtaining (2.33) from decision rule (2.15).

From (2.29a) we see that, for those who worked in the previous time period, the log of the lagged asking wage *evaluated at the actual hours of work* can be written as

$$\ln w^*_{-1} = \beta_{01} + Z^*_{-1}\beta_1 + I_{-1}\beta_2 + \beta_3 \ln w_{-1} + \beta_4 h_{-1} + u^*_{-1}$$

$$= (\beta_{01} + Z^*_{-1}\beta_1 + I_{-1}\beta_2 + u^*_{-1}) + \beta_3 \ln w_{-1} + \beta_4 h_{-1} . \qquad (2.34)$$

The term in parentheses on the right-hand side of the second expression for $\ln w^*_{-1}$ in (2.34) can be seen from (2.29b) to equal the lagged asking wage of the individual <u>evaluated at 0 hours of work</u>. Moreover, for those who worked in the previous time period we see from (2.22) that

$$\ln w_{-1} = \ln w^*_{-1}, \qquad (2.35)$$

where the asking wage on the right-hand side of (2.35) is evaluated at the actual hours of work. Thus, from (2.34) and (2.35) we have

$$\ln w_{-1} = (\beta_{0i} + Z^*_{-1}\beta_1 + I_{-1}\beta_2 + u^*_{-1}) + \beta_3 \ln w_{-1} + \beta_4 h_{-1}. \qquad (2.36)$$

Since the term in parentheses on the right-hand side of (2.36) is the asking wage evaluated at 0 hours of work, we see now that the second term on the right-hand side of our inequality decision rule, as given by (2.33), can be expressed as

$$\ln w_{-1} - \ln w^*_{-1} = \beta_3 \ln w_{-1} + \beta_4 h_{-1} \qquad (2.37)$$

where $\ln w^*_{-1}$ on the left-hand side of (2.37) is the log of the asking wage in the previous year evaluated at 0 hours of work. Thus, <u>for those who worked in the previous year</u> we see that (2.33) can be rewritten as

$$\ln w - \ln w_{-1} > (\ln w^* - \ln w^*_{-1}) - \beta_3 \ln w_{-1} - \beta_4 h_{-1}, \qquad (2.38)$$

where $\ln w^*$ and $\ln w^*_{-1}$ on the right-hand side of (2.38) are evaluated at 0 hours of work.

Notice that using (2.30) we have

$$\ln w - \ln w_{-1} = (\alpha_{0i} - \alpha_{0i}) + (Z - Z_{-1})\alpha_1 + (E - E_{-1})\alpha_2 \qquad (2.39)$$
$$+ u - u_{-1},$$

and using (2.29b) we have

$$(\ln w^* - \ln w^*_{-1}) = (\beta_{0i} - \beta_{0i}) + (Z^* - Z^*_{-1})\beta_1 \qquad (2.40)$$
$$+ (I - I_{-1})\beta_2 + (u^* - u^*_{-1}).$$

Thus, expression (2.38) no longer involves the individual fixed effects terms α_{0i} and β_{0i}, which cancel out of both (2.39) and (2.40). The error term associated with the inequality decision rule $\ln w > \ln w^*$, which is equivalent to (2.38) for those who worked in the previous time period, is given by

$$(u^* - u^*_{-1}) - (u - u_{-1}). \qquad (2.41)$$

If u^* and u obey the autoregressive relationships specified in (2.31a) and (2.31b), then (2.41) can be rewritten as

$$(u^*-u^*_{-1})-(u-u_{-1}) = (\rho^*-1)u^*_{-1} + \varepsilon^* - (\rho-1)u_{-1} - \varepsilon . \quad (2.42)$$

Moreover, if the autoregressive parameters ρ^* and ρ in (2.42) are both equal to 1, then (2.42) reduces to

$$(u^* - u^*_{-1}) - (u - u_{-1}) = \varepsilon^* - \varepsilon \quad (2.43)$$

where ε^* and ε are both normally distributed with 0 means over individuals and over time periods. We see now that the probability that an individual who worked in the last time period will also work in the current time period may be specified as

$$P(h > 0) = F(\phi') \quad (2.44)$$

where

$$\phi' = (1/\sigma')[(Z-Z_{-1})\alpha_1 - (Z^*-Z^*_{-1})\beta_1 - (I-I_{-1})\beta_2 \quad (2.45)$$
$$+ (E-E_{-1})\alpha_2 + \beta_3 \ln w_{-1} + \beta_4 h_{-1}] ,$$

with the variance of the error term $(\varepsilon^*-\varepsilon)$ given by $(\sigma')^2$.

Notice that the probability of work in (2.44) is <u>not</u> a conditional probability. This can be seen from the way in which (2.33) was derived from the original inequality decision rule given by (2.15). The issue is rather that it is only for those who worked in the previous period that we are able to evaluate the second term on the right-hand side of (2.33) as specified in (2.37). Thus, in estimating the parameters of (2.45) using standard probit analysis, we must limit our sample to those who worked in the previous time period for whom we observe values for w_{-1} and h_{-1}. Limiting, or censoring, the sample in this manner will undoubtedly cause sample selection bias problems if, ρ^* and ρ are not both precisely equal to 1, since in this case the true error term for the model giving the probability of work in the current time period will involve contributions from the error terms u^*_{-1} and u_{-1} for the previous time period. In general, we see that as ρ^* and ρ each tend from 1 to 0 in value, the numerical importance of the contributions from u^*_{-1} and u_{-1}, respectively, increases, leading to potentially more serious selection bias problems, while the autoregressiveness of the contributions from u^*_{-1} and u_{-1} diminishes. On the other hand, when ρ^* and ρ are very close to, but not exactly 1, the contributions of u^*_{-1} and u_{-1} to the error term given by (2.42) will be numerically unimportant, but

2 Methodology and Data

whatever contributions there are from u^*_{-1} and u_{-1} will be highly autocorrelated.

Following this formulation for the probability that an individual will work[9], wage and hours equations can be derived in a straightforward manner for individuals found to work in the current period and who also worked in the previous time period. We see from (2.30) that

$$\ln w - \ln w_{-1} = (\alpha_{0i} - \alpha_{0i}) + (Z - Z_{-1})\alpha_1 \qquad (2.46)$$
$$+ (E - E_{-1})\alpha_2 + (u - u_{-1}),$$

and hence that

$$\ln w = \ln w_{-1} + (Z - Z_{-1})\alpha_1 + (E - E_{-1})\alpha_2 + (u - u_{-1}). \qquad (2.47)$$

Moreover, if u obeys the autoregressive relationship given by (2.31b) with ρ equal to 1, then (2.47) becomes

$$\ln w = \ln w_{-1} + (Z - Z_{-1})\alpha_1 + (E - E_{-1})\alpha_2 + \varepsilon \qquad (2.48)$$

where ε will have a mean of 0 in both the uncensored populaton of all individuals and in the censored population of those who worked in the previous time period regardless of their work status in the current time period. However, in the doubly censored population of those who worked in the previous time period and who are also found to work in the current time period, we have

$$E(\varepsilon | h > 0, h_{-1} > 0) = (\sigma'_{12}/\sigma')\lambda' \qquad (2.49)$$

where

$$\sigma'_{12} = \text{cov}(\varepsilon, \varepsilon^* - \varepsilon) \qquad (2.50)$$

is most likely nonzero,

$$(\sigma')^2 = \text{var}(\varepsilon^* - \varepsilon), \qquad (2.51)$$

and

$$\lambda' = f(\phi')/F(\phi') \qquad (2.52)$$

with ϕ' given by (2.45). (The condition $h_{-1} > 0$ in (2.49) has no effect here since ε and ε_{-1}, the error terms for $\ln w$ and $\ln w_{-1}$, are assumed to be statistically independent.) Thus, we can rewrite the error term for equation (2.48) as

$$\varepsilon = (\sigma'_{12}/\sigma')\lambda' + v \qquad (2.53)$$

where v has a mean of 0 in the doubly censored sample of individuals who worked in the previous time period and who are also found to work in the current time period. Using (2.53) we can rewrite equation (2.48) as

$$\ln w = \ln w_{-1} + (Z-Z_{-1})\alpha_1 + (E-E_{-1})\alpha_2 + (\sigma'_{12}/\sigma')\lambda' + v. \qquad (2.54)$$

An estimated value of λ' can be computed for each individual who worked in the previous time period using probit estimation results for (2.45) to estimate ϕ' in (2.52). The parameters of equation (2.54) can then be estimated for individuals who worked in the previous time period and who are also found to work in the current time period using ordinary least squares regression analysis.

For those who work, we have the equilibrium condition that they will choose their hours of work so that their asking wage, evaluated at their actual hours of work, equals their offered wage. Thus, from (2.29a) and this equilibrium condition, we have the hours equation given by

$$h = (1/\beta_4)[(1-\beta_3)\ln w - \beta_{0i} - Z^*\beta_1 - I\beta_2 - u^*] , \qquad (2.55)$$

which is the same as equation (2.23) in the Standard Model except that now the constant term for the equation is person-specific. Since the error term of $\ln w$ in (2.55) is thought to be correlated with u^*, we rewrite equation (2.55) as

$$h = (1/\beta_4)[(1-\beta_3)\ln w_D - \beta_{0i} - Z^*\beta_1 - I\beta_2 + (1-\beta_3)u - u^*] \qquad (2.56)$$

where now we see from (2.54) that

$$\ln w_D = \ln w_{-1} + (Z-Z_{-1})\alpha_1 + (E-E_{-1})\alpha_2 + (\sigma'_{12}/\sigma')\lambda' \qquad (2.57)$$

is the deterministic portion of $\ln w$.

We can now rewrite (2.56) as

$$h - h_{-1} = (1/\beta_4)[(1-\beta_3)(\ln w_D - \ln w_{D,-1}) - (\beta_{0i} - \beta_{0i}) \qquad (2.58)$$
$$-(Z^*-Z^*_{-1})\beta_1 - (I-I_{-1})\beta_2 + (1-\beta_3)(u-u_{-1}) - (u^*-u^*_{-1})],$$

or as

$$h = h_{-1} + (1/\beta_4)[(1-\beta_3)(\ln w_D - \ln w_{D,-1}) - (Z^*-Z^*_{-1})\beta_1 \qquad (2.59)$$
$$- (I-I_{-1})\beta_2] + (1/\beta_4)[(1-\beta_3)(u-u_{-1}) - (u^*-u^*_{-1})] .$$

2 Methodology and Data

Moreover, if u and u^* obey (2.31b) and (2.31a) with ρ and ρ^* both equal to 1, then (2.59) becomes

$$h = h_{-1} + (1/\beta_4)[(1-\beta_3)(\ln w_D - \ln w_{D,-1}) - (Z^* - Z^*_{-1})\beta_1 \quad (2.60)$$
$$- (I - I_{-1})\beta_2] + (1/\beta_4)[(1-\beta_3)\varepsilon - \varepsilon^*].$$

where the error term $U' = (1/\beta_4)[(1-\beta_3)\varepsilon - \varepsilon^*]$ will have a mean of 0 in both the uncensored population of all individuals and in the censored population of those who worked in the previous time period regardless of their work status in the current time period. However, in the doubly censored population of those who worked in the previous time period and who are also found to work in the current time period we have

$$E(U' \mid h > 0, h_{-1} > 0) = (\sigma''_{12}/\sigma')\lambda' \quad (2.61)$$

where

$$\sigma''_{12} = \text{cov}(U', \varepsilon^* - \varepsilon), \quad (2.62)$$

$(\sigma')^2$ is given by (2.51) and λ' is given by (2.52). Thus, we can rewrite the error term for equation (2.60) as

$$U' = (\sigma''_{12}/\sigma')\lambda' + v^* \quad (2.63)$$

where v^* has a mean of 0 in the doubly censored sample of individuals who worked in the previous time period and who are also found to work in the current time period. Using this result we can rewrite equation (2.60) as

$$h = h_{-1} + (1/\beta_4)[(1-\beta_3)(\ln w_D - \ln w_{D,-1}) - (Z^* - Z^*_{-1})\beta_1 \quad (2.64)$$
$$- (I - I_{-1})\beta_2] + (\sigma''_{12}/\sigma')\lambda' + v^*.$$

The parameters of (2.64) can be estimated for individuals who worked in the previous time period and who are found to work in the current time period by substituting into (2.64) predicted values for $\ln w_D$ and $\ln w_{D,-1}$ from equation (2.54) and then applying ordinary least squares to (2.64).

For individuals who did not work in the previous time period, we cannot evaluate the term $(\ln w_{-1} - \ln w^*_{-1})$ on the right-hand side of (2.33) as $(\beta_3 \ln w_{-1} + \beta_4 h_{-1})$, nor can we estimate the parameters of the index (2.45) or of equation (2.54) or (2.64), since we do not observe values for w_{-1} and h_{-1}. Since the term $(\ln w_{-1} - \ln w^*_{-1})$ is essentially a measure of the strength of the individual's attachment to the labor force, we might be able to use the number or proportion of years the individual has worked since 18 years of age as a proxy for this term. (This approach is taken in Nakamura and Nakamura, 1983a). Otherwise for those who did not work we are left with the model

$$P(h > 0) = F(\phi''), \qquad (2.65)$$

where now

$$\phi'' = (1/\sigma)[(\alpha_{0i} - \beta_{0i}) + Z\alpha_1 - Z^*\beta_1 - I\beta_2 + E\alpha_2], \qquad (2.66)$$

for the decision to work. For those who do work in the current period we have

$$\ln w = \alpha_{0i} + Z\alpha_1 + E\alpha_2 + (\sigma_{12}/\sigma)\lambda + V \qquad (2.67)$$

and

$$h = (1/\beta_4)[(1-\beta_3)\ln w_D - \beta_{0i} - Z^*\beta_1 - I\beta_2] + (\sigma_{13}/\sigma)\lambda + V^*, \qquad (2.68)$$

where σ_{12} is the covariance of u with (u^*-u), σ_{13} is the covariance of $U = (1/\beta_4)[(1-\beta_3)u - u^*]$ with (u^*-u), σ^2 is the variance of (u^*-u), the random term in (2.65), and

$$\lambda = f(\phi'')/F(\phi'') \qquad (2.69)$$

with ϕ'' given by (2.66). The estimated constant terms for such a model will represent the central tendencies of the person-specific terms $(1/\sigma)(\alpha_{0i} - \beta_{0i})$ in (2.66), α_{0i} in (2.67) and $(1/\beta_4)(-\beta_{0i})$ in (2.68).

The extent of the bias problem involved in directly estimating the parameters of (2.66), (2.67) and (2.68) will depend on, among other factors, the extent to which the values of the person-specific terms are correlated with the explanatory variables in these relationships. Notice that if the relevant correlations between the person-specific terms and the explanatory variables in each relationship are all essentially 0, then the associated bias problem may be negligible. In this case, however, the estimated model will capture none of the continuity in individual work behavior due to unobservable person-specific effects. At the other extreme, suppose the person-specific effects are almost perfectly correlated with the included explanatory variables in our relationships. Now we will clearly have a bias problem in the sense that the coefficient estimates of our variables will embed both the direct effects of the variables and the sorting effects for different "types" of individuals as characterized by their person-specific unobservable attributes. Thus, our coefficient estimates cannot be used directly to predict the changes that would occur in our

2 Methodology and Data

dependent variables, given unit changes in each of our explanatory variables. However, now our estimated model will capture the continuity in individual work behavior due both to the continuity in our explanatory variables and to the person-specific effects that are correlated with these explanatory variables (see also Nakamura and Nakamura, 1983a).

FOOTNOTES TO ADDENDUM

1. See, for example, Mangasarian (1969) for necessary and sufficient conditions for maximization (or minimization) problems of the sort we discuss here.
2. The inclusion of the log of the offered wage in the asking wage equation when h is positive is in accord with Heckman's original specification of his behavioral model. See Heckman (1974, Appendix). For further discussion of this issue, see Nakamura, Nakamura and Cullen (1979, p.796, fn. 11), Nakamura and Nakamura (1981, p.457, fn. 5) and Heckman (1978).
3. For a comprehensive treatment of the selection bias problem and of Heckman's approach to dealing with this problem, see Heckman (1976, 1979, 1980). See also Smith (1980, Introduction) for a readable introductory summary of the selection bias problem. The statistical theory of the truncated normal distribution on which Heckman's estimation method is based is summarized in Johnson and Kotz (1970, 1972). The error term for an equation like (2.21) can be shown to be heteroscedastic under the assumptions that have been made about the error term for (2.14). Thus, Heckman (1976, 1979, 1980) suggests that an equation like (2.21) could be estimated using generalized least squares.
4. This procedure is followed, for instance, in Nakamura, Nakamura and Cullen (1979) and Nakamura and Nakamura (1981). In studies such as Heckman (1974, 1976), a reduced form hours equation is estimated. See Nakamura, Nakamura and Cullen (1979, p.796, fn. 11) for commentary on the difference between the two approaches. An hours equation like (2.28) is estimated by generalized least squares in, for instance, Nakamura, Nakamura and Cullen (1979). When an equation like (2.28) is estimated using ordinary least squares, the error term of this equation can be shown to be heteroscedastic under the assumptions that have been made about the error term for equation (2.23).
5. For simulation results showing that the Standard Model generates too many changes in work status, see Heckman (1981, Table 3.3, column 5) and Nakamura and Nakamura (1983a,

Table 5, method 1). Simulation results indicating the extent to which the Standard Model fails to capture the observed continuity in the hours of work and earnings, as well as the work status, of married women are presented in Nakamura and Nakamura (1983a,1984).

6. For sophisticated approaches to estimating the parameters of such a model, see, for instance, Heckman (1981,1981a,1981b).

7. Using maximum likelihood methods, and assuming that the disturbance term corresponding to the difference between our two disturbance terms for which first order autoregressive processes are postulated in (2.31a) and (2.31b) can be one-factor analyzed, Heckman (1981, p.106) finds that over a 3-year time horizon, the estimated correlation between the disturbance term in year 1 and year 2 is .915 and the estimated correlation between the disturbance term in year 2 and year 3 is .918.

8. See, for instance, Heckman (1981b, p.187, fn. 9). Such transformations are possible, however, for linear and logit models.

9. This model formulation and estimation method are given in Nakamura and Nakamura (1983a).

CHAPTER 3

ESTIMATION RESULTS FOR OUR INERTIA MODEL

> Each control variable was included in
> the model with a theoretical, or maybe
> a common-sense, justification, and the
> estimated effect of each was interesting
> in its own right. (Glen Cain commenting
> on Jacob Mincer's work on the labor
> force behavior of individuals)

In this chapter we present estimates for the coefficients of the probit index, wage equation and hours equation given in section 2.3. These equations have been estimated separately for individuals who did not and for individuals who did work in the previous year in each of the six demographic groups of women and for the youngest of our four demographic groups of men defined in section 2.7. For the remaining three groups of men we did not estimate separate sets of equations depending on work status in the previous year. The coefficients of the lagged wage rate and hours of work variables in the probit index, wage and hours equations are set equal to 0 for the subgroups of individuals who did not work in the previous year, since we do not observe values for these variables for these subgroups. The variables included in the equations that we have estimated are those that are defined in section 2.4 and for which mean values are given for our pooled data samples in section 2.7.

Instead of displaying our coefficient estimates in large tables that most readers would probably skip over, in each of the following sections of this chapter, we present and discuss the coefficient estimates for a small group of the explanatory variables in our model. Thus, section 3.2 is devoted to our marital status variables. Results for the age and other related variables are given in section 3.3. Results for the race variable are given in section 3.4. Section 3.5 contains the results for our education variable. Results for variables of special relevance to the work behavior of the young are presented in section 3.6. Section 3.7 is devoted to our child status variables. Results for other income variables are given in section 3.8. Section 3.9 contains the results for our macroeconomic variables. Section 3.10 contains the results for our lagged hours of work and wage rate variables. The results for our selection bias term are given in section 3.11. And the results for the current wage variable in the estimated hours equations for our different demographic groups are given in section 3.12. The various sets of coefficient estimates are thus presented in small tables that are an integral part of the text. This format of presenting the results for all relevant equations and demographic groups for a small set of variables also facilitates comparisons of results among demographic groups and allows us to look for patterns in our results for variables that appear in more than one of our behavioral relationships. Full-sized tables including coefficient estimates for all explanatory variables are also shown in Chapter 5 for the important demographic groups of wives 21-46 years of age and wives 47-64 years of age.

As explained in sections 2.5 and 2.6, we rely on replication of results over demographic groups and meaningful patterns of coefficient estimates for our various behavioral relationships for each demographic group, rather than on standard tests of significance as a means of concluding when the observed relationships between our dependent and explanatory variables are stronger than might be expected by pure chance. For descriptive purposes, however, in our coefficient tables, those coefficient estimates that are larger in magnitude than their estimated standard errors by a factor of at least 1.96 are denoted by two stars, while those coefficient estimates that are larger in magnitude than their estimated standard errors by a factor of at least 1.282 are denoted by one star.

Another unique aspect of the presentation of our results is that in each section, in addition to showing coefficient estimates, we show the probabilities of work, wage rates and hours of work implied by these coefficient estimates for hypothetical women in our various demographic groups, given specified changes in the variables of interest.[1] In these tables we refer to the probabilities of work, wage rates and hours of work for women who did not work in the previous year as probabilities of starting work, starting wage rates and starting hours of work, respectively. For those who did work in the previous year, we use the corresponding terms of probabilities of continuing to work, continuing wage rates, and continuing hours of work. These tables were bothersome to construct and add to the bulk of the book. Without them, however, many readers may find it difficult to think intuitively about the implications of the coefficient estimates shown. The magnitudes of the impacts implied by our probit coefficient estimates depend not only on the magnitudes

3 Estimation Results for Our Inertia Model

of these coefficient estimates but also on the initial probability value for the individual, or mean probability value for the group of individuals, in question. Few readers would be expected to be able to translate probit coefficient estimates into impacts for unit changes in the explanatory variables for various types of individuals without turning to a table for the cumulative standard normal distribution. The sizes of the impacts implied by estimated coefficients in log-linear relationships like our wage equations also depend on the initial values of the dependent variables. Again, many readers probably cannot conveniently think about the magnitude of the impacts on the wage rates for certain types of individuals that are implied by the coefficient estimates for a wage equation where the dependent variable is in log form. It is even more difficult to think about the _full_ impact implied by our coefficient estimates of a change in one of our explanatory variables because of all the interrelationships in our model. For instance, the age variable has a direct impact on the hours of work as an explanatory variable in our hours equations and an indirect impact through both the selection bias term and the current wage variable included in our hours equations. Thus, we feel that the tables of probabilities of work, wage rates and hours of work for various sorts of hypothetical women are an essential part of the presentation of our empirical results. We give the specifications of the hypothetical women for whom the values in these tables are calculated and the details of the calculation of these values in section 3.1.

  A summary of the material contained in Chapter 3 may be helpful to the reader. What follows, therefore, is an outline of the variables for which estimation results are shown in each of the sections of this chapter. We also briefly summarize our results concerning which of these variables are found to affect current work behavior after controlling for work behavior in the previous year. Further details concerning these variables can be found in sections 2.4 and 2.7.

  The variables for which estimation results are shown in section 3.2 are the following: (1) dummy for currently married, (2) dummy for married in previous year (t-1), (3) dummy for currently widowed, and (4) dummy for currently divorced. The dummy variable for currently married is only included in our relationships for those demographic groups where we did not differentiate by marital status in forming our data samples used in estimation. Thus, this dummy is included for women 14-20, women at least 65 years of age, and men. The estimation results for this variable are what might be expected. The dummy variables for currently widowed and currently divorced are only included for unmarried women 47-64 years of age and women at least 65 years of age. We obtain no results of interest for these variables. The dummy variable indicating which individuals were married in the previous year has been included in the appropriate behavioral relationships for all of our demographic groups of women. The results for this variable are striking and support conjectures and early empirical findings by researchers like Cain (1966).

In section 3.3 estimation results are shown for the variables: (1) age, (2) dummy for 60-62 years of age, (3) dummy for 63-64 years of age, (4) dummy for 65-66 years of age, and (5) disability dummy. For reasons explained in the text, only the first of these four variables -- the continuous variable for years of age -- is included in our relationships for women. We find clear age-related patterns in the work behavior of women, with these patterns differing in an interesting manner for women who did versus women who did not work in the previous year.

The race variable for which estimation results are shown in section 3.4 is a dummy variable set equal to 1 if an individual is black, and set equal to 0 otherwise. Our most interesting finding for this variable is that, after controlling for work behavior in the previous year, black women are no more, or even less, likely to work in the current year than nonblack women.

Estimation results for a continuous education variable are shown in section 3.5. This variable is found to have systematic effects on work behavior, as might be expected. We find some evidence that this variable affects the asking wage as well as the offered wage, contrary to the specification of our model.

Estimation results for two variables of special relevance to the work behavior of women and men 14-20 years of age are shown in section 3.6. These variables are a dummy set equal to 1 for those who were attending school in the previous year and a dummy set equal to 1 for those living with parents. These results are of some interest, despite the unsophisticated treatment of the interactions among school status, leaving home, and work status. Certainly they suggest some promising directions for further research.

Section 3.7 contains estimation results for the following child status variables: (1) baby dummy, (2) young child dummy, and (3) number of children younger than 18. Only the continuous variable for the number of children younger than 18 living at home is included in our relationships for men as well as women for all age groups. The results for this variable are weak for both women and men. For the other two dummy variables included in our relationships for women younger than 47, only the dummy for the presence of a new baby appears to be associated with a reduction in labor supply. Even the effects associated with this variable are quite modest, however. Thus, after controlling for work behavior in the previous year, we find little evidence of important

3 Estimation Results for Our Inertia Model

effects of child status on the work behavior of women. Further support for this position comes from results shown in Chapter 6. This finding has a variety of implications for modeling, forecasting and policy analyses related to the work behavior of women.

Section 3.8 contains our estimation results for our other income variables. These are (1) husband's income, (2) change in husband's income, (3) negative change in husband's income, (4) dummy for AFDC in t-1, (5) dummy for Social Security in t-1, and (6) wife's income in t-1. Obviously, each of these variables is included only for certain of our demographic groups. The most notable aspect of our estimation results for these variables is that we are able to identity few, if any, consistent and intuitively understandable patterns. Whether other income variables really have little effect on current work behavior after controlling for work behavior in the previous year, or whether effects would be found if these variables were modified or introduced into our relationships in some other manner, is a possible topic for further investigation.

In section 3.9 we show estimation results for a variable for the national unemployment rate and a national wage index variable. We do not manage to identify any consistent effects for these variables either.

Section 3.10 contains estimation results for our lagged hours of work and wage variables. The most interesting tables in this section are, perhaps, Tables 3.10.7 and 3.10.9 which show how the probability of continuing to work and the expected continuing hours of work for hypothetical women change depending on how many hours these women are assumed to have worked in the previous year. In particular, it may be of interest to compare the figures in the column in these tables for 2,000 hours of work in the previous year with the point estimates for the probability of work and for annual hours of work for men shown in section 2.7.

In section 3.11 we show estimation results for the selection bias term included in our wage rate and hours of work equations. The most interesting result to emerge from this section is that we find as much evidence that the selection bias term belongs in our wage and hours equations for men as for the inclusion of this variable in our wage and hours equations for women.

Finally, in section 3.12 we present coefficient estimates for the current log wage variable in our hours of work equations. We obtain estimates of the uncompensated wage elasticity of hours of work that lie in essentially the same range for women as for men, contrary to accepted beliefs about the ranges of the wage elasticities for women and men. We find that this result remains even when we make certain alterations in our estimation method and model. At the least, this result means that those claiming to have discovered responses in work behavior for women that are very different from the responses that are believed to characterize male work behavior should be required to show results obtained using essentially the same data and estimation method for both women and men.

We proceed now with the specifications of our hypothetical women given in section 3.1.

3.1. Hypothetical Women and the Calculation of Their Probabilities of Work, Wage Rates and Hours of Work

The baseline characteristics of our hypothetical women are given in Table 3.1.1 when it is assumed that these women did not work in the previous year and in Table 3.1.2 when it is assumed that these women did work in the previous year. Notice that when we assume that these hypothetical women worked in the previous year, we also assume that they did <u>not</u> work in the year prior to that, and in the baseline case, we assign each of them the wage rate and hours of work for the previous year that characterize the starting work behavior for that woman as specified in Table 3.1.1.

Suppose now that we want to show how our estimated coefficients imply that the starting work behavior of women differs depending, say, on their child status. In this case, we begin by considering hypothetical women with no children younger than 18 and with the characteristics given in Table 3.1.1. We then suppose that the circumstances for these hypothetical women are altered from the baseline case by the addition, for instance, of a new baby or of a youngest child less than 6 that is not a new baby or of a child younger than 18 but older than 5 years of age. For each of these changes, we calculate the corresponding changes from the baseline case that our coefficient estimates imply would occur in the probit indices. This allows us to calculate probabilities of starting work for women identical in all respects, except the specified child status characteristics, to our hypothetical women for the baseline case. The figures for the starting wage rates and starting hours of work for the specified alterations in child status are calculated in a similar manner, except that now we must also take into account the secondary impacts of the changes in the probit indices and hence in the selection bias terms that enter the wage and hours equations, as well as the changes in the current wage variable that enters the hours equations. Where the final wage or hours figures arrived at have been determined taking into account both direct and indirect impacts of the given change in circumstances from the

3 Estimation Results for Our Inertia Model

TABLE 3.1.1
CHARACTERISTICS OF HYPOTHETICAL WOMEN ASSUMING
THEY DID NOT WORK IN PREVIOUS YEAR

Age and marital status	Prob. of work	Value of probit index	Value of selection bias term	Current log wage if working	Current hours if working
17					
Married	.13	−1.12	1.61	.58	614
Unmarried	.30	−.53	1.16	.58	614
33					
Married	.21	−.81	1.37	.81	671
Unmarried	.38	−.31	1.00	.64	993
55					
Married	.09	−1.34	1.80	.51	734
Unmarried	.13	−1.13	1.62	.81	737
70					
Married	.00	−5.89			
Unmarried	.06	−1.56	1.99	−.97	96

baseline case, the figures accounting for only the direct changes are shown in parentheses next to the final figures.

Our figures for continuing work behavior, given specified changes in circumstances, are arrived at in a manner similar to that used for our figures for starting work behavior, except that now the characteristics of our hypothetical women for the baseline case are given in Table 3.1.2 instead of in Table 3.1.1. Also, some of the changes in current circumstances are ones that would have had to have prevailed in the previous year as well. In these cases, the indirect impacts include the changes from the baseline case in the wage rates and hours of work for the previous year.

The characteristics for our hypothetical women shown in Tables 3.1.1 and 3.1.2 are arrived at based on the sample means of the relevant variables for our six demographic groups of women (see section 2.7). Due to sample size considerations, we did not form separate groups for married and unmarried

TABLE 3.1.2
CHARACTERISTICS OF HYPOTHETICAL WOMEN ASSUMING
THEY STARTED TO WORK IN PREVIOUS YEAR

Age and marital status	Prob. of work	Value of probit index	Value of selection bias term	Wage in t-1	Hours in t-1	Current log wage if working	Current hours if working
17							
Married	.47	-.08	.85	$1.78	614	.68	1112
Unmarried	.76	.71	.40	1.78	614	.68	1112
33							
Married	.85	1.04	.28	2.24	671	.93	1359
Unmarried	.92	1.41	.16	1.89	993	.97	1676
55							
Married	.86	1.08	.26	1.67	734	.99	1378
Unmarried	.92	1.41	.16	2.25	737	.90	1711
70							
Unmarried	.74	.65	.44	.38	96	.71	1070

women in the 14-20 and 65 and over age brackets. For these groups we have assigned the sample point estimates for the mean probabilities of work to the hypothetical unmarried woman in each group, and then we have calculated the probabilities of starting and of continuing to work for the corresponding hypothetical married women using the estimated coefficients for our dummy variable for currently married. This resulted in a probability of starting to work of 0 for our hypothetical married 70-year-old woman. Thus, we treat the probability of continuing to work, which presumes having started to work in the previous year, as 0 as well for this hypothetical married woman. This is why we show no figures in our tables for a hypothetical married woman in our oldest age bracket. We have assigned the sample means for the wage rate and hours of work for those in the age groups of 14-20 and 65 and older both to our unmarried and married hypothetical women in the younger group and to the unmarried hypothetical woman in the older group.

We have included an explanation of these details in the

3   Estimation Results for Our Inertia Model

text simply to make the tables for starting and continuing work behavior presented in the rest of Chapter 3 and in Chapter 4 understandable. We do not intend that our hypothetical women should be viewed as displaying representative behavior. On the basis of the details presented in this section, it should be clear that while we have attempted to assign reasonable behavior to our hypothetical women in the baseline circumstances, our assignment of characteristics to these women is largely arbitrary. We proceed now with the presentation of the empirical results for our Inertia Model developed in section 2.3.

3.2. Marital Status Variables

It has long been recognized that the labor force behavior of women differs systematically by marital status. A higher proportion of unmarried women work, and unmarried women tend to work longer hours and receive higher wage rates than married women. If these observed differences in work behavior by current marital status are due to relatively fixed tastes and preferences formed in the late teens or early twenties for home-oriented versus market-oriented activities, we might expect to find little change in individual labor force behavior with changes in marital status. A finding to the contrary would suggest that tastes for work change either together with or as a result of changes in marital status, with these tastes perhaps being molded by economic need and by changed future expectations concerning income flows from a husband.

For women who did not work in the previous year, probit index and hours equation coefficient estimates for a dummy variable set equal to 1 if a woman was married in the previous year are shown in Tables 3.2.1 and 3.2.2. If only current marital status matters, then all of the coefficient estimates for this dummy variable should be essentially 0. We see from Tables 3.2.1 and 3.2.2 that this is not the case. What we find, instead, is that for unmarried women, the impacts of having been married in the previous year are positive on both the probability of starting work and the starting hours of work. On the other hand, for currently married women the impacts of having been married in the previous year on the probability of starting work and on the starting hours of work are generally negative. In other words, one direct effect or corollary of changes in marital status for women who did not work in the previous year is increases in labor supply, with these increases tending to be largest for women whose marriages have recently terminated.

TABLE 3.2.1
COEFFICIENT ESTIMATES FOR MARITAL STATUS VARIABLES
IN PROBIT INDICES FOR PROBABILITY OF WORK:
WOMEN WHO DID NOT WORK IN t-1

Group	Dummy for currently married	Dummy for married in t-1	Dummy for currently widowed	Dummy for currently divorced
Women 14-20	-.595*	-.180		
Wives 21-46		-.195		
Unmarried women 21-46		1.264**		
Wives 47-64		-.997**		
Unmarried women 47-64		1.496**	.017	-.166
Women 65+	-4.330**	1.293**	-1.252**	-.925*

TABLE 3.2.2
IV COEFFICIENT ESTIMATES FOR MARITAL STATUS
VARIABLES IN HOURS EQUATIONS:
WORKING WOMEN WHO DID NOT WORK IN t-1

Group	Dummy for currently married	Dummy for married in t-1	Dummy for currently widowed	Dummy for currently divorced
Women 14-20	-736.7**	95.9		
Wives 21-46		-313.7*		
Unmarried women 21-46		806.1**		
Wives 47-64		219.8		
Unmarried women 47-64		228.0	776.1**	1061.6**
Women 65+		-112.5	1061.6**	396.4*

3 Estimation Results for Our Inertia Model

For women who did work in the previous year, probit index and hours equation coefficient estimates for our dummy variable set equal to 1 if a woman was married in the previous year are shown in Tables 3.2.3 and 3.2.4. From these tables we see that for women who worked in the previous year, the impacts on current labor supply of having also been married in the previous year are generally positive, regardless of current marital status. The one exception is the negative coefficient in the hours equation for unmarried women 47-64 years of age. Ignoring this one coefficient, we see also that the positive impacts on the continuing labor supply of women of having been married in the previous year are largest for women who are currently unmarried.

In addition to our coefficient estimates for our marital status variable set equal to 1 if a woman was married in the previous year, in Tables 3.2.1 through 3.2.4, we also show coefficient estimates for unmarried women 47-64 and women 65 and over for dummy variables for being currently widowed and for being currently divorced, and we show coefficient estimates for women 14-20 and women 65 and over for a dummy variable set equal to 1 if a women is currently married. We find little consistency in our coefficient estimates for our dummy variables for currently widowed and for currently divorced. However, in both the probit indices and the hours equations for both starting and continuing work behavior, we find the coefficient estimates for our dummy for currently married to be negative in sign. This finding is consistent both with prior expectations and with the marital status patterns in the point estimates shown in section 2.7 for the probability of work and hours of work for the 21-46- and 47-64-year-old age groups of women.

We now consider hypothetical women who were not married in the previous year and who had the age and marital status characteristics in the current year and the probabilities of starting work, starting wage rates and starting hours of work shown in Table 3.1.1. Tables 3.2.5 through 3.2.7 show how our coefficient estimates in Tables 3.2.1 and 3.2.2 imply that the starting work behavior of these women would differ if they had been married instead of unmarried in the previous year. From Table 3.2.5 we see that in every age group except the oldest, our currently married hypothetical woman is more likely to start work if she was unmarried in the previous year than if she was married. Also, however, in every age group except the youngest, our currently unmarried hypothetical woman is much more likely to start work if she was married than if she was unmarried in the previous year. In other words, married women who were married and did not work in the previous year are more likely than otherwise to persist in not working, and unmarried women who were unmarried and did not work in the previous year are also more likely than otherwise to persist

TABLE 3.2.3
COEFFICIENT ESTIMATES FOR MARITAL STATUS
VARIABLES IN PROBIT INDICES
FOR PROBABILITY OF EMPLOYMENT: WOMEN WHO WORKED IN t-1

Group	Dummy for currently married	Dummy for married in t-1	Dummy for currently widowed	Dummy for currently divorced
Women 14-20	-.792**	.359*		
Wives 21-46		.404**		
Unmarried women 21-46		1.939		
Wives 47-64		1.443**		
Unmarried women 47-64		1.945	.154	-.279
Women 65+	-.229		.180	-.266

TABLE 3.2.4
IV COEFFICIENT ESTIMATES FOR MARITAL
STATUS VARIABLES IN HOURS EQUATIONS:
WORKING WOMEN WHO WORKED IN t-1

Group	Dummy for currently married	Dummy for married in t-1	Dummy for currently widowed	Dummy for currently divorced
Women 14-20	-67.6	124.3		
Wives 21-46		3.9		
Unmarried women 21-46		343.1*		
Wives 47-64		479.7*		
Unmarried women 47-64		-1192.8**	-92.7*	-92.7*
Women 65+	-120.8		-237.4*	148.6

TABLE 3.2.5
PROBABILITIES OF STARTING WORK FOR WOMEN
DEPENDING ON WHETHER THEY ARE MARRIED
IN t OR WERE MARRIED IN t-1

Marital status in t-1 and age	Marital status in t			
	Married		Unmarried	
Married	17	.10	17	.24
	33	.16	33	.83
	55	.01	55	.64
	70	.00	70	.39
Unmarried	17	.13	17	.30
	33	.21	33	.38
	55	.09	55	.13
	70	.00	70	.06

TABLE 3.2.6
STARTING WAGE RATES FOR HYPOTHETICAL
WOMEN DEPENDING ON WHETHER THEY ARE
MARRIED IN t OR WERE MARRIED IN t-1

Marital status in t-1 and age	Marital status in t			
	Married		Unmarried	
Married	17	$1.66	17	$1.66
	33	2.39	33	2.41
	55	1.52	55	2.32
			70	.52
Unmarried	17	1.78	17	1.78
	33	2.24	33	1.89
	55	1.67	55	2.25
			70	.38

TABLE 3.2.7
STARTING HOURS OF WORK FOR HYPOTHETICAL
WOMEN DEPENDING ON WHETHER THEY ARE
MARRIED IN t OR WERE MARRIED IN t-1

Marital status in t-1 and age		Marital status in t			
		Married		Unmarried	
Married	17	129	(-27)	17	845 (710)
	33	307	(357)	33	1778 (1799)
	55	518	(954)	55	1308 (965)
				70	165 (16)
Unmarried	17	614		17	614
	33	671		33	993
	55	734		55	737
				70	96

TABLE 3.2.8
PROBABILITIES OF CONTINUING TO WORK
FOR HYPOTHETICAL WOMEN DEPENDING ON
WHETHER THEY ARE MARRIED IN t OR
WERE MARRIED IN t-1 and t-2

Marital status in t-1 and t-2 and age		Marital status in t		
		Married	Unmarried	
Married	17	.49 (.61)	17	.78 (.86)
	33	.88 (.92)	33	1.00 (1.00)
	55	.99 (.99)	55	1.00 (1.00)
Unmarried	17	.47	17	.76
	33	.85	33	.92
	55	.86	55	.92

in not working. Because of the nature of these responses and the baseline probabilities of starting work, which are higher for our unmarried than for our married hypothetical women, our hypothetical women who were not married in the previous year are only 4 to 17 percentage points more likely to start work if they are currently unmarried as opposed to married, but our hypothetical women who were married in the previous year are 14 to 67 percentage points more likely to start work if they are currently unmarried as opposed to married.

In Table 3.2.7 we find the same pattern of labor supply responses as in Table 3.2.5. In every age group, our married hypothetical woman is estimated to start work with fewer hours in the year if she was married than if she was unmarried in the previous year. On the other hand, in every age group our unmarried hypothetical woman is estimated to start out working substantially more hours if she was married rather than unmarried in the previous year. Because of the nature of these responses, our hypothetical 17-, 33- and 55-year-old women who were not married in the previous year start our working 0 to 322 more hours if they are currently unmarried as opposed to married. However, our hypothetical 17-, 33- and 55-year-old women who were married in the previous year start out working 716 to 1471 more hours if they are currently unmarried as opposed to married.

The impacts of previous marital status on the wage rate are only indirect via the selection bias term. From Table 3.2.6 we see that, with the exception of our 17-year-old hypothetical women, for both our married and unmarried hypothetical women the starting wage rate is estimated to be higher for those who were married in the previous year as opposed to unmarried.

Consider hypothetical women with the current age and marital status attributes, the probabilities of continuing to work, the continuing wage rates, and the continuing hours of work shown in Table 3.1.2, who were unmarried in both the previous year and the year before that, and who started work in the previous year with the probabilities, wage rates and hours of work shown in Table 3.1.1. Tables 3.2.8 through 3.2.10 show how our coefficient estimates imply that the continuing work behavior of these hypothetical women would differ if they had been married as opposed to unmarried in both the previous year when they started to work and in the year before that.

From Table 3.2.8 we see that the probabilities of continuing to work for our hypothetical 17-, 33- and 55-year-old currently married women would be 2 to 13 percentage points higher if they had been married instead of unmarried in the preceeding two years. Likewise for our 17-, 33- and 55-year-old currently unmarried women, the probabilities of continuing to work would have been 2 to 8 percentage points higher if they had been married instead of unmarried in the preceeding two years.

If we look at the figures in parentheses ignoring indirect impacts in Table 3.2.10, we see the same pattern of labor supply responses as in Table 3.2.8. That is, we see that considering only direct effects, with one exception, our

TABLE 3.2.9
CONTINUING WAGE RATES FOR HYPOTHETICAL WOMEN
DEPENDING ON WHETHER THEY ARE MARRIED IN t OR
WERE MARRIED IN t-1 AND t-2

Marital status in t-1 and t-2 and age	Marital status in t — Married		Marital status in t — Unmarried	
Married	17	$1.88	17	$1.88
	33	2.54	33	2.97
	55	2.89	55	3.29
Unmarried	17	1.98	17	1.98
	33	2.54	33	2.65
	55	2.69	55	2.46

TABLE 3.2.10
CONTINUING HOURS OF WORK FOR HYPOTHETICAL
WOMEN DEPENDING ON WHETHER THEY ARE
MARRIED IN t OR WERE MARRIED IN t-1 AND t-2

Marital status in t-1 and t-2 and age	Marital status in t — Married		Marital status in t — Unmarried	
Married	17	1067 (1236)	17	1067 (1236)
	33	1206 (1363)	33	1786 (2019)
	55	1721 (1858)	55	469 (518)
Unmarried	17	1112	17	1112
	33	1359	33	1676
	55	1378	55	1711

hypothetical women would work longer hours if they had been married rather than unmarried in the preceeding two years. The picture becomes mixed, however, when we also consider indirect effects. The most important indirect effect is that all of the hypothetical women are found, from Table 3.2.7, to have had very low starting hours of work if they were married in both the previous year when they started work and in the year before that. As with the starting wage rates, we find from

3   Estimation Results for Our Inertia Model

TABLE 3.2.11
COEFFICIENT ESTIMATES FOR DUMMY VARIABLE FOR
CURRENTLY MARRIED IN PROBIT INDICES FOR
PROBABILITY OF WORK: MEN

Work status in t-1	Age 14-20	21-46	47-64	65+
Did not work	2.789	.402**	-.130	-.119
Worked	.307			

TABLE 3.2.12
IV COEFFICIENT ESTIMATES FOR DUMMY VARIABLE
FOR CURRENTLY MARRIED IN HOURS EQUATIONS: WORKING MEN

Work status in t-1	Age 14-20	21-46	47-64	65+
Did not work	-247.3	157.5**	89.4**	131.1
Worked	146.5*			

Table 3.2.9 that indirect effects imply that the continuing wage rates for hypothetical 33- and 55-year-old women would be generally higher if they had been married instead of unmarried in the preceeding two years.

The impacts of <u>changes</u> in marital status on work behavior cannot be considered in studies based on cross-sectional data that include information about current marital status but not about marital status in the previous year.[2] Nor can such impacts be considered in panel data studies based on <u>continuously married</u> women.[3] We are not the first, however, to suggest that changes in marital status might have important effects on the work behavior of women. For instance, in commentary on the participation rates for nonwhite versus white wives, Cain (1966, pp. 82-83) speculates: "Given the relatively high probability that the Negro wife will be without her husband during part of her married life, it seems likely that she would maintain closer ties to the labor force while married." He goes on to state:

> To test the marital instability hypothesis ...
> we can look for differential labor force behavior
> among those wives in the white population who have
> remarried or separated .... I use survey data for
> this test, and the results ... do conform to this
> stated expectation.

Also Sweet (1973, pp. 105-106) reports: "Data from our 1/1000 sample of women with children show that if either spouse has been married more than once the probability of the wife working is increased." Our results suggest that more attention should be directed toward gaining a better understanding of the relationships between the work behavior and patterns of family formation and dissolution.[4]

In Tables 3.2.11 and 3.2.12, we show coefficient estimates for men for our dummy variable for being currently married. These coefficient estimates are seen to be generally positive. This is the reverse of what we find to be the direction of the response to being currently married for women.

We draw the following conclusions:

1. Currently married women supply less labor, and currently married men supply more labor, than their unmarried counterparts, even after controlling for child status and other factors including work behavior in the preceding year.
2. Changes in marital status have powerful impacts on the work behavior of women. Women who did not work in the previous year are more likely to start work and have higher starting hours of work if their marital status has changed, with the positive effects being greater by far for those whose marriages have terminated. Married and unmarried women who worked in the previous year are more likely to continue working if they were married in the previous year and the year before that, with the positive effects being greatest for those who are currently unmarried. Because of these relationships and the way in which hours of work in one year affect the probability of work and hours of work in the following year, we see that martial breakdown can greatly increase a woman's labor supply for years to come, whether or not she subsequently remarries.

3.3. Age

Age cannot directly affect work behavior, except to the extent that work is prohibited by law for the very young and discouraged by collective agreements for the older age groups. We enter age into our models of work behavior as a proxy for other factors on which we do not have data, such as cumulative work experience, job seniority, depreciation of job skills or education, health status, personal attitudes toward work at various stages of the life cycle, discrimination against older people in the labor market, and so forth. Thus, a finding that age plays an important role in a model of labor force behavior is really a finding that factors for which age is serving as a proxy have important effects on labor force behavior.[5]

If we do not control for age in a model of labor force behavior, the responses to unobserved factors correlated with age will remain in the model error terms. These components of the error terms may be correlated with other variables such as husband's income, that change systematically over the life cycle. Also, with more variability in the error term, parameter estimates for other variables will be less precise.

In this study we are particularly interested in the question of whether there are systematic differences in the estimated responses to the age variable depending on whether or not a woman worked in the previous year.

The coefficient estimates for the age variable in the probit indices for the probability of work and in our log wage and hours equations are shown in Tables 3.3.1 through 3.3.6. Factors which affect the offered wage should affect the probability of work and the hourly wage, with the direction of the effect being the same in both cases. Likewise, factors that affect the asking wage should affect the probability of work and the hours of work in the same direction.

Looking at Tables 3.3.1 and 3.3.3, we see that for both married and unmarried women in the 21-46- and 47-64-year-old age groups who did not work in the previous year, the age coefficients are negative in both the probit indices for the probability of work and the hours equations. On the other hand, for women 14-20 who did not work in the previous year, both the probit index and hours equation age coefficients are positive. From Tables 3.3.2 and 3.3.1, we see also that there is agreement in sign between the negative age coefficients in the log wage equations and the negative age coefficient estimates in the probit indices for married women aged 21-46 and 47-64 who did not work in the previous year. This sign agreement is not present for unmarried women in these age groups, however, nor is it present for the 14-20 age group.

Looking now at Tables 3.3.4 and 3.3.6, we find that for both married and unmarried women 47-64 years of age who worked

TABLE 3.3.1
COEFFICIENT ESTIMATES FOR AGE VARIABLE IN
PROBIT INDICES FOR PROBABILITY OF WORK:
WOMEN WHO DID NOT WORK IN t-1

Marital status	Age			
	14-20	21-46	47-64	65+
Married		-.020**	-.055**	
	.176**			-.035*
Unmarried		-.023*	-.014	

TABLE 3.3.2
OLS COEFFICIENT ESTIMATES FOR AGE VARIABLE
IN LOG WAGE EQUATIONS:
WORKING WOMEN WHO DID NOT WORK IN t-1

Marital status	Age			
	14-20	21-46	47-64	65+
Married		-.014**	-.014	
	-.018			-.006
Unmarried		.007*	.011	

TABLE 3.3.3
IV COEFFICIENT ESTIMATES FOR AGE VARIABLE
IN HOURS EQUATIONS:
WORKING WOMEN WHO DID NOT WORK IN t-1

Marital status	Age			
	14-20	21-46	47-64	65+
Married		-4.4	-62.8	
	230.2**			10.4
Unmarried		-10.5	-4.8	

TABLE 3.3.4
COEFFICIENT ESTIMATES FOR AGE VARIABLE IN
PROBIT INDICES FOR PROBABILITY OF WORK:
WOMEN WHO WORKED IN t-1

Marital status	Age			
	14-20	21-46	47-64	65+
Married	.069	.020**	-.029*	.011
Unmarried		.001	-.026*	

TABLE 3.3.5
OLS COEFFICIENT ESTIMATES FOR AGE VARIABLE
IN LOG WAGE EQUATIONS:
WORKING WOMEN WHO WORKED IN t-1

Marital status	Age			
	14-20	21-46	47-64	65+
Married	.007	.001	.007	-.028*
Unmarried		-.001	.001	

TABLE 3.3.6
IV COEFFICIENT ESTIMATES FOR AGE VARIABLE IN
HOURS EQUATIONS:
WORKING WOMEN WHO WORKED IN t-1

Marital status	Age			
	14-20	21-46	47-64	65+
Married	5.7	-5.0**	-10.4*	-52.5**
Unmarried		3.1*	-7.7**	

in the previous year, the estimated coefficients of the age variable in the probit indices for the probability of work and in the hours equations are all negative. The age coefficients in the probit indices and hours equations are all positive for women 14-20 and unmarried women 21-46 who worked in t-1, but there is a sign conflict for married women 21-46 who worked in t-1. There is also a sign conflict for the oldest age group. Comparing the results in Tables 3.3.5 and 3.3.4, it is difficult to find any sort of systematic impacts of the age variable on wage rates.

Since the age variable is acting primarily as a proxy for other unobserved age-related factors, it is interesting to compare our coefficient estimates for women with coefficient estimates for this variable for men. One of the factors for which age probably acts as a proxy in our equations for women is disability due to illness or accident. We are not able to control directly for disability status in our equations for women since this information is not available in our data source for married women. In our equations for men in the 21-46, 47-64 and 65-and-over age groups, however, we have introduced a dummy variable set equal to 1 if an individual has a disability that limits or prevents work and set equal to 0 otherwise. Also, many more men than women retire abruptly due to company and pension plan regulations. Thus, in our equations for men 47-64 years of age, we have included a dummy set equal to 1 if a man is 60-62 years of age and set equal to 0 otherwise and another dummy set equal to 1 if a man is 63-64 years old and set equal to 0 otherwise; and in our equations for men 65 or more years of age, we have included a dummy set equal to 1 if a man is 65-66 years of age and set equal to 0 otherwise.

The coefficient estimates for our continuous age variable and for our disability and retirement age dummies in our probit indices for the probability of work and in our log wage and hours equations for men are shown in Tables 3.3.7 through 3.3.12.

From Table 3.3.7 we see that for those 14-20 who did not work in the previous year, the age-related rise in the probability of work is much less steep for men than it is for women and is not apparent at all for men 14-20 who worked in the previous year. The proxy effects on the probability of work are less important for men than for women in this age bracket.

Men who have a disability limiting work in the 21-46, 47-64 and 65-and-over age brackets are seen from Table 3.3.8 to be far less likely to work than otherwise-similar men, with the negative effects being greatest in the 47-64 age bracket. Also, we see from Table 3.3.8 that for men there are large 60-62 and 65-66 "retirement effects." After controlling for these disability and retirement effects, we see from Table

3 Estimation Results for Our Inertia Model

TABLE 3.3.7
COEFFICIENT ESTIMATES FOR AGE VARIABLE IN
PROBIT INDICES FOR PROBABILITY OF WORK: MEN

		Age		
Work status in t-1	14-20	21-46	47-64	65+
Did not work	.053*	.001	-.011	-.035**
Worked	-.018			

TABLE 3.3.8
COEFFICIENT ESTIMATES FOR DISABILITY AND
RETIREMENT AGE DUMMIES IN PROBIT
INDICES FOR PROBABILITY OF WORK: MEN

	Age		
Dummy variable	21-46	47-64	65+
Disability dummy	-.454**	-.600**	-.085
Dummy for 60-62 years of age		-.297*	
Dummy for 63-64 years of age		.212	
Dummy for 65-66 years of age			-.403**

TABLE 3.3.9
OLS COEFFICIENT ESTIMATES FOR AGE VARIABLE
IN LOG WAGE EQUATIONS: WORKING MEN

		Age		
Work status in t-1	14-20	21-46	47-64	65+
Did not work	.089**	.007**	.005*	-.030**
Worked	.086**			

TABLE 3.3.10
OLS COEFFICIENT ESTIMATES FOR DISABILITY
AND RETIREMENT AGE DUMMIES IN LOG
WAGE EQUATIONS: WORKING MEN

Dummy variable	Age 21-46	Age 47-64	Age 65+
Disability dummy	-.084**	-.049*	-.089
Dummy for 60-62 years of age		-.049	
Dummy for 63-64 years of age		-.044	
Dummy for 65-66 years of age			.063

3.3.7 for men, and Tables 3.3.1 and 3.3.4 for women, that in the age bracket of 47-64 the negative proxy effect of age on the probability of work is not as strong for men as it is for women. In the oldest age bracket for men, however, even after controlling for disability and retirement effects, the direct negative impact of age on the probability of work is at least as great as it is for women in the oldest age bracket.

From Table 3.3.9 we see that, in marked contrast to our results for women shown in Tables 3.3.2 and 3.3.5, there are strong positive age effects on the wage rates for men 14-20 and 21-46. From Table 3.3.10 we see that having a disability depresses the wage rates for men 21-46, 47-64 and 65 and over. We had thought, too, that following mandatory retirement, many men might find new jobs paying substantially lower wage rates than their old jobs. The evidence in Table 3.3.10 concerning abrupt age-specific effects of this sort is weak, however. After controlling for disability effects and any effects on wage rates of reaching ages commonly associated with retirement, from Table 3.3.9 we find negative impacts of age on the wage rates of men 47-64 and 65 and over, with the negative impact being considerably greater for the 65-and-over group. For women aged 47-64, we find no clear evidence of any impact of age on wage rates. The negative direct impact of age on the probability of work for women 65 and over who worked in the previous year is comparable in magnitude to the negative impact of age for men in this age group, however.

3   Estimation Results for Our Inertia Model

TABLE 3.3.11
IV COEFFICIENT ESTIMATES FOR AGE VARIABLE
IN HOURS EQUATIONS: WORKING MEN

Work status in t-1	14-20	21-46	47-64	65+
Did not work	324.5**	-1.1	-7.7	1.2
Worked	133.6**			

TABLE 3.3.12
IV COEFFICIENT ESTIMATES FOR DISABILITY AND
RETIREMENT AGE DUMMIES IN HOURS EQUATIONS: WORKING MEN

Dummy variable	21-46	47-64	65+
Disability dummy	-147.0**	-147.1**	60.4
Dummy for 60-62 years of age		-43.0	
Dummy for 63-64 years of age		-134.5**	
Dummy for 65-66 years of age			-51.3

From Table 3.3.12 we see that there are negative disability affects for men 24-46 and 47-64 years of age, and also negative retirement effects, on the hours of work of men. After controlling for these effects, we find small negative impacts of age on hours of work for men 24-46 and 47-64 that are similar in magnitude to the age effects reported in Table 3.3.6 for women in these same age groups who worked in the previous year. Contrary to our results for women 65 and over who worked in the previous year, however, we find no negative impact of age on the hours of work of men who are 65 and over, after controlling for 64-65-year-old retirement effects. For the 14-20 age group, we see from Table 3.3.11 that there are

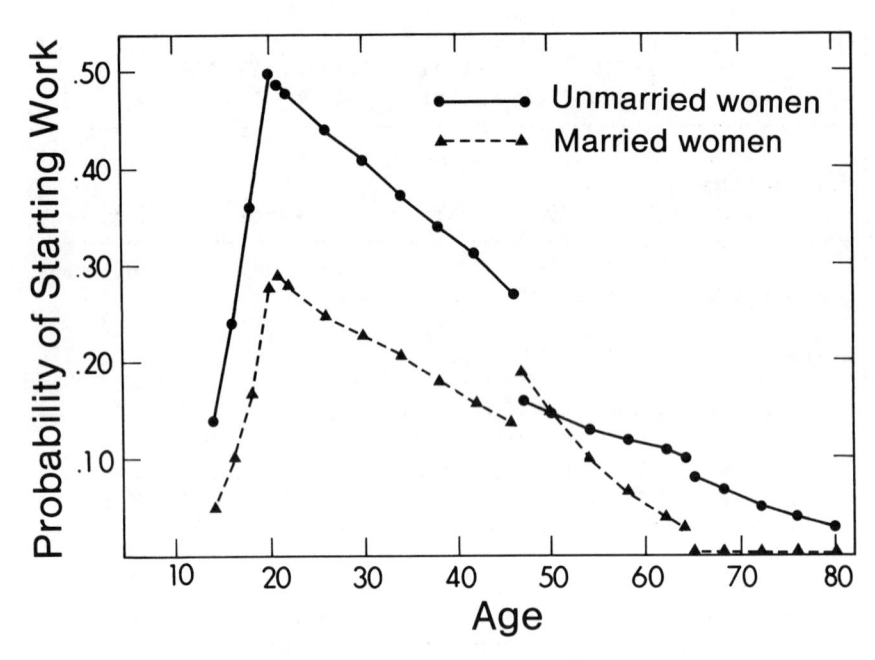

Fig. 3.3.1. Effects of age on probabilities of starting work.

strong positive effects of age on hours of work for both young men who did not and who did work in the previous year, with the larger effect being for young men who did not work in the previous year. A large positive impact of age on hours of work is also shown for women 14-20 years of age who did not work in the previous year in Table 3.3.3.

Suppose we again consider hypothetical women with the characteristics shown in Table 3.3.1. Assuming that nothing changes about each of these women over time except age, we can use the coefficient estimates shown in Tables 3.3.1 through 3.3.3 to determine the probabilities of starting to work and the accompanying starting wage rates and starting hours of work for our hypothetical women over the age brackets for which our behavioral relationships have been estimated. These results are shown graphically for women who did not work in the previous year in Figures 3.3.1 through 3.3.3. The dotted lines in Figures 3.3.2 and 3.3.3 show the estimated wage rates ignoring the indirect impact of age through the selection bias term, and the estimated hours ignoring the indirect impacts of age through the selection bias term and the log wage rate. Estimated starting wage rates and hours of work are not shown beyond age 64, since the probability of starting work for our hypothetical wife in the oldest category is assumed to be 0.

3 Estimation Results for Our Inertia Model

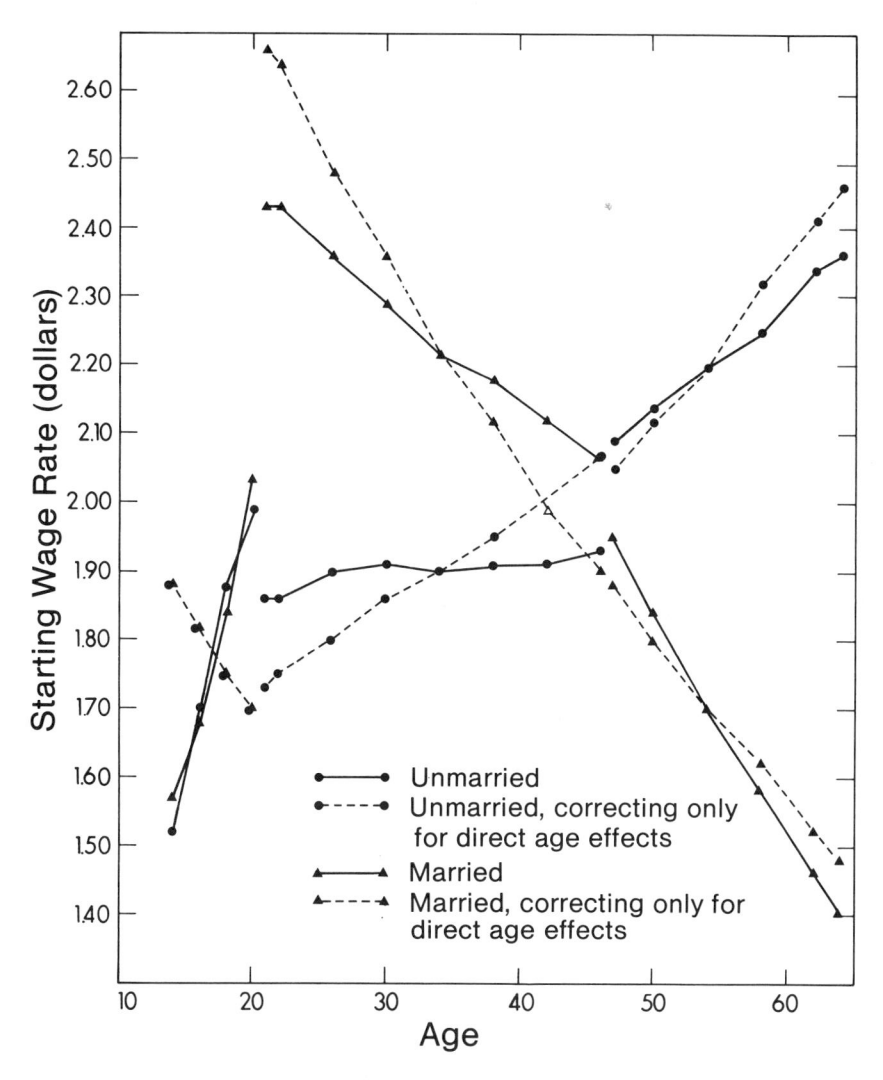

Fig. 3.3.2. Effects of age on starting wage rates.

What we see in Figure 3.3.1 for both married and unmarried women is a steep rise in the probabilities of starting work over the 14-20 age interval, followed by steady declines over the 21-46 and 47-64 age intervals. This pattern is repeated in Figure 3.3.2 for the wage rates for our hypothetical married women. For married women who did not work in the previous year, wage rates rise rapidly over the 14-20 age interval and then fall steadily over the 21-46 and 47-64

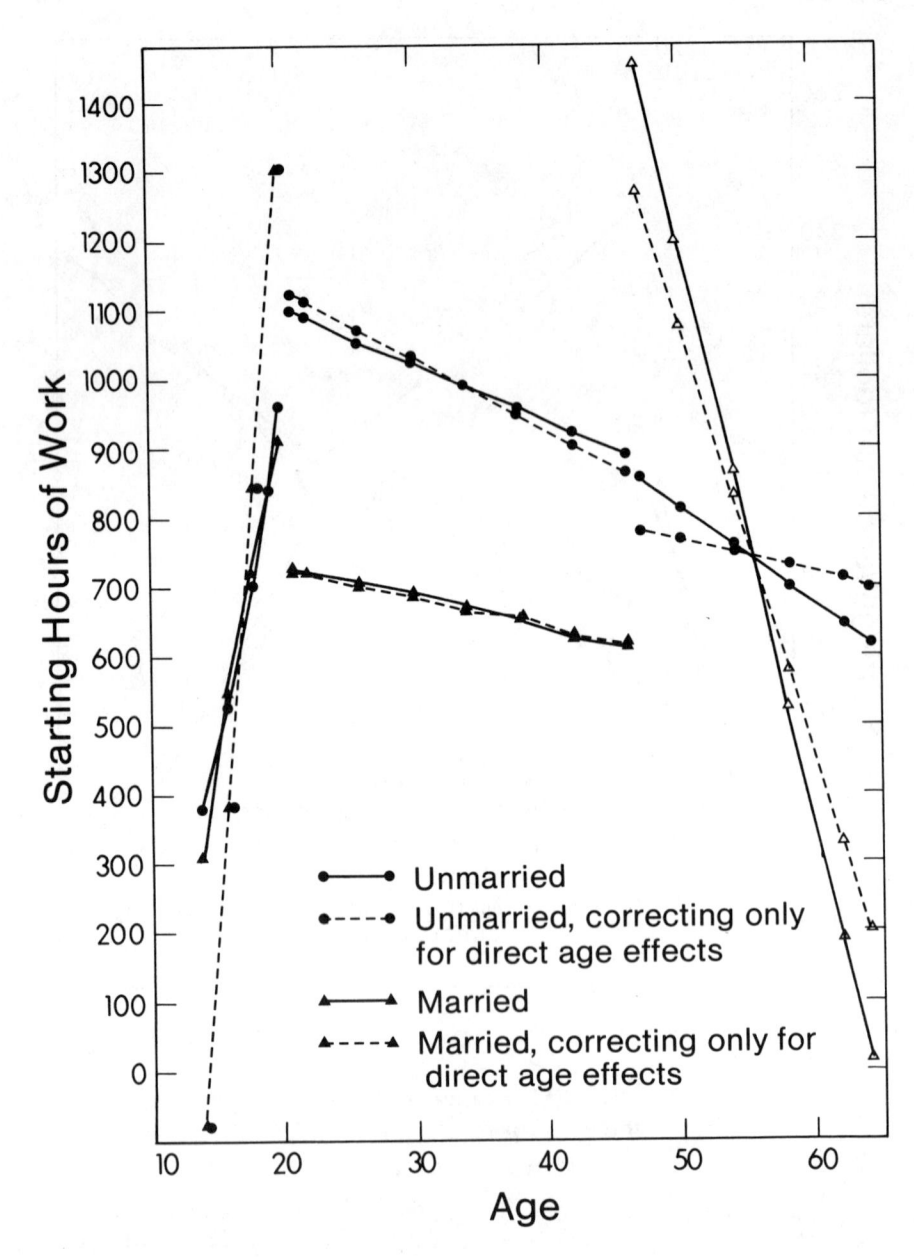

Fig. 3.3.3. Effects of age on starting hours of work.

3 Estimation Results for Our Inertia Model 111

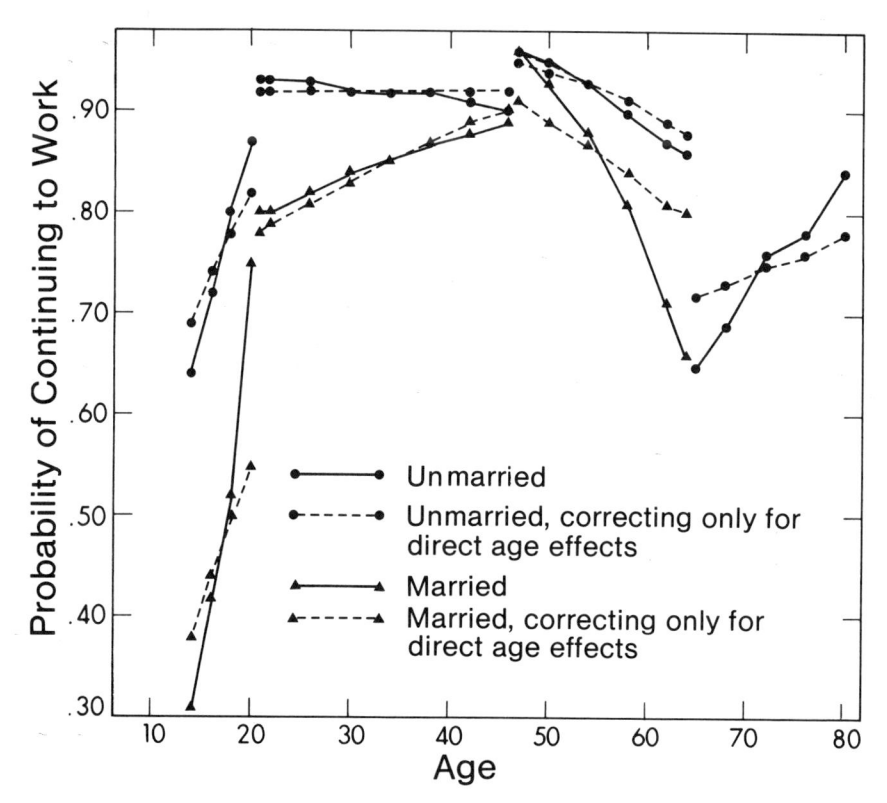

Fig. 3.3.4. Effects of age on probabilities
of continuing to work.

age intervals. Notice that the rise in starting wage rates
over the 14-20 age interval is due to the indirect impact of
age on the wage rate via the selection bias term since the
direct impact of age for this age bracket is negative. For
unmarried women, however, we see from Figure 3.3.2 that
starting wage rates are estimated to rise over all three age
intervals of 14-20, 21-46 and 47-64. After taking into account
the indirect impact of age through the selection bias term,
the rise in the middle age interval is found to be very
gentle. Also, the rise in the youngest age group is again due
to the indirect impact of age through the selection bias term
outweighing the direct negative impact of age. The picture
that emerges from Figure 3.3.3 for the starting hours of work
is again the same as in Figure 3.3.1. For both married and
unmarried women, starting hours of work rise steeply over the
14-20 age interval and then fall over the 21-46 interval.

We will now consider hypothetical women who started work
in the previous year and who have the characteristics shown in

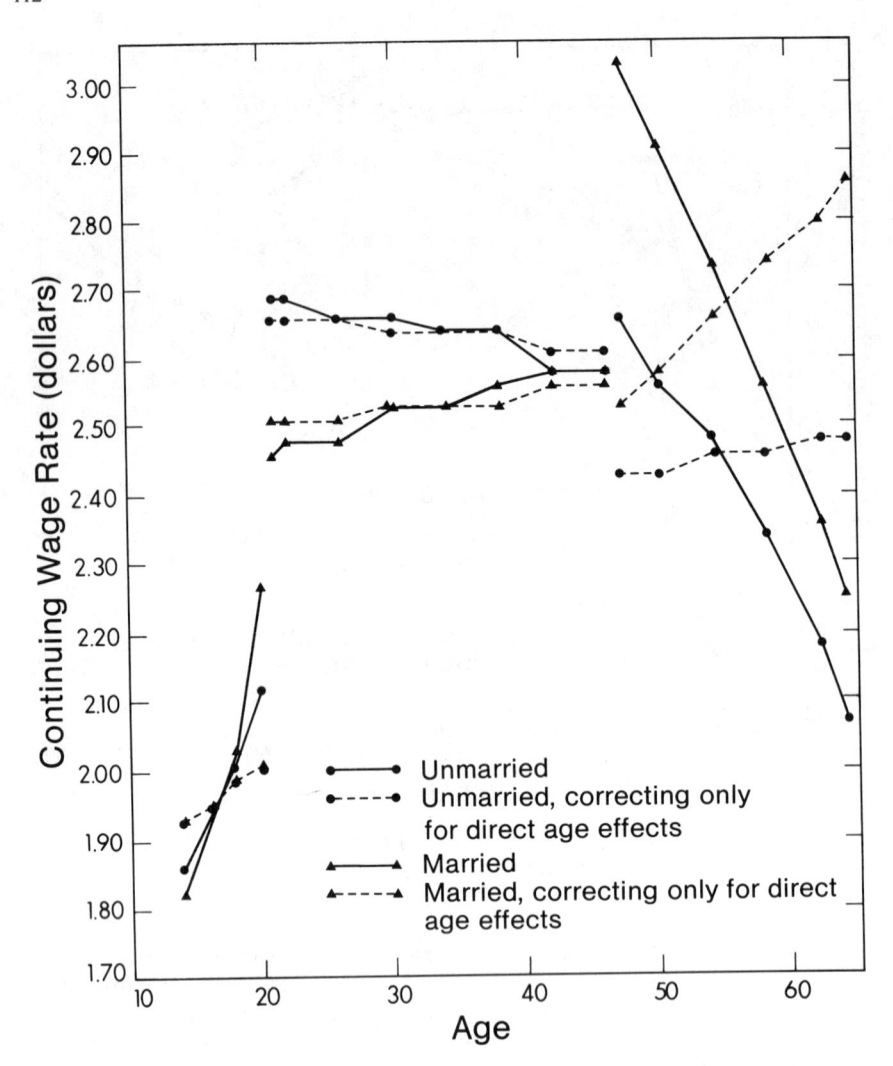

Fig. 3.3.5. Effects of age on continuing wage rates.

Table 3.3.2. We again assume that nothing about these hypothetical women changes over the relevant age brackets except age, and hence also the wage rates and hours of work at which these women are assumed to have started work in the previous year. The coefficient estimates shown in Tables 3.3.4 through 3.3.6 can thus be used to determine the probabilities of continuing to work, and the wage rates and the hours of work for women who continue to work, for our hypothetical women over the same age intervals of 14-20, 21-46 and

3   Estimation Results for Our Inertia Model   113

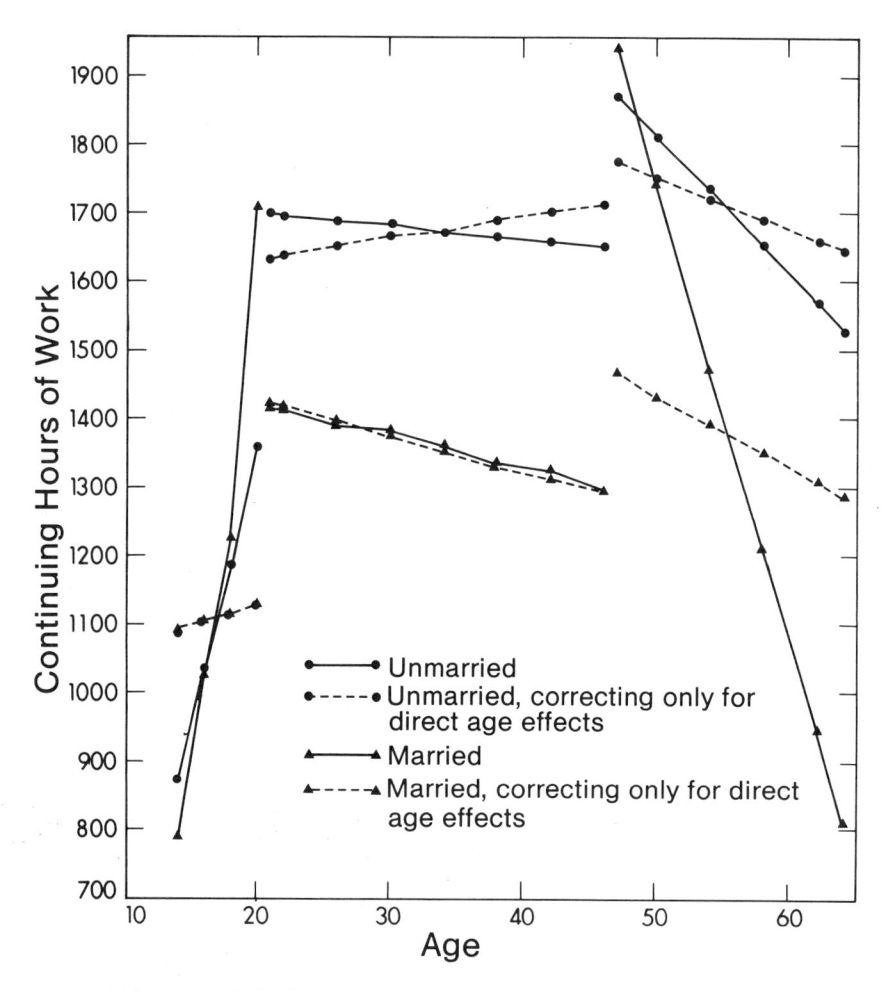

Fig. 3.3.6. Effects of age on continuing hours of work.

47-64. These results are shown graphically in Figures 3.3.4-3.3.6.

Looking at Figures 3.3.4 through 3.3.6 we find that, just as for starting work behavior, the probabilities of continuing to work and the continuing wage rates and continuing hours of work all rise steeply over the 14-20 age group for both married and unmarried women. For unmarried women over the 21-46-year-old interval the probabilities of continuing to work and continuing wage rates and hours of work all fall slightly. For married women there are slight rises in the probabilities of continuing to work and in the continuing wage rates and hours of work over this age interval. In the

47-64-year-old interval the probabilities of continuing to work and the accompanying wage and hours figures all drop steeply for both marital status groups. Notice that the declines in the wage rates for both married and unmarried women over the 47-64-year-old age group are due to the indirect impacts of age, primarily through the selection bias term, outweighing its positive direct impacts.

The following conclusions seem to emerge from these results:

1. Comparing our results for women for starting versus continuing work behavior, we find that the probabilities of starting work, the starting wage rates, the starting hours of work, and also the probabilities of continuing to work, the continuing wage rates and continuing hours of work all rise steeply over the 14-20 age interval. Over the intermediate years of 21-46, however, the probabilities of starting work, starting wage rates and starting hours all fall except for the starting wage rates for unmarried women. On the whole, there is considerably less change in the dependent variables of interest for this age group for women who worked in the previous year. Moreover, for married women the changes in the probabilities of continuing to work and in the continuing wages over the 21-46 age interval are in the positive direction. Thus, the difference between the probabilities of work for a hypothetical woman depending on whether or not she worked in the previous year tends to widen with increases in her assumed age. The difference between the estimated earnings of a woman depending on whether or not she worked last year also tends to widen with age.
2. Probabilities of work and annual hours of work are found to decline with advancing age for men 47-64 and 65 and over, as they do for women, even after controlling for disability status and retirement effects for men. This result suggests that the declines in the probability of work and annual hours of work that we observe for women over 46 are not due primarily to the fact that we are unable to control for the disability status of women in this study.
3. Wage rates rise sharply with age for men in the 14-20 age group, and continue to rise much less sharply with age for men in the 21-46 and 47-64 age groups. For women in the 21-46 and 47-64 age groups, on the other hand, wage rates rise very slightly or actually decline with age.[6] In the 65-and-over age group the direct impacts of age on wage rates are similar for

both men and for women who worked in the previous year.

3.4. Race

The signs of dummy variables set equal to 1 if a wife is black, or is nonwhite, have long been a puzzle in studies of female labor force behavior. Many would argue that there is widespread job and wage discrimination against blacks, including black women. At the same time, employers and others studying the employment problems of blacks often argue that the lower quality of formal education that blacks receive is an important cause of their employment and wage problems. According to either of these lines of argument, the coefficient of a race dummy in a standard wage or log wage equation should be found to be negative. Moreover, if race-related factors primarily affect the offered wage function, the coefficient of a race dummy in a probit index for the probability of work should also be negative and the direct impact of the race dummy in the hours equation should be insignificantly different from 0. What has been found, however, in study after study is that the coefficient of the race dummy is negative as expected in the wage or log wage equation, but it is positive and highly significant in the probit index for the probability of work. This sort of finding is typically justified by suggesting other possible omitted race-related factors that might affect the asking wage, such as the greater earnings variability of black versus nonblack husbands, the large discrepancy in the asset holdings of black versus nonblack households, and the availability of lower-cost childcare in black households due to higher unemployment rates for black men and a tendency among blacks toward an extended family system.[7] If effects of this sort on the asking wage were really strong enough, however, to outweigh the race-related impacts on the probability of work of discrimination and lower-quality education, we would expect not only to find a direct positive impact of the race dummy in the probit index for the probability of work but also in the hours of work equation.

Our estimates for the coefficients of a dummy variable set equal to 1 if a woman is black are shown in Tables 3.4.1 through 3.4.3 for women who did not work in the previous year and in Tables 3.4.4 through 3.4.6 for women who did work in the previous year. The results shown in these tables are surprising in the context of the existing literature. For both women who did and did not work in the previous year, the coefficients of the race dummy in the probit indices for the

TABLE 3.4.1
COEFFICIENT ESTIMATES FOR RACE DUMMY IN
PROBIT INDICES FOR PROBABILITY OF WORK:
WOMEN WHO DID NOT WORK IN t-1

Marital status	Age			
	14-20	21-46	47-64	65+
Married	-.399**	-.051	.014	-.440*
Unmarried		-.028	-.187	

TABLE 3.4.2
OLS COEFFICIENT ESTIMATES FOR RACE DUMMY
IN LOG WAGE EQUATIONS:
WORKING WOMEN WHO DID NOT WORK IN t-1

Marital status	Age			
	14-20	21-46	47-64	65+
Married	-.018	-.066	.053	-.084
Unmarried		-.164*	-.448*	

TABLE 3.4.3
IV COEFFICIENT ESTIMATES FOR RACE DUMMY
IN HOURS EQUATIONS:
WORKING WOMEN WHO DID NOT WORK IN t-1

Marital status	Age			
	14-20	21-46	47-64	65+
Married	-280.9*	252.8**	-117.3	228.8**
Unmarried		69.6	-378.8	

3 Estimation Results for Our Inertia Model

TABLE 3.4.4
COEFFICIENT ESTIMATES FOR RACE DUMMY IN
PROBIT INDICES FOR PROBABILITY OF WORK:
WOMEN WHO WORKED IN t-1

Marital status	Age			
	14-20	21-46	47-64	65+
Married	-.317**	-.059	.062	-.001
Unmarried		-.389**	-.200	

TABLE 3.4.5
OLS COEFFICIENT ESTIMATES FOR RACE DUMMY
IN LOG WAGE EQUATIONS:
WORKING WOMEN WHO WORKED IN t-1

Marital status	Age			
	14-20	21-46	47-64	65+
Married	-.156*	-.065**	-.071	-.044
Unmarried		-.021	-.011	

TABLE 3.4.6
IV COEFFICIENT ESTIMATES FOR RACE DUMMY
IN HOURS EQUATIONS:
WORKING WOMEN WHO WORKED IN t-1

Marital status	Age			
	14-20	21-46	47-64	65+
Married	228.3*	82.6**	59.9	-153.8
Unmarried		-25.3	2.9	

probability of work are always negative except for married women 47-64 years of age. Thus, in this study there is almost complete agreement between the negative signs of the race coefficients in the log wage equations, shown in Tables 3.4.2 and 3.4.5, and the negative signs of the race variable in the probit indices for the probability of work, shown in Tables 3.4.1 and 3.4.4. The coefficient estimates shown in Tables 3.4.3 and 3.4.6 for the race dummy in the hours equations are generally erratic in sign. We believe that the differences between these results and those reported in earlier studies are due to the fact that in this study, separate equations have been estimated for women who did not and for women who did work in the previous year. Women who worked last year are substantially more likely to work this year than are women who did not work last year, even after controlling for the education, child status and other variables typically included in studies of the work behavior of married women. In any one year, a higher proportion of black women are found to have worked in the previous year. When relationships are estimated using data for both women who did not and for women who did work in the previous year, the difference in the mean levels of the unobservable factors for women who did not versus women who did work in the previous year is captured in part by the race dummy.

From Table 3.4.8 we see that in all four age groups, black men receive lower wage rates than otherwise-similar nonblack men, just as Tables 3.4.2 and 3.4.5 show that the direct impact of being black on the hourly wage is negative for all groups of women. The negative impacts of being black on the wage rate are generally larger for men than for women who worked in the previous year, particularly for the 65-and-over age group. In fact, for men, but not for women, there is a clear tendency for these negative wage impacts of being black to become larger in magnitude as one moves from the younger to older age groups. From Table 3.4.9 we see that black men also seem to work fewer hours than otherwise similar nonblack men, although there is no age-group pattern in these hours equation coefficient estimates for men. Recall that for women, in Tables 3.4.3 and 3.4.6, we also find no regular pattern of race dummy impacts on hours of work.

The negative impacts for men of the race dummy on the wage rate suggest that being black lowers the offered wage. The negative impacts for men of the race dummy on hours of work suggest that being black raises the asking wage. A factor that lowers the offered wage and raises the asking wage should unambiguously lower the probability of work. Yet, from Table 3.4.7 we find that being black only lowers the probability of work for men 14-20 who worked in the previous year and for men 65 and over.

Suppose now that we consider hypothetical nonblack women

TABLE 3.4.7
COEFFICIENT ESTIMATES FOR RACE DUMMY IN PROBIT INDICES FOR PROBABILITY OF WORK: MEN

Work status in t-1	14-20	21-46	47-64	65+
Did not work	.053*	.022	.180	-.356*
Worked	-.018			

TABLE 3.4.8
OLS COEFFICIENT ESTIMATES FOR RACE DUMMY IN LOG WAGE EQUATIONS: WORKING MEN

Work status in t-1	14-20	21-46	47-64	65+
Did not work	-.048	-.065**	-.117**	-.359**
Worked	-.294**			

TABLE 3.4.9
IV COEFFICIENT ESTIMATES FOR RACE DUMMY IN HOURS EQUATIONS: WORKING MEN

Work status in t-1	14-20	21-46	47-64	65+
Did not work	-114.9	-77.8**	-1.8	-21.2
Worked	-22.2			

with the age and marital status attributes shown in Table 3.1.1, and the probabilities of starting work, the starting wage rates and the starting hours of work also shown in this table. Tables 3.4.10 through 3.4.12 show how the coefficient estimates shown in Tables 3.4.1 through 3.4.3 imply these probabilities of starting to work, starting wage rates and

TABLE 3.4.10
PROBABILITIES OF STARTING WORK FOR
HYPOTHETICAL NONBLACK WOMEN VERSUS
OTHERWISE-IDENTICAL BLACK WOMEN

Age	Nonblack	Black
\multicolumn{3}{c}{Unmarried women}		

Age	Nonblack	Black
17	.30	.18
33	.38	.37
55	.13	.09
70	.06	.02

Married women

Age	Nonblack	Black
17	.13	.06
33	.21	.19
55	.09	.09

TABLE 3.4.11
STARTING WAGE RATES FOR HYPOTHETICAL
NONBLACK WOMEN AND FOR
OTHERWISE-IDENTICAL BLACK WOMEN

Age	Nonblack	Black

Unmarried women

Age	Nonblack	Black
17	$1.78	$1.52 ($1.75)
33	1.89	1.60 (1.62)
55	2.25	1.43 (1.43)
70	.38	.31 (.35)

Married women

Age	Nonblack	Black
17	1.49	1.49 (1.75)
33	2.24	2.09 (2.09)
55	1.67	1.75 (1.75)

TABLE 3.4.12
STARTING HOURS OF WORK FOR
HYPOTHETICAL NONBLACK WOMEN, AND FOR
OTHERWISE-IDENTICAL BLACK WOMEN

Age	Nonblack	Black
\multicolumn{3}{c}{Unmarried women}		
17	614	620 (333)
33	993	1028 (1063)
55	737	608 (358)
70	96	296 (385)
\multicolumn{3}{c}{Married women}		
17	614	659 (333)
33	671	948 (924)
55	734	611 (617)

TABLE 3.4.13
PROBABILITIES OF CONTINUING TO WORK
FOR HYPOTHETICAL NONBLACK WOMEN VERSUS
OTHERWISE-IDENTICAL BLACK WOMEN

Age	Nonblack	Black
\multicolumn{3}{c}{Unmarried women}		
17	.76	.65 (.65)
33	.92	.85 (.85)
55	.92	.86 (.89)
70	.74	.79 (.74)
\multicolumn{3}{c}{Married women}		
17	.47	.35 (.34)
33	.85	.88 (.84)
55	.86	.86 (.87)

TABLE 3.4.14
CONTINUING WAGE RATES OF HYPOTHETICAL
NONBLACK WOMEN AND OF
OTHERWISE-IDENTICAL BLACK WOMEN

Age	Nonblack	Black
\multicolumn{3}{c}{Unmarried women}		
17	$1.98	$1.66 ($1.68)
33	2.65	2.27 (2.58)
55	2.46	1.75 (2.43)
70	2.04	1.86 (1.95)
\multicolumn{3}{c}{Married women}		
17	1.98	1.65 (1.68)
33	2.54	2.46 (2.36)
55	2.69	2.48 (2.51)

TABLE 3.4.15
CONTINUING HOURS OF WORK FOR HYPOTHETICAL
NONBLACK WOMEN AND FOR
OTHERWISE-IDENTICAL BLACK WOMEN

Age	Nonblack	Black
\multicolumn{3}{c}{Unmarried women}		
17	1112	1059 (1340)
33	1676	1594 (1651)
55	1711	1605 (1714)
70	1070	1010 (916)
\multicolumn{3}{c}{Married women}		
17	1112	1034 (1340)
33	1359	1564 (1442)
55	1378	1354 (1438)

3 Estimation Results for Our Inertia Model

hours of work would differ if these hypothetical women were black. Tables 3.4.13 through 3.4.15 show how our coefficient estimates given in Tables 3.4.4 through 3.4.6 imply the probabilities of continuing to work and the continuing wage rates and hours of work for hypothetical nonblack women with the characteristics shown in Table 3.1.2 would change if these hypothetical women were black. The figures shown in parentheses in Tables 3.4.11 through 3.4.15 ignore all indirect impacts of the race dummy.

We find from Table 3.4.10 that being black lowers the probability of a woman starting work by 0 to 12 percentage points. Notice that for the one group, wives 47-64, where the coefficient of the race dummy in the probit index for the probability of starting work is positive, this positive impact is not enough to increase the probability of work by even 1 percentage point for our hypothetical woman in this demographic group. From Table 3.4.11 we see that being black lowers the offered wage by 7 to 36 percent, except for our hypothetical 55-year-old wife, whose wage would be estimated to be 5 percent higher if she were black. The picture that emerges from Table 3.4.12 for the impact of being black on hours of work is erratic both in terms of sign and magnitude.

From Table 3.4.13 we see that, at least for unmarried women, being black seems to lower the probability of continuing to work, too. The hypothetical woman for whom we find no change is the same 55-year-old wife for whom we found that being black did not change the probability of starting work either. The impacts of being black on the probability of continuing to work are positive for our hypothetical 70-year-old unmarried woman and our 33-year-old married woman because the large indirect positive impacts of being black via the starting hours of work outweigh the direct negative impacts of the race variable for these groups. From Table 3.4.14 we see that the continuing wage rates would be 3 to 29 percent lower if our hypothetical women were black. As with the starting wage, the largest negative effect on the continuing wage in percentage terms is for our hypothetical 55-year-old unmarried woman. From Table 3.4.15 we find that with one exception, the continuing hours of work for our hypothetical women would be 2 to 7 percent lower if they were black.

Our findings with respect to the impacts of our race dummy may be summarized as follows:

1. After controlling for other factors, including work status in the previous year, being black is associated with lower probabilities of starting to work for all categories of women except for wives 47-64, for whom there seems to be virtually no residual race differential. Being black is also

associated with lower probabilities of continuing to work for unmarried women younger than 65. For married women who worked in the previous year the picture is unclear. There is certainly no consistent evidence, however, of a positive race effect for these women.
2. The balance of the evidence indicates that after controlling for other factors, including work status in the previous time period, the wage rates for black women are 3 to 36 percent lower than for their nonblack counterparts. These results, and our results for the impact of being black on the probabilities of starting and continuing to work, are generally consistent with the hypothesis that discrimination and poorer-quality school training lead to lower wage distributions for black compared with otherwise-similar nonblack women and that this in turn leads to lower probabilities of starting and continuing to work for black women after controlling for other factors.
3. Being black is found also to have substantial negative impacts on the wage rates of men in all age groups, and black men are found to work somewhat fewer hours than otherwise-similar nonblack men. However, we find no consistent tendency for black men to be less likely to work than nonblack men after controlling for work behavior in the previous year. This result may be due to the fact that we did not estimate separate sets of equations for men who did and did not work in the previous year except for men 14-20.

3.5. Education

Years of formal education is the most important variable in the wage equations of most models of the labor force behavior of women. It is usually argued that the more education an individual has, the larger the individual's stock of human capital is and hence, the higher the individual's offered wage will be. Factors that raise the offered wage should also increase the probability that a woman will work. The empirical results published in earlier studies are consistent with these behavioral hypotheses.[8] Questions can still be raised, however, about the true role of education in models of female labor force behavior.[9]

Perhaps underlying tastes largely determine a woman's educational attainment, leading to a spurious relationship between education and labor force behavior that might

3 Estimation Results for Our Inertia Model

TABLE 3.5.1
COEFFICIENT ESTIMATES FOR EDUCATION VARIABLE IN
PROBIT INDICES FOR PROBABILITY OF WORK:
WOMEN WHO DID NOT WORK IN t-1

Marital status	Age			
	14-20	21-46	47-64	65+
Married	.002	.114**	.038	.027
Unmarried		.084**	.078**	

TABLE 3.5.2
OLS COEFFICIENT ESTIMATES FOR EDUCATION VARIABLE
IN LOG WAGE EQUATIONS:
WORKING WOMEN WHO DID NOT WORK IN t-1

Marital status	Age			
	14-20	21-46	47-64	65+
Married	.038*	.141**	.102*	-.024
Unmarried		.078**	.122**	

disappear if we were to control for these tastes by controlling for observed work behavior in the previous year. If tastes for work are acquired through the educational process, this could also result in the same sort of spurious relationship between education and work behavior. If there is an impact of human capital accumulation, as we and most others believe, on the employment and earnings of individuals, is this a "one time" effect that would be fully reflected in last year's employment and earnings behavior, or perhaps the relationships between this year's and the previous year's employment and earnings differ depending on how much education an individual has. Perhaps wages increase more rapidly over time for those with more education.

From Tables 3.5.1 and 3.5.2, we see that the estimated coefficients of the education variable are always positive in both the probit indices for the probability of work and the log wage equations for women who did not work in the previous year, except for women at least 65 years of age in the log

TABLE 3.5.3
COEFFICIENT ESTIMATES FOR EDUCATION VARIABLE IN PROBIT INDICES FOR PROBABILITY OF WORK: WOMEN WHO WORKED IN t-1

Marital status	Age 14-20	21-46	47-64	65+
Married	-.080**	.036*	.044	.050
Unmarried		.072**	.060**	

TABLE 3.5.4
OLS COEFFICIENT ESTIMATES FOR EDUCATION VARIABLE IN LOG WAGE EQUATIONS: WORKING WOMEN WHO WORKED IN t-1

Marital status	Age 14-20	21-46	47-64	65+
Married	.035*	.086**	.072**	.020
Unmarried		.035**	.024**	

TABLE 3.5.5
COEFFICIENT ESTIMATES FOR EDUCATION VARIABLE IN PROBIT INDICES FOR PROBABILITY OF WORK: MEN

Work status in t-1	Age 14-20	21-46	47-64	65+
Did not work	.030	.036*	-.020	-.002
Worked	.009			

wage equation. From Tables 3.5.3 and 3.5.4, we see that the same is true for women who did work in the previous year, except for women 14-20 in the probit index. Thus, after controlling for work behavior in the previous year, we still

TABLE 3.5.6
OLS COEFFICIENT ESTIMATES FOR EDUCATION VARIABLE IN LOG WAGE EQUATIONS: WORKING MEN

Work status in t-1	14-20	21-46	47-64	65+
		Age		
Did not work	.027	.029**	.038**	.056**
Worked	.022*			

TABLE 3.5.7
PROBABILITIES OF STARTING WORK FOR HYPOTHETICAL WOMEN WITH 12 YEARS OF EDUCATION, AND FOR OTHERWISE-IDENTICAL WOMEN WITH 10 AND WITH 14 YEARS OF EDUCATION

Age	10	12	14
	Years of education		
	Unmarried women		
17	.30	.30	.30
33	.31	.38	.44
55	.10	.13	.17
70	.05	.06	.06
	Married women		
17	.13	.13	.13
33	.15	.21	.28
55	.08	.09	.10

find that the impacts of education are generally positive on both the probability of work and the wage rate.

It is often argued that in the job market, men benefit more than women from having additional years of education.[10] We should look, therefore, at the impacts of education on the probabilities of work and the offered wage rates for men. The coefficient estimates for our education variable in probit

TABLE 3.5.8
STARTING WAGE RATES FOR HYPOTHETICAL
WOMEN WITH 12 YEARS OF EDUCATION, AND FOR
OTHERWISE-IDENTICAL WOMEN WITH 10
AND WITH 14 YEARS OF EDUCATION

	Years of education		
Age	10	12	14

Unmarried women

Age	10		12	14	
17	$1.65	($1.65)	$1.78	$1.93	($1.93)
33	1.55	(1.62)	1.89	2.32	(2.22)
55	1.75	(1.77)	2.25	2.89	(2.86)
70	.40	(.39)	.38	.36	(.36)

Married women

Age	10		12	14	
17	1.65	(1.65)	1.78	1.93	(1.93)
33	1.86	(1.70)	2.24	2.72	(2.97)
55	1.35	(1.36)	1.67	2.05	(2.03)

indices for the probability of work and in log wage equations for men are shown in Tables 3.5.5 and 3.5.6. Looking first at Table 3.5.6, and comparing these results with the results for women shown in Tables 3.5.2 and 3.5.4, we see that the direct impacts of education on the wage rate are systematically positive for men, as they are for women. Except for the 65-and-over category, however, the magnitudes of the impacts for men are generally smaller than they are for women in the corresponding age categories who worked in the previous year. The impacts for women continuing to work are in turn systematically smaller than the impacts shown in Table 3.5.2 for women who did not work in the previous year. On the other hand, it can be seen from Tables 3.5.2 and 3.5.4 that for women the positive impacts of education seem, on the whole, to become smaller the older the age group; while the positive impacts for men shown in Table 3.5.6 become steadily larger as we go from younger to older age groups. The results for women are generally consistent with the hypothesis that the value of their formal education is depreciating with age. The results for men are consistent with the hypothesis that the value of their formal education is enhanced over time by on-the-job

TABLE 3.5.9
STARTING HOURS OF WORK FOR HYPOTHETICAL
WOMEN WITH 12 YEARS OF EDUCATION, AND FOR
OTHERWISE-IDENTICAL WOMEN WITH 10
AND WITH 14 YEARS OF EDUCATION

	Years of education		
Age	10	12	14
Unmarried women			
17	599	614	629
33	962	993	1023
55	863	737	614
70	100	96	90
Married women			
17	599	614	629
33	713	671	631
55	721	734	742

training and experience, with those men with more formal training receiving more or higher quality on-the-job training and experience (see, for instance, Lazear, 1976). We would also observe results of this sort, however, if education and sex were used as screening critera by employers in allocating opportunities for training and career advancement.

If education raises the offered wage distribution for men but does not alter the asking wage distribution, we would expect to find that education also raises the probability of work for men, as it does for women. In Table 3.5.5, however, we find no indication of a positive impact of education on the probability of work for men except for men 21-46 years of age. Perhaps this is because there are proxy effects of education on the asking wage that outweigh its positive impacts on the offered wage.

We will now consider hypothetical women who each have 12 years of formal education and the age and marital status attributes, the probabilities of the starting to work, the starting wage rates and the starting hours of work shown in Table 3.1.1. Tables 3.5.7 through 3.5.9 show how the coefficient estimates given in Tables 3.5.1 and 3.5.2 imply

TABLE 3.5.10
PROBABILITIES OF CONTINUING TO WORK FOR
HYPOTHETICAL WOMEN WITH 12 YEARS OF EDUCATION,
AND FOR OTHERWISE-IDENTICAL WOMEN WITH
10 AND WITH 14 YEARS OF EDUCATION

	Years of education		
Age	10	12	14
	Unmarried women		
17	.80 (.81)	.76	.71 (.71)
33	.89 (.90)	.92	.94 (.94)
55	.92 (.90)	.92	.92 (.94)
70	.71 (.71)	.74	.77 (.77)
	Married women		
17	.52 (.53)	.47	.41 (.40)
33	.84 (.83)	.85	.86 (.87)
55	.83 (.84)	.86	.88 (.88)

that these probabilities of starting to work and these starting wage rates and hours of work would differ if these hypothetical women had either 10 or 14 instead of 12 years of education. We also consider hypothetical women who each have 12 years of education and the age and marital status attributes, the probabilities of continuing to work, the continuing wage rates and the continuing hours of work shown in Table 3.1.2; and who started work in the previous year with the probabilities, wage rates and hours shown in Table 3.1.1. Tables 3.5.10 through 3.5.12 show how our coefficient estimates imply that the probabilities of continuing to work and the continuing wage rates and hours of work would differ if these hypothetical women had 10 or 14 instead of 12 years of education. The numbers in parentheses in Tables 3.5.8, 3.5.10, and 3.5.11 ignore all indirect effects of education.

If we compare the values for 10 versus 14 years of education, we find that the additional four years of education have no impact on the probabilities of starting to work for our hypothetical women in the 14-20 age bracket. For the older hypothetical women the additional four years of education increase the probabilities of starting to work by 1 to 13

3 Estimation Results for Our Inertia Model

TABLE 3.5.11
CONTINUING WAGE RATES FOR HYPOTHETICAL WOMEN WITH 12 YEARS OF EDUCATION, AND FOR OTHERWISE-IDENTICAL WOMEN IN 10 AND WITH 14 YEARS OF EDUCATION

	Years of education		
Age	10	12	14

Unmarried women

Age	10		12	14	
17	$1.84	($1.84)	$1.98	$2.12	($2.12)
33	2.22	(2.46)	2.65	3.13	(2.83)
55	2.09	(2.34)	2.46	2.94	(2.58)
70	2.01	(1.95)	2.04	2.05	(2.12)

Married women

Age	10		12	14	
17	1.84	(1.84)	1.98	2.12	(2.12)
33	2.07	(2.14)	2.54	3.13	(3.00)
55	2.20	(2.34)	2.69	3.29	(3.09)

percentage points, with the percentage point magnitudes of the increases declining with age for both the unmarried and married women. Looking at Table 3.5.8, we find that four additional years of education also increase the starting wage rates for all except the hypothetical women in the over 64-years-of-age category. These increases are quite substantial, ranging from 17 to 65 percent with the percentage magnitudes of the increases rising rather than declining with age for both the unmarried and married women. Thus, even though the magnitudes of the coefficients of the education variable in the wage equations seem to decline with increasing age for women, the <u>total</u> impacts of education increase with age for women as for men. The impacts of four additional years of education on the starting hours can be seen, from Table 3.5.9, to range from -29 to 6 percent.

From Table 3.5.10 we see that, as with the probabilities of starting work, an additional four years of education in general increases the probabilities that a woman will continue to work. In the case of the probabilities of continuing to work, however, there is no age pattern in the magnitudes of the percentage point increases. From Table 3.5.11 we see that,

TABLE 3.5.12
CONTINUING HOURS OF WORK FOR HYPOTHETICAL
WOMEN WITH 12 YEARS OF EDUCATION, AND FOR
OTHERWISE-IDENTICAL WOMEN WITH 10 AND
WITH 14 YEARS OF EDUCATION

	Years of education		
Age	10	12	14

Unmarried women

17	1044	1112	1162
33	1636	1676	1718
55	1766	1711	1660
70	1033	1070	1106

Married women

17	1066	1112	1162
33	1359	1359	1369
55	1359	1378	1393

ignoring the hypothetical woman in the oldest age group, the continuing wage rates increase with four more years of education by 15 to 63 percent. As in the case of the starting wage rates, the magnitudes of the education-related percentage increases in the continuing wage rates increase with age. From Table 3.5.12 we find that with the exception of the hypothetical unmarried 55-year-old woman, the continuing hours of work rise by 1 to 11 percent with an additional four years of education.

The following conclusions can be drawn from these results:

1. The positive impacts of increased education on the probabilities of work and the observed wage rates for women do not disappear if we control for unobserved tastes for home-oriented versus market-oriented activities by controlling for work behavior in the previous year. Moreover, the positive impacts observed are consistent with the hypothesis that years of education is a meaningful measure of one dimension of human capital and that for individual

3 Estimation Results for Our Inertia Model

women, the stock of human capital affects the wage distribution.

2. The fact that for women the positive impacts of additional education on the starting and continuing wage rates seem to be much stronger and display a different age pattern than the positive impacts on the probabilities of starting and of continuing to work, suggests that education may also affect the work behavior of women by affecting their asking wage rates. In this case, we are ignoring the direct effects of education on the hours of work by not including education as a separate explanatory variable in our equations for starting and continuing hours of work. Mark Killingsworth (1983, p.200) suggests this may affect our estimates of the coefficient of the wage variable in our hours equations. Including education in the hours equations, however, results in substantial problems of multicollinearity between education and the instrumental wage variable. If education has important effects on the asking wage rate, in addition to the effects of education on the offered wage, it may be impossible to get reliable estimates of the response of hours of work to a change in the offered wage using conventional procedures for estimating hours of work equations.

3. Further evidence that education has impacts on the asking wage rate, in addition to its impacts on the offered wage, comes from our estimation results for men. For men we find that the impacts of education on the offered wage are consistently positive, but we find no consistent evidence of positive impacts of education on the probability of work for men. As for women, these results suggest that we are ignoring negative direct impacts of education on the hours of work by not including education as an explanatory variable in our hours of work equations for men. The econometric problems involved in including an education variable directly in the hours equations are the same for men as those outlined above for women.

3.6. Special Circumstances Affecting Young Women

Even after controlling for all other factors for which we have data, we find that women in the 21-46 age group are more likely to work in the current year, the more they worked in

TABLE 3.6.1
PROBABILITY OF STARTING WORK FOR WOMEN
14-20 WHO DID NOT WORK IN t-1 DEPENDING
ON WHETHER THEY LIVE WITH PARENTS
AND THEIR STUDENT STATUS IN t-1

Living with parents	Student in t-1 No	Student in t-1 Yes
	Unmarried women	
No	.30	.57
Yes	.19	.38
	Married women	
No	.13	.28
Yes	.07	.18

the previous year. Thus, to understand and predict the work behavior of women in the 21-46 age group, we must also consider the work behavior of young women 14-20 years of age.[11] In addition to the factors included in our equations for older women, certain special circumstances would be expected to have important impacts on the labor force behavior of this youngest group of women. Prominent among these special circumstances are the student status of a young woman and the issue of whether or not she is still living in her parents' home.

The usual one-period theoretical models of the labor force behavior of women, built on a dichotomous choice between market and nonmarket uses of time (work versus "leisure"), cannot easily accommodate the intertemporal trade-offs that accompany nonmarket uses of time for activities like education that may alter the future offered wage distributions of an individual.[12] These models cannot take direct account of the costs and benefits, for instance, of borrowing or foregoing earned income to go to school in the hopes that this schooling will lead to higher earnings in the future.

We have found that women with more education have higher starting and continuing wage rates than those with less

3 Estimation Results for Our Inertia Model

TABLE 3.6.2
STARTING WAGE RATES OF HYPOTHETICAL 17-YEAR-OLD WOMEN DEPENDING ON WHETHER THEY LIVE WITH PARENTS AND THEIR STUDENT STATUS IN t-1

Living with parents	Student in t-1 No	Student in t-1 Yes
Unmarried women		
No	$1.78	$2.09
Yes	1.58	1.91
Married women		
No	1.78	2.18
Yes	1.57	1.93

education. Thus, decisions that young women make about whether or not to stay in school do affect the future offered wage distributions they will face. Casual observation also suggests that because being a student is so time consuming, being a student must inhibit the labor market activities of a young woman.[13]

Since young women who are attending school are more likely than otherwise to be living with their parents, if we do not also control for whether or not a young woman is living with her parents, our variable for student status might become a proxy for living in the parental home. Young women, whether unmarried or married, who are still living in the parental home may enjoy income-in-kind and direct financial support from their parents in excess of the financial assistance normally received by young women who are no longer living with their parents.[14]

In this study, in the probit indices for the probabilities of starting and of continuing to work and in the starting and continuing equations for hours of work for women 14-20, we have included a dummy set equal to 1 if a young woman was a student in the previous year and another dummy set equal to 1 if she is living with her parents. The estimated coefficients of the dummy for student status in the probit

TABLE 3.6.3
STARTING HOURS OF WORK OF HYPOTHETICAL
17-YEAR-OLD WOMEN DEPENDING ON WHETHER THEY
LIVE WITH PARENTS AND THEIR STUDENT STATUS IN t-1

Living at home	Student in t-1 No	Student in t-1 Yes
Unmarried women		
No	614	744 (1085)
Yes	558 (316)	641 (787)
Married women		
No	614	678 (1085)
Yes	588 (316)	622 (787)

indices are .549 for women who did not work in the previous year and .217 for women who did work in the previous year. The coefficient estimates for this dummy in the hours equations are 470.7 for women who did not work in the previous year and 34.7 for women who did work in the previous year. Thus, the direct impact of a young woman having been a student in the previous year is that she is more, not less, likely to start work if she did not work in the previous year or to continue working if she was already working in the previous year and that in either case she will tend to work more, not fewer, hours if she was a student in the previous year.

The estimated coefficients of the dummy for living with parents in the probit indices are -.334 for women who did not work in the previous year and .001 for women who did work in the previous year. The associated coefficient estimates in the hours equations are -298.0 and -140.3 for women who did not and for women who did work in the previous year, respectively. We find, as was expected, that the direct impact of living at home is that a young woman is less likely than otherwise to start work if she did not work in the previous year; and that, whether or not she worked in the previous year, she will tend to work fewer hours than would otherwise be the case. This may, of course, be because young women with little or no

TABLE 3.6.4
PROBABILITY OF CONTINUING TO WORK FOR WOMEN
14-20 WHO WORKED IN t-1 DEPENDING ON
WHETHER THEY LIVE WITH PARENTS
AND THEIR STUDENT STATUS IN t-1

Living with parents	Student in t-1 No	Student in t-1 Yes
Unmarried women		
No	.76	.84 (.82)
Yes	.75 (.76)	.83 (.82)
Married women		
No	.47	.57 (.55)
Yes	.46 (.47)	.55 (.55)

earned income cannot afford to leave home.

Consider hypothetical unmarried and married 17-year-old women who have the probabilities of starting work and the starting wage rates and hours of work shown in Table 3.1.1 and who were not students in the previous year and are not living with their parents. Tables 3.6.1 through 3.6.3 show how our coefficient estimates imply their starting work behavior would differ if these hypothetical women had been students in the previous year, or were living with their parents, or both. The numbers in parentheses in Table 3.6.3 ignore indirect effects.

From Table 3.6.1 we find that the positive impacts of having been a student in the previous year on the probabilities of our hypothetical young women starting work are substantial in magnitude, ranging from 11 to 21 percentage points. The negative impacts of living with parents range in magnitude from 6 to 13 percentage points. We had expected to find the lowest probabilities of starting work for young women who were in school in the previous year and who are living with parents. What we have found, instead, is that the probabilities of starting work are higher if our hypothetical young women were in school in the previous year, whether or not they are living with parents. The highest probabilities of

TABLE 3.6.5
CONTINUING WAGE RATES OF HYPOTHETICAL 17-YEAR-OLD WOMEN DEPENDING ON WHETHER THEY LIVE WITH PARENTS AND THEIR STUDENT STATUS IN t-1

Living with parents	Student in t-1 No	Student in t-1 Yes
Unmarried women		
No	$1.98	$2.03
Yes	1.95	1.99
Married women		
No	1.98	2.03
Yes	1.95	1.99

of starting work for our hypothetical unmarried and married young women come with having been a student in the previous year and not living at home.

From Table 3.6.2 we see that, due to indirect impacts through the selection bias term, starting wage rates are 17 to 23 percent higher for our hypothetical young women who were in school in the previous year compared with what their wage rates would have been otherwise. Also, living with parents lowers the starting wage rates of our hypothetical young women by 9 to 13 percent. The starting wage rates are higher for both our unmarried and married 17-year-olds if they were in school in the previous year, whether or not they are living at home. The highest wage rates are associated with having been a student in the previous year and with not living at home.

We see from Table 3.6.3 that the starting hours of work are 6 to 21 percent higher if our hypothetical 17-year-olds were students in the previous year, and 10 to 16 percent lower if they live at home. Again the hours of work are uniformly higher if a hypothetical woman was a student in the previous year, regardless of whether or not she is living at home. Also, the highest values for the starting hours of work are associated with having been a student in the previous year and with not living at home.

TABLE 3.6.6
CONTINUING HOURS OF WORK OF HYPOTHETICAL
17-YEAR-OLD WOMEN DEPENDING ON WHETHER THEY LIVE
WITH PARENTS AND THEIR STUDENT STATUS IN t-1

Living with parents	Student in t-1 No	Student in t-1 Yes
Unmarried women		
No	1112	1317 (1198)
Yes	936 (964)	1091 (1050)
Married women		
No	1112	1327 (1198)
Yes	940 (964)	1127 (1050)

Now consider hypothetical unmarried and married 17-year-old women who have the probabilities of continuing to work and the continuing wage rates and hours of work shown in Table 3.1.2, who started work in the previous year with the probabilities, wage rates and hours of work shown in Table 3.1.1, and who were not students in the previous year and are not living at home. Tables 3.6.4 through 3.6.6 show how our coefficient estimates imply that the continuing work behavior of these young women would differ if they had been students in the previous year or were currently living at home. The patterns observed in Tables 3.6.4 through 3.6.6 for continuing work behavior are identical in terms of the signs and relative magnitudes of the effects of student status and living at home to those already described for starting work behavior in discussing Tables 3.6.1 through 3.6.3.

It is interesting to compare our coefficient estimates for women aged 14-20 for our dummy variables for having been a student in the previous year and for living with parents with our coefficient estimates for these dummy variables for men 14-20 years of age. Our estimates for women and for men 14-20 for our dummy variables in our probit indices for the

TABLE 3.6.7
COEFFICIENT ESTIMATES IN PROBIT INDICES FOR PROBABILITY OF WORK, AND OLS COEFFICIENT ESTIMATES IN LOG WAGE EQUATIONS, FOR DUMMY VARIABLE FOR HAVING BEEN A STUDENT IN t-1 AND FOR DUMMY VARIABLE FOR LIVING WITH PARENTS

	Women 14-20		Men 14-20	
Dummy variable	Worked in t-1	Did not work in t-1	Worked in t-1	Did not work in t-1
Probit indices for probability of work				
Dummy for student in t-1	.217	.549**	.813**	.656**
Dummy for living with parents	.001	-.334*	-.862**	.088
Hours equations				
Dummy for student in t-1	34.7	470.7**	26.9	182.8
Dummy for living with parents	-140.3*	-298.0*	-70.1	56.4

probability of work and in our hours equations are shown in Table 3.6.7. We see from this table that the coefficient estimates for men 14-20 display the same sign pattern as for women with the exception that we find no negative impact of living at home on labor supply for young men who did not work in the previous year.

The conclusions that we draw from these results are as follows:

1. The longer a woman stays in school during her teenage years, the more likely it is she will enter her early twenties with recent labor market experience, and the more substantial this experience is likely to have been in terms of both accumulated hours of work and

the wages received for this work. This is because for women 14-20 the current probabilities of either starting or continuing to work, and the expected starting or continuing wage rates and the starting or continuing hours of work if she works, are all higher if the woman was in school in the previous year.
2. Living at home depresses the probability that a woman 14-20 years of age will start or continue to work, and it depresses her expected hours of work and wage rate if she does work.
3. Just as for young women, the longer a young man remains in school during his teenage years, the more likely it is that he will enter his early twenties with recent labor market experience and the more substantial this experience is likely to have been in terms of hours of work. This is because, as for young women, the direct impacts for men 14-20 of having been a student in the previous year on the probabilities of starting or continuing to work, and on the starting or continuing hours of work for those who work, are all positive.
4. Living at home depresses the probability of continuing to work and the continuing hours of work for men 14-20, which is also the case for women 14-20 who worked in the previous year if we take into account indirect as well as direct impacts. However, in contrast to our results for young women, living at home does not seem to depress the probability of work or the hours of work for men 14-20 years of age who did not work in the previous year.
5. The magnitudes of the impacts of student status in the previous year and living with parents on the current work behavior of both women and men 14-20 years of age are large enough that we must consider developing theoretical models that can properly incorporate these variables.

3.7. Child Status Variables

Interest in forecasting female labor supply, econometric concerns and current policy issues all point to a need for gaining a better understanding of how child status affects the labor force behavior of women. Casual observation confirms that there are large differences in labor force behavior between women with small children or large numbers of children at home and those with no children or with grown children. But

TABLE 3.7.1
COEFFICIENT ESTIMATES FOR CHILD
STATUS VARIABLES IN PROBIT INDICES
FOR PROBABILITY OF WORK:
WOMEN WHO DID NOT WORK IN t-1

Group	Baby dummy	Young child dummy	Number of children younger than 18
Women 14-20	-.196	.180*	
Wives 21-46	-.188	-.458**	.072
Unmarried women 21-46	.255	.022	-.066**
Wives 47-64			.010
Unmarried women 47-64			.136**
Women 65+			.210*

are the differences in labor force behavior that we observe among women in different child status groups due to contemporaneous responses to current child status or are they largely the reflection of long-standing tastes for home-oriented versus market-oriented activities? For instance, if a home-oriented woman begins her married life as a full-time homemaker and then fails, for some reason, to have the children she desires, is it more likely than otherwise that she will ultimately start to work outside the home? Or, if a market-oriented woman has a baby, which may or may not have been planned, how likely is she to quit work?

There are also many policy questions where the debate really centers on how child status affects female labor force behavior. Many women in impoverished families who have children at home do not work in the market place and also receive some sort of government support or welfare. Is it really the problems of caring for children that cause these women not to work? Given their past work histories, if their childcare responsibilities were suddenly lifted from them, making their situations more like those of childless women, how much more likely would these women be to start work? If

3 Estimation Results for Our Inertia Model

TABLE 3.7.2
IV COEFFICIENT ESTIMATES FOR CHILD STATUS
VARIABLES IN HOURS EQUATIONS:
WORKING WOMEN WHO DID NOT WORK IN t-1

Group	Baby dummy	Young child dummy	Number of children younger than 18
Women 14-20	-290.7*	46.4	
Wives 21-46	-135.2	70.2	-26.7
Unmarried women 21-46	69.6	-193.8**	6.7
Wives 47-64			-59.9
Unmarried women 47-64			-101.8
Women 65+			8.6

they did start work, how much would they be likely to work and earn? The validity of many of the cost-benefit-type arguments put forth for publicly-funded day care hinge on the answers to questions of this sort.

A first stumbling block on the path toward understanding how child status affects female labor force behavior is the problem of quantifying child status. There are many dimensions to child status including the ages, number, timing and spacing of children. The child status variables appearing in published studies of female labor force behavior usually deal with only one or two of these dimensions of child status.[15]

In addition to the fact that most of the commonly used child status variables deal with only limited aspects of a woman's child status, there are also end-point and linearity problems with some of these variables. Suppose that the only child status variable used in a study is a dummy set equal to 1 if a woman has a child younger than 6, and set equal to 0 otherwise. This means, for instance, that a woman with no children and an otherwise-similar woman with three children aged 6 to 13 will have the same expected profiles of labor force behavior. In the case of a variable for the age of the youngest child living at home, care must be taken to define

TABLE 3.7.3
PROBABILITIES OF STARTING WORK FOR HYPOTHETICAL
WOMEN WITH NO CHILDREN YOUNGER THAN 18
AT HOME, AND FOR OTHERWISE-IDENTICAL
WOMEN WITH CHILDREN AT HOME

Age	No children	New baby	Child less than 6 but no new baby	Child less than 18 but older than 5
Unmarried women				
17	.30	.23	.36	
33	.38	.45	.36	.35
55	.13			.16
70	.06			.09
Married women				
17	.13	.09	.17	
33	.21	.18	.11	.23
55	.09			.09
70	.00			.00

the variable as the age of the youngest child plus 1. Otherwise, childless women and otherwise-similar women with a baby under a year of age will have the same expected labor force behavior profiles. Even so, if the true labor supply response to this variable is negative and declining in magnitude as the age of the youngest child increases, there will be a serious discontinuity problem between the values of 0 and 1. This problem might be overcome by the addition of a dummy variable set equal to 1 if a woman has no children at home. For continuous variables, such as the number of children ever born, the number living at home, or the numbers in specified age groups, the implicit assumption is that 2 children will have twice the impact of 1, and so forth. Many would argue that in reality, the impact on labor force behavior of an additional child declines with each increase in the birth parity.

Attempts to define child status variables that more fully reflect the complexity of child status have not met with consistent success. Attempts to reflect the spacing as well as the ages and number of children in full detail, for instance,

3 Estimation Results for Our Inertia Model

typically result in the introduction of a large number of child status variables, the coefficients of which turn out to be erratic in sign and magnitude and statistically insignificant (see, for instance, Gramm, 1975).

Despite its complexity, however, many aspects of child status change over time in a manner that is both gradual and largely predictable. For instance, the age of each existing child increases by one each year, and the number and spacing of existing children remain fixed. Thus, unless a woman has had a new baby, the impact of her current child status on her current labor force behavior should be largely reflected in her previous year's labor force behavior. One might hope to control for the impact of child status, therefore, by introducing a dummy variable for the presence of a new baby and controlling for a woman's labor force behavior in the previous year.

Child status variables may also serve as proxies for a variety of omitted variables, including the number of years of previous labor force experience, a family's child-related needs for income, desired child quality, and a woman's preferences for home-oriented versus market-oriented activities. All of these factors, also, change slowly, or not at all, from one year to the next; and hence, these factors should also be reflected in a woman's labor force behavior in the previous year. If long-standing preferences for home-oriented versus market-oriented activities largely determine both the fertility and labor force behavior of women, we might expect that child status variables, including even a dummy for a new baby, would explain very little of the variability in current labor force behavior after controlling for a woman's labor force behavior in the previous year.[16]

Of course, even career women can have preferences or beliefs that dictate that they will quit work for a year or so, if and when they have a baby. Contingency plans of this sort will result in abrupt and systematic changes in labor force behavior that may not be foreshadowed by a woman's labor force behavior in the previous year. Thus, even after controlling for labor force or work behavior in the previous year, a baby dummy variable may pick up premeditated responses reflecting the longstanding beliefs and preferences of women, as well as responses directly attributable to the time requirements of caring for a new baby and the problems and costs of purchasing substitutes for the mother's time.

In this study, a dummy set equal to 1 if a woman has a new baby, a dummy set equal to 1 if a woman has a child younger than 6 that is not a new baby, and a continuous variable for the total number of children younger than 18 living at home are included in the indices for the probability of work and in the equations for annual hours of work for appropriate demographic groups. The estimated coefficients of

TABLE 3.7.4
STARTING WAGE RATES OF HYPOTHETICAL WOMEN WITH NO
CHILDREN YOUNGER THAN 18 AT HOME, AND OF
OTHERWISE-IDENTICAL WOMEN WITH CHILDREN AT HOME

Age	No children	New baby	Child less than 6 but no new baby	Child less than 18 but older than 5
		Unmarried women		
17	$1.78	$1.66	$1.90	
33	1.89	1.99	1.88	$1.88
55	2.24			2.24
70	.38			.40
		Married women		
17	1.78	1.65	1.91	
33	2.24	2.34	2.61	2.18
55	1.67			1.67

our child status variables reflect the impacts of these variables after controlling for the impacts of child status in the previous year and other persistent observable and unobservable factors as reflected, or embedded, in a woman's work behavior in the previous year.

The coefficient estimates for our child status variables for women who did not work in the previous year are shown in Tables 3.7.1 and 3.7.2. Sign patterns that are replicated for more than one age group, or for both married and unmarried women, would suggest the presence of relationships between work behavior and our child status variables. Also, we might expect the coefficients of the child status variables to have the same signs in both the probit indices for the probability of work and the equations for hours of work. Looking at Tables 3.7.1 and 3.7.2, we see that only the negative impact of the baby dummy is replicated for two demographic groups, women 14-20 and wives 21-46, for both the probit indices for the probability of work and the equations for hours of work.

Suppose we consider hypothetical childless women with the age and marital status attributes, the probabilities of starting work, the starting wage rates and the starting hours of work shown in Table 3.1.1. Tables 3.7.3 through 3.7.5 show

3 Estimation Results for Our Inertia Model   147

TABLE 3.7.5
STARTING HOURS OF WORK FOR HYPOTHETICAL WOMEN
WITH NO CHILDREN YOUNGER THAN 18 AT HOME, AND
FOR OTHERWISE-IDENTICAL WOMEN WITH
CHILDREN AT HOME

Age	No children	New baby	Child less than 6 but no new baby	Child less than 18 but older than 5
\multicolumn{5}{c}{Unmarried women}
17	614	469 (323)	534 (660)	
33	993	1065 (1069)	806 (806)	1002 (1000)
55	737			674 (635)
70	96			138 (105)
\multicolumn{5}{c}{Married women}
17	614	488 (323)	515 (660)	
33	671	478 (509)	713 (714)	665 (644)
55	734			679 (674)

how the coefficient estimates given in Tables 3.7.1 and 3.7.2 imply that these probabilities of starting work and starting wage rates and hours of work would differ if these hypothetical women had a new baby, a youngest child less than 6 that is not a new baby, or a child younger than 18 but older than 5.

As in Tables 3.7.1 and 3.7.2, the only consistent pattern that emerges from Tables 3.7.3 through 3.7.5 is that the presence of a new baby depresses both the probabilities of starting to work and the expected hours of work if a woman does start work for both of our hypothetical 17-year-olds and for our married 33-year-old. We can detect no patterns whatever in the starting wage rates shown in Table 3.7.4.

The coefficient estimates for our child status variables for women who did work in the previous year are shown in Tables 3.7.6 and 3.7.7. Our variable for the number of children younger than 18 was not included for these women. The coefficient estimates for our baby and young child dummies shown in Table 3.7.6 are negative for both married and unmarried women 21-46, with the impact of the baby dummy being larger in magnitude in each case as might be expected. Thus,

TABLE 3.7.6
COEFFICIENT ESTIMATES FOR CHILD STATUS VARIABLES
IN PROBIT INDICES FOR PROBABILITY OF WORK:
WOMEN WHO WORKED IN t-1

Group	Baby dummy	Young child dummy
Women 14-20	.594*	.172
Wives 21-46	-.528**	-.130*
Unmarried women 21-46	-.679**	-.083

TABLE 3.7.7
IV COEFFICIENT ESTIMATES FOR CHILD STATUS
VARIABLES IN HOURS EQUATIONS:
WORKING WOMEN WHO WORKED IN t-1

Group	Baby dummy	Young child dummy
Women 14-20	-285.7*	-151.0*
Wives 21-46	58.0	4.0
Unmarried women 21-46	-162.6*	2.9

the results in Table 3.7.6 suggest that the presense of a new baby or young child depresses the probabilities of continuing to work for women 21-46 years of age.

The results shown in Table 3.7.7 suggest that a woman 14-20 years of age whose youngest child is a new baby or a child younger than 6 and who, nevertheless, continues to work, will tend to work fewer hours. Again, we find the negative impacts of a new baby to be numerically greater than the corresponding impacts of a young child that is not a new baby. However, the signs of the coefficients of the child status variables in the probit indices for the probability of work only agree with the signs of the coefficients of these variables in the hours equations for unmarried women 21-46.

Consider hypothetical childless women who started work in

3 Estimation Results for Our Inertia Model

TABLE 3.7.8
PROBABILITIES OF CONTINUING TO WORK FOR
HYPOTHETICAL WOMEN WITH NO CHILDREN YOUNGER
THAN 18 AT HOME, AND FOR OTHERWISE-IDENTICAL
WOMEN WITH CHILDREN AT HOME

Age	No children	New baby	Child less than 6 but no new baby
Unmarried women			
17	.76	.89 (.90)	.80 (.81)
33	.92	.77 (.77)	.87 (.91)
Married women			
17	.47	.67 (.69)	.51 (.53)
33	.85	.65 (.69)	.83 (.82)

TABLE 3.7.9
CONTINUING WAGE RATES OF HYPOTHETICAL WOMEN
WITH NO CHILDREN YOUNGER THAN 18 AT HOME,
AND OF OTHERWISE-IDENTICAL WOMEN
WITH CHILDREN AT HOME

Age	No children	New baby	Child less than 6 but no new baby
Unmarried women			
17	$1.98	$2.01	$1.98
33	2.65	2.29	2.61
Married women			
17	1.98	2.03	1.98
33	2.54	2.29	2.56

TABLE 3.7.10
CONTINUING HOURS OF WORK FOR HYPOTHETICAL
WOMEN WITH NO CHILDREN YOUNGER THAN 18
AT HOME, AND FOR OTHERWISE-IDENTICAL
WOMEN WITH CHILDREN AT HOME

Age	No children	New baby	Child less than 6 but no new baby
	Unmarried women		
17	1112	945 (846)	914 (961)
33	1676	1546 (1513)	1560 (1673)
	Married women		
17	1112	1068 (826)	958 (961)
33	1359	1322 (1417)	1369 (1363)

TABLE 3.7.11
COEFFICIENT ESTIMATES FOR VARIABLE FOR NUMBER OF
CHILDREN YOUNGER THAN 18 IN PROBIT INDICES
FOR PROBABILITY OF WORK AND HOURS EQUATIONS:
MEN AND WORKING MEN, RESPECTIVELY

	Age	
Equation	21-46	47-64
Probit index	-.046*	-.024
Hours equation	-9.1	-1.6

the previous year with the probabilities, wage rates and hours shown in Table 3.1.1, and with the probabilities of continuing to work, the continuing wage rates and the continuing hours of work shown in Table 3.1.2. Tables 3.7.8 through 3.7.10 show how our coefficient estimates in Tables 3.7.1 and 3.7.2 and Tables 3.7.6 and 3.7.7 imply that the continuing work behavior would differ if these hypothetical women had a new baby, a youngest child less than 6 that was not a new baby, or a child

3 Estimation Results for Our Inertia Model

younger than 18 in the previous year.

Looking at the results in Tables 3.7.8 through 3.7.10, we find that when indirect effects on the continuing hours of work are also taken into account, the presence of a new baby depresses the probabilities of continuing to work and the hours of work if the woman does work for our married and unmarried hypothetical 33-year-old women. The continuing wage rates are also depressed. The presence of a youngest child less than 6 also causes the probability of continuing to work to be depressed, the continuing hours of work to fall, and the continuing wage rate to fall for our unmarried hypothetical 33-year-old. This pattern is not replicated for the hypothetical married 33-year-old, however.

For comparative purposes, we have also included our variable for the number of children younger than 18 in probit indices for the probability of work and equations for annual hours of work for men 21-46 and 47-64 years of age. The coefficient estimates for men for this child status variable are shown in Table 3.7.11. All of these coefficient estimates are negative. However, comparing the magnitudes of these coefficients with those shown in Tables 3.7.1 and 3.7.2, and also in Tables 3.7.6 and 3.7.7, for women, we see that the negative impacts of children on the labor supply of men are relatively small. Can it be true that men with more children tend to supply less labor because they place higher values on home time and hence, have higher asking wage rates, as is argued for women? An alternative explanation is that there are personal as well as regional, cultural and economic traits that lead men and women in certain parts of the country to both have more children and to work less and that these characteristics are not fully controlled for by controlling for the work behavior of the individual in the previous year.

Our findings with respect to the impact of child status variables on female and male work behavior may be summarized as follows:

1. When work behavior in the previous year is taken into account, we find little evidence that child status affects a woman's current work behavior. Only the presence of a new baby seems to consistently depress the probabilities of starting and of continuing to work, as well as the starting and continuing hours of work, for married women 21-46 years of age. This pattern is replicated for the 14-20 age group, except in the case of the probabilities of continuing to work. For unmarried women 21-46 years of age, this pattern is replicated in the case of the continuing, but not the starting, work behavior. We note that the direct effect of the presence of a new baby on the continuing hours of work for 21-46-year-old wives is

positive. For this group, the negative total impact
of the presence of a new baby on the continuing hours
of work comes about because of the impact of a new
baby on the selection bias term in the hours
equation.
2. The presence of children younger than 18 also seems
to slightly depress the labor supply of men.

3.8. Other Income Variables

In most studies of the labor force behavior of married
women, the earned income of the husband is found to depress
the labor supply of the wife.[17] But maybe young women with
strong preferences for home-oriented activities are more
successful in finding husbands with high permanent incomes,
and maybe the observed relationship between the current
incomes of husbands and the work activities of their spouses
is largely due to this marital sorting. If this is the case,
if we control for preferences for home-oriented versus
market-oriented activities by controlling for a woman's labor
force behavior in the previous year, we should find the
remaining relationships between the husband's income and the
wife's labor force behavior to be relatively weak.
Unanticipated changes in the husband's earnings might still
bring about changes in the wife's labor force behavior, of
course, due to changes in the relationship between family
income and the economic needs of the family.[18]

It is also generally believed that women who receive
transfer income will tend to supply less labor, both because
of the negative income effects of this transfer income on
labor supply and because factors such as the presence of young
children, poor earnings potential, disability or illness, or
old age, which are common reasons for an individual to receive
transfer income, tend to persist over time and tend to inhibit
labor force activities. In addition, there are regulations
that inhibit work behavior while an individual is receiving
certain types of transfer income.

We have included a continuous variable for the current
level of the husband's income in our probit indices for the
probability of starting work for women 14-20, wives 21-46,
wives 47-64 and women at least 65 years of age; and we have
included this variable in our starting hours equations for all
of these demographic groups except women at least 65 years of
age. A continuous variable for the change from the previous to
the current year in the husband's income has been included in
both our probit and hours equations for women 14-20 who did
not work in the previous year and in our probit and hours

3 Estimation Results for Our Inertia Model

TABLE 3.8.1
COEFFICIENT ESTIMATES FOR OTHER INCOME VARIABLES IN
PROBIT INDICES FOR PROBABILITY OF WORK:
WOMEN WHO DID NOT WORK IN t-1

Group	Husband's income	Change in husband's income	Negative change in husband's income	Dummy for AFDC in t-1	Dummy for Social Security in t-1
Women 14-20	.060	-.168*			
Wives 21-46	-.033**	.011		.154	
Unmarried women 21-46				.003	
Wives 47-64	-.029*		.042		-.486
Unmarried women 47-64					-.589*
Women 65+	-.009		.063		-.615*

equations for wives 21-46 who did not and who did work in the previous year. A variable set equal to the change in the husband's income if this change is negative and set equal to 0 otherwise has been included in our probit index for the probability of starting work for women at least 65 years of age, and it has been included in both our probit indices and our hours equations for wives 47-64 and for women at least 65 years of age who worked in the previous year. Finally, we have included a dummy variable set equal to 1 if a woman's family received Aid for Families of Dependent Children (AFDC) in the previous year in our probit and hours equations for women 21-46, and we have included another dummy set equal to 1 if a woman or her husband received Social Security benefits in the previous year in both our probit and hours equations for women 47-64 and women at least 65 years of age.

The coefficient estimates for the other income variables included in our probit and hours of work equations are shown in Tables 3.8.1 through 3.8.4. Our initial expectation was that all of these coefficient estimates would be negative, except for the coefficients for a negative change in the husband's income, which were expected to be positive if older wives tend to reduce their work effort and eventually retire

TABLE 3.8.2
IV COEFFICIENT ESTIMATES FOR OTHER INCOME VARIABLES IN HOURS EQUATIONS: WORKING WOMEN WHO DID NOT WORK IN t-1

Group	Husband's income	Change in husband's income	Negative change in husband's income	Dummy for AFDC in t-1	Dummy for Social Security in t-1
Women 14-20	70.2*	-58.7			
Wives 21-46	-6.3	-15.4		-204.4	
Unmarried women 21-46				-169.9*	
Wives 47-64	-57.5*		-52.7		-594.6
Unmarried women 47-64					-545.4
Women 65+					142.1

along with their husbands.[19] The coefficient estimates shown in Tables 3.8.1 and 3.8.3 for the probit indices for the probabilities of starting to and of continuing to work, respectively, often have the "wrong" signs. The coefficient estimates shown in Tables 3.8.2 and 3.8.4 for the starting and the continuing hours of work equations, respectively, often have the "wrong" signs, too. Also, we might expect to find agreement in the coefficient signs between our probit indices and our hours equations, between our relationships for women who did not work in the previous year and for women who did work in the previous year, and over age groups for married and for unmarried women. Except for consistency between our estimation results for starting versus continuing work behavior, these expected correspondences are not to be found in Tables 3.8.1 through 3.8.4. In these respects our results are equally weak for all our other income variables and offer, at best, weak support for the notion that income from sources other than a woman's own work acts to increase her asking wage and thereby to reduce her probability of working and her hours of work if she does work. This picture does not change when we consider the total impacts of our other income variables. Thus, tables for our hypothetical women are not shown for

3 Estimation Results for Our Inertia Model

TABLE 3.8.3
COEFFICIENT ESTIMATES FOR OTHER INCOME VARIABLES IN PROBIT INDICES FOR PROBABILITY OF WORK: WOMEN WHO WORKED IN t-1

Group	Change in husband's income	Negative change in husband's income	Dummy for AFDC in t-1	Dummy for Social Security in t-1
Wives 21-46	.019*		-.509*	
Unmarried women 21-46			-.459**	
Wives 47-64		.113**		-.373
Unmarried women 47-64				-.173
Women 65+		.336*		.269

TABLE 3.8.4
IV COEFFICIENT ESTIMATES FOR OTHER INCOME VARIABALES IN HOURS EQUATIONS: WORKING WOMEN WHO WORKED IN t-1

Group	Change in husband's income	Negative change in husband's income	Dummy for AFDC in t-1	Dummy for Social Security in t-1
Wives 21-46	-10.1**		218.0	
Unmarried women 21-46			-51.6	
Wives 47-64		9.3		101.8
Unmarried women 47-64				190.9*
Women 65+		-221.7		77.4

TABLE 3.8.5
COEFFICIENT ESTIMATES FOR OTHER INCOME VARIABLES
IN PROBIT INDICES FOR PROBABILITY OF WORK: MEN

Group	Wife's income in t-1	Dummy for AFDC in t-1	Dummy for Social Security in t-1
Men 14-20 who did not work in t-1		2.739*	
Men 14-20 who worked in t-1		-.025	
Men 21-46	-.005	-.128	
Men 47-64	.042*		.091
Men 65+	.036		.025

TABLE 3.8.6
IV COEFFICIENT ESTIMATES FOR OTHER INCOME
VARIABLES IN HOURS EQUATIONS: WORKING MEN

Group	Wife's income in t-1	Dummy for AFDC in t-1	Dummy for Social Security in t-1
Men 14-20 who did not work in t-1		-1643.1*	
Men 14-20 who worked in t-1		157.9	
Men 21-46	-4.5*	-436.4**	
Men 47-64	-2.2		-312.2**
Men 65+	9.3		55.5

3 Estimation Results for Our Inertia Model

these variables.

Our coefficient estimates for other income variables in probit indices for the probability of work and in hours of work equations for men are shown in Tables 3.8.5 and 3.8.6. Here again, we find little consistency in coefficient signs over age groups or between the results for probit indices and the results for the hours equations. Certainly there is little, if any, evidence in these two tables of negative impacts of other income on the labor supply of men. Of course, we might not expect the income effects of other income on labor supply to be as strong for men as for women.

We draw the following conclusions from these results:

1. There seem to be weak negative relationships between the probability of a wife younger than 47 starting to work and the level of her husband's income, even after controlling for long-standing preferences for home-oriented versus market-oriented activities by controlling for the wife's work behavior in the previous year.
2. The causal basis of the negative relationships between the labor supply of wives younger than 47 and the income levels of their husbands is unclear since, with the exception of wives younger than 21, we find a positive relationship between the probabilities of a wife starting or continuing to work and the <u>change</u> in her husband's income from the previous to the current year.
3. There is weak evidence of a mutual husband-wife retirement effect for wives older than 46; that is, there is some evidence that wives older than 46 have lower probabilities of work if the husband's income fell from the previous to the current year. We find, on the other hand, that older wives who do work start out working or continue working work longer hours than would otherwise be the case if the husband's income has fallen from the previous to the current year.
4. Despite the difficulties in interpreting the estimated coefficients of the husband's income variables, there is considerable consistency between our estimation results for starting versus continuing work behavior. In a study such as this one that includes only national variables as controls for macroeconomic conditions, the estimated responses to the husband's income variables may reflect the fact that these variables are acting, in part, as proxies for differences in the levels and changes in local versus national macroeconomic variables. In this case, the coefficients of the husband's income

variables could not be interpreted as measuring pure income effects on the labor supply of wives. The level of the husband's income may also be a proxy, of course, for other unmeasured traits, such as preferences for child quality, that are not adequately controlled for by controlling for the wife's work behavior in the previous year and that do not change from year to year with changes in the level of the husband's income.

5. There is weak evidence that, all else being equal, women in families that received AFDC or Social Security benefits in the previous year are less likely to work in the present year and will probably work fewer hours than would otherwise be the case if they do work.

6. We find no evidence that other income sources in the previous year, such as the earnings of a wife or AFDC benefits or Social Security benefits, have any impact on the probabilities of work or hours of work of men in the current year.

3.9. Macroeconomic Variables

There is a great deal of public and academic interest in questions concerning the existence, direction and magnitude of impacts of macroeconomic conditions on the labor force behavior of women. Numerous questions come to mind. When the unemployment rate goes up, will wives be more likely to work because of economic pressures within families? That is, is there an added worker effect? Or will women be less likely to start, or to continue, to work because those who have not been working or have recently been laid off think it will not be possible to find work and hence, do not look, or look without success? That is, is there a discouraged worker effect? Or do added and discouraged worker effects (see, for instance, Ehrenberg and Smith, 1982, pp. 190-192), acting in opposite directions, lead to a finding of no effect of rising unemployment on the probability of a wife working? For married women, do discouraged worker effects operate through the impact of macro unemployment on the offered wage distributions that wives face, and do added worker effects operate through the impacts of macro unemployment on the husband's income variables that help to determine the asking wage distributions of wives? Are married women, as secondary workers, more sensitive than unmarried women and men to changes in macroeconomic conditions, such as the level of unemployment? Do unmarried women and men exhibit only discouraged worker

3 Estimation Results for Our Inertia Model

effects operating through the impacts of unemployment on their offered wage distributions? Are there differences in the effects of unemployment on the starting versus the continuing work behavior of women?[20] Are there impacts of other macroeconomic variables,[21] such as the general wage level? After controlling for the real earned incomes of husbands, do increases in the nominal wage level cause wives to be more likely to start, or to continue, working? Do married women respond as unmarried women do, and do women respond as men do, to changes in the nominal wage level?

We have included the national unemployment rate and a national wage index in our probit indices for the probability of work and in our log wage equations. Our coefficient estimates for these variables for women are shown in Tables 3.9.1 and 3.9.3 for our probit indices for the probabilities of starting, and of continuing, to work, respectively. We see that, with the exception of the coefficient estimates for the national unemployment rate for women 14-20, there is perfect agreement in sign for the corresponding coefficient estimates in these two tables. The coefficient estimates for women 21-46 and 47-64 years of age also display clear patterns. In particular, a rise in unemployment has negative impacts on the probabilities of starting and of continuing to work for unmarried women in these age groups, indicating a possible discouraged worker effect for unmarried women. On the other hand, a rise in unemployment has positive impacts on the probabilities of starting and of continuing to work for married women in these age groups, indicating a possible added worker effect for married women even after controlling for changes in the husband's income. Also, a rise in the national wage index seems to increase the probabilities of work for both married and unmarried women in these age groups.

Comparing the coefficient estimates shown in Table 3.9.1 with the coefficient estimates shown in Table 3.9.2, however, we find little evidence of any correspondence of signs for the coefficients of our macro variables in our probit indices for the probability of starting work and in the starting log wage equations. Nor is it possible to interpret the signs of the coefficient estimates of the macroeconomic variables in the log wage equations in any meaningful way. A similar picture emerges when we compare the coefficient estimates shown in Table 3.9.3 for our probit indices for the probability of continuing to work with the coefficient estimates shown in Table 3.9.4 for the log wage equations for women who worked in the previous year. We find little correspondence in sign between the two sets of coefficient estimates, and we are unable to offer any behavioral explanation for the sign patterns of the estimated coefficients of our macroeconomic variables in our log wage equations for women who worked in the previous year. Thus, we find no evidence that impacts of

TABLE 3.9.1
COEFFICIENT ESTIMATES FOR MACROECONOMIC
VARIABLES IN PROBIT INDICES FOR
PROBABILITY OF WORK:
WOMEN WHO DID NOT WORK IN t-1

Group	National unemployment rate	National wage index
Women 14-20	.007	-.0113*
Wives 21-46	.018	.0068**
Unmarried women 21-46	-.012	.0024
Wives 47-64	.033	.0041
Unmarried women 47-64	-.101*	.0062
Women 65+	-.169*	-.0100*

TABLE 3.9.2
OLS COEFFICIENT ESTIMATES FOR MACROECONOMIC
VARIABLES IN LOG WAGE EQUATIONS:
WORKING WOMEN WHO DID NOT WORK IN t-1

Group	National unemployment rate	National wage index
Women 14-20	.018	.0015
Wives 21-46	-.046	.0002
Unmarried women 21-46	.050*	-.0042**
Wives 47-64	.067	-.0038
Unmarried women 47-64	.207*	.0073
Women 65+	-.082	.0099

TABLE 3.9.3
COEFFICIENT ESTIMATES FOR MACROECONOMIC VARIABLES
IN PROBIT INDICES FOR PROBABILITY OF WORK:
WORKING WOMEN WHO WORKED IN t-1

Group	National unemployment rate	National wage index
Women 14-20	-.057	-.0140*
Wives 21-46	.028	.0019
Unmarried women 21-46	-.029	.0031
Wives 47-64	.001	.0041
Unmarried women 47-64	-.058	.0071*
Women 65+	-.057	-.0016

TABLE 3.9.4
OLS COEFFICIENT ESTIMATES FOR MACROECONOMIC
VARIABLES IN LOG WAGE EQUATIONS:
WORKING WOMEN WHO WORKED IN t-1

Group	National unemployment rate	National wage index
Women 14-20	-.022	.0046
Wives 21-46	-.024**	-.0008
Unmarried women 21-46	-.000	.0014
Wives 47-64	.006	-.0012
Unmarried women 47-64	.047*	-.0026**
Women 65+	-.022	.0013

TABLE 3.9.5
COEFFICIENT ESTIMATES FOR MACROECONOMIC VARIABLES
IN PROBIT INDICES FOR PROBABILITY OF WORK: MEN

Group	National unemployment rate	National wage index
Men 14-20 who did not work in t-1	.005	-.0021
Men 14-20 who worked in t-1	-.012	-.0143
Men 21-46	-.028	-.0009
Men 47-64	-.064	-.0050*
Men 65+	-.087*	-.0047

TABLE 3.9.6
OLS COEFFICIENT ESTIMATES FOR MACROECONOMIC
VARIABLES IN LOG WAGE EQUATIONS: WORKING WOMEN

Group	National unemployment rate	National wage index
Men 14-20 who did not work in t-1	-.009	.0013
Men 14-20 who worked in t-1	-.049**	-.0010
Men 21-46	-.010**	-.0004
Men 47-64	-.010*	.0012
Men 65+	.087**	.0006

the national unemployment rate or the national wage index on the labor force behavior of women are transmitted via the impacts of these variables on the offered wage distributions of individual women who work. The nature of any possible macroeconomic effects on the work behavior of women is not

3 Estimation Results for Our Inertia Model

clarified by looking at the total impacts of our macroeconomic variables. Thus, we do not show tables for our hypothetical women for these variables either.

In Tables 3.9.5 and 3.9.6, we show the coefficient estimates for our two macroeconomic variables in our probit indices for the probability of work and in our log wage equations for men. For men we find that an increase in the national unemployment rate acts to decrease the probability of work for all groups except men 14-20 who did not work in the previous year and also acts to decrease the wage rate for all groups except for men at least 65 years of age. Thus, our results for men are consistent with the hypothesis of a discouraged worker effect that operates via the depressing effects of increased unemployment on the offered wage distributions of men. Our coefficient estimates for men for the national wage index, however, are always negative in the probit indices but sometimes positive and sometimes negative in the log wage equations. Thus, we find little consistent evidence of any impact of the national wage index on the work behavior of men.

The conclusions we draw from our empirical results for our two macroeconomic variables are as follows:

1. Increases in the national unemployment rate decrease both the probabilities of work for men and the wage rates for those men who do work. These results are consistent with the hypothesis that increases in unemployment decrease the labor supply of men by decreasing their offered wage distributions.
2. Increases in the national unemployment rate also decrease the probabilities of starting and of continuing to work for unmarried women. Moreover, we find accompanying decreases in the starting and continuing hours of work for those unmarried women who do work, due to indirect impacts of the unemployment rate on hours of work. However, we find no evidence that increases in the national unemployment rate cause decreases in the starting or continuing wage rates of unmarried women who work. Thus, we find no evidence that the decreases in the labor supply of unmarried women with increasing national unemployment rates are due to decreases in their offered wage distributions.
3. Increases in the national unemployment rate cause increases in the probabilities of starting and of continuing to work for married women, even after taking into account the changes in the earned income of the husband. Moreover, we find accompanying increases in the starting and continuing hours of work for those married women who work, due to

indirect impacts. As for unmarried women, however, we find no evidence of any systematic changes in the wage rates of married women with changes in the national unemployment rate.
4. We find no evidence that changes in our national wage index have any effects on the work behavior of women or men.

3.10. Lagged Hours of Work and Wage Rate Variables

For individuals who worked in the previous year, their hours of work and wage rates in the previous year give us an indication of the strength of their attachment to the labor force. These lagged hours of work and wage rate variables reflect, or embed, all of the factors affecting the offered and asking wage rates of an individual in the previous year, including the values of both measured and unmeasured characteristics and random shocks in that year. If nothing changed from the previous year and there were no random shocks, we would expect an individual to display the same labor force behavior in the current year as in the previous year. A finding that the lagged hours of work and wage rate variables play important roles in our behavioral equations for individuals who worked in the previous year is consistent with the hypothesis that measured and unmeasured variables that change slowly or not at all, including individual tastes for market-oriented activities, are responsible for a substantial portion of the differences among individuals in their current labor force behavior. This is the portion of labor force behavior for the existing adult population that may not be easily altered by short-run government programs.

In Table 3.10.1 we show our coefficient estimates for women who worked in the previous year for our lagged hours of work and wage rate variables in our probit indices for the probability of work in the current year. We see that the lagged hours coefficient estimates are always positive as expected. These coefficients seem to be larger in magnitude for unmarried than for married women, with the magnitudes of these coefficient estimates showing some tendency to decline with age for both married and unmarried women. The estimated coefficients of the lagged wage variable are positive as expected except for unmarried women aged 47-64 and for women older than 64.

In Table 3.10.2 we show our coefficient estimates for men for our lagged hours of work and wage rate variables in our probit indices for the probability of work. We see that these coefficient estimates are always positive. The coefficient

3 Estimation Results for Our Inertia Model

TABLE 3.10.1
COEFFICIENT ESTIMATES FOR LAGGED HOURS OF WORK
AND WAGE RATE VARIABLES IN PROBIT INDICES
FOR PROBABILITY OF WORK:
WOMEN WHO WORKED IN t-1

Group	Hours in t-1	Wage in t-1
Women 14-20	.00064**	.0025
Wives 21-46	.00067**	.0187
Unmarried women 21-46	.00103**	.0536*
Wives 47-64	.00057**	.0501*
Unmarried women 47-64	.00090**	-.0315
Women 65+	.00076*	-.0603

TABLE 3.10.2
COEFFICIENT ESTIMATES FOR LAGGED HOURS OF WORK
AND WAGE RATE VARIABLES IN PROBIT INDICES:
MEN

Group	Hours in t-1	Wage in t-1
Men 14-20 who worked in t-1	.00038**	.0318
Men 21-46	.00085**	.1799**
Men 47-64	.00127**	.1189**
Men 65+	.00109**	.1015**

estimates for the lagged hours variable show some tendency to increase in magnitude with increasing age, rather than to decline as for women. The coefficient estimates for the lagged wage variable fall in magnitude from the 21-46 through the over-65 age group but are smallest of all for the 14-20 age group. Looking at both Tables 3.10.1 and 3.10.2, we find, in fact, that the coefficient estimates for our lagged hours and wage rate variables are always smallest in magnitude for the youngest age group. This suggests, as might be expected, that relatively unchanging factors play a much less important role in determining the labor force behavior of women and men in the 14-20 age group than for older women and men.

In Tables 3.10.3 and 3.10.4 we show our coefficient estimates for women and for men, respectively, for our lagged hours of work and wage rate variables in our log wage equations. The coefficient estimates of the lagged hours variable are positive for all groups except unmarried women 47-64 years of age and men 47-64 years of age. The coefficient estimates for the lagged wage variable shown in Tables 3.10.3 and 3.10.4 are always positive for both women and men. The coefficient estimates for men decline in magnitude from the 21-46-year-old age group onward, as is also the case for the coefficient estimates of our lagged wage variable in our probit indices for men.

Coefficient estimates for our lagged hours of work variable in our hours equations for women and for men are shown in Tables 3.10.5 and 3.10.6, respectively. These coefficient estimates are always positive, as is consistent with both our expectations and our probit results for the lagged hours variable shown in Tables 3.10.1 and 3.10.2. Also, in agreement with our probit results, these coefficient estimates rise in magnitude with age for men and tend to fall in magnitude with age from the 21-46 age group on for women.

Consider hypothetical women with the age and marital status characteristics and the continuing work behavior shown in Table 3.1.2, having started work in the previous year with the probabilities, hours of work and wage rates shown in Table 3.1.1. Suppose now that these women had started work in the previous year working 500, 1,000 or 2,000 hours instead of the number of hours designated for each of our hypothetical women in Table 3.1.1. Tables 3.10.7 through 3.10.9 show how our estimated coefficients imply the probabilities of continuing to work, the continuing wage rates and the continuing hours of work of these women would be expected to differ depending on their hours of work in the previous year.

From Table 3.10.7 we see that the probabilities of continuing to work rise by 11 to 20 percentage points for our hypothetical unmarried women, and by 13 to 35 percentage points for our hypothetical married women, in response to a rise in hours of work in the previous year from 500 to 2,000 hours. From Table 3.10.8 we see that the rise from 500 to 2,000 hours of work in the previous year raises wage rates by 5 to 26 percent for our hypothetical unmarried women, and by 21 to 30 percent for our hypothetical married women. Notice that positive indirect effects of the lagged hours variable via the selection bias term make the total impact of lagged

3 Estimation Results for Our Inertia Model

TABLE 3.10.3
OLS COEFFICIENT ESTIMATES FOR LAGGED HOURS
OF WORK AND WAGE RATE VARIABLES IN
LOG WAGE EQUATIONS:
WORKING WOMEN WHO WORKED IN t-1

Group	Hours in t-1	Wage in t-1
Women 14-20	.0001**	.020
Wives 21-46	.0001**	.067**
Unmarried women 21-46	.0000	.186**
Wives 47-64	.0001*	.105**
Unmarried women 47-64	-.0001**	.191**
Women 65+	.0001	.375**

TABLE 3.10.4
OLS COEFFICIENT ESTIMATES FOR LAGGED HOURS
OF WORK AND WAGE RATE VARIABLES IN LOG WAGE EQUATIONS:
WORKING MEN

Group	Hours in t-1	Wage in t-1
Men 14-20 who worked in t-1	.0002**	.041**
Men 21-46	.0000**	.135**
Men 47-64	-.0001**	.109**
Men 65+	.0000	.065**

hours on the wage rate positive for our hypothetical 55-year-old women, despite the negative direct effect of the lagged hours variable for this one age group. We see also from Table 3.10.9 that the increase in hours of work in the previous year from 500 to 2,000 hours raises the hours of work in the current year by 28 to 70 percent for our hypothetical

TABLE 3.10.5
IV COEFFICIENT ESTIMATES FOR LAGGED HOURS OF
WORK VARIABLE IN HOURS EQUATIONS:
WORKING WOMEN WHO WORKED IN t-1

Marital status	Age			
	14-20	21-46	47-64	65+
Married		.496**	.650**	
	.257*			.093
Unmarried		.595**	.568**	

TABLE 3.10.6
IV COEFFICIENT ESTIMATES FOR LAGGED HOURS
OF WORK VARIABLE IN HOURS EQUATIONS: WORKING MEN

Work status in t-1	Age			
	14-20	21-46	47-64	65+
Did not work	----	.589**	.663**	.840**
Worked	.334**			

unmarried women and by 69 to 81 percent for our hypothetical married women.

Suppose we again consider hypothetical women who have the age and marital status characteristics and the continuing work behavior shown in Table 3.1.2 and who started work in the previous year with the probabilities, hours of work and wage rates shown in Table 3.1.1. Suppose now that these hypothetical women had started work in the previous year with wage rates of $2.00, $3.00 or $4.50 instead of the values designated for each of our hypothetical women in Table 3.1.1. Tables 3.10.10 through 3.10.12 show how our coefficient estimates imply that the probabilities of continuing to work, continuing wage rates, and continuing hours of work would be expected to differ for these women depending on their wage rates in the previous year.

From Table 3.10.10 it can be seen that the probabilities of continuing to work change from -6 to 3 percentage points for our hypothetical women as the wage rate in the previous year rises from $2.00 to $4.50. From Table 3.10.11 we see that

3 Estimation Results for Our Inertia Model

TABLE 3.10.7
PROBABILITIES OF CONTINUING TO WORK FOR HYPOTHETICAL
WOMEN DEPENDING ON THEIR HOURS OF WORK IN THE PREVIOUS YEAR

	Hours of work in t-1		
Age	500	1,000	2,000

Unmarried women

Age	500	1,000	2,000
17	.74	.83	.94
33	.81	.92	.99
55	.88	.95	.99
70	.83	.91	.98

Married women

Age	500	1,000	2,000
17	.44	.57	.79
33	.82	.90	.97
55	.83	.89	.96

TABLE 3.10.8
CONTINUING WAGE RATES FOR HYPOTHETICAL WOMEN
DEPENDING ON THEIR HOURS OF WORK IN THE PREVIOUS YEAR

	Hours of work in t-1		
Age	500	1,000	2,000

Unmarried women

Age	500		1,000		2,000	
17	$1.95	($1.95)	$2.07	($2.05)	$2.32	($2.27)
33	2.39	(2.65)	2.65	(2.65)	2.86	(2.65)
55	2.25	(2.51)	2.58	(2.39)	2.83	(2.16)
70	1.91	(2.04)	1.95	(2.22)	2.01	(2.46)

Married women

Age	500		1,000		2,000	
17	1.95	(1.95)	2.07	(2.05)	2.36	(2.27)
33	2.43	(2.48)	2.72	(2.61)	3.16	(2.89)
55	2.56	(2.64)	2.83	(2.77)	3.32	(3.06)

TABLE 3.10.9
CONTINUING HOURS OF WORK FOR HYPOTHETICAL WOMEN
DEPENDING ON THEIR HOURS OF WORK IN THE PREVIOUS YEAR

	Hours of work in t-1		
Age	500	1,000	2,000

Unmarried women

17	1052 (1083)	1313 (1211)	1792 (1468)
33	1405 (1383)	1680 (1680)	2256 (2275)
55	1551 (1576)	1876 (1860)	2481 (2428)
70	1223 (1108)	1367 (1154)	1564 (1247)

Married women

17	1052 (1083)	1345 (1211)	1906 (1468)
33	1251 (1274)	1560 (1522)	2119 (2018)
55	1223 (1226)	1554 (1551)	2212 (2201)

TABLE 3.10.10
PROBABILITIES OF CONTINUING TO WORK FOR HYPOTHETICAL
WOMEN DEPENDING ON THEIR WAGE RATES IN THE PREVIOUS YEAR

	Wage rate in t-1		
Age	$2.00	$3.00	$4.50

Unmarried women

17	.76	.76	.76
33	.92	.93	.94
55	.92	.92	.91
70	.71	.69	.65

Married women

17	.47	.47	.47
33	.85	.85	.86
55	.86	.87	.89

3 Estimation Results for Our Inertia Model

this same rise in the wage rate in the previous year causes the wage rates in the current year to rise by 4 to 164 percentage points for our hypothetical unmarried women, and from 4 to 35 percentage points for our hypothetical married women. Moreover, these increases are almost entirely due to the direct, rather than the indirect, effects of the lagged wage variable on the current wage rates. Finally, we see from Table 3.10.12 that the change from $2.00 to $4.50 in the wage rate in the previous year causes the hours of work to change by -30 to 5 percent for our hypothetical unmarried women and by 1 to 5 percent for our hypothetical married women, due to the indirect effects of the lagged wage variable via the current log wage variable and the selection bias term in our hours equations. If we ignore the 70-year-old unmarried hypothetical woman, all of these indirect changes lie between 2 and 5 percent.

In considering these results, it is important to remember that they reflect the estimated sensitivity of our model to observed differences among individuals in lagged hours of work and wage rates; not the responses that we would expect to observe for women whose lagged hours of work or wage rates were exogenously changed. Among other considerations, it should be recalled that these lagged variables have been included in our relationships because they are thought to embed unobservable factors that change slowly or not at all over time for individuals.

The present study is cast in an annual framework because of the nature of the data used. Lagged hours of work and wage variables could also be used in a model based on quarterly, monthly or weekly data. Notice, however, that as the unit time period becomes shorter, the proportion of women for whom we have this information about strength of attachment to the work force in the previous time period will decline because the proportion of women who work in any given week, say, is less than the proportion who work in a year. Second, seasonal factors (summer vacation, Christmas holidays, and so forth) become more important as the unit time period becomes shorter. Third, the ratio of information about fixed and persistent factors affecting a woman's attachment to the work force to random noise will probably decrease as the unit time period is shortened. Thus, there are advantages to our unit time period of a year in estimating a model such as our Inertia Model.

The conclusions that we draw from our empirical results for the lagged hours of work and wage rate variables are:

1. Measured and unmeasured factors embodied in the previous year's hours of work and wage rates are important in explaining the current work behavior of individual women and men.
2. The direct effects of the previous year's hours of

TABLE 3.10.11
CONTINUING WAGE RATES FOR HYPOTHETICAL WOMEN
DEPENDING ON THEIR WAGE RATES IN THE PREVIOUS YEAR

	Wage rate in t-1		
Age	$2.00	$3.00	$4.50

Unmarried women

17	$1.98 ($1.98)	$2.01 ($2.01)	$2.07 ($2.07)
33	2.69 (2.69)	3.25 (3.25)	4.35 (4.26)
55	2.34 (2.34)	2.83 (2.83)	3.63 (3.78)
70	3.82 (3.74)	5.64 (5.42)	10.07 (9.49)

Married women

17	1.98 (1.98)	2.01 (2.01)	2.07 (2.07)
33	2.48 (2.48)	2.66 (2.66)	2.97 (2.94)
55	2.72 (2.69)	3.13 (3.09)	3.67 (3.63)

TABLE 3.10.12
CONTINUING HOURS OF WORK FOR HYPOTHETICAL WOMEN
DEPENDING ON THEIR WAGE RATES IN THE PREVIOUS YEAR

	Wage rate in t-1		
Age	$2.00	$3.00	$4.50

Unmarried women

17	1112	1137	1174
33	1680	1716	1769
55	1706	1725	1746
70	890	788	619

Married women

17	1112	1137	1174
33	1357	1367	1380
55	1378	1386	1394

3 Estimation Results for Our Inertia Model

work are always positive on both the probabilities of continuing to work and the continuing hours for both men and women. However, the direct effects of this lagged variable on the continuing wage rates are negative for unmarried women 47-64 and men 47-64, while they are slightly positive for all other groups of women and men. It would seem that the measured and unmeasured factors embodied in the lagged hours of work have more important impacts on the asking wage than on the offered wage.

3. The direct effects of the previous year's wages rates on the current log wages are positive for both women and men, with the magnitudes of the impacts growing with age for both married and unmarried women but becoming smaller beyond age 21 for men. The direct effects of the previous year's wage rates on the probabilities of continuing to work are also always positive for men, with the magnitudes of the coefficient estimates displaying an age pattern similar to the age pattern of the coefficient estimates of the lagged wage variable in our log wage equations for men. The direct effects of the previous year's wage rates on the probabilities of continuing to work, however, are small in magnitude for women compared with men, and they are negative for unmarried women 47-64 years of age and for women older than 64.

3.11. Selection Bias

The coefficients of the selection bias term in the log wage and hours of work equations supposedly have the signs of the correlation coefficients between the unobservables affecting the determination of which individuals work in a year and the unobservables affecting the dependent variables of interest. From Figure 3.11.1 we see that the value of the selection bias term falls in a smooth, nonlinear fashion as the probability of work rises, approaching 0 as the individual probability of work in the year approaches 1. Since the total impact of the selection bias term in an equation for the log wage or hours of work is the <u>product</u> of the coefficient of this term multiplied by the value of the selection bias term for the given individual, we see that the impact of this term will tend to be numerically small for individuals with probabilities of work close to 1. This fact in no way implies, however, that the <u>coefficient</u> of the selection bias term in a log wage or hours equation should be small or insignificantly

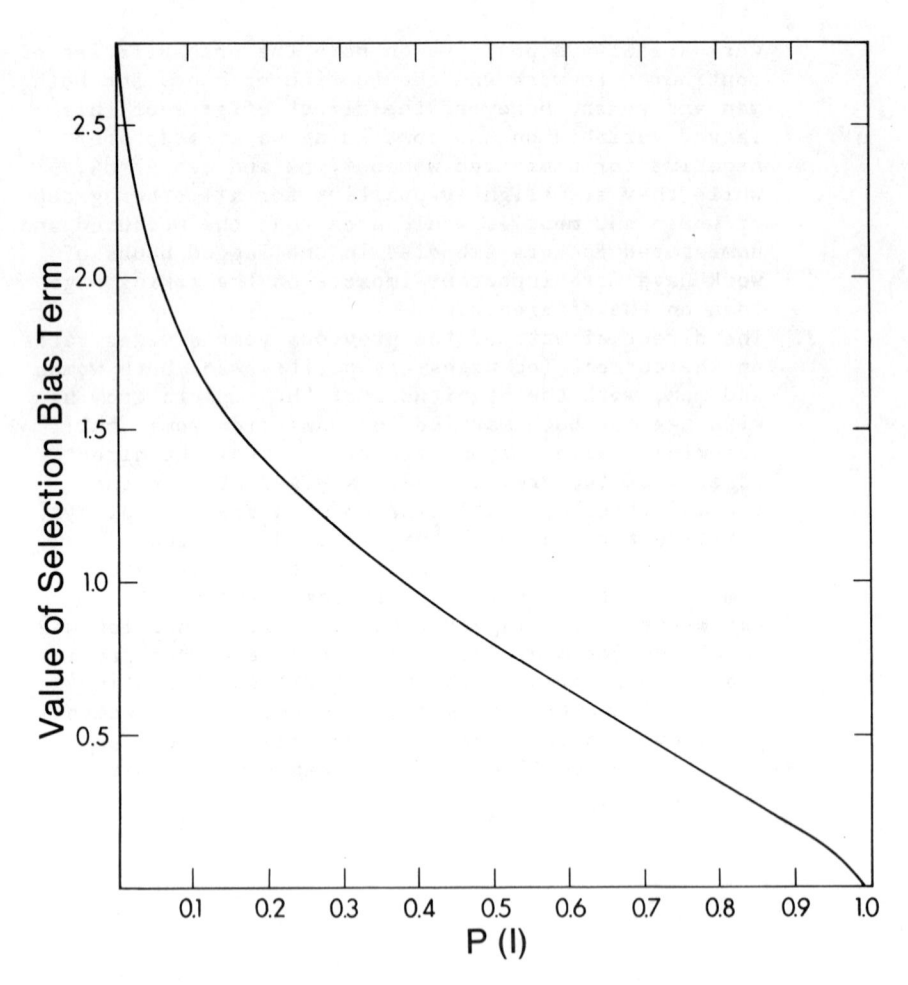

Fig. 3.11.1. Relationship between value of selection bias term and probability of work.

different from 0 for a group, such as prime-aged men, with an employment rate close to 1.

The coefficient estimates for the selection bias term in our log wage equations are shown in Table 3.11.1 for women who did not work in the previous year, in Table 3.11.2 for women who did work in the previous year, and in Table 3.11.3 for men. These coefficient estimates are predominantly negative for both women and men. This suggests that the correlations between the unobservables affecting the determination of who works and the unobservables affecting the offered wage are negative.

3 Estimation Results for Our Inertia Model

TABLE 3.11.1
OLS COEFFICIENT ESTIMATES FOR SELECTION
BIAS TERM IN LOG WAGE EQUATIONS:
WORKING WOMEN WHO DID NOT WORK IN t-1

Marital status	_ Age _			
	14-20	21-46	47-64	65+
Married		.497*	-.104	
	-.465*			-.303*
Unmarried		-.350**	-.029	

TABLE 3.11.2
OLS COEFFICIENT ESTIMATES FOR SELECTION
BIAS TERM IN LOG WAGE EQUATIONS:
WORKING WOMEN WHO WORKED IN t-1

Marital status	Age			
	14-20	21-46	47-64	65+
Married		-.437**	-.450**	
	-.082			.497
Unmarried		-.601**	-1.877**	

TABLE 3.11.3
OLS COEFFICIENT ESTIMATES FOR SELECTION
BIAS TERM IN LOG WAGE EQUATIONS: MEN

Work status in t-1	Age			
	14-20	21-46	47-64	65+
Did not work	-.023			
		-.131**	-.558**	.077
Worked	.691**			

If we rank the average employment rates for women who did not work in the previous year, women who worked in the previous year and men, in each age category, men have the highest rate and women who did not work in the previous year

TABLE 3.11.4
IV COEFFICIENT ESTIMATES FOR SELECTION BIAS TERM
IN HOURS EQUATIONS: WORKING WOMEN WHO DID NOT WORK IN t-1

Marital status	Age			
	14-20	21-46	47-64	65+
Married		-187.3	-505.5	
	1060.1**			-113.1
Unmarried		102.6	-356.6	

TABLE 3.11.5
IV COEFFICIENT ESTIMATES FOR SELECTION
BIAS TERM IN HOURS EQUATIONS:
WORKING WOMEN WHO WORKED IN t-1

Marital status	Age			
	14-20	21-46	47-64	65+
Married		-329.9*	-2.4	
	-447.0*			-786.4
Unmarried		251.9*	-270.7	

TABLE 3.11.6
IV COEFFICIENT ESTIMATES FOR SELECTION
BIAS TERM IN HOURS EQUATIONS: WORKING MEN

Work status in t-1	Age			
	14-20	21-46	47-64	65+
Did not work	-686.0			
		516.5**	171.0**	269.9*
Worked	-831.9**			

have the lowest rate. Average employment rates vary systematically over age groups, too. Looking at the coefficient estimates for the selection bias term, however, we see no tendency for these to be systematically smaller (or larger) in magnitude as the employment rate rises.

3 Estimation Results for Our Inertia Model

The coefficient estimates for the selection bias term in our hours equations are shown in Table 3.11.4 for women who did not work in the previous year, in Table 3.11.5 for women who worked in the previous year, and in Table 3.11.6 for men. Ignoring the youngest age group and unmarried women 21-46 years of age, we find that the coefficient estimates are always positive for men and negative for women. For the youngest age group, all of the coefficient estimates are negative, except for women 14-20 who did not work in the previous year. Thus, there is weak evidence that the correlations between the unobservables affecting the determination of who works and the unobservables affecting hours of work are positive for men at least 21 years old, but they are negative for women and younger men who are more loosely attached to the labor force on the average. There is no systematic tendency, however, for the coefficient estimates for the selection bias term to be more negative for women who did not work in the previous year than for otherwise-similar women who did work in the previous year.

Consider hypothetical women with the age and marital status characteristics and the starting work behavior shown in Table 3.1.1. Suppose it were possible, which it is not, to change the probabilities of work and selection bias terms for these hypothetical women without changing any of their observable characteristics. Tables 3.11.7 and 3.11.8 show how the starting wage rates and hours of work for these women would change if their probabilities of starting work were varied from .20 to .90 and hence, their selection bias terms were varied in value from .19 to 1.40. We see from Table 3.11.7 that the starting wage rates rise by 3 to 75 percent, except for our married 33-year-old hypothetical woman, for whom the wage rate falls by 24 percent. From Table 3.11.8 we see that the starting hours of work rise for all of the hypothetical women, except those in the younger two age groups for unmarried women and the youngest group for married women, with the increases ranging from 51 to 102 percent.

We will now consider hypothetical women who have the age and marital status characteristics and the continuing work behavior shown in Table 3.1.2 and who started work in the previous year with the probabilities, wage rates and hours of work shown in Table 3.1.1. Suppose it were possible, which it is not, to change the probabilities of continuing to work and the selection bias terms for these women without changing anything about their designated work behavior in the previous year or their observable characteristics in the current year. Tables 3.11.9 and 3.11.10 show how the continuing wage rates and continuing hours of work for these women would change if their probabilities of continuing to work were varied from .20 to .90 and hence, their selection bias terms were varied in value from .19 to 1.40. We see from Table 3.11.9 that except

TABLE 3.11.7
STARTING WAGE RATES FOR HYPOTHETICAL WOMEN
DEPENDING ON THEIR PROBABILITIES OF STARTING WORK

	Probability of starting work		
Age	.20	.50	.90
	Unmarried women		
17	$1.60	$2.12	$2.80
33	1.65	2.03	2.51
55	2.27	2.29	2.34
70	.45	.54	.66
	Married women		
17	1.97	2.61	3.45
33	2.27	1.70	1.25
55	1.73	1.84	1.97

TABLE 3.11.8
STARTING HOURS OF WORK FOR HYPOTHETICAL WOMEN
DEPENDING ON THEIR PROBABILITIES OF STARTING WORK

	Probability of starting work		
Age	.20	.50	.90
17	847 (868)	265 (232)	−328 (−414)
33	1005 (1034)	987 (972)	969 (910)
55	808 (815)	1016 (1029)	1219 (1247)
70	202 (163)	309 (231)	408 (300)
	Married women		
17	411 (391)	−171 (−245)	−764 (−891)
33	661 (665)	889 (778)	1126 (892)
55	932 (936)	1229 (1239)	1530 (1548)

TABLE 3.11.9
CONTINUING WAGE RATES FOR HYPOTHETICAL WOMEN
DEPENDING ON THEIR PROBABILITIES OF CONTINUING TO WORK

	Probability of continuing to work		
Age	.20	.50	.90
Unmarried women			
17	$1.86	$1.95	$2.05
33	1.25	1.79	2.58
55	.24	.74	2.32
70	3.29	2.43	1.79
Married women			
17	1.88	1.98	2.07
33	1.63	2.01	2.64
55	1.62	2.12	2.77

TABLE 3.11.10
CONTINUING HOURS OF WORK FOR HYPOTHETICAL WOMEN
DEPENDING ON THEIR PROBABILITIES OF CONTINUING TO WORK

	Probability of continuing to work		
Age	.20	.50	.90
Unmarried women			
17	729 (804)	1059 (1072)	1394 (1344)
33	1837 (1988)	1759 (1837)	1679 (1683)
55	1133 (1375)	1413 (1538)	1697 (1703)
70	8 (115)	747 (787)	1297 (1267)
Married women			
17	804 (866)	1134 (1134)	1469 (1407)
33	881 (919)	1135 (1155)	1398 (1394)
55	1349 (1375)	1364 (1377)	1380 (1378)

for our unmarried 70-year-old hypothetical woman, continuing wage rates rise substantially. From Table 3.11.10 we see that, except for our unmarried 33-year-old hypothetical woman, continuing hours of work also rise.

The conclusions that we draw are as follows:

1. There is as much evidence that the selection bias term belongs in our log wage and hours equations for men as there is for the inclusion of this term in our equations for women. In particular, there is no tendency for the coefficients of the selection bias term to become smaller in magnitude as we move from groups with low to those with high employment rates.
2. For women in most age-marital status groups, the effect of an increase in the probability of work as transmitted through a decrease in the value of the selection bias term is to increase both the starting, or continuing, wage rates and the starting, or continuing, hours of work. We find no systematic differences in the responses of married versus unmarried or younger versus older women. Nor do we find any systematic age-related response differences for women. The coefficient estimates for men indicate that their responses are similar to those of women in the case of the log wage, but they are opposite in sign for men at least 21 years of age in the case of hours of work.

3.12. Current Wage Rate

There has been a great deal of academic and public interest in the question of how, or whether, individuals adjust their hours of work in response to changes in their wage rates. Theoretically, the coefficient of the log wage variable in the hours equation should reflect the tradeoff between positive substitution effects and negative income effects. That is, as an individual's wage rate rises, we might expect this person to work longer hours because the opportunity cost of each hour of leisure is higher; but at the same time the individual will enjoy a higher income level for the same number of hours of work and hence, might be expected to consume more of all desirable goods, including leisure, leading to less work. The consensus that is often reported to emerge from the empirical literature is that the response of hours of work to a change in the wage rate is negative or insignificant for men, but strongly positive for women.[22] One rational offered for this apparent difference in the responses

3 Estimation Results for Our Inertia Model

of men and women is that women spend a substantial portion of their nonmarket time performing cooking, cleaning and childcare services that are not really leisure time activities and that can be purchased in the marketplace. Thus, the positive substitution effect should be stronger for women than for men who must substitute work in the marketplace for true leisure if they choose to work longer hours. Another rational is that the income effect will be weak for those working small numbers of hours, since in this case a change in the wage rate will necessarily result in a small income change. Many more women than men work small numbers of hours, of course.[23]

The unconditional labor supply function can always be written as the product of a function for the probability of work and a conditional labor supply function for the hours of work given that an individual does work. Thus, the full impact of a change in an individual's offered wage will consist of the impacts on the probability of work and on the expected hours of work given that an individual works. Theoretically, the impact of an increase in the offered wage on the hours of work of an individual who works may be either positive or negative because the income and substitution effects associated with such a wage change have impacts of opposite sign. However, following the reasoning of Ben-Porath (1973, p. 702), for those who are not working, there is no income effect from a wage rise, and hence, there will be only a substitution effect leading to an increase in the probability of work. We know of no empirical evidence contrary to this hypothesis concerning the effect of wage changes on participation.

However, _not all_ the findings reported in the literature support the conclusion that the response of hours of work to a wage change is positive _for working women_. It is true that except for the studies of Nakamura, Nakamura and Cullen (1979) and Nakamura and Nakamura (1981), the uncompensated wage elasticities of hours of work for women from the various studies summarized in Killingsworth (1983, Table 4.3, pp. 194-199) range in magnitude from -.89 to 15.24, with _most_ of the estimates being positive. However, estimates of the uncompensated wage elasticity of hours of work for wives from experimental data are found from Killingsworth (1983, Table 6.2, pp. 398-399) to range from -.36 to .94. Thus, while the estimates for wives from nonexperimental data are predominantly positive, and sometimes very large in magnitude; the estimates for wives from experimental data span roughly the same range as the estimates for men from both nonexperimental and experimental data (-.38 to .28).[24] Using nonexperimental data, Nakamura, Nakamura and Cullen (1979, p. 800) obtain uncompensated wage elasticities of hours of work for married women who work of -.320 to .299; Nakamura and Nakamura (1981, p. 483) report values of -.495 to .654; and values of -.197 to -.030 are reported in Nakamura and Nakamura

TABLE 3.12.1
IV COEFFICIENT ESTIMATES FOR OWN LOG
WAGE RATE IN HOURS EQUATIONS:
WORKING WOMEN WHO DID NOT WORK IN t-1

Marital status	Age 14-20	21-46	47-64	65+
Married		-397.3*	-106.2	
	192.7			217.9
Unmarried		210.3	-690.6**	

TABLE 3.12.2
IV COEFFICENT ESTIMATES FOR OWN LOG
WAGE RATE IN HOURS EQUATIONS:
WORKING WOMEN WHO WORKED IN t-1

Marital status	Age 14-20	21-46	47-64	65+
Married		85.2*	51.3	
	1241.8**			-222.6*
Unmarried		201.5**	104.0**	

TABLE 3.12.3
IV COEFFICIENT ESTIMATES FOR OWN LOG WAGE
RATE IN HOURS EQUATIONS: WORKING MEN

Work status in t-1	Age 14-20	21-46	47-64	65+
Did not work	-1185.8			
		112.1**	85.9*	105.2
Worked	-142.7			

(1983, p. 246). Although these results are dismissed as a "striking anomaly" by Killingsworth (1983, p. 192), we note that these results are similar to both the findings for wives from experimental data and to the results obtained by others for men using both nonexperimental data and experimental data.

3 Estimation Results for Our Inertia Model

Also, using yet another data set for Canada with an improved wage variable, Chris Robinson and Nigel Tomes (1985) have obtained results for married women that support our findings.

If it really is true that men work less, but working women work longer and longer hours as their wage rates rise, there are numerous implications. If real wage rates are eroded over time by inflation or higher taxes, for instance, men should fail to show any response or should increase their hours of work while women should work fewer hours. In a country like Canada where all spouses must file separate returns, all else being equal, wives should work more hours than in the United States, since the marginal tax rates that Canadian wives filing separately face are on the whole lower than for U.S. wives, who often file jointly with their husbands. Legislation resulting in higher wage rates for women should also lead them to work longer hours. In fact, according to this scenario, if women's wage rates are increased at the expense of male wage rates, everyone will work more.

In Tables 3.12.1 through 3.12.3, we show the coefficient estimates for our instrumental log wage variable in our hours equations. From Table 3.12.1 we see that for women who did not work in the previous year, the coefficient estimates are negative for three out of the six groups. Both for women who worked in the previous year and for men, however, the coefficient estimates are predominantly positive. These results suggest that there is a weak positive response of hours of work to a change in the wage rate for women who worked in the previous year and for men, at least for those between 21 and 64 years of age, but that the response for women who did not work in the previous year is negative.

Consider hypothetical women with the probabilities of starting work, and the starting wage rates and hours of work shown in Table 3.1.1. Suppose now that the starting wage rates for these women are instead set at $2.00, $3.00 or $4.50. We see from Table 3.12.4 that a 125 percent increase in the starting wage rate from $2.00 to $4.50 would cause our hypothetical women to alter their starting hours of work by −68 to 38 percent. Or suppose that we consider hypothetical women who worked last year and who have the probabilities of continuing to work, the continuing wage rates and the continuing hours of work shown in Table 3.1.2. Suppose that continuing wage rates for these women are set at $2.00, $3.00 or $4.50. From Table 3.12.5 we see that, except for the hypothetical 17-year-olds, a 125 percent increase in the continuing wage rate from $2.00 to $4.50 would cause these women to alter their continuing hours of work by only −14 to 8 percent. Thus, except for the youngest group, where there is a positive response of hours of work to a wage change, we find that the responsiveness of hours of work to a wage change is slight for women who worked last year compared to the

TABLE 3.12.4
STARTING HOURS OF WORK FOR HYPOTHETICAL
WOMEN DEPENDING ON THEIR STARTING WAGE RATES

	Starting wage rate		
Age	$2.00	$3.00	$4.50

Unmarried women

17	635	714	791
33	1002	1090	1174
55	820	537	260
70	458	547	634

Married women

17	635	714	791
33	719	556	397
55	715	671	629

TABLE 3.12.5
CONTINUING HOURS OF WORK FOR HYPOTHETICAL WOMEN
DEPENDING ON THEIR CONTINUING WAGE RATES

	Continuing wage rate		
Age	$2.00	$3.00	$4.50

17	1124	1633	2130
33	1619	1702	1783
55	1689	1732	1773
70	1074	983	894

Married women

17	1124	1633	2130
33	1338	1373	1407
55	1363	1384	1404

3 Estimation Results for Our Inertia Model

TABLE 3.12.6
ALTERNATIVE COEFFICIENT ESTIMATES FOR OWN
LOG WAGE RATE IN HOURS EQUATIONS:
WORKING WOMEN WHO DID NOT WORK IN t-1

Group	IV estimates	OLS estimates
Women 14-20	192.7	-38.1
Wives 21-46	-397.3*	-68.4*
Unmarried women 21-46	210.3	-16.3
Wives 47-64	-106.2	-263.5*
Unmarried women 47-64	-690.6**	-257.2**
Women 65+	217.9	-108.7**

TABLE 3.12.7
ALTERNATIVE COEFFICIENT ESTIMATES FOR OWN
LOG WAGE RATE IN HOURS EQUATIONS:
WORKING WOMEN WHO WORKED IN t-1

Group	IV estimates including lagged hours	OLS estimates including lagged hours	IV estimates without lagged hours
Women 14-20	1241.8**	-110.2**	1925.0**
Wives 21-46	85.2	-134.1**	-138.3**
Unmarried women 21-46	201.5**	-48.9*	-31.5
Wives 47-64	51.3	-111.3**	-398.2**
Unmarried women 47-64	104.0**	-55.4*	52.9
Women 65+	-222.6*	-279.0**	-210.6*

situation for women who did not work last year. This is what we would expect if women starting work have some degree of choice among jobs offering different wage and hours of work combinations and if women continuing on in the same job have little opportunity to alter their hours of work even if their wage rates change, due, for instance, to pay raises.

How sensitive to our estimation method are our estimates of the response of hours of work to a wage change? The wage variable is constructed by dividing reported earnings for the given calendar year by our measure of hours of work for this year. Hours figures that are erroneously low will result in erroneously high wage figures. This is the main reason that we use predicted, rather than actual, values for the log wage rate in our hours equations. We would expect the OLS (ordinary least squares) estimates of the coefficient of the log wage variable to be negatively biased due to the errors-in-variables problem involving the wage rate and hours of work figures. But the R^2 values for the equations from which we obtain our instrumental log wage variable range from only .056 to .223 for women who did not work in the previous year, from .081 to .490 for women who did work in the previous year, and from .078 to .523 for men. Thus, our auxiliary log wage equations are weak. The inclusion of the lagged dependent variable in equations for annual hours of work is not standard practice either and may result in special econometric problems.

We were curious as to how the IV (instrumental variables) coefficient estimates presented in Tables 3.12.1 through 3.12.3 would compare with IV estimates obtained without including the lagged dependent variable in the hours equations for men and for women who worked in the previous year and with OLS estimates of the coefficient of the log wage variable in the hours equations. These alternative sets of coefficient estimates are shown in Tables 3.12.6 through 3.12.8. We see that the OLS estimates of the coefficient of the log wage variable are always negative for both men and women. Comparing these coefficient estimates with the IV coefficient estimates shown in column one in each table, we find considerable support for the claim that the OLS coefficient estimates are negatively biased for both women <u>and</u> men.

The coefficient estimates shown in Table 3.12.6 are for women who did not work in the previous year, and hence, no information about hours of work in the previous year is included in the hours equations for these women. The IV estimates shown in the first column of Tables 3.12.7 and 3.12.8, however, are for hours equations that include hours of work in the previous year as an explanatory variable. Thus, in the last column of Tables 3.12.7 and 3.12.8, we show IV estimates for the coefficient of the log wage variable in the more standard hours equations that do not include the lagged

3 Estimation Results for Our Inertia Model

TABLE 3.12.8
ALTERNATIVE COEFFICIENT ESTIMATES FOR OWN
LOG WAGE RATE IN HOURS EQUATIONS: WORKING MEN

Group	IV estimates including lagged hours	OLS estimates including lagged hours	IV estimates without lagged hours
Men 14-20 who did not work in t-1	1185.8	-166.0**	
Men 14-20 who worked in t-1	-142.7	-232.9**	511.2**
Men 21-46	112.1**	-160.1**	-72.2**
Men 47-64	85.9**	-133.3**	-135.3**
Men 65+	105.2	-238.3**	-181.8*

TABLE 3.12.9
WAGE ELASTICITIES OF HOURS OF WORK EVALUATED
AT MEAN HOURS OF WORK:
WORKING WOMEN WHO DID NOT WORK IN t-1

Group	Using IV estimates	Using OLS estimates
Women 14-20	.32	-.06
Wives 21-46	-.59	-.10
Unmarried women 21-46	.21	-.02
Wives 47-64	-.14	-.32
Unmarried women 47-64	-.94	-.35
Women 65+	2.27	-1.13

TABLE 3.12.10
WAGE ELASTICITIES OF HOURS OF WORK EVALUATED AT MEAN
HOURS OF WORK: WORKING WOMEN WHO WORKED IN t-1

Group	Using IV estimates including lagged hours	Using OLS estimates including lagged hours	Using IV estimates without lagged hours
Women 14-20	1.12	-.10	1.73
Wives 21-46	.06	-.10	-.10
Unmarried women 21-46	.12	-.03	-.02
Wives 47-64	.04	-.08	-.29
Unmarried women 47-64	.06	-.03	.03
Women 65+	-.21	-.26	-.20

TABLE 3.12.11
WAGE ELASTICITIES OF HOURS OF WORK EVALUATED
AT MEAN HOURS OF WORK: WORKING MEN

Group	Using IV estimates including lagged hours	Using OLS estimates including lagged hours	Using IV estimates without lagged hours
Men 14-20 who did not work in t-1	-1.44	-.20	
Men 14-20 who worked in t-1	-.11	-.18	.39
Men 21-46	.05	-.07	-.03
Men 47-64	.04	-.06	-.06
Men 65+	.09	-.21	-.16

3 Estimation Results for Our Inertia Model

dependent variable on the right-hand side. The coefficient estimates for the log wage variable are now negative for four out of our six groups of women who worked in the previous year and for three out of four groups of men.

From the alternative coefficient estimates shown in Tables 3.12.6 through 3.12.8 for the log wage variable in our hours equations, we can calculate uncompensated wage elasticities of hours of work. These are shown in Tables 3.12.9 through 3.12.11. Some of the elasticity estimates for the youngest and oldest age groups do exceed 1 in magnitude. However, for prime-aged women who did not work in the previous year, the elasticities computed using IV coefficient estimates range from -.94 to .21, while those computed using OLS coefficient estimates range from -.35 to -.02. And for women 21 to 65 who worked in the previous year, the elasticities computed using IV coefficient estimates from hours equations including the lagged dependent variable range from .04 to .12, those computed using OLS coefficient estimates range from -.10 to -.03, and those computed using IV coefficient estimates from hours equations not including the lagged dependent variable range from -.29 to .03. For men 21 to 65, the elasticities computed using IV coefficient estimates from hours equations including the lagged dependent variable range from .04 to .09, those computed using OLS coefficient estimates range from -.21 to -.06, and those computed using IV coefficient estimates from hours equations not including the lagged dependent variable range from -.16 to -.03.

Several conclusions emerge from these empirical results:

1. No matter whether we use OLS or IV estimation, or whether or not we include the lagged dependent variable in the hours equation, for prime-aged men and women we find the wage elasticities of hours of work to be consistently less than 1 in magnitude. In fact, for prime-aged men and for prime-aged women who worked in the previous year, we find the wage elasticities of hours of work to be consistently less than .3 in magnitude.
2. Regardless of the estimation method, we find no clear evidence of a systematic difference between men and women in the signs of the wage elasticities of hours of work. However, there _may_ be some differences in the wage elasticities of hours of work over age groups. There may also be some differences in the wage elasticities for entering versus continuing workers.
3. Our findings with respect to the direction of the response of hours of work to a change in the wage rate depend crucially, and in the _same_ manner for both women and men, on whether an instrumental wage

variable is used and whether the lagged dependent variable is included in the hours equations. Our results suggest that OLS estimates of the coefficient of the log wage variable in our hours equations are negatively biased. If we stick to the usual specification of the hours equations without the lagged dependent variable on the right-hand side, the wage elasticities of hours of work computed using IV coefficient estimates are predominantly negative for both men and women. On the other hand, the wage elasticities of hours of work computed using IV coefficient estimates from hours equations including the lagged dependent variable on the right-hand side are predominantly positive for both men and for women who worked in the previous year, but they have a tendency to be negative for women who did not work in the previous year. At the very least, these results suggest that those claiming to have found substantial differences in the work behavior of women and men should be required to show empirical results for both women and men using essentially the same data source and estimation methods.[25]

FOOTNOTES TO CHAPTER 3

1. Hall (1973, Tables 3.2 and 3.3) presents similar tables for hypothetical individuals along with his tables of coefficient estimates.
2. Information about marital status in the year prior to the "current" year for which earnings and weeks of work data are collected could easily be collected on a recall basis, of course, in cross-sectional surveys.
3. Many interesting policy questions about women and work also involve women who may have been married, but who are currently unmarried (that is, single parents, widows, and so forth).
4. See Sweet (1973, pp. 164-165), Ross and Sawhill (1975), and SRI International (1983, Part V) for discussion and evidence relating to possible effects of work behavior and income on marital stability.
5. The effects of these factors are not always in the same direction. For example, poor health is negatively correlated with labor supply while cumulative work experience is probably positively correlated with labor supply. Since age picks up the effects of negative factors like poor health, as well as the effects of positive factors like experience, the signs of the coefficients of the age variable are difficult to

3 Estimation Results for Our Inertia Model

predict.

6. This part of our results and the rise in wage rates that we find over the 14-20 age bracket are in general agreement with the findings of other researchers. For instance, Hall (1973, p. 116) reports: "The striking characteristic of the age pattern of wages for women of both races is the failure of wages to rise with age after the early twenties." We see from the results in this section, however, that a much richer pattern of overall age effects emerges once we take account of work behavior in the previous year.

7. See Nakamura and Nakamura (1981, p. 465, fn. 11) for further references on what Heckman (1978, p. 205) terms, "the perverse association between wage rates and participation status ... found in demographic groups ... such as married black women."

8. See, for instance, Heckman (1974, 1976, 1980), Heckman and Macurdy (1980), Nakamura, Nakamura and Cullen (1979), and Nakamura and Nakamura (1981, 1983).

9. We have already mentioned the possibilities that employers may use education as a screening criterion and that an education variable may act as a proxy for variables such as ability or socioeconomic background. (See Thurow, 1972, 1975; Gintis, 1971; and Fraker, 1984.) There are also those who argue convincingly that education affects tastes and hence, that education should be included as an explanatory variable in the hours of work equations for married women, in contrast to the usual practice of assuming a priori that education will only affect the hours of work of a married woman indirectly through the impact of education on the wife's wage rate. (See, for instance, Michael, 1973.) The main reason for not doing this in studies like Nakamura, Nakamura and Cullen (1979) and Nakamura and Nakamura (1981, 1983a, 1983b) is that the predicted values of the wage rate that enter the hours equations are strongly affected by education, leading to severe problems of multicollinearity if education is also introduced into the hours equations as an independent explanatory variable. We were not even able to get around this problem by using a nonconventional instrument for the wage variable in the hours of work equations (Nakamura and Nakamura, 1983). This problem may be circumvented to some extent, however, in studies like this one that control for previous work behavior and that therefore control to some degree for education-related circumstances and tastes for work that are reflected in the person's previous work behavior.

10. See Mincer and Polachek (1974), Becker (1975), and Wachtel (1975). Becker (1975, p. 179) concludes that "even when the gain from a more lucrative marriage is included, the money rate of return from college seems less for women!"

11. In her study of the consequences of teenage women's nonemployment, Corcoran (1982, p. 393) concludes that "control

for differences in women's labor force attachment did not reduce the long-run costs associated with teenage nonemployment." Meyer and Wise (1982, p. 277) also find that "work experience acquired while in high school is strongly related to later employment."

12. See Meyer and Wise (1982) for an analysis of the relationship between high school curriculum, work experience, and academic achievement, on the one hand, and early labor force employment and wage rates, on the other. We note, however, that the log-linear functional form for wage or earnings equations in many models formally presented as one-period models is sometimes interpreted as arising from a cost function whose only components are the rising costs of income foregone in order to attend school (see Mincer, 1974).

13. Employment rates are somewhat higher for young persons who are currently out-of-school than for those who are attending school. See, for instance, Freeman and Medoff (1982, p. 45, Table 3.2).

14. Feldstein and Ellwood (1982, p. 24) suggest that "the family acts as an alternative source of income when young people are not working."

15. For instance, Heckman and Macurdy (1980) and Heckman (1981) include continuous variables for the number of children younger than 6 and for the total number of children at home. Nakamura, Nakamura and Cullen (1979) and Nakamura and Nakamura (1981) include continuous variables for the number of children younger than 6, the number of children 6 to 14 years of age, the number of children 19 to 24 years of age who are living at home and attending school, the number of children ever born, the product of the numbers of children in the younger than 6 and 6 to 14 age categories, and an interaction term created by dividing family income exclusive of the wife's earnings by family size.

16. T. Paul Schultz (1974, p. 287) notes:

A problem in the analysis of household behavior ... is whether short- or long-run response parameters are to be estimated. Estimates are usually obtained of the responsiveness of current flows of labor market services, (1) to current observed market wages, that are a reflection of past accumulated market experience and other human capital investments such as schooling, (2) nonearned income, that is associated with past accumulated savings, and (3) family composition, that represents past reproductive behavior.

In this study we are trying to estimate short-run response parameters. We are trying to isolate the current impacts of variables, such as our child status variables, on current work

3 Estimation Results for Our Inertia Model

behavior <u>after</u> <u>controlling</u> <u>for</u> <u>the</u> <u>cumulative</u> <u>impacts</u> of these variables, or of any unobservable factors like tastes for work, on work behavior. The realization that work behavior and child status, and perhaps other attributes such as education and marital status, may all be jointly determined to some extent <u>in</u> <u>a</u> <u>lifetime</u> <u>context</u> by common underlying preferences and circumstances can lead, as well, to a different sort of research effort aimed at measuring long-run response parameters. In this long-run context, an attempt is made to estimate the <u>total</u> impacts on both work behavior and fertility, for instance, of "exogenous" variables, like a person's place of residence at age 16 or his or her education (see T. Paul Schultz, 1974, p. 291), which are believed to determine or be associated with a person's unobservable tastes for home-oriented versus market-oriented activities. T. Paul Schultz (1974, p. 275) also asserts that "age is unassailably exogenous." See, for instance, T. Paul Schultz (1978,1980), Rosenzweig and Wolpin (1980), and Cain and Dooley (1976) for discussion and empirical evidence concerning these issues of endogeneity. See also Carliner, Robinson and Tomes (1980) and Robinson and Tomes (1982). The findings of T. Paul Schultz (1974) are consistent, for instance, with the hypothesis that the background factors that he considers (wife's residential origins at age 16, her age and the schooling of both spouses) largely determine both the observed child status and work behavior of married women. Having accepted this hypothesis, though, one still might want to determine, for instance, whether there are any short-run responses of current work behavior to changes in child status, after controlling for the cumulative effects of child status embedded in the previous year's work behavior.

17. Examples of studies that find that, after controlling for other factors, wives with husbands who earn more can be expected to work less include the cross-sectional studies of Heckman (1974,1976), Nakamura, Nakamura and Cullen (1979), and Nakamura and Nakamura (1981); and the panel data studies of Heckman (1978,1981).

18. In this regard, a married woman's life-time behavior may be based on the perceived permanent income of her husband, while adjustments to life-time behavior may be made based on the transitory component of her husband's income. See Mincer (1962) and Cain (1966), for instance, for further discussion and evidence related to this issue.

19. We found evidence of such a mutual retirement effect, for instance, in Nakamura and Nakamura (1983a).

20. Unemployment rate variables have been included in numerous studies of the labor force behavior of married women. For instance, Heckman (1981), in a study of the probability of employment for married women using data from the Michigan

Panel Study of Income Dynamics, includes among his explanatory variables both the unemployment rate in the county in which each woman resides and the national unemployment rate for prime-age males. Also Nakamura et al. (1979, Chapter 4) and Nakamura, Nakamura and Cullen (1979) include the provincial unemployment rate in a study based on micro data from the 1971 Census of Canada of the probabilities of work, wage rates and hours of work of married women. Nakamura and Nakamura (1981) include the state unemployment rate in the U.S. portion and the provincial unemployment rate in the Canadian portion of their analysis of the probabilities of work, wage rates and hours of work of U.S. and Canadian wives. The general consensus seems to be that higher rates of unemployment are associated with lower probabilities of employment for married women. We are not aware of any empirical work showing definitively that higher unemployment rates depress the wage rates of working women, however. It may be difficult to establish this empirically partly because it is difficult to control for changes in the type of women working as the level of unemployment changes.

21. In line with Bowen and Finegan's (1969) early work, Nakamura et al. (1979), Nakamura, Nakamura and Cullen (1979), and Nakamura and Nakamura (1981,1983) include indices of the local job opportunities for women in their studies, with the index included in Nakamura and Nakamura (1983) measuring job opportunities in terms of expected hours of work per expected working woman instead of as the expected number of jobs per woman in the potential labor force as is the case in the other studies cited. However measured, job opportunities per potential working woman seem to be positively associated with the probability of employment for women. These indices summarizing the job opportunities for women also seem to be positively related to the wage rates of women who work. The results reported in Nakamura, Nakamura and Cullen (1979, pp. 802-803) can provide the interested reader with a feel for the estimated responsiveness of the work behavior of individual wives to changes in the job opportunities for women. We did not include such a variable in the present study, largely because individuals are not identified by state of residence in the microanalytic simulation environment within which our labor force equations will be used.

Heckman (1981) also includes in his study the wage of unskilled labor in the county in which a woman resides. And Nakamura and Nakamura (1983a) include the state unemployment rate, the state average hourly wage rate in manufacturing measured in 1967 dollars, and first differences for both these variables in various models for the probability of work of married women. The results obtained for these macro variables are suggestive, but they do not provide us with clear evidence about how macroeconomic conditions influence or constrain the

3 Estimation Results for Our Inertia Model

employment and earnings behavior of individual wives.

22. For instance, Ehrenberg and Smith (1982, p. 166) write in their textbook:

> Numerous studies of labor-supply behavior have relied on cross-sectional data. These studies basically analyze labor-force participation or annual hours of work as they are affected by wage rates .... The findings discussed here are of <u>nonexperimental studies</u> .... Just about all studies of male labor-supply behavior indicate ... males have (individual) negatively sloped supply curves .... The estimates for women ... usually indicate ... a positively sloped labor supply curve.

23. Deaton and Muellbauer (1980, p. 276) argue, for instance:

> For men, whose shadow wage is low and who work relatively long hours, the income effect is dominant so that the labor supply curve is backward sloping, at least in the observed range. For women, however, the high value of time spent in the home sets a relatively high shadow wage and both participation and hours at work are lower than for men. With shorter working hours, the income effect is necessarily relatively unimportant, so that rising real wages account for greater labor supply by married women through increased participation and longer hours.

We attempted to test this hypothesis that the response of hours of work to a wage change differs depending on the number of hours worked in Nakamura and Nakamura (1983).

See Perlman (1969, pp. 4-24) for an introductory overview of some of the main ideas that have been advanced in the literature concerning the relationships among work time, leisure and nonmarket work time. Nonmarket work may include activities such as commuting and cleaning the house, for instance. Perlman summarizes Mincer's (1962) position that the fact that income from market work can be used to purchase substitutes for homework tends to make the labor supply curve for married women forward-sloping, since an increase in labor supply need not result in an equal reduction in leisure time in this case. Possibilities for men to substitute market time for nonmarket time are considered to be much less because they spend so little time, on the average, in nonmarket work.

See also Sharir (1975) for a simple graphical exposition of related issues.

24. Summarizing the results from a large number of more

recent studies of the work behavior of men based on nonexperimental data, Killingsworth (1983, pp. 193-194, Table 4.3) reports uncompensated wage elasticities of hours of work for men ranging from -.38 to .14. Killingsworth (1983, pp. 398-399, Table 6.2) also reports wage elasticities of hours of work for husbands from various studies based on negative income tax experimental data ranging in value from -.19 to .28. Thus, for men the range of values obtained using nonexperimental and experimental data is roughly the same and spans 0.

25. T. Paul Schultz (1973, p. 259) argues that "there are few instances ... where either pure wage or income effects can be identified and estimated from existing data." Da Vanzo, De Tray, and Greenberg (1976) report that, whereas the response of hours worked per week or per year to either an observed or imputed offered wage is always significantly negative when the sample is restricted to men who worked, this response is generally positive when men who did not work are included in the sample using imputed wage rates. Similar results are also reported by Garfinkel (1973, pp. 215-217). Thus, other researchers have also found the wage elasticities for men to be sensitive to the estimation method used.

CHAPTER 4

COMPARISONS OF OUR INERTIA MODEL
WITH VARIOUS SIMPLER MODELS

> Everything should be made
> as simple as possible,
> but not simpler. (Albert Einstein)

Our Inertia Model differs in at least two potentially important respects from other models of work behavior that have been presented in the literature. First, we have estimated separate sets of behavioral relationships for those who did not and for those who did work in the previous year. Second, in the behavioral relationships for those who did work in the previous year, we have included lagged variables for the wage rate and hours of work in the previous year. In section 4.1 we assess how these innovations in model specification affect our empirical results. In section 4.2 we use simulation methods to explore the extent to which our Inertia Model is an improvement over the simpler models for which empirical comparisons are made in section 4.1.

In section 3.12 we show that the estimates of a key parameter, the coefficient of the wage rate variable in the hours equations for those who worked in the previous year, are sensitive to whether or not the lagged hours of work variable is included in the specification of the hours equations for those who worked in the previous year. In section 4.3 we investigate the question of whether there are other empirical implications of this change in model specification. In this section we also explore the empirical implications of two aspects of the specification of models of the work behavior of women that have become standard practice: the incorporation of a selection bias term into the wage and hours of work equations as proposed by Heckman (1976),[1] and the use of a log-linear specification for the wage equation.[2] In section 4.4 we examine the differences in simulation results for the model variations for which differences in empirical results are explored in section 4.3.

In comparing alternative model specifications, even

though one may be found to be superior to the others in some overall sense, others may nevertheless be superior in the treatment of interactions involving one or more particular explanatory variables. This question is explored using simulation methods in section 4.5. We divide the individuals in our simulation population into subgroups depending on characteristics such as their child status or age, and then we check the ability of our alternative models to simulate the employment and work behavior of these subgroups. The variables used in forming these subgroups are variables for which substantial differences in the estimated coefficients or predictions for our hypothetical married women were identified in the first four sections of this chapter.

All of the simulation results presented in sections 4.2, 4.4 and 4.5 are in-sample simulation results in the sense that essentially the same data were used in the estimation of our model variations and in the simulation checks on these model variations. Since the data have been used in pooled form in the estimation of our behavioral relationships, there is no definitional reason why in-sample simulation results using these estimated relationships must capture aspects of the distributions for the dependent variables of interest viewed over time, such as the observed continuity in the actual employment and earnings histories of individuals. Moreover, in our simulations the wage rates and hours of work of individuals are generated in each time period for those individuals who are simulated to work, rather than for those individuals who actually did work; and after the first simulation period, the values for all lagged endogenous variables included in our models are the simulated, rather than the actual, values. Thus, there is no reason why even the distributions for our pooled in-sample simulation results must mirror the actual pooled distributions. We feel that in-sample simulations can often provide valuable insights into questions of model specification without, at the same time, requiring that some of the available data, which could otherwise be used for estimation of a model, be reserved for out-of-sample simulations. Nevertheless, there may be questions that could be more adequately settled with out-of-sample simulation results. Moreover, we are aware that many of our colleagues have an inherent mistrust of in-sample simulation checks. Thus, in section 4.6 we present simulation comparisons for all of our alternative model specifications using additional years of data from the PSID that were not available to us when we first began the research on which the rest of this book is based.

Finally, in section 4.7 we examine the issue of the sensitivity of the simulation comparisons presented in sections 4.2, 4.4, 4.5 and 4.6 to our treatment in our simulations of extreme wage estimates. As part of this examination, we report the results for additional simulations in which a more conventional truncation approach was used for dealing with the problem of extreme wage estimates. Our findings from these additional simulations are in agreement with the findings presented in the earlier sections of this chapter.

4.1. How Are Our Empirical Results Affected by the Incorporation of Information Concerning Work Behavior in the Previous Year?

Until quite recently, it was standard practice in empirical studies of the work behavior of individuals not to use any information about work behavior in previous years. Would empirical results for such a model differ in any important respects from the results presented in Chapter 3 for our Inertia Model? It is difficult to answer this question by making comparisons between the estimation results for our Inertia Model and those presented in the literature for models not incorporating information about previous work behavior, since these other studies are all based on other data sets and include different sets of explanatory variables. Thus, we have reestimated the coefficients of our probit indices and wage and hours equations using the same methodology used in estimating our Inertia Model, except that no differentiation is made between individuals depending on whether or not they worked in the previous year and the coefficients of the lagged wage and hours of work variables in these equations have all been set equal to 0. This is an empirical implementation, therefore, of the Standard Model described in section 2.2 and in the Addendum to Chapter 2. In addition to providing us with a basis for making comparisons, the Standard Model is of interest in its own right since this is the only sort of model that can be estimated in countries where data sets, like the PSID data, that contain information on both current and past work behavior do not exist or are not available for research purposes. This latter statement covers most of the world.

Heckman has suggested that what we call the Standard Model could be improved upon by adding a simple dummy variable set equal to 1 if the person worked in the previous year and set equal to 0 otherwise.[3] Thus, we have also reestimated the coefficients of our behavioral relationships for all relevant individuals in each demographic group without regard for their work status in the previous year, with the coefficients of the lagged wage and hours of work variables set equal to 0 and with a dummy variable added into each of our equations that is set equal to 1 if the individual worked in the previous year and set equal to 0 otherwise. We call this our Dummy Model.

Another way of using the same information incorporated into the Dummy Model would be to estimate the coefficients of our behavioral relationships separately for those who did and for those who did not work in the previous year, with the coefficients of the lagged wage and hours of work variables still set equal to 0. We call this our Split Model. The Split Model differs from the Dummy Model in that not only the constant terms, but also the slope coefficients of our behavioral relationships, are allowed to differ for individiuals who did versus individuals who did not work in the previous year.

The Dummy and Split Models are of special interest in the current Canadian context since the additional information required to estimate Canadian versions of these models could be collected by a simple rewording of a single question on a census questionnaire, such as the one used in either of the last two decennial censuses of population in Canada.[4] Presumably this information could also be easily collected on a recall basis as part of cross-sectional surveys in other countries where panel data are not available. There might even be reasons for collecting this information as part of the U.S. census of population. The information could be collected, as in the Canadian case, by the simple rewording of an existing question;[5] and national census data have certain advantages over PSID and other panel data in terms of the numbers of individuals of different types who are surveyed and the self-weighting nature of the data. Comparisons of the Dummy and Split Models versus the Standard Model should allow us to assess the value of having information for individuals on whether or not they worked in the previous year. Comparisons between the Dummy and Split Models should allow us to assess which would be the better way to use information of this sort if it were available. And comparisons of the Dummy and Split Models versus our Inertia Model should allow us to assess the value of collecting information about earnings and hours of work in the previous year in addition to collecting information on whether each individual worked in the previous year.

To conserve space we only show our comparative estimation results for the Standard, Dummy, Split and Inertia Models for wives 21-46 and wives 47-64 years of age, since the focus of this book is on the work behavior of married women. In Tables 4.1.1 and 4.1.2, we show coefficient estimates for our probit indices and hours equations for these four different model variants for our dummy variable set equal to 1 if a person was married in the previous year. The top number in each group of four lines of coefficient values in these and the following tables in this section is the coefficient estimate for the Standard Model. The next line is the coefficient estimate for

4 Comparisons of Our Inertia Model

TABLE 4.1.1
COEFFICIENT ESTIMATES FOR DIFFERENT METHODS
FOR DUMMY VARIABLE FOR MARRIED IN t-1 IN
PROBIT INDICES FOR PROBABILITY OF WORK: WOMEN

Wives 21-46	Wives 47-64
-.071	-.035
.179*	.209
-.195,.280**	-.997**,1.032**
-.195,.404**	-.997**,1.443**

TABLE 4.1.2
COEFFICIENT ESTIMATES FOR DIFFERENT METHODS
FOR DUMMY VARIABLE FOR MARRIED IN t-1 IN
HOURS EQUATIONS: WORKING WOMEN

Wives 21-46	Wives 47-64
11.3	68.8
-24.5	-150.1
-315.8*,-66.8	224.0,-311.0
-313.7*, 3.9	219.8, 479.7*

TABLE 4.1.3
COEFFICIENT ESTIMATES FOR DIFFERENT METHODS
FOR AGE, RACE DUMMY AND EDUCATION VARIABLES
IN PROBIT INDICES FOR PROBABILITY OF WORK: WOMEN

Group	Age	Race dummy	Education
Wives 21-46	.005*	.171**	.132**
	.006*	.072	.076**
	-.020**,-.025**	-.051, .111	.114**,.058**
	-.020**, .020**	-.051,-.059	.114**,.036*
Wives 47-64	-.070**	.426**	.113**
	-.036**	.096	.052**
	-.055**,-.023*	.014,.155	.038,.059*
	-.055**,-.029**	.014,.062	.038,.044

the Dummy Model. The next line gives the coefficient estimates for the Split Model for those who did not and those who did work in the previous year, in this order. The last line in each group gives the coefficient estimates of the Inertia Model for those who did not and those who did work in the previous year, in this order. The coefficient estimates for the Inertia Model for wives 21-46 and wives 47-64 have already been presented, along with the estimation results for other demographic groups in Chapter 3. These selected estimation results for the Inertia Model are shown again in the tables in this section for convenience. In the following discussion we will only mention aspects of our results where there are systematic differences among our models.

From the estimation results for the Standard and Dummy Models reported in Tables 4.1.1 and 4.1.2, we would probably conclude that the dummy variable for marital status in the previous year does not belong in the model. On the other hand, our results for the Split and Inertia Models indicate that wives who did not work in the previous year are less likely to start work if they were married in the previous year as well, while the reverse is true for wives who did work in the previous year. These effects are particularly large in magnitude for wives 47-64 years of age. In other words, wives who have not changed marital status in the last year are more likely than otherwise to continue in the same work status category as in the previous year, particularly as they get older.

In Tables 4.1.3 through 4.1.5, we show our probit index, log wage and hours equation coefficient estimates for the Standard, Dummy, Split and Inertia Models for our age, race dummy and education variables.

From Table 4.1.3 we find that the effect of increasing age on the probability of work for wives 21-46 is positive for the Standard and Dummy Models, negative for both those who did not and those who did work in the previous year for the Split Model, and negative for those who did not work in the previous year but positive for those who did for the Inertia Model. For wives 47-64 years of age, the impact of increasing age on the probability of starting work is negative according to all four model variants; but according to the Split and Inertia Models, the negative impact of increasing age is larger in magnitude for those who did not versus those who did work in the previous year. From Table 4.1.4 we find that according to the Standard and Dummy Models, wage rates rise with increasing age for wives 21-46 years of age and fall with increasing age for wives 47-64 years of age. According to the Split and Inertia Models, however, wage rates fall with increasing age for wives 21-46 years of age who did not work in the previous year, while the evidence of change in wage rates as age increases is unclear for wives 47-64 years of age. From Table 4.1.5 we see

4 Comparisons of Our Inertia Model   203

TABLE 4.1.4
COEFFICIENT ESTIMATES FOR DIFFERENT METHODS
FOR AGE, RACE DUMMY AND EDUCATION VARIABLES
IN WAGE EQUATIONS: WORKING WOMEN

Group	Age	Race dummy	Education
Wives 21-46	.004**	-.021	.116**
	.005**	-.018	.120**
	-.014**,.003*	-.239*,-.037	.140**,.110**
	-.014**,.001	-.066, -.065**	.141**,.086**
Wives 47-64	-.027**	.204**	.171**
	-.011*	-.068	.138**
	-.014,.005	.052, .022	.102*,.125**
	.011,.007	.053,-.071	.102*,.072**

TABLE 4.1.5
COEFFICIENT ESTIMATES FOR DIFFERENT METHODS
FOR AGE VARIABLE AND RACE DUMMY IN HOURS EQUATIONS:
WORKING WOMEN

Group	Age	Race dummy
Wives 21-46	-1.1	171.6**
	-3.1*	203.2**
	-4.6,-8.4**	313.0**,167.2**
	-4.4,-5.0**	252.8**, 82.6**
Wives 47-64	4.2	46.1
	-17.7	141.7*
	-62.4,-14.3**	-117.8,149.4*
	-62.8,-10.4*	-117.3, 59.9

that the Dummy, Split and Inertia Models all predict more rapid declines in hours of work in response to increasing age than does the Standard Model, particularly for wives 47-64 years of age.

According to the Standard Model, from Table 4.1.3 we find that black wives in both age groups have a considerably higher probability of work than otherwise similar nonblack wives.[6] Also, for the Standard Model we find from Table 4.1.4 that 21-46-year-old black wives have slightly lower wage rates, while 47-64-year-old black wives have higher wage rates on the average than otherwise similar nonblack wives; and from Table 4.1.5 we find that black wives tend to work longer hours. The Standard Model seems to suggest, therefore, that the expected earnings for black wives are higher than for otherwise-similar nonblack wives. In the case of the Dummy Model, the estimated increases in the probit indices for the probability of work for wives 21-46 and 47-64 years of age associated with being black are much smaller than for the Standard Model, and black wage rates are found to be systematically lower after controlling for other factors for both age groups of wives. For the Split Model the probability of work is found to be lower for 21-46-year-old black wives who did not work in the previous year than for otherwise-similar nonblack wives, and for the Inertia Model the probability of work is found to be lower for black wives 21-46 years of age who did not or did work in the previous year compared with otherwise-similar nonblack wives. Moreover, both the Split and Inerita Models predict substantially lower wage rates for 21-46-year-old black wives than for otherwise-similar nonblack wives compared with the results for the Standard and Dummy Models.

From Table 4.1.3 we see that the Standard Model predicts relatively large positive impacts of the education variable on the probability of work for both age groups of wives, while the Dummy Model predicts smaller positive impacts for both age groups. The Split and Inertia Models, on the other hand, predict a large positive impact of the education variable on the probability of work for 21-46-year-old wives who did not work in the previous year and relatively small positive impacts for this variable for wives 21-46-years-old who worked in the previous year and for wives 47-64 years of age. This pattern for the magnitudes of the coefficient estimates for the education variable can be seen from Table 4.1.4 to be approximately replicated for the log wage equations. However, for the education variable the coefficient estimates are all positive for all model variants.

The probit index and hours equation coefficient estimates for the different model variants for our three child status variables are shown in Tables 4.1.6 and 4.1.7.

From the results for the Split and Inertia Models shown in Table 4.1.6, we see that the birth of a baby is more likely to cause a change in work status from the previous to the current year for wives who worked in the previous year than for wives who did not, while the reverse is true if the youngest child is less than 6 but not a new baby. That is, the coefficient estimates for the Split and Inertia Models for the baby dummy are larger in magnitude for wives who worked in the

TABLE 4.1.6
COEFFICIENT ESTIMATES FOR DIFFERENT METHODS FOR CHILD STATUS VARIABLES IN PROBIT INDICES FOR PROBABILITY OF WORK: WOMEN

Group	Baby dummy	Young child dummy	Number of children younger than 18
Wives 21-46	-.558**	-.512**	-.058**
	-.395**	-.302**	-.003
	-.188,-.636**	-.458**,-.187**	.072**,-.068**
	-.188,-.528**	-.458**,-.130*	.072**, ----
Wives 47-64			-.030
			-.044
			.010,.045
			-.010,-----

TABLE 4.1.7
COEFFICIENT ESTIMATES FOR DIFFERENT METHODS FOR CHILD STATUS VARIABLES IN HOURS EQUATIONS: WORKING WOMEN

Group	Baby dummy	Young child dummy	Number of children younger than 18
Wives 21-46	-73.6	58.6	-42.2**
	-148.6*	-61.6	-44.8**
	-141.0,23.3	58.9,-30.3	-25.2,-31.8
	-135.2,58.0	70.2, 4.0	-26.7, ----
Wives 47-64			-59.9**
			-67.2**
			-60.1,-58.7**
			-59.9, ----

previous year than for those who did not, while the reverse is true for the coefficient estimates for these models for the young child dummy. Response differences of this sort cannot be captured in the Standard and Dummy Models. From Table 4.1.7 we see that the impacts on hours of work of the baby dummy are negative for both the Standard and Dummy Models, but they are negative only for wives who did not work in the previous year for the Split and Inertia Models.

TABLE 4.1.8
COEFFICIENT ESTIMATES FOR DIFFERENT METHODS
FOR HUSBAND'S INCOME VARIABLES IN PROBIT
INDICES FOR PROBABILITY OF WORK: WOMEN

Group	Husband's income	Change in husband's income	Negative change in husband's income
Wives 21-46	-.055**	.041**	
	-.029**	.024**	
	-.033**,-.029**	.011,.043**	
	-.033**, ----	.011,.019*	
Wives 47-64	-.005		.068**
	-.004		.079**
	-.029*,.015		.042,.096**
	-.029*,----		.042,.113**

TABLE 4.1.9
COEFFICIENT ESTIMATES FOR DIFFERENT METHODS
FOR HUSBAND'S INCOME VARIABLES IN HOURS EQUATIONS:
WORKING WOMEN

Group	Husband's income	Change in husband's income	Negative change in husband's income
Wives 21-46	-.6	-3.2	
	-10.4**	2.7	
	-7.2,-3.8	-15.1*, -4.4	
	-6.3, ---	-15.4*,-10.1**	
Wives 47-64	10.4*		-49.8*
	5.8		-28.3
	-57.4*,9.0*		-53.1,-33.1
	-57.5*,---		-52.7, 9.3

In Tables 4.1.8 through 4.1.11, we show the probit index and hours equation coefficient estimates for our four different model variants for the other income variables. We see from Tables 4.1.8 and 4.1.9 that for all methods the signs are predominantly negative for the coefficients of the husband's income variable, but they are positive for the

TABLE 4.1.10
COEFFICIENT ESTIMATES FOR DIFFERENT METHODS
FOR AFDC AND SOCIAL SECURITY DUMMY VARIABLES IN
PROBIT INDICES FOR PROBABILITIY OF WORK: WOMEN

Group	Dummy for AFDC in t-1	Dummy for Social Security in t-1
Wives 21-46	-.485** -.380* .154,-1.004** .154, -.509*	
Wives 47-64		-.554** -.495* -.486,-.448 -.486,-.373

TABLE 4.1.11
COEFFICIENT ESTIMATES FOR DIFFERENT METHODS
FOR AFDC AND SOCIAL SECURITY DUMMY VARIABLES
IN HOURS EQUATIONS: WORKING WOMEN

Group	Dummy for AFDC in t-1	Dummy for Social Security in t-1
Wives 21-46	-263.3* -207.9 -196.2, 17.8 -204.4,218.0	
Wives 47-64		-10.7 -204.6 -592.8,-111.0 -594.6, 101.8

coefficients for our variables for change in the husband's income. From Tables 4.1.10 and 4.1.11, we see that based on the Standard or Dummy Model, we would conclude that AFDC payments in the previous year are associated with lower labor supply in the current year, while the Split and Inertia Models provide weak support, at best, for this position.

TABLE 4.1.12
COEFFICIENT ESTIMATES FOR DIFFERENT METHODS
FOR MACROECONOMIC VARIABLES IN PROBIT INDICES
FOR PROBABILITY OF WORK: WOMEN

Group	National unemployment rate	National wage index
Wives 21-46	.007	.0047**
	.021	.0047**
	.018, .027	.0068**, .0032*
	.018, .028	.0068**, .0019
Wives 47-64	-.023	.0038*
	.011	.0037
	.033, -.020	.0041, .0044
	.033, .001	.0041, .0041

TABLE 4.1.13
COEFFICIENT ESTIMATES FOR DIFFERENT METHODS
FOR MACROECONOMIC VARIABLES IN LOG WAGE EQUATIONS:
WORKING WOMEN

Group	National unemployment rate	National wage index
Wives 21-46	-.021*	-.0004
	-.017*	.0003
	-.046, -.017*	.0001, -.0003
	-.046, -.024**	.0002, -.0008
Wives 47-64	.006	.0003
	.025	.0000
	.067, .012	-.0038, -.0005
	.067, .006	-.0038, -.0012

We show the probit index and log wage equation coefficient estimates for the four model variants for the macroeconomic variables in Tables 4.1.12 and 4.1.13. There are no interesting model-specific differences in our estimation results for these variables.

The log wage and the hours equation coefficient estimates

TABLE 4.1.14
COEFFICIENT ESTIMATES FOR DIFFERENT METHODS FOR SELECTION BIAS TERM IN LOG WAGE EQUATIONS: WORKING WOMEN

Wives 21-46	Wives 47-64
-.001	.659**
.309**	.817**
.478*,-.223*	-.107,-.001
.497*,-.437**	-.104,-.450**

TABLE 4.1.15
COEFFICIENT ESTIMATES FOR DIFFERENT METHODS FOR SELECTION BIAS TERM IN HOURS EQUATIONS: WORKING WOMEN

Wives 21-46	Wives 47-64
-608.7**	-624.3*
-256.5	-391.0
-165.5,-868.4*	-510.4,-568.9
-187.3,-392.9*	-505.5, -2.4

TABLE 4.1.16
COEFFICIENT ESTIMATES FOR DIFFERENT METHODS FOR OWN LOG WAGE RATE IN HOURS EQUATIONS: WORKING WOMEN

Wives 21-46	Wives 47-64
-217.0*	-194.3
23.1	40.1
-376.0* ,-39.8	-109.2, 7.0
-397.3**, 85.2*	-106.2,51.3

for our model variants for the selection bias term are shown in Tables 4.1.14 and 4.1.15. The coefficient of the selection bias term in the log wage equation is found to be essentially 0 or positive using the Standard and Dummy Models, but it is found to be positive for wives 21-46 who did not work in the previous year and negative otherwise using the Split and

Inertia Models. From Table 4.1.15 we see that the coefficient of the selection bias term in the hours equation is generally smaller in magnitude for the model variants other than the Standard Model, all of which include some information about work behavior in the previous year.

The coefficient estimates for our Standard, Dummy, Split and Inertia Models for the own log wage variable in our hours equations are shown in Table 4.1.16. We find the coefficient estimates for both age groups are negative for the Standard Model in line with the results published in our earlier cross-sectional studies using U.S. and Canadian census data.[7] In contrast, these coefficient estimates are positive and small in magnitude for the Dummy Model, and negative for wives who did not work in the previous year and positive with one exception for wives who did work in the previous year for the Split and Inertia Models.

4.2. Simulation Comparisons for Our Standard, Dummy, Split and Inertia Models

In section 4.1 we establish that there are differences in sign and magnitude for the coefficient estimates of our Inertia Model versus the Standard, Dummy and Split Models. The most striking differences are between the Standard and Dummy Models versus the Split and Inertia Models. These differences are probably primarily due to the fact that for the Split and Inertia Models, separate sets of behavioral relationships are estimated for those who did not and for those who did work in the previous year, whereas this is not the case for the Standard and Dummy Models. We also note in the introductory remarks to this chapter that there are important differences in the data requirements of these four models. In particular, the Standard Model can be estimated using cross-sectional data of the sort commonly available from national population censuses. The Dummy and Split Models require information about work status in the previous year that could be easily collected on a recall basis as part of cross-sectional surveys. The Inertia Model requires information on hours of work and earnings, as well as work status, in the previous year. This additional information could also be collected on a recall basis as part of cross-sectional surveys, such as population censuses.

An estimated model, including an estimated parametric description of the disturbance terms of the model, specifies a predicted joint distribution for all of the dependent variables of the model for any given set of initial conditions for lagged dependent variables and values for variables being treated as exogenous to the model. We will now examine how various aspects of the predicted joint distributions of the dependent variables of our Inertia, Standard, Dummy and Split Models compare with these aspects of the actual joint distributions of the dependent variables of interest.

All of the simulations for which results are given in this section are for the years of 1971 through 1977.[8] In each year of the simulation for each individual included in the simulation (that is, for each individual in the simulation population), we calculate the value of the appropriate estimated probit index depending on which model is being used and which of our ten demographic groups the individual belongs to. The values of all explanatory variables, except those dependent and lagged dependent variables for which values are generated in the simulation, are the actual observed values. The probability of work for the individual in the given year is found from the computed value of the individual's probit index using a subroutine for the cumulative standard normal distribution. A drawing is then taken from a uniform distribution; and if the value drawn is less than the computed probability of work, the individual is simulated to work in that year. For each individual simulated to work in a year, a predicted value of the selection bias term is calculated using the computed value of the probit index. Next, a predicted conditional expected value is calculated for the log wage using the appropriate estimated relationship for the given model and the individual's demographic group. Then, a predicted conditional expected value is calculated for the hours of work using the estimated relationship for the given model and demographic category and using the value already calculated for the predicted expected log wage. Random drawings are taken from normal distributions with 0 means and with standard deviations set equal to the appropriate regression standard errors, and these are added to the predicted conditional expected values for the log wage and hours of work in order to obtain a predicted log wage and a predicted value for hours of work. The predicted wage is calculated as the antilog of the predicted log wage. Finally, the predicted income for the year is calculated as the product of the predicted wage and the predicted hours of work. In the first year of the simulation, the values used for all lagged endogenous variables are the actual values reported for the year prior to the first simulation year. After this, the values used are the simulated values generated in the previous year. Using this simulation procedure, therefore, we create the joint distribution of the dependent variables of interest for each of our models. The characteristics of these distributions for our models are compared in this section with the actual joint distribution for the relevant variables. The simulation data set for all of our in-sample simulations, including the simulations for which results are presented in this section, consists of the first 7 of the 8 years of data that make up the pooled data base used in estimating all of our models.

It is the characteristics of the predicted versus the actual distributions of the dependent variables that are of concern to us, rather than the extent to which we are actually able to reproduce the work histories of the individuals in our simulation population. If several individuals in our simulation population are virtually the same in terms of their observed characteristics but exhibit different work behavior over the relevant time period, all that matters is that we correctly simulate the mix of work behaviors. We must, of course, carefully consider which characteristics of the mix of work behaviors are the characteristics of concern to us.

Notice that in all of the models that use information about work behavior in the previous year, errors made in determining the work behavior of an individual in one year will feed into and distort our determination of the work behavior of the individual in years to come. Also, errors in prediction that are systematic for any of our models, coming from any sort of a bias or misspecification of the model, will probably recur for relevant individuals in more than 1 year over the 7-year simulation period. Thus, these sorts of errors in the yearly determination of the work behavior of individuals should be magnified when we look at characteristics concerning the joint distribution of the dependent variables that have to do with the work histories of individuals over the 7-year simulation period. In particular, since earnings histories summarize the work decisions, wage rates, and hours of work of individuals over the given period of years, the predicted distribution of individual incomes cumulated over the 7-year simulation period should provide a good summary of the overall performance of a model. The distribution of individual earnings cumulated over time may also be of special interest since it is often earnings, rather than wage rates, hours of work or the work decision itself, that are the focus of interest.[9]

We begin by looking at the simulation results for our Standard, Dummy, Split and Inertia Models on a yearly basis. For each year for each of our models, we have computed the proportion of all individuals, as well as the proportion of individuals who were in each of our ten demographic groups in the first year of the simulation period, who are simulated to work in the given year. These results are shown in Tables A.1 through A.7 in Appendix A for all individuals and for the six groups of women. All four models can be seen to capture the gross differences among different demographic groups in the employment rate. All four models also capture, in a rough sense, the slight increase over the simulation period in the

4 Comparisons of Our Inertia Model

proportion of all individuals found to work, as well as the more marked increase over the simulation period in the proportion of women 21-46 years of age and married at the start of the simulation who are found to work. The Standard and Inertia Models also capture the considerable drop over time in the employment rate for women at least 65 years of age at the start of the simulation, but this drop is not captured by the Dummy or Split Model. None of the models captures the drop in 1975 and 1976 in the employment rate for women who were 14-20 years of age at the start of the simulation, though all of the models capture the rise from 1971 to 1974 in the employment rate for this group. Finally, all of the models capture, to some extent, the lack of trends over time in the employment rates for women who were 21-46 and unmarried, women who were 47-64 and married, and women who were 47-64 and unmarried at the start of the simulation, except for the Dummy Model for the 47-64 year old and married group.

For each year and each of our models, we have also computed the average simulated wage rate for all individuals and for the individuals who were in each of our ten demographic groups in the first year of the simulation period. These results are shown in Tables A.8 through A.14 in Appendix A for all individuals and for our six groups for women. From these tables we see that all models capture to some degree the rise over the simulation period in the average wage rate for all individuals, the elevation of wage rates from 1974 to 1976 for women 14-20 at the start of the simulation, the rise with time in the average wage for women 21-46 years of age and unmarried at the start of the simulation, and the 1972 dip in the average wage for women at least 65 years of age at the start of the simulation. All of the models also reflect the lack of any clear pattern of change over time in the average wage for women 47-64 years of age and unmarried at the start of the simulation. All of the models except the Split Model capture both the 1974 dip in the average wage and the general rise in the average wage over the 7-year simulation period for women 21-46 years of age and married in the first year of the simulation, and all of the models except the Dummy and Split Models capture the 1975 dip in the average wage and the general rise in the average wage over the simulation period for women 47-64 years of age and married at the start of the simulation. None of the models, however, captures the drop in the average wage from 1971 to 1973 for women 14-20 at the start of the simulation.

Average simulated hours of work per year were also computed for each model for all individuals and for the individuals in each of our ten demographic groups at the beginning of the simulation period. These results are shown in Tables A.15 through A.21 for all individuals and for our six groups for women. We see from these tables that all of the

TABLE 4.2.1
GROUPS FOR WHICH STANDARD MODEL IS WORSE THAN DUMMY,
SPLIT AND INERTIA MODELS IN TERMS OF MAGNITUDES
OF AVERAGE DEVIATIONS FOR VARIABLES OF INTEREST

Group	Proportion simulated to work each year	Average wage	Average hours	Average income
All individuals				
Women 14-20		*		
Wives 21-46				
Unmarried women 21-46				
Wives 47-64		*		
Unmarried women 47-64				*
Women 65+				

models capture the general rise over the simulation period in the average hours of work for all individuals, the steep rise over time in the average hours of work for women 14-20 at the start of the simulation, the rise over time in average hours for women 21-46 and married in the first simulation year, and the fall in average hours from 1974 through 1977 for women 21-46 years of age and unmarried at the beginning of the simulation. All four models also reflect the lack of trend over time in average hours of work for women 47-64 and married, women 47-64 and unmarried, and women at least 65 years of age at the start of the simulation.

The income for each individual found to work in each year is computed as the product of the individual's wage rate and hours of work for that year. Average simulated annual income figures were computed for each model for all individuals and for the individuals in each of our ten demographic groups at the start of the simulation. These figures are shown in Tables A.22 through A.28 for all individuals and for our six groups of women. From these tables it can be seen that all four of our models capture the general rise over time in the average annual income for all individuals and for women 14-20 years of age at the start of the simulation, as well as the steep drop

4 Comparisons of Our Inertia Model 215

TABLE 4.2.2
GROUPS FOR WHICH DUMMY OR SPLIT MODEL IS AS GOOD OR
BETTER THAN STANDARD MODEL IN TERMS OF MAGNITUDES
OF AVERAGE DEVIATIONS FOR VARIABLES OF INTEREST

Group	Proportion simulated to work each year	Average wage	Average hours	Average income
All individuals				
Women 14-20		*	*	*
Wives 21-46	*		*	
Unmarried women 21-46			*	*
Wives 47-64		*		*
Unmarried women 47-64		*	*	*
Women 65+			*	

from 1971 to 1972 in the average income of women at least 65 years of age at the start of the simulation. All of the models reflect the lack of any clear trend in average incomes over the simulation period for women 21-46 and unmarried, women 47-64 and married, and women 47-64 and unmarried in the first year of the simulation period, except perhaps the Split Model for the latter two groups of women. All of the models except the Split Model also capture the rise in the average income for women 21-46 years of age and married at the start of the simulation.

Another way of judging the yearly averages for our four models shown in Tables A.1 through A.28 is in terms of the magnitudes of the average differences over the simulation period between the actual and simulated average values. These averages of averages, so to speak, are shown in the bottom row on each of these tables. To calculate the 0.0 shown at the bottom of column one on Table A.1, for instance, we took the difference between the actual percentage point employment rate and the proportion, measured in percentage points, of individuals simulated to work using the Standard Model for each of the 7 years in our simulation period. We summed these 7 differences and then divided by 7.

TABLE 4.2.3
GROUPS FOR WHICH SPLIT MODEL IS AS GOOD OR BETTER
THAN DUMMY MODEL IN TERMS OF MAGNITUDES OF AVERAGE
DEVIATIONS FOR VARIABLES OF INTEREST

Group	Proportion simulated to work each year	Average wage	Average hours	Average income
All individuals	*	*		
Women 14-20		*		
Wives 21-46			*	*
Unmarried women 21-46	*		*	*
Wives 47-64	*		*	*
Unmarried women 47-64				
Women 65+	*			

The magnitudes of these average differences provide us with one sort of performance ranking for our four alternative models. (The following comparative results are not changed, in general, by using average squared or absolute differences to rank our models.) Using this criterion, in Table 4.2.1 we indicate with a star the demographic groups for which the Standard Model is worse than the Dummy, Split and Inertia Models in terms of the proportion of individuals simulated to work each year, the simulated average wage, the simulated average hours of work, or the simulated average income. In Table 4.2.2 we indicate with a star the groups for which the Dummy or Split Model is as good as or better than the Standard Model for each of the same average simulated variables. In Table 4.2.3 the Split Model is compared with the Dummy Model. Finally, in Table 4.2.4 we indicate those groups for which the Inertia Model outperforms our other three models in terms of the stated measure of performance for each of the dependent variables of interest. No clear differences among our models emerge from Tables 4.2.1 through 4.2.4. If we had to choose a model on the basis of the summary results contained in Tables A.1 through A.28, we would probably choose the Standard Model since the performance for this model does not appear worse

4 Comparisons of Our Inertia Model

TABLE 4.2.4
GROUPS FOR WHICH INERTIA MODEL IS AS GOOD OR BETTER
THAN STANDARD, DUMMY AND SPLIT MODELS IN TERMS OF
MAGNITUDES OF AVERAGE DEVIATIONS FOR VARIABLES OF INTEREST

Group	Proportion simulated to work each year	Average wage	Average hours	Average income
All individuals				
Women 14-20	*			
Wives 21-46				
Unmarried women 21-46				
Wives 47-64			*	
Unmarried women 47-64	*			
Women 65+	*			

than the performance for the other three models and the Standard Model does not require information on work behavior in the previous year.

The results displayed in Tables A.1 through A.28 and summarized in Tables 4.2.1 through 4.2.4 reveal nothing, however, about the extent to which there are systematic prediction errors that occur year after year for particular individuals. Stated somewhat differently, Tables A.1 through A.28 show us nothing about the extent to which our four alternative models succeed in capturing the observed continuity over time in individual work behavior and earnings. Nor do these tables tell us anything about the extent to which our four alternative models succeed in capturing the distributions, as contrasted with the averages, for relevant dependent variables.

The pooled distributions for simulated annual hours of work are shown in Tables B.1 through B.7 in Appendix B for all individuals and for each of our six groups of women classified according to their demographic group in the first year of the simulation. For all groups except women at least 65 years of age in the first year of the simulation period, these pooled distributions display essentially the same pattern of shortcomings for all four alternative models. With a few exceptions for the unmarried groups, this pattern is that there are too many observations in the 0 hours, or no work, category; too few observations in the 1 to 600 hours category; too many observations in the 601 to 1,200, 1,201 to 1,400, and 1,401 to 1,800 hours categories; too few, often many too few, observations in the 1,801 to 2,200 category; and too many observations in the 2,201-and-over category. Nevertheless, the simulated distributions of pooled annual hours of work for all four of our models have the same basic shape, at least, as the actual distributions for all individuals and for all six of our demographic groupings for women.

The pooled distributions for simulated annual income are shown in Tables B.8 through B.14. Again, all of these pooled distributions for all four models, with a small number of exceptions, display the same pattern of deficiencies. There are too few observations in the $1 - 1,000 category, too many in the $1,001 - 2,000 and $2,001 - 5,000 categories, and too few in the $10,000 - 20,000 category. However, all four models capture the overall shape of the pooled annual income distributions.

In Tables B.15 through B.21, we show the simulated distributions of individuals classified by number of years of work out of 7 for all four of our models. For the first time, a clear-cut difference can be seen between the results for the Standard Model versus our results for the other three models. For the Standard Model we always find far too many observations in two or more of the middle three groups of 1-2, 3-4, and 5-6 years of work out of 7, and we find way too few observations in the groups of 0 and of 7 years of work. For the other three models there is also some tendency to place too many observations in the intermediate categories for years of work and too few in the categories of no years of work or all years of work; but the degree of distortion is, on the whole, small and always much less than for the Standard Model.

It is those who work full-time year after year who take home the largest share of total personal income and who are most likely to accumulate substantial pension and Social Security benefits. Thus, in Tables B.22 through B.28, we show the simulated distributions of individuals classified by the number of years out of 7 when they worked any positive number of hours up to 1,400 hours, or part-time, and by the number of years out of 7 when they worked more than 1,400 hours, or full-time. From these tables, as from Tables B.15 through B.21, we see that the Standard Model consistently underestimates the proportion of individuals not working at all over the 7-year period, with the other models all performing much better for this category. We also see that all four models almost always overestimate the proportion of individuals in the intermediate category of 1-3 years of

4 Comparisons of Our Inertia Model

part-time work and 1-3 years of full-time work. The degree of overestimation for this intermediate category is always most serious for the Standard Model, followed by the Dummy and Split Models, sometimes in this order and sometimes in reverse order, and then followed by the Inertia Model. The Standard, Dummy and Split Models all underestimate the proportion of individuals who worked 4-6 part-time years and no full-time years, except for women who were 47-64 years of age and unmarried in the first year of the simulation period, while the Inertia Model generally performs well for this category. Finally, except for women 47-64 years of age and unmarried and for women 65 years of age or older at the start of the simulation, the Standard, Dummy and Split Models always substantially underestimate the proportion of individuals who worked full-time in all 7 years. The Inertia Model generally underestimates the proportion of individuals in this important full-time category too, but the degree of underestimation is somewhat less. At least for the Inertia Model, there is a clear resemblance between the shapes of the simulated and actual distributions of individuals classified by years of part-time and full-time work.

In many applied settings, the main reason for studying the work behavior of individuals is to gain some understanding of the determinants of the income distribution for these individuals. Moreover, in applications related to individual or family welfare, poverty status, consumption or savings, it is really the distribution of individual income cumulated over substantial numbers of years that matters, rather than the distribution of individual income in any one year. We noted earlier as well that the simulated cumulative income distributions are of special interest to us from the point of view of detecting errors in model specification since these distributions will reflect and magnify systematic errors related to any component of the model, except to the extent that these errors systematically cancel out in the calculation of predicted individual incomes.

The simulated distributions for individual income cumulated over a 7-year period are shown for all four alternative models in Tables B.29 through B.35. For all individuals and for our six demographic groupings of women, the Standard Model always considerably underestimates the proportion of individuals with no income over the 7-year simulation period and considerably overestimates the proportion of individuals with $10,000 - 19,999 in earnings over this time period. For all individuals and all demographic groups of women except the oldest, the Dummy and Split Models also tend to overestimate the proportions of individuals with cumulative earnings of $10,000 - 19,999 and $20,000 - 29,999, although the degree of distortion is generally moderate. The Inertia Model appears to reproduce very accurately the shape

TABLE 4.2.5
GROUPS FOR WHICH STANDARD MODEL IS WORSE THAN DUMMY, SPLIT AND
INERTIA MODELS IN TERMS OF VARIOUS DISTRIBUTIONAL COMPARISONS

Group	Pooled hours	Pooled income	Years of work out of 7	Years of full/part time work	Income over 7 years
All individuals	*	*	*	*	*
Women 14-20			*	*	*
Wives 21-46	*	*	*	*	*
Unmarried women 21-46		*	*	*	*
Wives 47-64		*	*	*	*
Unmarried women 47-64	*		*	*	*
Women 65+		*	*	*	*

of the cumulative income distribution for all individuals and
for all demographic groups of women, except for women 47-64
years of age and unmarried in the first year of the simulation
for whom the Inertia Model places too many individuals in the
lowest positive income category of up to $10,000 and too few
individuals in the $10,000 - 19,999 category, and for the
oldest group of women for whom the Inertia Model places too
few individuals in the $0 earnings category and too many in
the lowest category of positive earnings.

One descriptive measure of the degree of fit of simulated
distributions of the sort shown in Tables B.1 through B.35 to
the corresponding actual distributions observed for the
individuals in our data base is the chi-square statistic for
goodness-of-fit, where the actual and simulated frequencies
are calculated as the products of the actual and simulated
proportions, respectively, times the number of observations,
n, for the sample from which the actual frequencies are
computed.[10] We will refer to this descriptive statistic as a
pseudo chi-square statistic. The values of this pseudo
chi-square statistic provide us with one measure of relative
performance for our alternative models, with smaller values of
the statistic indicating better fits. Values for this pseudo

4 Comparisons of Our Inertia Model

TABLE 4.2.6
GROUPS FOR WHICH DUMMY OR SPLIT MODEL IS AS
GOOD OR BETTER THAN STANDARD MODEL IN
TERMS OF VARIOUS DISTRIBUTIONAL COMPARISONS

Group	Pooled hours	Pooled income	Years of work out of 7	Years of full/part time work	Income over 7 years
All individuals	*	*	*	*	*
Women 14-20				*	*
Wives 21-46	*	*	*	*	*
Unmarried women 21-46		*	*	*	*
Wives 47-64	*	*	*	*	*
Unmarried women 47-64	*		*	*	*
Women 65+	*	*	*	*	*

chi-square statistic are shown in the bottom row of Tables B.1 through B.35. (We note that in computing the pseudo chi-square values shown at the bottom of our tables, we have summed the proportions in each column below the line across the body of each table that has such a horizontal line across it.)

In Table 4.2.5 we indicate with a star the demographic categories for which the Standard Model performs less well than the Dummy, Split and Inertia Models according to our pseudo chi-square criterion. We see that according to this criterion the Standard Model is rejected for all individuals and for all six of our demographic groups for women. Using the same pseudo chi-square criterion, we indicate with a star the demographic groups for which either the Dummy or Split Model is better than or as good as the Standard Model in Table 4.2.6, and the demographic groups for which the Split Model outperforms or does as well as the Dummy Model in Table 4.2.7. From these two tables and Table 4.2.5, we see that both the Dummy and Split Models are to be preferred to the Standard Model according to the pseudo chi-square criterion. There is no clear basis for preferring either the Dummy or Split Model, although the Split Model appears to more adequately

TABLE 4.2.7
GROUPS FOR WHICH SPLIT MODEL IS AS GOOD OR BETTER THAN
DUMMY MODEL IN TERMS OF VARIOUS DISTRIBUTIONAL COMPARISONS

Group	Pooled hours	Pooled income	Years of work out of 7	Years of full/part time work	Income over 7 years
All individuals	*	*			
Women 14-20			*		
Wives 21-46	*	*			*
Unmarried women 21-46	*				*
Wives 47-64	*	*		*	*
Unmarried women 47-64	*		*	*	
Women 65+	*	*	*	*	*

capture the shape of the pooled distribution of annual hours of work except for women 14-20 years of age in the first year of the simulation period.

Finally, in Table 4.2.8 we indicate with a star the demographic groups for which the Inertia Model performs as well as or better than all three of our other models according to our pseudo chi-square statistic criterion. We see from the last two columns of this table that if we are concerned with the distributions of cumulative hours of work or income, then for women younger than 65 the Inertia Model seems to be superior to the Standard, Dummy and Split Models. If we are simply concerned with the distribution of number of years of work, then we might use the Dummy or Split Model instead.

From Table B.29 we find that both the Dummy and Split Models perform as well as or better than the Inertia Model in terms of the pseudo chi-square statistic for the cumulative income distribution for all individuals. The reason for this is that in the Inertia Model we did not estimate separate sets of behavioral relationships for men over age 20 depending on work status in the previous year, although we did include lagged wage and hours of work variables. We thought that, since most men work most of the time, it would not be

4   Comparisons of Our Inertia Model   223

TABLE 4.2.8
GROUPS FOR WHICH INERTIA MODEL IS AS GOOD OR BETTER THAN
STANDARD, DUMMY AND SPLIT MODELS
IN TERMS OF VARIOUS DISTRIBUTIONAL COMPARISONS

Group	Pooled hours	Pooled income	Years of work out of 7	Years of full/part time work	Income over 7 years
All individuals		*		*	
Women 14-20	*	*	*	*	*
Wives 21-46		*		*	*
Unmarried women 21-46			*	*	*
Wives 47-64	*	*		*	*
Unmarried women 47-64		*		*	*
Women 65+					

important to take into account differences in work status in the previous year for men, provided that we did take into account differences in their wage rates and hours of work in the previous year. Further investigation has shown that this is not true, and that the differences in current work behavior between men who did not and men who did work in the previous year cannot be fully captured without either allowing the constant terms of our behavioral relationships to shift depending on lagged work status or estimating separate sets of relationships.

In section 4.1 we find that for the Split and Inertia Models there are systematic differences in the responses to our child status variables for wives who did not versus wives who did work in the previous year. The estimation results for the Split and Inertia Models also reveal systematic response differences depending on work status in the previous year for our age, race dummy and education variables and for our dummy variable set equal to 1 if a person was married in the previous year. Since the Standard and Dummy Models cannot capture coefficient differences between those who did not and those who did work in the previous year, and since the

simulation results are not better for these two models than
for the Split and Inertia Models (the results for the Standard
Model are found, in some ways, to be substantially worse), we
reject the Standard and Dummy Models in favor of the Split and
Inertia Models. Moreover, since certain key simulation results
are systematically better for women for the Inertia Model than
for the Split Model, to the extent that our estimation results
for these two models differ, we reject the Split Model in
favor of the Inertia Model for women. (Recall that we find the
coefficient estimates for the Split and Inertia Models to be
generally similar in both sign and magnitude).

Our results suggest that collecting information on work
status for the year prior to the year for which income and
weeks of work data are collected in cross-sectional population
surveys would lead to clear improvements in behavioral
inference and forecasting concerning the work behavior and
earnings of individuals. When information of this sort is
available, separate behavioral relationships should be
estimated for those who did not and those who did work in the
previous year, as opposed to simply introducing into the
behavioral relationships a dummy set equal to 1 if the person
worked in the previous year. Finally, if lagged information
could also be collected on a recall basis for hours of work
and earnings, in addition to the lagged information on work
status, this would lead to further, though more marginal,
improvements in inference and forecasting.

4.3. Sensitivity of Results to Inclusion of Lagged Dependent Variable in Hours Equation, Correction for Selection Bias, and Log-Linear Wage Equation

To test the sensitivity of our estimation results for the
Inertia Model to small variations in this model, we have
reestimated the model with the following three variations:

1. The lagged dependent variable has been omitted from the hours equations for those who worked in the previous year (Model A).[11]
2. The selection bias term has been omitted from the log wage and hours equations (Model B).
3. The selection bias term has been omitted from the wage and hours equations, and we have used a linear specification for the wage equation (Model C).

In all of the tables in this section, in each group of four
numbers the top one is the value for the Inertia Model, and

4 Comparisons of Our Inertia Model   225

the following three numbers correspond to our three variations of this model in the order in which these variations are listed above. For each group of explanatory variables, we will first consider how the coefficient estimates differ depending on the variation of the model used. We will then consider differences among the models in the total impacts of the explanatory variables, after taking selection bias and lagged endogenous variables into account where relevant.

Notice that none of the model variations involves alterations in our probit relationships for the probabilities of starting and of continuing to work. Nevertheless, different predictions for the starting wage rate or hours of work can result in different predictions for the probability of continuing to work due to the impacts of lagged variables for the wage rate and hours of work. In the following tables, results are only shown for married women in the 21-46 and 47-64 year old age groups.

4.3.1. Dummy for married in previous year

From Table 4.3.1 we see that the coefficient estimates of our dummy variable for married in the previous year in our starting hours equations for wives 47-64 years of age are positive for our Inertia Model and Model A but negative for Models B and C. From Table 4.3.2 we see that the coefficient estimates for this same dummy variable in our continuing hours equations are negative and large in magnitude for Model A for both wives 21-46 and 47-64 years of age, but positive for our Inertia Model and Models B and C. We might expect that these large differences in coefficient estimates would result in clear-cut differences among the predicted values of the dependent variables of interest for these different model variants.

Looking at Tables 4.3.3 through 4.3.7, however, we find that at least the direction of change in each of the dependent variables of interest, depending on whether our hypothetical wives were married as opposed to unmarried in the previous year, is always the same for all four model variations, except for the continuing hours of work for our 55-year-old hypothetical wife. The predicted values shown in these tables, of course, take into account indirect impacts of our lagged marital status dummy through the selection bias term and lagged dependent variables. In terms of magnitudes, the starting wage rates, starting hours, continuing wage rates and continuing hours for our 33-year-old hypothetical wife, assuming she was also married in the previous two years, are higher for our Inertia Model and Model A than for Models B and C, which do not include the selection bias term. Also, the continuing hours of work for our 55-year-old hypothetical wife

4.3.1. Dummy for Married in Previous Year

TABLE 4.3.1
IV COEFFICIENT ESTIMATES FOR DIFFERENT METHODS FOR
DUMMY VARIABLE FOR MARRIED IN t-1 IN HOURS EQUATIONS:
WORKING WOMEN WHO DID NOT WORK IN t-1

Wives 21-46	Wives 47-64
-313.7*	219.8
-313.7*	219.8
-370.6*	-142.2
-367.5*	-146.9

TABLE 4.3.2
IV COEFFICIENT ESTIMATES FOR DIFFERENT METHODS FOR
DUMMY VARIABLE FOR MARRIED IN t-1 IN HOURS EQUATIONS:
WORKING WOMEN WHO WORKED IN t-1

Wives 21-46	Wives 47-64
3.9	479.7*
-295.2**	-1745.9**
62.5	496.2**
62.1	497.3**

TABLE 4.3.3
STARTING WAGE RATES FOR DIFFERENT METHODS FOR
HYPOTHETICAL MARRIED WOMEN DEPENDING ON
WHETHER THEY WERE MARRIED IN t-1

	Marital status in t-1	
Age	Unmarried	Married
33	$2.24	$2.39
		2.39
		2.24
		2.24
55	1.67	1.52
		1.52
		1.67
		1.67

TABLE 4.3.4
STARTING HOURS OF WORK FOR DIFFERENT METHODS
FOR HYPOTHETICAL MARRIED WOMEN DEPENDING ON
WHETHER THEY WERE MARRIED IN t-1

	Marital status in t-1	
Age	Unmarried	Married
33	671	307
		307
		300
		303
55	734	518
		518
		592
		587

TABLE 4.3.5
PROBABILITIES OF CONTINUING TO WORK FOR DIFFERENT
METHODS FOR HYPOTHETICAL MARRIED WOMEN DEPENDING ON
WHETHER THEY WERE MARRIED IN t-1 AND t-2

	Marital status in t-1 and t-2	
Age	Unmarried	Married
33	.85	.88
		.88
		.88
		.88
55	.86	.99
		.99
		.99
		.99

4.3.1. Dummy for Married in Previous Year

TABLE 4.3.6
CONTINUING WAGE RATES FOR DIFFERENT METHODS FOR
HYPOTHETICAL MARRIED WOMEN DEPENDING ON
WHETHER THEY WERE MARRIED IN t-1 AND t-2

	Marital status in t-1 and t-2	
Age	Unmarried	Married
33	$2.54	$2.54
		2.54
		2.36
		2.43
55	2.69	2.89
		2.89
		2.66
		2.67

TABLE 4.3.7
CONTINUING HOURS OF WORK FOR DIFFERENT METHODS
FOR HYPOTHETICAL MARRIED WOMEN DEPENDING ON
WHETHER THEY WERE MARRIED IN t-1 AND t-2

	Marital status in t-1 and t-2	
Age	Unmarried	Married
33	1359	1206
		1221
		1120
		1201
55	1378	1721
		441
		1781
		1778

TABLE 4.3.8
OLS COEFFICIENT ESTIMATES FOR DIFFERENT METHODS
FOR AGE VARIABLE IN LOG WAGE EQUATIONS:
WORKING WOMEN WHO DID NOT WORK IN t-1

Wives 21-46	Wives 47-64
-.014**	.011
-.014**	.011
-.011*	.066
-.039*	.068

TABLE 4.3.9
IV COEFFICIENT ESTIMATES FOR DIFFERENT METHODS
FOR AGE VARIABLES IN HOURS EQUATIONS:
WORKING WOMEN WHO DID NOT WORK IN t-1

Wives 21-46	Wives 47-64
-4.4	-62.8
-4.4	-62.8
-7.0	-81.8**
-7.3	-82.7**

TABLE 4.3.10
OLS COEFFICIENT ESTIMATES FOR DIFFERENT METHODS
FOR AGE VARIABLE IN LOG WAGE EQUATIONS:
WORKING WOMEN WHO WORKED IN t-1

Wives 21-46	Wives 47-64
.001	.007
.001	.007
.005**	.002
.013**	.019

are drastically lower for Model A than for our Inertia Model.

4.3.2. Age

From Tables 4.3.8 through 4.3.11, we find that the signs

TABLE 4.3.11
IV COEFFICIENT ESTIMATES FOR DIFFERENT METHODS
FOR AGE VARIABLE IN HOURS EQUATIONS:
WORKING WOMEN WHO WORKED IN t-1

Wives 21-46	Wives 47-64
-5.0**	-10.4*
-17.8**	23.1**
-2.9*	-10.3**
-2.9*	-10.6**

TABLE 4.3.12
STARTING WAGE RATES FOR DIFFERENT METHODS FOR
HYPOTHETICAL MARRIED WOMEN DEPENDING ON AGE

Base age	Woman at base age	Woman 5 years older than base age
33	$2.24	$2.16
		2.16
		2.12
		2.04
55	1.67	1.72
		1.72
		2.32
		2.01

of the estimated coefficients of the age variable do not vary with the model used, except for the estimate of the age coefficient in the equation for continuing hours of work for wives 47-64, although there are some differences in the magnitudes of the coefficient estimates. Prediction results for our hypothetical 33- and 55-year-old wives are shown in Tables 4.3.12 through 4.3.16. We see from these tables that the direction of change with increased age is always the same for all model variations, except for the continuing wage rate for our 55-year-old hypothetical wife and the continuing hours of work for our 33-year old hypothetical wife. Looking more carefully at Tables 4.3.12 through 4.3.16, however, we find that there are systematic differences among the results for our model variations. In particular, compared with the

4 Comparisons of Our Inertia Model

TABLE 4.3.13
STARTING HOURS OF WORK FOR DIFFERENT METHODS FOR
HYPOTHETICAL MARRIED WOMEN DEPENDING ON AGE

Base age	Woman at base age	Woman 5 years older than base age
33	993	978
		978
		972
		972
55	737	314
		314
		339
		321

TABLE 4.3.14
PROBABILITIES OF CONTINUING TO WORK FOR DIFFERENT
METHODS FOR HYPOTHETICAL MARRIED WOMEN DEPENDING ON AGE

Base age	Woman at base age	Woman 5 years older than base age
33	.85	.87
		.87
		.87
		.87
55	.86	.76
		.76
		.77
		.76

predictions for our Inertia Model the starting wage, starting hours and continuing hours predictions for Models B and C are systematically lower for our hypothetical 33-year-old wife. On the other hand, for our hypothetical 55-year-old wife, the starting wage, starting hours, continuing wage and continuing hours predictions are systematically higher for Models B and C than for our Inertia Model. The prediction for continuing hours for our 33-year-old hypothetical wife is considerably

TABLE 4.3.15
CONTINUING WAGE RATES FOR DIFFERENT METHODS FOR
HYPOTHETICAL MARRIED WOMEN DEPENDING ON AGE

Base age	Woman at base age	Woman 5 years older than base age
33	$2.54	$2.56
		2.56
		2.56
		2.56
55	2.69	2.51
		2.51
		2.80
		2.87

TABLE 4.3.16
CONTINUING HOURS OF WORK FOR DIFFERENT METHODS FOR
HYPOTHETICAL MARRIED WOMEN DEPENDING ON AGE

Base age	Woman at base age	Woman 5 years older than base age
33	1359	1343
		1374
		1334
		1333
55	1378	1047
		999
		1070
		1055

higher for Model A than for our Inertia Model.
 From Tables 4.3.12 through 4.3.16, we see then that, all else being the same, we might expect that Models B and C, which do not include the selection bias term, will yield lower income predictions with increasing age for wives 21-46 years of age and higher income predictions with increasing age for wives 47-64 years of age than will our Inertia Model. Also, we might expect that Model A will yield higher income predictions

TABLE 4.3.17
OLS COEFFICIENT ESTIMATES FOR DIFFERENT METHODS
FOR RACE DUMMY IN LOG WAGE AND WAGE EQUATIONS:
WORKING WOMEN WHO DID NOT WORK IN t-1

Wives 21-46	Wives 47-64
-.066	.053
-.066	.053
-.080	.070
-.653	.359

TABLE 4.3.18
IV COEFFICIENT ESTIMATES FOR DIFFERENT METHODS
FOR RACE DUMMY IN HOURS EQUATIONS:
WORKING WOMEN WHO DID NOT WORK IN t-1

Wives 21-46	Wives 47-64
252.8**	-117.3
252.8**	-117.3
248.7**	-107.1
217.9**	-120.2

TABLE 4.3.19
OLS COEFFICIENT ESTIMATES FOR DIFFERENT METHODS
FOR RACE DUMMY IN LOG WAGE AND WAGE EQUATIONS:
WORKING WOMEN WHO WORKED IN t-1

Wives 21-46	Wives 47-64
-.065**	-.071
-.065**	-.071
-.068**	-.074
-.066	.223

with increasing age for wives 21-46 years of age who worked in the previous year than will our Inertia Model. We see also that the differences in predicted values for Model B versus Model C are quite slight, except for the starting wage rates where the predictions for Model C are substantially lower. Our key behavioral findings with respect to the impact of age on

TABLE 4.3.20
IV COEFFICIENT ESTIMATES FOR DIFFERENT METHODS
FOR RACE DUMMY IN HOURS EQUATIONS:
WORKING WOMEN WHO WORKED IN t-1

Wives 21-46	Wives 47-64
82.6**	59.9
104.4**	-24.4
82.0**	60.8
74.8**	52.4

TABLE 4.3.21
STARTING WAGE RATES FOR DIFFERENT METHODS
FOR HYPOTHETICAL MARRIED NONBLACK WOMEN,
AND FOR OTHERWISE-IDENTICAL BLACK WOMEN

Age	Nonblack	Black
33	$2.24	$2.09
		2.09
		2.07
		1.59
55	1.67	1.75
		1.75
		1.79
		2.03

work behavior remain the same no matter which model variation is used though.

4.3.3. Race

From Tables 4.3.17 through 4.3.20, we see that the signs of our coefficient estimates for our race dummy variable do not change depending on the model variation, except for the coefficient estimates in the equations for the continuing wage rate and hours of work for wives 47-64 years of age. Looking now at Tables 4.3.21 through 4.3.25, we find only two differences in the predictions for our hypothetical wives depending on the model variation used that seem worth noting.

TABLE 4.3.22
STARTING HOURS OF WORK FOR DIFFERENT METHODS
FOR HYPOTHETICAL MARRIED NONBLACK WOMEN, AND
FOR OTHERWISE-IDENTICAL BLACK WOMEN

Age	Nonblack	Black
33	671	948
		948
		938
		939
55	734	611
		611
		629
		611

TABLE 4.3.23
PROBABILITIES OF CONTINUING TO WORK FOR DIFFERENT
METHODS FOR HYPOTHETICAL MARRIED NONBLACK WOMEN
AND FOR OTHERWISE-IDENTICAL BLACK WOMEN

Age	Nonblack	Black
33	.85	.88
		.88
		.88
		.87
55	.86	.86
		.86
		.86
		.86

First, using Model C, both the starting and continuing wage predictions are lower for our 33-year-old hypothetical black wife, and both the starting and continuing wage predictions are higher for our 55-year-old hypothetical black wife, than is the case for any of our other model variations. Thus, the use of a linear wage equation results in the finding of larger race-related wage differentials than when the dependent variable of the wage equation is in log form. Also, using

TABLE 4.3.24
CONTINUING WAGE RATES FOR DIFFERENT METHODS FOR
HYPOTHETICAL MARRIED NONBLACK WOMEN, AND FOR
OTHERWISE-IDENTICAL BLACK WOMEN

Age	Nonblack	Black
33	$2.54	$2.46
		2.46
		2.46
		2.44
55	2.69	2.48
		2.48
		2.51
		3.04

TABLE 4.3.25
CONTINUING HOURS OF WORK FOR DIFFERENT METHODS
FOR HYPOTHETICAL MARRIED NONBLACK WOMEN, AND
AND FOR OTHERWISE-IDENTICAL BLACK WOMEN

Age	Nonblack	Black
33	1359	1564
		1599
		1590
		1586
55	1378	1354
		1385
		1367
		1356

Model A the continuing hours of work are predicted to be higher for both our 33- and 55-year-old hypothetical black wives than for any of our other model variations including our Inertia Model. Overall our behavioral findings with respect to our race dummy variable appear largely unchanged, however, no matter which of the four model variations is used.

4 Comparisons of Our Inertia Model

TABLE 4.3.26
OLS COEFFICIENT ESTIMATES FOR DIFFERENT METHODS
FOR EDUCATION VARIABLE IN LOG WAGE AND WAGE EQUATIONS:
WORKING WOMEN WHO DID NOT WORK IN t-1

Wives 21-46	Wives 47-64
.141**	.102*
.141**	.102*
.118**	.101*
.329**	.236**

TABLE 4.3.27
OLS COEFFICIENT ESTIMATES FOR DIFFERENT METHODS
FOR EDUCATION VARIABLE IN LOG WAGE AND WAGE EQUATIONS:
WORKING WOMEN WHO WORKED IN t-1

Wives 21-46	Wives 47-64
.086**	.072**
.086**	.072**
.092**	.078**
.258**	.213**

4.3.4. Education

From Tables 4.3.26 and 4.3.27, we see that the coefficient estimates of the education variable in our wage equations are always positive no matter which model variation is used. Thus, our finding that women with more education have higher wage rates does not depend on which of the model variations being considered is used. We also find that the predictions for our hypothetical wives are very similar, on the whole, no matter which model variation is used. Thus, these predictions are not shown.

4.3.5. Child status variables

Alternative estimation results for our child status variables in the equations for starting and continuing hours of work are shown in Tables 4.3.28 and 4.3.29. From Table 4.3.29 we see that omission of the lagged dependent variable from the equation for continuing hours of work for wives 21-46

4.3.5. Child status variables

TABLE 4.3.28
COEFFICIENT ESTIMATES FOR DIFFERENT METHODS FOR
CHILD STATUS VARIABLES IN HOURS EQUATIONS:
WORKING WOMEN WHO DID NOT WORK IN t-1

Group	Baby dummy	Young child dummy	Number of children younger than 18
Wives 21-46	-135.2	70.2	-26.7
	-135.2	70.2	-26.7
	-196.9*	-61.9	-11.1
	-196.3*	-61.5	-10.8
Wives 47-64			-59.9
			-59.9
			-52.2
			-53.9

TABLE 4.3.29
COEFFICIENT ESTIMATES FOR DIFFERENT METHODS FOR
CHILD STATUS VARIABLES IN HOURS EQUATIONS:
WORKING WOMEN WHO WORKED IN t-1

Group	Baby dummy	Young child dummy
Wives 21-46	58.0	4.0
	521.5**	88.9**
	-39.1	-14.8
	-39.0	-15.6

years old results in the finding that wives who worked in the previous year, and who continue to work in the current year despite the presense of a baby or young child, work substantially longer hours than otherwise-similar wives. Omission of the selection bias term from the equations for starting and for continuing hours of work can be seen from Tables 4.3.28 and 4.3.29 to result in the consistent finding that working wives with a baby or a young child, or with more children younger than 18, work fewer hours than otherwise-similar working wives. The coefficient estimates for the child status variables remain virtually unchanged whether the dependent variable for our wage equations is in log or

TABLE 4.3.30
STARTING WAGE RATES FOR DIFFERENT METHODS FOR
HYPOTHETICAL MARRIED WOMEN WITH NO CHILDREN
YOUNGER THAN 18 AT HOME, AND FOR
OTHERWISE-IDENTICAL WOMEN WITH CHILDREN AT HOME

Age	No children	New baby	Child less than 6 but no new baby	Child less than 18 but older than 5
33	2.24	2.34	2.61	2.18
		2.34	2.61	2.18
		2.24	2.24	2.24
		2.24	2.24	2.24
55	1.67			1.67
				1.67
				1.67
				1.67

TABLE 4.3.31
STARTING HOURS OF WORK FOR DIFFERENT METHODS FOR
HYPOTHETICAL MARRIED WOMEN WITH NO CHILDREN
YOUNGER THAN 18 AT HOME, AND FOR
OTHERWISE-IDENTICAL WOMEN WITH CHILDREN AT HOME

Age	No children	New baby	Child less than 6 but no new baby	Child less than 18 but older than 5
33	671	478	713	665
		478	713	665
		463	598	660
		464	599	660
55	734			679
				679
				682
				680

TABLE 4.3.32
PROBABILITIES OF CONTINUING TO WORK FOR DIFFERENT
METHODS FOR HYPOTHETICAL MARRIED WOMEN WITH NO
CHILDREN YOUNGER THAN 18 AT HOME, AND FOR
OTHERWISE-IDENTICAL WOMEN WITH CHILDREN AT HOME

Age	No children	New baby	Child less than 6 but no new baby
33	.85	.65	.83
		.65	.83
		.64	.80
		.64	.80

TABLE 4.3.33
CONTINUING WAGE RATES FOR DIFFERENT METHODS FOR
HYPOTHETICAL MARRIED WOMEN WITH NO CHILDREN
YOUNGER THAN 18 AT HOME, AND FOR
OTHERWISE-IDENTICAL WOMEN WITH CHILDREN AT HOME

Age	No children	New baby	Child less than 6 but no new baby
33	$2.54	$2.29	$2.56
		2.29	2.56
		2.54	2.48
		2.54	2.52

TABLE 4.3.34
CONTINUING HOURS OF WORK FOR DIFFERENT METHODS FOR
HYPOTHETICAL MARRIED WOMEN WITH NO CHILDREN
YOUNGER THAN 18 AT HOME, AND FOR
OTHERWISE-IDENTICAL WOMEN WITH CHILDREN AT HOME

Age	No children	New baby	Child less than 6 but no new baby
33	1359	1322	1369
		1315	1341
		1320	1300
		1320	1300

4 Comparisons of Our Inertia Model

linear form.

We will now consider hypothetical childless wives with the starting work behavior described in Table 3.1.1, and hypothetical childless wives with the continuing work behavior given in Table 3.1.2 and who started work in the previous year with the probabilities, wage rates and hours given in Table 3.1.1. For our Inertia Model and Model A, starting wage rates can be seen from Table 4.3.30 to vary depending on child status, due to the impacts of the selection bias term. The starting wage rates for our hypothetical wives will always be identical for our Inertia Model and Model A for those who did not work in the previous year. For Models B and C, which do not include the selection bias term, starting wage rates do not vary with child status. From Table 4.3.31 we see that Models B and C consistently predict lower starting hours of work for our hypothetical wives if they have a child at home than if they are childless. The picture is similar for our Inertia Model and Model A except that our hypothetical 33-year-old wife is predicted to work longer hours if she has a child younger than 6 that is not a new baby.

From Table 4.3.32 we see that both the arrival of a new baby and the presence of a child less than 6 that is not a new baby reduce the probability of our hypothetical wives continuing work for our Inertia Model and Models A, B and C. The differences between the predicted probabilities for Models B and C versus our Inertia Model for our hypothetical 33-year-old wife if she has a young child are relatively large, however.

The variations with child status in the predicted values for the continuing wage rate shown in Table 4.3.33 are due to the impacts of the selection bias term for our Inertia Model and Model A, and to the impacts of the lagged wage rate and hours of work variables for all model variations including our Inertia Model. For Models B and C, we see that the predicted wage rate is consistently the same or lower if our hypothetical wife has a new baby or a young child as opposed to having no children. For our Inertia Model and Model A, the predicted wage is lower for our hypothetical 33-year-old wife if she has a new baby, but it is higher if she has a young child that is not a new baby.

From Table 4.3.34 we see that Models A, B and C predict lower continuing hours of work for our hypothetical 33-year-old wife if she has either a new baby or a young child than if she is childless. On the other hand, our Inertia Model predicts lower hours of work for our hypothetical wife if she has a new baby but higher hours if she has a young child.

Looking back we find that our Inertia Model predicts a higher starting wage rate and higher starting hours of work for our hypothetical 33-year-old wife if she has a young child than do Models B and C. Moreover, from Tables 4.3.32 and

4.3.5. Child status variables

TABLE 4.3.35
IV COEFFICIENT ESTIMATES FOR DIFFERENT METHODS FOR
OTHER INCOME VARIABLES IN HOURS EQUATIONS:
WORKING WOMEN WHO DID NOT WORK IN t−1

Group	Husband's income	Change in husband's income	Negative change in husband's income	Dummy for AFDC in t−1	Dummy for Social Security in t−1
Wives 21−46	−6.3	−15.4*		−204.4	
	−6.3	−15.4*		−204.4	
	−15.1*	−12.6		−129.8	
	−15.6*	−12.6		−133.9	
Wives 47−64	−57.5*		−52.7		−594.6
	−57.5*		−52.7		−594.6
	−69.3**		−40.5		−741.5
	−68.6**		−40.4		−744.1

TABLE 4.3.36
IV COEFFICIENT ESTIMATES FOR DIFFERENT METHODS FOR
OTHER INCOME VARIABLE IN HOURS EQUATIONS:
WORKING WOMEN WHO WORKED IN t−1

Group	Change in husband's income	Negative change in husband's income	Dummy for AFDC in t−1	Dummy for Social Security in t−1
Wives 21−46	−10.1**		218.0	
	−21.5**		832.0**	
	−7.7*		87.9	
	−7.7*		86.9	
Wives 47−64		9.3		101.8
		−125.7**		576.2**
		10.3		97.1
		10.5		96.0

4 Comparisons of Our Inertia Model   243

4.3.33, we find that our Inertia Model predicts a higher
probability of continuing to work and a higher continuing wage
rate for our hypothetical 33-year-old wife with a young child
than do Models B and C. Making the same sort of comparisons in
Table 4.3.34, we find a higher value for the continuing hours
of work for our Inertia Model than for any of our three model
variations. All else being equal then, we might expect that
our Inertia Model will yield higher predictions for earned
income for wives 21-46 years of age with a young child than
Models A, B or C, with the discrepancies being largest between
our Inertia Model versus Models B and C which do not include a
selection bias term. Looking back at Tables 4.3.30 through
4.3.34, we find virtually no differences in the predicted
responses to child status between Models B and C.

4.3.6. Other income variables

   From Tables 4.3.35 and 4.3.36, we see that the
coefficient estimates for our other income variables always
have the same signs regardless of the model variation used,
except for the coefficient estimates for our variable for a
negative change in the husband's income in our equation for
continuing hours of work for wives 47-64 years of age, which
are positive for all of the models except Model A. We see also
from Table 4.3.36 that the coefficient estimates for our dummy
variables for AFDC and for Social Security benefits in the
previous year are substantially larger for Model A. No other
substantial differences of interest emerge when we consider
the total impacts of these variables. Thus, we do not show
comparative tables for our hypothetical wives for our other
income variables.

4.3.7. Macroeconomic variables

   The two macroeconomic variables included in this study
are the national unemployment rate and a national wage index.
From Tables 4.3.37 and 4.3.38, we see that the coefficient
estimates for these variables always have the same sign for
all four of our model variants except for the coefficient
estimates for the national wage index in our wage equation for
wives 21-46 years of age who did not work in the previous
year. And no interesting model-specific differences emerge
when we consider the total impacts of these variables. Thus,
we do not show tables of comparative values for our
hypothetical wives for these variables.

TABLE 4.3.37
OLS COEFFICIENT ESTIMATES FOR DIFFERENT METHODS FOR
MACROECONOMIC VARIABLES IN LOG WAGE EQUATIONS:
WORKING WOMEN WHO DID NOT WORK IN t-1

Group	National unemployment rate	National wage index
Wives 21-46	-.046	.0002
	-.046	.0002
	-.051	-.0002
	-.060	-.0075
Wives 47-64	.067	-.0038
	.067	-.0038
	.073	-.0035
	.106	-.0105

TABLE 4.3.38
OLS COEFFICIENT ESTIMATES FOR DIFFERENT METHODS FOR
MACROECONOMIC VARIABLES IN LOG WAGE AND WAGE EQUATIONS:
WOMEN WHO WORKED IN t-1

Group	National unemployment rate	National wage index
Wives 21-46	-.024**	-.0008
	-.024**	-.0008
	-.020*	-.0006
	-.020	-.0033*
Wives 47-64	.006	-.0012
	.006	-.0012
	.007	-.0006
	.031	-.0010

4.4. Simulation Comparisons of Inertia Model
with Models A, B and C

In section 4.3 we found that there are certain
differences in empirical results for our Inertia Model versus

4 Comparisons of Our Inertia Model

Model A where the lagged hours variable is omitted from the hours equation, for our Inertia Model versus Model B where the selection bias term has been omitted from the wage and hours equations, and for our Inertia Model versus Model C which is the same as Model B except that the wage equation is linear instead of log-linear in form. The Inertia Model and Models A, B and C all share the same estimated probit equations for the determination of who works. In simulation, however, there are systematic differences in the choice of individuals simulated to work each year that arise after the first simulation period because of model-specific differences in the simulated values of the lagged wage rate and hours of work variables in the probit indices.

We thought that if it were really true that fixed or slowly changing unobservable factors like tastes for work are major determinants of hours of work, then the omission of the lagged hours variable from our hours equations should result in a marked deterioration in our ability to simulate hours of work for individuals over periods of years. There should also be some accompanying deterioration in our ability to simulate the earnings of individuals over periods of years. Thus, we would expect the major differences between the Inertia Model and Model A to show up in the simulated distributions for years out of 7 of full-time and part-time work and in the distributions for the incomes of individuals cumulated over our 7-year simulation period. We might also expect the Inertia Model to outperform Model A in terms of the simulated distributions for pooled annual hours of work.

Omission of the selection bias term from the wage and hours equations, as in Model B, means that variables like our child status variables, which are hypothesized to enter the asking but not the offered wage equation, no longer have any impact on the determination of wage rates. It also means that variables like education and the macroeconomic variables, which are specified to enter the offered but not the asking wage equation, affect the determination of hours of work only through their impacts on the wage variable in the hours equations. Of course, if selection bias is not really important, or if it is not properly corrected for by the introduction of a Heckman-style selection bias term (see fn. 1 to this chapter), or if the problems of multicollinearity resulting from the inclusion of our selection bias term in our wage and hours equations are sufficiently severe, then we should find that Model B outperforms our Inertia Model.

There are theoretical and empirical arguments suggesting that the education variable should be related to the log of the wage rate (see fn. 2 to this chapter). In addition, there are practical reasons for preferring a log-linear specification for wage equations in a simulation model. Linear wage equations can generate predicted wage rates that are less than 0 and that must be arbitrarily set to small positive number. This assignment of some small positive values in place of simulated negative wage rates distorts both the overall shape and the mean, or central tendency, of the simulated wage and income distributions.

On the other hand, there are problems with log-linear wage equations. First, if we generate log wage rates for individuals in our simulations and then take the antilogs of these log wage rates and use these in our calculations of simulated wage rates and incomes, the arithmetic means for these simulated wage rates and incomes are not mathematically equivalent to the arithmetic means for the actual wage rates and incomes of individuals that are often available over historical periods in the publications of government statistical agencies. Thus, whether we use a log-linear or a linear wage equation, problems arise in making comparisons with published arithmetic means for wage rates or the earned incomes of individuals. Also, for a small number of individuals the simulated wage rates explode over time for our log-linear wage equations. We handle this problem in sections 4.2, 4.4, 4.5 and 4.6 by simply eliminating these individuals from our simulation population for each model for which the problem arises. Fortunately, as is shown in section 4.7 and Appendix F, this censoring does not result in any detectable distortions for the distributions of actual values for the dependent variables of interest. In section 4.7 we explain more fully why we have adopted this approach to dealing with extreme estimated wage rates in this chapter. Nevertheless, in a full-blown microanalytic simulation model with individuals embedded in families and where the initial population is a careful representation of the national population in some base year, dropping individuals because of exploding wage rates would be an unacceptable practice. It would be a costly one, too, since each simulation run would have to be repeated from the start, once all individuals with exploding wage rates had been identified. As noted in the introduction to this chapter, in section 4.7 we explore the consequences of, instead, truncating the simulated wage distributions for all models at $20 per hour. This procedure is more conventional and would be easier to implement in a microanalytic simulation model, but it has a variety of other associated drawbacks which are discussed in section 4.7.

For Model C, which contains a linear wage equation, this problem of exploding predicted wage rates for certain individuals does not arise. Thus, our comparisons between Models B and C are designed to investigate how our distributional results for the simulated pooled and cumulative incomes of individuals would change if we used linear rather than log-linear wage equations. We have chosen to make this comparison for a model not including a selection bias term

4 Comparisons of Our Inertia Model

TABLE 4.4.1
GROUPS FOR WHICH MODEL A IS AS GOOD OR BETTER
THAN INERTIA MODEL IN TERMS OF VARIOUS
DISTRIBUTIONAL COMPARISONS

Group	Pooled hours	Pooled income	Years of work out of 7	Years out of 7 of full-time and part-time work	Income cumulated over 7 years
All individuals	*	*	*		
Women 14-20			*		
Wives 21-46	*	*	*		
Unmarried women 21-46	*	*	*		
Wives 47-64				*	
Unmarried women 47-64	*		*	*	*
Women 65+	*	*	*		*

because this is the model that, in fact, has been incorporated as the new labor force module into a microanalytic simulation model of the U.S. household sector.[12] Comparisons between our Inertia Model and Model C reveal differences in results due to both the omission of the selection bias term and to the use of a linear wage equation in Model C.

As in section 4.2, we began our comparison of the alternative models of interest in this section by looking at our simulation results for these models on a year-by-year basis. As in section 4.2, however, this analysis reveals no clear distinction among the model variants being considered. Thus again we turn our attention to distributional comparisons.

The pooled distributions for simulated annual hours of work are shown in Tables C.1 through C.7 in Appendix C for all individuals and for our six groups of women classified according to their age and marital status in the first year of the simulation time period. On the basis of a visual

TABLE 4.4.2
GROUPS FOR WHICH MODEL B IS AS GOOD OR BETTER
THAN INERTIA MODEL IN TERMS OF VARIOUS
DISTRIBUTIONAL COMPARISONS

Group	Pooled hours	Pooled income	Years of work out of 7	Years out of 7 of full-time and part-time work	Income cumulated over 7 years
All individuals	*	*	*	*	*
Women 14-20		*		*	
Wives 21-46	*	*	*	*	*
Unmarried women 21-46	*	*	*	*	
Wives 46-64		*	*	*	*
Unmarried women 47-64		*	*		
Women 65+					

inspection of these results, we are not able to observe any clear differences in performance among our four model variants. Nor are we able to observe any clear distinctions among our models in terms of the pooled distributions for simulated annual income shown in Tables C.8 through C.14, except that Model C places too many observations in the $1 - 1,000 income category for women who were 21-46 or 47-64 years of age and unmarried in the first year of our simulation period, while the Inertia Model and Models A and B place too many observations in the $1,001 - 2,000 income category for these same groups of women. Also, Model B performs much less well than our other models for our oldest group of women.

In Tables C.15 through C.21, we show the simulated distributions of individuals classified by number of years of work out of 7 for all four of the model variants. Again, it is difficult to identify any systematic differences in performance among our models on the basis of a visual inspection of these results.

4 Comparisons of Our Inertia Model

TABLE 4.4.3
GROUPS FOR WHICH MODEL C IS AS GOOD OR BETTER THAN
MODEL B IN TERMS OF VARIOUS DISTRIBUTIONAL COMPARISONS

Group	Pooled hours	Pooled income	Years of work out of 7	Years out of 7 of full-time and part-time work	Income cumulated over 7 years
All individuals	*		*	*	
Women 14-20			*	*	*
Wives 21-46			*	*	
Unmarried women 21-46	*			*	*
Wives 47-64					
Unmarried women 47-64	*			*	*
Women 65+	*	*		*	*

In Tables C.22 through C.28, we show the simulated distributions of individuals classified by the number of years out of 7 when they worked any positive number of hours up to 1,400 hours, or part-time, and by the number of years out of 7 when they worked more than 1,400 hours, or full-time. As was found for the Standard, Dummy, Split and Inertia Models in section 4.2, we find here that Models A, B and C, also, generally overestimate the number of individuals in the intermediate category of 1-3 years of part-time work and 1-3 years of full-time work. For all individuals, taken together, for women 21-46 and married in the first simulation year, for women 21-46 and unmarried in the first simulation year, and for women 47-64 and married in the first simulation year, all of the model variants underestimate the number of individuals working full-time in all 7 years of the simulation time period. Thus, all of these models have failings in terms of the extent to which they capture the observed distributions of individuals by years of part-time versus full-time work, but it is not easy to draw distinctions concerning the relative

TABLE 4.4.4
GROUPS FOR WHICH INERTIA MODEL IS AS GOOD OR BETTER
THAN MODELS A, B AND C IN TERMS OF VARIOUS
DISTRIBUTIONAL COMPARISONS

Group	Pooled hours	Pooled income	Years of work out of 7	Years out of 7 of full-time and part-time work	Income cumulated over 7 years
All individuals					
Women 14-20	*				*
Wives 21-46					
Unmarried women 21-46					*
Wives 47-64	*				
Unmarried women 47-64					
Women 65+				*	

performance of these models on the basis of casual inspections of results such as those presented in Tables C.22 through C.28. Nor have we been able to draw relative performance distinctions on the basis of visual inspection for the simulated distributions for individual income cumulated over the 7-year simulation period, which are shown for the Inertia Model and for Models A, B and C in Tables C.29 through C.35.

Values for the pseudo chi-square statistic defined in section 4.2 are shown in the bottom row of Tables C.1 through C.35 and can be used as a more formal means of ranking our Inertia Model and Models A, B and C in terms of relative performance. (We note again that a horizontal line across the body of a table indicates that the proportions below this line in each column have been summed for the purpose of computing our pseudo chi-square values.)

In Tables 4.4.1 and 4.4.2 we indicate with stars the demographic categories for which Models A and B, respectively, perform as well or better than the Inertia Model for various

TABLE 4.4.5
RANKINGS OF INERTIA MODEL AND MODELS A, B AND C

Model	All individuals	Women 14-20	Wives 21-46	Unmarried women 47-64	Wives 47-64	Unmarried women 47-64	Women 65+
				Pooled hours			
Inertia	4	1	3	4	1.5	3	2
A	2	3	2	2	1.5	1	1
B	3	2	1	3	3	4	4
C	1	4	4	1	4	2	3
				Pooled income			
Inertia	3	2	3	3	2	2	3
A	1	3	1	1	3	3	2
B	2	1	2	2	1	1	4
C	4	4	4	4	4	4	1
				Years of work out of 7			
Inertia	4	2	4	2.5	3	4	2
A	1	1	1	1	4	1	1
B	3	4	3	2.5	1	2	3
C	2	3	2	4	2	3	4

distributional comparisons, using our pseudo chi-square criterion as the basis for ranking our models. Model A seems to perform particularly well in terms of the distributions of individuals by number of years worked out of 7, and Model B

TABLE 4.4.5 (cont.)

Model	All individuals	Women 14-20	Wives 21-46	Unmarried women 47-64	Wives 47-64	Unmarried women 47-64	Women 65+
	Years out of 7 of full-time and part-time work							
Inertia	3	3	3	3	4	2	1
A	4	4	4	4	3	1	3
B	2	2	2	2	1	4	4
C	1	1	1	1	2	3	2
	Income cumulated over 7 years							
Inertia	2	1.5	2	1	1.5	2.5	3
A	4	4	4	2	4	1	2
B	1	3	1	4	1.5	4	4
C	3	1.5	3	3	3	2.5	1

performs well in this respect also and performs particularly well in terms of the pooled distributions for annual income. However, neither Model A nor Model B consistently performs as well as or better than the Inertia Model in terms of the key distributions of individual income cumulated over the 7-year simulation period.

In Table 4.4.3 a star indicates that Model C performs as well as or better than Model B for the given demographic group and distributional comparison in terms of our pseudo chi-square criterion. In the column for the distribution of income cumulated over 7 years, we find a star for four out of six groups of women. Thus, the comparison between Model C and Model B, as summarized in Table 4.4.3, is quite favorable to Model C.

In Table 4.4.4 a star indicates the demographic groups for each set of distributional comparisons for which the Inertia Model is found to perform as well as or better than Models A, B and C. In the column for income cumulated over 7

4 Comparisons of Our Inertia Model

years, we find a star for three out of our six groups for women. Nevertheless, the results in Table 4.4.4 certainly cannot be interpreted as strong evidence in favor of accepting the Inertia Model in preference to Model A, B or C.

Of course, summaries of the rankings of these models of the sort given in Tables 4.4.1 through 4.4.4 may be misleading. For instance, sampling variability might lead one model sometimes to be ranked below and sometimes to be ranked above another, even though the performance of both is very similar and is really superior to the remaining two models. Thus, in Table 4.4.5 we show the actual rankings of our Inertia Model and Models A, B and C. These are the rankings on which all of the summary comparisons presented in Tables 4.4.1 through 4.4.4 are based. As we expected, Model A, which does not include the lagged hours variable in the hours equations, performs particularly poorly in terms of the distributions of individuals by years of full-time and years of part-time work. Model B is often found to compare favorably with our other three models. Nevertheless, if we look at the final rows in Table 4.4.5 for the distributions of income cumulated over 7 years, we find that all of the fourth place rankings are in the rows for Models A and B. Comparing the rankings for the Inertia Model and Model C, we find also that the Inertia Model is to be preferred to Model C for all individuals and all except the oldest group of women.[13] We take these results to be weak confirmation of our choice of the empirical results for the Inertia Model over the results for Models A, B and C.

4.5. How Well Can Our Alternative Models Capture the Impacts of Key Explanatory Variables?

In sections 4.1 and 4.3, we identify many similarities, but also some differences, among the Dummy and Split Models, Models A, B and C, and the Inertia Model in terms of the estimated impacts of various explanatory variables. In section 4.2 we conclusively reject the Standard Model on the basis that it fails to capture the observed continuity and earnings of individuals. Thus, we will not consider the Standard Model in this section. We also present evidence in section 4.2 that the Split Model is to be preferred to the Dummy Model, and the Inertia Model is to be preferred to both the Dummy and Split Models. In section 4.4 we give weak evidence that the Inertia Model should be preferred to Models A, B and C. Does this mean then that the coefficient estimates for the Inertia Model accurately portray the impacts of our explanatory variables on the various aspects of work behavior considered, or at least that the estimated coefficients of the Inertia Model are better estimates of the impacts of our explanatory variables than the estimated coefficients for any of our other models?

We have no direct evidence concerning how well our estimated models would capture the changes in the endogenous variables of interest if we were able to exogenously change the values of the explanatory variables. We can at least examine, however, the goodness-of-fit of these models for various simulated distributions of interest for subgroups of our data set. Evidence that the simulated distributions for a model are good approximations of the actual distributions of interest for population subgroups defined in terms of the values of particular explanatory variables is not proof that the estimated coefficients of the model accurately reflect the changes that would occur in endogenous variables if the values of the variables used in forming the population subgroups were changed exogenously. But evidence of poor fit of the simulated to the actual distributions strongly suggests that the model in question would not properly reflect the impacts of exogenous changes in the explanatory variable or variables of interest. Evidence of poor fit also suggests possible forecasting problems for particular population subgroups if the model were used to project behavior patterns into the future, even if this future is assumed to be similar to the present in a structural sense.

We will concentrate on checking the fit of our models for population subgroups defined in terms of the values of explanatory variables for which there are clear differences in the estimated coefficient values among our models. We will make the same distributional comparisons for the Dummy Model, the Split Model, and Models A, B and C as for the Inertia Model since it is possible for a model, to reflect the behavior of certain population subgroups better than other models, even though its performance is not optimal in some overall sense.

In this section we examine distributional results for six different partitions of the six demographic groups of women in our simulation population. In our first partition, we divide these groups of women into those who had a new baby or a young child sometime during the 7-year simulation period and those who did not have a baby or young child during this period. In our second partition, we split our groups for women 21-46 years of age in the first year of the simulation period into subgroups of women 21-33 and 34-46 years of age in this first year, and we split our groups for women 47-64 years of age in the first year of the simulation period into subgroups of women 47-55 and 56-65 years of age in this first year. In our third partition, we split our groups of women who were married in the first year of the simulation period into those married in all 7 years of the simulation period and those who were not married in at least 1 of these 7 years, and we split our

4 Comparisons of Our Inertia Model

groups of women who were unmarried in the first year of the simulation period into those unmarried in all 7 years of the simulation period and those who were married in at least 1 of these years. Our fourth partition consists of splitting our sample of women 47-64 years of age and married in the first year of the simulation period into those with husbands whose incomes, measured in 1967 dollars, never dropped by more than $3,000 from one year to the next, and those with husbands whose incomes did drop by this amount or more in a year sometime during the simulation period. In our fifth partition, we divide the women in each of our six demographic groups by whether they are black or nonblack. And in our sixth partition we divide our sample of women who were 21-46 years of age and unmarried in the first year of our simulation period into those who were and those who were not in households that received AFDC benefits sometime during our simulation period, and we divide our sample of women who were 47-64 years of age and unmarried in the first year of the simulation period into those who were and those who were not in households that received Social Security benefits sometime during the simulation period.

In Tables D.1 through D.12 in Appendix D, we show the actual distributions for years of work out of 7 and for individual income cumulated over 7 years. We also show the corresponding distributions for our simulation results for the models being compared for our child status partition for women 14-20, for women 21-46 and married, and for women 21-46 and unmarried in the first year of the simulation period. The actual proportion of women in the category of 7 years of work is, for all three age and marital status groups, smaller for women who did than for women who did not have a baby or small child; and women who had a baby or small child are particularly concentrated in a relative sense in the categories of 1-2 and 3-4 years of work out of 7. Women who had a baby or small child are also concentrated, in a relative sense, in the category for under $10,000 in the observed distributions for individual income cumulated over 7 years. Thus there are clear-cut differences in the relevant actual distributions of women who had a baby or small child versus those who did not. In Tables 4.5.1 and 4.5.2, we show the rankings of our models according to the values of the pseudo chi-square statistic for the distributional results shown in Tables D.1 through D.12. From these two tables, we are not able to detect any pattern of differences in the relative rankings of our models depending on the child-status category compared with the rankings of these models for the unpartitioned demographic groups.

In Tables D.13 through D.34, we show the actual and simulated distributions for years of work out of 7 and cumulative individual income for our age partition for women

TABLE 4.5.1
RANKINGS OF MODELS BY PSEUDO CHI-SQUARE
STATISTIC FOR DISTRIBUTIONS FOR NUMBER
OF YEARS WORKED OUT OF 7: CHILD STATUS SPLITS

Group	Inertia	Dummy	Split	A	B	C
Women 14-20	2	3.5	3.5	1	6	5
Women 14-20 with baby or young child	2.5	4.5	1	6	2.5	4.5
Women 14-20 with no baby or young child	5	1	4	2	6	3
Wives 21-46	6	3	5	1	4	2
Wives 21-46 with baby or young child	6	2	5	4	3	1
Wives 21-46 with no baby or young child	3	1	6	5	4	2
Unmarried women 21-46	2.5	4	6	1	2.5	5
Unmarried women 21-46 with baby or young child	6	3.5	3.5	1.5	1.5	5
Unmarried women 21-46 with no baby or young child	6	4	5	1	2.5	2.5

21-46 years of age and married, for women 21-46 years of age and unmarried, for women 47-64 years of age and married, and for women 47-64 years of age and unmarried in the first year of the simulation period. Again, there are systematic differences in the <u>actual</u> distributions of interest for the age subgroups. For instance, for women 21-46 years of age, we find lower proportions in the 7 years of work category for those in the younger than for those in the older age subgroups, while for women 47-64 we find higher proportions in the seven years of work category for those in the younger than for those in the older age subgroups. In Tables 4.5.3 and

TABLE 4.5.2
RANKINGS OF MODELS BY PSEUDO CHI-SQUARE
STATISTIC FOR DISTRIBUTIONS FOR EARNED INCOME
CUMULATED OVER 7-YEAR PERIOD: CHILD STATUS SPLITS

Group	Inertia	Dummy	Split	A	B	C
Women 14-20	1.5	3	6	5	4	1.5
Women 14-20 with baby or young child	1.5	3	4.5	1.5	4.5	6
Women 14-20 with no baby or young child	2	1	6	5	3	4
Wives 21-46	2	6	3	5	1	4
Wives 21-46 with baby or young child	2	6	3	5	1	4
Wives 21-46 with no baby or young child	2	4.5	4.5	3	1	6
Unmarried women 21-46	1	5	4	2	6	3
Unmarried women 21-46 with baby or young child	2	3.5	5	1	3.5	6
Unmarried women 21-46 with no baby or young child	1	6	3	2	5	4

4.5.4, we show the rankings of our models according to our pseudo chi-square statistic for the distributional results shown in Tables D.13 through D.34. On the whole, we are unable to find clear differences in the pattern of rankings depending on the age subgroup compared with the rankings for the unpartitioned demographic groups, except that the Inertia Model performs more poorly in a relative sense for the age subgroups for older women in terms of the ability of the model to capture the distributions of income cumulated over 7 years.

In Tables D.29 through D.40, we show the actual and simulated distributions for years of work out of 7 and for

TABLE 4.5.3
RANKINGS OF MODELS BY PSEUDO CHI-SQUARE STATISTIC
FOR DISTRIBUTIONS FOR NUMBER OF YEARS
WORKED OUT OF 7: AGE SPLITS

Group	Inertia	Dummy	Split	A	B	C
Wives 21-46	6	3	5	1	4	2
Wives 21-33	6	3	5	4	2	1
Wives 34-46	3	1.5	5	4	6	1.5
Unmarried women 21-46	2.5	4	6	1	2.5	5
Unmarried women 21-33	4.5	3	6	1	4.5	2
Unmarried women 34-46	3	5.5	2	1	4	5.5
Wives 47-64	4	1.5	6	5	1.5	3
Wives 47-55	6	4	5	2.5	1	2.5
Wives 56-64	2	1	5	6	4	3
Unmarried women 47-64	6	5	3	1	2	4
Unmarried women 47-55	4	3	6	1	2	5
Unmarried women 56-64	6	5	2.5	1	2.5	4

cumulative individual income for our marital status partition. There are very substantial differences in the actual distributions of interest for the subgroups created by our marital status partition. For instance, the proportion of women with no years of work is much higher for those subgroups of women who were either married or unmarried for all 7 years of the simulation period versus those subgroups consisting of women who changed marital status at least once during this period. For women 21-46 years of age, in those subgroups of women who changed marital status we also find much higher proportions in the upper income categories of our cumulative income distributions than for those women who were either

4 Comparisons of Our Inertia Model

TABLE 4.5.4
RANKINGS OF MODELS BY PSEUDO CHI-SQUARE
STATISTIC FOR DISTRIBUTIONS FOR EARNED INCOME
CUMULATED OVER 7-YEAR PERIOD: AGE SPLITS

Group	Inertia	Dummy	Split	A	B	C
Wives 21-46	2	6	3	5	1	4
Wives 21-33	1	6	4	5	3	2
Wives 34-46	1.5	5	3.5	3.5	1.5	6
Unmarried women 21-46	1	5	4	2	6	3
Unmarried women 21-33	2	3.5	5	1	6	3.5
Unmarried women 34-46	1	4	5.5	2.5	2.5	5.5
Wives 47-64	1.5	6	5	4	1.5	3
Wives 47-55	2.5	6	5	2.5	1	4
Wives 56-64	3	6	1	4	2	5
Unmarried women 47-64	2.5	5	6	1	4	2.5
Unmarried women 47-55	4	5	6	1.5	1.5	3
Unmarried women 56-64	5	6	3	2	1	4

married or unmarried for all 7 years. In Tables 4.5.5 and 4.5.6, we show the rankings of our models for the distributional results shown in Tables D.29 through D.40. Again, we find no systematic pattern of differences in the rankings of our models for the subgroups formed by our marital status partition compared with the rankings for the unpartitioned demographic groups.

In Tables D.41 through D.44, we show the same set of actual and simulated distributions for women who were 47-64 years of age and married in the first year of the simulation period partitioned by whether or not their husbands' incomes, measured in 1967 dollars, dropped in any year over the

TABLE 4.5.5
RANKINGS OF MODELS BY PSEUDO CHI-SQUARE
STATISTIC FOR DISTRIBUTIONS FOR NUMBER OF
YEARS WORKED OUT OF 7: MARITAL STATUS SPLITS

Group	Inertia	Dummy	Split	A	B	C
Wives 21-46	6	3	5	1	4	2
Women 21-46 and always married	6	3	4	2	5	1
Women 21-46 and not always married	5.5	2	3	4	5.5	1
Wives 47-64	4	1.5	6	5	1.5	3
Women 47-64 and always married	3.5	3.5	5	6	1.5	1.5
Unmarried women 21-46	2.5	4	6	1	2.5	5
Women 21-46 and always unmarried	3	5	6	1.5	1.5	4
Women 21-46 and not always unmarried	6	1	3.5	2	5	3.5
Unmarried women 47-64	6	5	3	1	2	4
Women 47-64 and always unmarried	5.5	5.5	4	1	2	3

simulation period by more than $3,000. The differences between the actual distributions for these two subgroups of women are not very substantial. Thus, it is not surprising to find in Tables 4.5.7 and 4.5.8 that the rankings of our models for the cumulative income distribution are quite similar for these population subgroups compared with the rankings for our whole group of women 47-64 and married in the first year of the simulation period. There is one important difference in rankings that appears in both Tables 4.5.7 and 4.5.8, however. For both the distribution of years of work out of 7 and the

TABLE 4.5.6
RANKINGS OF MODELS BY PSEUDO CHI-SQUARE
STATISTIC FOR DISTRIBUTIONS FOR EARNED INCOME
CUMULATED OVER 7 YEAR PERIOD: MARITAL STATUS SPLITS

Group	Inertia	Dummy	Split	A	B	C
Wives 21-46	2	6	3	5	1	4
Women 21-46 and always married	2	6	4	5	1	3
Women 21-46 and not always married	1.5	5	4	1.5	3	6
Wives 47-64	1.5	6	5	4	1.5	3
Women 47-64 and always married	1	4	6	4	2.5	2.5
Unmarried women 21-46	1	5	4	2	6	3
Women 21-46 and always unmarried	1	6	4.5	2	3	4.5
Women 21-46 and not always unmarried	2	4.5	4.5	1	6	3
Unmarried women 47-64	2.5	5	6	1	4	2.5
Women 47-64 and always unmarried	2.5	5	6	1	2.5	4

cumulative income distribution, Model A performs most poorly among the models being considered for the subgroup of women whose husbands experienced an income drop of more than $3,000 sometime during the simulation period. It should be recalled from section 4.3 that the coefficient of our variable for a negative change in the husband's income is very much larger in magnitude for Model A than for the Inertia Model.

In Tables D.45 through D.58, we show the actual and simulated distributions for years of work out of 7 and for cumulative individual income for black versus nonblack women.

TABLE 4.5.7

RANKINGS OF MODELS BY PSEUDO CHI-SQUARE STATISTIC FOR DISTRIBUTIONS FOR NUMBER OF YEARS WORKED OUT OF 7: SPLITS FOR DECLINE IN HUSBAND'S INCOME

Group	Inertia	Dummy	Split	A	B	C
Wives 47-64	4	1.5	6	5	1.5	3
Wives 47-64 with husbands whose incomes never dropped by more than $3,000 from one year to the next	2.5	1	6	2.5	4	5
Wives 47-64 with husbands whose incomes, from one year to the next, declined at least once by $3,000 or more	4.5	4.5	2.5	6	1	2.5

TABLE 4.5.8

RANKINGS OF MODELS BY PSEUDO CHI-SQUARE STATISTIC FOR DISTRIBUTIONS FOR EARNED INCOME CUMULATED OVER 7-YEAR PERIOD: SPLITS FOR DECLINE IN HUSBAND'S INCOME

Group	Inertia	Dummy	Split	A	B	C
Wives 47-64	1.5	6	5	4	1.5	3
Wives 47-64 with husbands whose incomes never dropped by more than $3,000 from one year to the next	1	6	5	4	2	3
Wives 47-64 with husbands whose incomes, from one year to the next, declined at least once by $3,000 or more	1	5	4	6	3	2

4 Comparisons of Our Inertia Model

TABLE 4.5.9
RANKINGS OF MODELS BY PSEUDO CHI-SQUARE
STATISTIC FOR DISTRIBUTIONS FOR NUMBER OF YEARS
WORKED OUT OF 7: BLACK VERSUS NONBLACK SPLITS

Group	Inertia	Dummy	Split	A	B	C
Wives 21-46	6	3	5	1	4	2
Black wives 21-46	6	4	5	2	3	1
Nonblack wives 21-46	5	3	6	1	4	2
Unmarried women 21-46	2.5	4	6	1	2.5	5
Black unmarried women 21-46	2	6	5	1	3	4
Nonblack unmarried women 21-46	6	1	5	4	2	3
Wives 47-64	4	1.5	6	5	1.5	3
Black wives 47-64	6	2.5	1	2.5	4	5
Nonblack wives 47-64	2	2	5	6	2	4
Unmarried women 47-64	6	5	3	1	2	4
Black unmarried women 47-64	3.5	6	5	1	2	3.5
Nonblack unmarried women 47-64	2	5	3	1	4	6

For women who were unmarried in the first year of the simulation period, larger proportions of the black subgroups never worked and smaller proportions worked all 7 years than for the nonblack subgroups, while the converse is true for women who were married in the first year of the simulation period. Also, for women who were unmarried in the first year of the simulation period, we find much smaller proportions of the black subgroups in the income categories of the cumulative

TABLE 4.5.10
RANKINGS OF MODELS BY PSEUDO CHI-SQUARE
STATISTIC FOR DISTRIBUTIONS FOR EARNED INCOME
OVER 7 YEAR PERIOD: BLACK VERSUS NONBLACK SPLITS

Group	Inertia	Dummy	Split	A	B	C
Wives 21-46	2	6	3	5	1	4
Black wives 21-46	4	3	6	1	2	5
Nonblack wives 21-46	1	6	5	4	2	3
Unmarried women 21-46	1	5	4	2	6	3
Black unmarried women 21-46	4	6	3	1	2	5
Nonblack unmarried women 21-46	4.5	4.5	2	3	6	1
Wives 47-64	1.5	6	5	4	1.5	3
Black wives 47-64	5	3	3	3	6	1
Nonblack wives 47-64	1.5	6	5	3	1.5	4
Unmarried women 47-64	2.5	5	6	1	4	2.5
Black unmarried women 47-64	4	6	3	5	1	2
Nonblack unmarried women 47-64	1	4	5	2	6	3

income distribution for at least $20,000 than for the nonblack subgroups, but this is not true for women who were married at the start of the simulation. In Tables 4.5.9 and 4.5.10, we show the rankings of our models for the distributional results shown in Tables D.45 through D.58. From the results as summarized in Table 4.5.10, we find that the Inertia Model performs more poorly for the black subgroups in terms of its relative ability to reflect the shapes of the observed

4 Comparisons of Our Inertia Model   265

cumulative income distributions compared with the relative performance of this model without the partitioning of our samples of women by race. Looking at the more detailed results in Tables D.52, D.54 and D.57, we find that for all black subgroups the Inertia Model substantially underestimates the proportion of women with no income over the 7-year simulation period. Also, for the black subgroups for women 21-46 years of age and married, and for women 47-64 who were unmarried in the first year of the simulation period, the Inertia Model considerably overestimates the proportions of individuals in the lowest positive income category while underestimating the proportions in the next lowest cumulative income category. For the black subgroup for women 21-46 years of age and unmarried in the first year of the simulation period, on the other hand, the Inertia Model overestimates the proportion of women in the cumulative income category of $30,000 - 39,999. We see from Table 4.5.10 that, in terms of the cumulative income distribution, Model A performs best for both black subgroups for women 21-46 years of age in the first year of the simulation period, while Model C performs consistently well in a comparative sense for the older black subgroups. It should be recalled that in section 4.3 we found substantially higher continuing hours of work for black wives compared with otherwise-similar nonblack wives for Model A than for the Inertia Model. These results suggest that in further research we should reexamine the role of the race dummy in the Inertia Model, with special attention to possible race-related differences in the impact of hours in the previous year on hours of work in the current year and to the way in which the race dummy impacts the estimated wage rate depending on the functional form of the wage equation.

Finally, in Tables D.59 through D.66, we show the actual and simulated distributions for years of work out of 7 and for cumulative individual income for women who were unmarried in the first year of the simulation period, partitioned according to whether or not their families ever received AFDC or Social Security benefits during the simulation period. The differences between the actual distributions for those women who did versus those who did not receive benefits during the simulation period are striking. For instance, of the 68 women who were 21-46 years of age and unmarried at the start of the simulation period and who received AFDC benefits during this period 29 percent never worked during this period and 15 percent worked all 7 years, while for the 179 women in this same demographic group who never received AFDC during this period 4 percent never worked and 62 percent worked all 7 years. Likewise, of the 32 women who were 47-64 years of age and unmarried at the start of the simulation period and who received Social Security benefits during the simulation period 72 percent never worked during the simulation period and none

TABLE 4.5.11
RANKINGS OF MODELS BY PSEUDO CHI-SQUARE
STATISTIC FOR DISTRIBUTIONS FOR NUMBER OF
YEARS WORKED OUT OF 7: AFDC/SOCIAL SECURITIY SPLITS

Group	Inertia	Dummy	Split	A	B	C
Unmarried women 21-46	2.5	4	6	1	2.5	5
Unmarried women 21-46 who received AFDC	3	6	4.5	1	4.5	2
Unmarried women 21-46 who did not receive AFDC	4	3	6	2	5	1
Unmarried women 47-64	6	5	3	1	2	4
Unmarried women 47-64 who received Social Security	1	6	5	4	3	2
Unmarried women 47-64 who did not receive Social Security	6	5	1	2	3	4

worked all 7 years, compared to percentage figures of 15 and 51, respectively, for those 113 women in this same group who never received Social Security benefits during the simulation period.

In Tables 4.5.11 and 4.5.12, we show the rankings of our models for the distributional results shown in Tables D.59 through D.66. From Table 4.5.12 we see that, in terms of the cumulative income distribution, the performance of the Inertia Model is unsatisfactory in a relative sense for one of the two subgroups for this partition for both age groups of unmarried women. Only Model A performs well in this respect for both subgroups for the younger age group, while none of our models appear to perform well in a relative sense for both subgroups for the older age group.

Tables D.59 through D.66 present a detailed picture of the dimensions in which further improvements are needed in modeling the labor force responses of unmarried women to the receipt of transfer payments. From Tables D.59 through D.62 for the distributions of individuals by years of work out of 7, we find that all of our models drastically underestimate

TABLE 4.5.12
RANKINGS OF MODELS BY PSEUDO CHI-SQUARE STATISTIC FOR DISTRIBUTIONS FOR EARNED INCOME CUMULATED OVER 7-YEAR PERIOD: AFDC/SOCIAL SECURITY SPLITS

Group	Inertia	Dummy	Split	A	B	C
Unmarried women 21-46	1	5	4	2	6	3
Unmarried women 21-46 who received AFDC	4	6	5	1	3	2
Unmarried women 21-46 who did not receive AFDC	1	5	4	2	6	3
Unmarried women 47-64	2.5	5	6	1	4	2.5
Unmarried women 47-64 who received Social Security	1	6	5	4	2	3
Unmarried women 47-64 who did not receive Social Security	3.5	1	2	3.5	5	6

the proportions of women who never work and overestimate the proportions of women who always work for the subgroups of women who were unmarried in the first year of the simulation period and who received AFDC or Social Security benefits sometime during the simulation period. For the subgroups of women who never received benefits during the simulation period, we find that our Inertia Model and Models B and C estimate approximately the correct proportions of women who are never found to work during the simulation period, with Model A overestimating these proportions; but all of our models underestimate the proportions of these women who worked all 7 years.

From Tables D.63 through D.66 for the distributions of individual income cumulated over the simulation period, we find that the simulated cumulative income distributions for all of our models place too many individuals in the upper income categories and too few in the $0 and lower income categories for the subgroups of women who were unmarried in the first year of the simulation period and received AFDC or Social Security benefits. The simulated cumulative income distributions for the subgroups of women who did not receive AFDC or Social Security benefits during the simulation period are much more satisfactory for all of our models. If we confine our attention to the Inertia Model and Models A, B and C, the Inertia Model performs as well as or better than the other three for the two subgroups of women who were unmarried in the first year of the simulation period and who did not receive AFDC or Social Security benefits during the simulation period. The lesson that emerges from these tables is that there are important differences in work behavior between women whose families do versus women whose families do not receive AFDC or Social Security benefits, particularly in the case of unmarried women; and these differences are not adequately captured by the introduction of simple dummy variables for the receipt of AFDC or Social Security benefits in the previous year as we have done in this study. This phenomenon is less important for married women, in part because relatively few married women younger than 65 are in families which receive AFDC or Social Security benefits.

Looking back over Tables 4.5.1 through 4.5.12, which summarize the results for our different partitions of the data, a few additional observations can be made. From the summary tables for the cumulative income distributions, we find clear evidence that the Inertia Model and Models A, B and C perform better than the Dummy and Split Models; and it is also clear that the Split Model is to be preferred to the Dummy Model when only information on lagged work status is available. Thus, we find clear evidence in favor of estimating separate sets of behavioral relationships for women who did and for women who did not work in the previous year; and we also find evidence of the importance of having available to us information on the lagged wage rate and hours of work, in addition to information on work status for the previous year. In our tables for the cumulative income distribution, we see that the Inertia Model does outperform Models A, B and C. Nevertheless, we find the performance of the simplest of these models, Model C, to be surprisingly good.

Little has been said about the tables for our distributions for years of work out of 7. This is because the rankings of our models displayed in these tables are somewhat erratic. Nevertheless, looking at these summary tables for years of work out of 7, we find a clear tendency for Model A to perform particularly well in this respect for the groups of women who were unmarried in the first year of the simulation period, and for Model C or Model B to yield the best results in this sense for those groups of women who were married in the first year of the simulation period. We are not sure what lessons can be learned from these results for years of work out of 7, except that it is clear that it can be misleading to judge the relative performance of alternative models of the

4 Comparisons of Our Inertia Model

work and earnings behavior of individuals solely on the basis of the ability of these models to properly simulate years of work and nonwork without regard to the ability of these models to properly simulate the amount of work and earnings in years of work as well.

4.6. Out-of-Sample Simulation Results

In sections 4.2, 4.4 and 4.5, we examine the ability of our alternative models to reflect the observed distributions of the dependent variables of interest for the same individuals, over essentially the same time period, whose pooled data were used in the estimation of our models. On the basis of these in-sample comparisons, we have found the Standard Model to perform far more poorly than our other six model variants. We have also found that the Dummy and Split Models, which use only lagged information about work status, perform somewhat more poorly than our Inertia Model and Models A, B and C which all use lagged information about the wage rate and hours of work in addition to lagged information about work status. Finally, we have found more tenuous evidence that the Inertia Model is to be preferred to Models A, B and C.

In our discussion of biases in section 2.5 we note that all of the explanatory variables included in this study are really composite variables that pick up the impacts of family and social background, abilities, preferences, and so forth in addition to the effects of these variables that are more commonly the focus of attention in theoretical models of labor force behavior. If this is the case, can any of our models satisfactorily explain the work behavior of individuals other than those whose data were used in the estimation of these models? Would any of our models even be able to explain the behavior of the same individuals in a different time period from the time period spanned by the data used in estimating our model?

When we began preliminary work for this study, PSID data were available only through 1979. Because we must obtain data on the current year's earnings and weeks of work from the records for the next year's wave of PSID data and because information on our lagged Social Security dummy variable is not available prior to the 1970 wave, our estimation was carried out using 1971-1978 data from the 1970-1979 waves of the PSID. Our in-sample simulation studies of these estimation results are for 1971-1977 since by 1978 there are no individuals in our category of women 14-20 years of age in 1971. By the time we were ready to write up these results, however, data from the 1980-1983 waves of the PSID were available, making it possible for us to perform out-of-sample simulation studies for 1981-1982.

In forming our in-sample 1971-1978 data base, we eliminated any individuals who were not in the PSID for all of the waves from 1970 through 1979. We also eliminated individuals who did not have usable data on any of our variables over the entire relevant time period. Thus, data for a total of only 2,657 individuals were included in our in-sample simulation population. In forming our out-of-sample simulation population, we have eliminated individuals who were not in the PSID for the four waves from 1980 through 1984 or who did not have usable data on any of our variables over the relevant time period. Because the out-of-sample time period is much shorter, we are left with 9,747 individuals in our out-of-sample simulation population. Thus, when individuals are grouped according to their demographic classification in the first out-of-sample simulation year, the number of individuals in each of these groupings is also much larger for our out-of-sample compared with our in-sample simulation population. These numbers are shown in the first column of Table 4.6.1. Of course, many of the 2,657 individuals included in our in-sample simulation population may also be included in the out-of-sample simulation population, but the out-of-sample simulation population contains at least 7,090 individuals not included in the in-sample simulation population. Also, none of the data from the 1970-1979 waves of the PSID that were used in estimating our models are used in our out-of-sample simulations because of the choice of the time period for the out-of-sample simulations.

Certainly the observed work behavior of the individuals in our out-of-sample simulation population over the 1981-1982 period is quite different from the observed work behavior of the individuals in our in-sample simulation population over the 1971-1977 period. From Table 4.6.1 we see, for instance, that for all of our demographic groupings except the oldest group of women, the average wage for those who work, measured in 1967 dollars, is considerably lower for our out-of-sample than for our in-sample population. (In each pair of numbers in Table 4.6.1, the upper number corresponds to the out-of-sample population while the lower number corresponds to the in-sample-population.) Average earnings are also lower for the out-of-sample than for the in-sample population, except for women 21-46 years of age and married and for women at least 65 years of age in the first year of the relevant simulation period. Employment rates and average annual hours of work are higher, on the other hand, for the out-of-sample than for the in-sample population for both groups of women 21-46 years of age and for women 47-64 years of age and married in the first simulation year.

In earlier sections of this chapter, we demonstrate that

TABLE 4.6.1
MEANS CALCULATED FROM POOLED DATA FOR OUR SIMULATION POPULATIONS FOR 1981-1982 (OUT-OF-SAMPLE) AND 1971-1978 (IN-SAMPLE), RESPECTIVELY

Group in first year of relevant simulation period	Number of individuals per year	Annual proportion who worked	Wage rate for workers	Annual hours of work for workers	Annual income for workers
All individuals	9747	.68	$2.84	1721	$5101
	2657	.73	3.36	1804	6307
Women 14-20	792	.42	1.52	904	1455
	172	.49	1.93	942	1609
Wives 21-46	1715	.68	2.37	1479	3333
	441	.59	2.53	1288	2980
Unmarried women 21-46	912	.79	2.28	1644	3793
	256	.73	2.51	1566	3972
Wives 47-64	599	.51	2.31	1440	3288
	149	.47	2.65	1336	3361
Unmarried women 21-46	391	.58	2.08	1591	3356
	156	.62	2.47	1656	4113
Women 65+	487	.14	1.57	936	1378
	88	.22	1.54	855	1372

the fits between the simulated and actual distributions of individual earned income cumulated over a number of years provide us with a meaningful basis for evaluating the performance of our alternative models. The simulated income of an individual in a year reflects whether or not the individual was simulated to work that year, and it reflects both the simulated wage rate and annual hours of work if the individual was found to work. Thus, errors in any one of our behavioral relationships, or concerning our specification of the distributions of the random error terms for the wage and hours equations, will affect the simulated earnings in a year for individuals found to work. Errors that are systematic will be magnified, and hence easier to detect, when the earnings of individuals are cumulated over many years. This will be

particularly true for all of our model variants where
information about work behavior in the previous year is used
in determining work behavior in the current year. The
cumulative individual income distributions are also of
particular interest because of recent concern and evidence
that many estimated models of labor force behavior do not
adequately capture the observed continuity over time in the
employment status and earnings of individuals.

Since we are able to cumulate individual incomes only
over a 2-year period for our out-of-sample simulations, we are
not able to discriminate among our models as well in terms of
their out-of-sample performance as we are able to in terms of
the in-sample performance of these models. Nevertheless, from
Tables E.1 through E.7, we find that the performance of the
Standard Model is clearly inferior to our other model variants
for all except the youngest and oldest groups of women. There
is little basis in these results for discriminating among the
remaining six models. All of them greatly overestimate the
proportion of women in the youngest age group with no earnings
over the 2-year period and tend also to overestimate the
proportion of women in this group with cumulative earnings
over this 2-year period in excess of $7,500. For all
individuals and the other five demographic groupings of women,
however, all of the models other than the Standard model quite
accurately predict the distribution of the income of
individuals cumulated over the 1981-1982 time period. Thus,
these models are able to properly predict the earnings
behavior for individuals whose average employment and earnings
behavior is quite different from the average behavior that
characterizes the data used in the estimation of our models.

4.7. Sensitivity of Our Simulation Results to Our Treatment of Extreme Wage Estimates

The simulation results for all of our model variants,
except Model C, which we present in the earlier sections of
this chapter, are based on simulation populations from which
we have eliminated those individuals for whom extreme wage
values are generated. Thus, for each model variant a different
number and selection of individuals have been eliminated. It
was necessary to do this because all of our model variants,
except Model C which incorporates a linear wage equation,
generate some estimated wage rates that are so large that our
simulation program will not continue properly. We could modify
our program so that it could accomodate these large values.
However, due to the dependence in most of our model variants
of a person's work behavior in the current year on the wage

rate and hours of work of the person in the previous year, once an enormous wage figure has been generated for an individual, all subsequent probabilities of work, wage rates and hours of work generated for this individual are badly distorted as well.

The fact that a particular model generates extreme, or otherwise unreasonable, values for a small number of individuals does not necessarily mean the model is misspecified in any important respect. For one thing, the reported values for some of the explanatory variables may be erroneous for some individuals. Or the model may fail to properly reflect the behavior of individuals with certain odd combinations of values for the explanatory variables, but it may provide a good representation of the behavior of most individuals. Another possibility is that the specified distributions for the error terms of the model do not have the proper shapes in the tails of these distributions.

It is common practice to set negative values generated for quantities like wage rates or hours of work equal to some small positive value. We do this for the negative wage rates generated by the estimated linear wage equations for Model C, and for the small number of negative figures for hours of work generated by all of our models. When either a person's wage rate or hours of work are set equal to some very small positive number, we virtually guarantee that the generated earned income for that person will also be very small. Suppose we were to truncate the generated wage distribution from the top as well. Suppose, for instance, that we simply set any generated wage rate that is larger than some cutoff value, such as $20, equal to this cutoff value. The generated income figures for those individuals whose wage rates were arbitrarily set equal to the cutoff value could fall almost anywhere in the distribution of simulated income figures. Thus, in examining our results for such a simulation, it would be impossible to say what effect these aberrant cases were having on the shape of the simulated income distribution.

Our justification for removing individuals for whom extreme wage values are simulated is that all aspects of the actual distributions of the dependent variables of interest that we have checked are virtually identical for our original populations and for our various populations from which individuals have been deleted for whom extreme wage values have been simulated. In Tables F.1 through F.7 in Appendix F, we show the actual proportions of individuals classified by the number of years of work out of 7 over the in-sample simulation period of 1971 through 1977 for our entire sample for each demographic group and for the various censored samples from which individuals with extreme simulated wage values have been deleted. The values for the chi-square statistic at the bottom of each of these tables are for tests of the null hypothesis that the distributions for these censored samples are identical to the distribution for the relevant uncensored sample. We see that this null hypothesis is accepted in all cases using a standard 5 percent critical region. In Tables F.8 through F.14, similar results are shown for the distributions of the earned income of individuals cumulated over the 7-year simulation period. We have checked numerous other aspects of the distributions of the dependent variables of interest as well. Thus, the actual distributions that we are trying to explain are virtually the same for our original population of individuals as they are for the populations of individuals that we have censored by removing individuals for whom extreme wage values were generated. In particular, we note that it is the simulated, not the reported, wage values of the individuals in question that are extreme. The actual wage values for these individuals have the appearance of being random samples from the uncensored wage distributions for the individuals in our demographic groups.

Still, concerns could be raised that the simulation comparisons among our various model variants might be sensitive to, or somehow distorted by, the way in which we have censored our simulation populations. Also, the censoring scheme we have adopted could not be used in a full-blown microanalytic simulation model of the household sector, because such a scheme could distort the representativeness of the simulation population with respect to characteristics other than the labor force characteristics of individuals and because the elimination of individuals in such a manner would wreak havoc with the family structure of the simulation population. Thus, we have repeated many of our simulation comparisons among our Standard, Dummy and Split Models; Models A, B and C; and our Inertia Model using a $20 cutoff for the generated wage rate. In Tables F.15 through F.18, we show a selection of our in-sample and out-of-sample results from our simulation studies using a $20 wage cutoff. Our finding from these additional simulations is that all of our conclusions given in the earlier sections of this chapter remain essentially unchanged. Thus, the results presented in the earlier sections of this chapter are not unduly sensitive to the treatment in our simulations of extreme wage estimates.

FOOTNOTES TO CHAPTER 4

1. Goldberger (1983), for instance, considers the effectiveness of the selection bias correction proposed by Heckman for the case where the normality assumption is violated. He concludes (p. 79) that this selection bias

correction procedure "will be quite sensitive to modest departures from normality." For further related studies see Arabmazar and Schmidt (1982) and Wales and Woodland (1980).

2. A log-linear functional form relating the wage rate and the education variable is sometimes justified as arising from a cost function whose only components are the rising interest costs of foregone income (see Mincer, 1974, p. 19). There is also some empirical evidence in favor of this functional form (see, for instance, Heckman and Polachek, 1974).

3. Heckman (1978a) suggests: "It is plausible to conjecture that 'lagged participation' might serve as a good 'proxy' for the effect of heterogeneity." In the revision of this working paper which was ultimately published, Heckman (1981, p. 118) refutes this conjecture on the basis of out-of-sample simulation results, stating:

> "Proxy methods" for solving the problems raised by heterogeneity such as ad hoc introduction of lagged work experience variables lead to dynamic models that yield exceedingly poor forecast equations for labor force turnover. Models that neglect recent market experience and heterogeneity actually perform better in forecasting turnover on fresh data, but these forecasts are still poor, and considerably overestimate the amount of turnover in the labor force.

It would appear, however, that the poor out-of-sample simulation results for his model incorporating a dummy variable for lagged participation are, in fact, due to peculiarities of his model that have nothing to do with the introduction of the dummy variable for lagged participation. In particular, the out-of-sample simulation problems stem from the impact of a national unemployment rate variable, for which the coefficient is poorly determined because the variable took on only two different values over the 3-year period covered by the panel data used in the estimation of the model, and from the impact of the in-sample experience variable, where this variable has a range of 0 to 3 in-sample and a range of 0 to 6 in the out-of-sample setting. Nakamura and Nakamura (1983a) present both in-sample and out-of-sample simulation results showing that the incorporation of a lagged dummy for work in the previous year, which is Heckman's lagged 'participation', can greatly improve the ability of a model of the labor force behavior of married women to capture the observed continuity over time in the employment and earnings behavior of individual women.

4. In the 1971 Census of Canada, for instance,

respondents were asked: "When did you last work at all, even for a few days?" The possible answers, from which the respondent was supposed to choose one, were "In 1971", "In 1970", "Before 1970", and "Never worked" (see Statistics Canada, 1975, question 32 in 1971 Census Questionnaire). To obtain the information needed for our Dummy and Split Models, this question would need to be reworded to ask: "Indicate all of the following time periods in which you worked at all, even for a few days: In 1971, In 1970, In 1969, Before 1969, Never worked." For the Dummy and Split Models we need to know if the person worked in the "lagged" year of 1969, with 1970 being the year for which "current" data were reported on weeks of work and earnings in the 1971 Census of Canada.

5. In the 1970 U.S. Census, respondents reported whether they last worked in 1970, 1969, 1968, 1964-1967, 1960-1963, 1959 or earlier, or never worked (see U.S. Department of Commerce, 1972, p. 73). What we need to know is all of these time periods in which the person worked, rather than just the last one. In particular, for the Dummy and Split Models we need to know if the person worked in the "lagged" year of 1968, with 1969 being the year for which "current" data were reported on weeks of work and earnings in the 1970 U.S. Census.

6. This result for the Standard Model is in qualitative agreement with the results reported by most other researchers. See Chapter 3, fn. 7.

7. See Nakamura et al. (1979), Nakamura, Nakamura and Cullen (1979), and Nakamura and Nakamura (1981,1983). For similar results based on PSID data, as was this study, but using different explanatory variables, different models, and more years of data for a sample of continuously married women, see Nakamura and Nakamura (1983a, Appendix).

8. No simulation results are presented for 1978 since there are no individuals left in our youngest age groups for women and men (14-20 years of age in the first simulation year) by this year.

9. See Nakamura and Nakamura (1983a, 1983b, 1984) for other applications of, and commentary on, simulation comparisons of this sort.

10. See Heckman (1978a, 1981) and Nakamura and Nakamura (1983a, 1983b, 1984) for other examples of the use of a chi-square statistic for comparing the relative performance of different models. Comparisons among the values for the pseudo chi-square statistic are valid for pseudo chi-square values computed using the same value of n. Massy, Montgomery and Morrison (1970,p. 36) suggest that "the chi-square statistic may be more useful for comparing the fit of two different models than it is in evaluating the correctness of either model."

11. The equations are identical for Method A and for our

4 Comparisons of Our Inertia Model

Inertia Method for those who did not work in the previous year. The differences in our estimation results between these two methods for those who did not work in the previous year are due to an inadvertent difference in the number of digits used in our intermediate computations for these two methods. For the most part, the differences are very small.

12. See Orcutt and Glazer (1980, section 3) for a description of this microanalytic simulation model prior to the most recent changes that have been made in the model by James D. Smith and his associates, in collaboration with Orcutt, at the Survey Research Center of the University of Michigan's Institute for Social Research.

13. If the application of our Inertia Model and Models A and B (as well as the Standard, Dummy and Split Models considered in sections 4.1 and 4.2) did <u>not</u> include dropping individuals with exploding wage estimates from our simulation populations, however, the wage and income means would be found to be ridiculously high for all of our models except Model C. (No individuals were dropped in our simulations for Model C.)

CHAPTER 5

PREVIOUS WORK EXPERIENCE

Work experience since reaching adulthood, or since marriage, has been found by other researchers to be an important determinant of the current work behavior of married women (see, for instance, Heckman, 1981, 1981a; Corcoran, 1982). We originally hoped to include such a variable in this study. We wanted to examine how previous work experience affects the work behavior not only of married women, but also of unmarried women and men. We found, however, that whereas values for the variable in the PSID data for years of work experience since turning 18 years of age are available for most of the women who were in the PSID and married over the time period spanned by our data, figures for this variable are missing for large numbers of the other types of women in our sample.[1] Moreover we found that even for those women who were married in all years for our sample period, figures for this variable are missing for disproportionally large numbers of women who worked small numbers of hours per year or on an intermittent basis over the years spanned by our data sample. We decided, therefore, that for the main portion of our analysis, it would be unacceptable to limit our sample of individuals to those for whom usable data are available on previous work experience.

Nevertheless, there are at least two reasons why we do want to investigate the impact of previous work experience on current work behavior. The first is that a measure of work experience over a period of years, as opposed to measures for just the previous year, may more adequately reflect tastes for work, capabilities for work, and other unobservable factors that may have important effects on current work behavior and that change slowly or not at all over substantial periods of time. Thus, controlling for previous work experience may allow us to obtain better measures of the current impacts of variables such as our child status and husband's income variables. A second reason for our interest in examining the role of previous work experience in determining current work behavior is that we want to be able to gauge how important it is for data collection agencies to collect recall information

5 Previous Work Experience

TABLE 5.1
COEFFICIENT ESTIMATES FOR PROBIT INDICES FOR
PROBABILITY OF WORK:
WIVES 21-46 YEARS OF AGE WHO DID NOT WORK IN t-1

	New sample			Old sample
Proportion of years worked since 18	.388*			
Years worked since 18		.026*		
Dummy for never worked since 18	-.178	-.198		
Dummy for married in t-1	-.355	-.362	-.368	-.195
Age	-.008	-.017*	-.008	-.020**
Race dummy	-.051	-.067	-.038	-.051
Education	.117**	.113**	.137**	.114**
Baby dummy	-.285*	-.287*	-.232	-.188
Young child dummy	-.300**	-.309**	-.274**	-.458**
Number of children younger than 18	.075*	.073*	.064*	.072**
Husband's income	-.030**	-.030**	-.030**	-.033**
Change in husband's income	.015	.015	.015	.011
Dummy for AFDC in t-1	.134	.124	.210	.154
National unemployment rate	-.708**	-.705**	-.702**	.018
National wage index	-.0572**	-.0571**	-.0569**	.0068**
Pseudo R^2 for model	.281	.282	.272	.074

TABLE 5.2
COEFFICIENT ESTIMATES FOR PROBIT INDICES FOR
PROBABILITY OF WORK:
WIVES 21-46 YEARS OF AGE WHO WORKED IN t-1

	New sample			Old sample
Proportion of years worked since 18	.050			
Years worked since 18		.013		
Hours in t-1	.00068**	.00067**	.00068**	.00067**
Wage in t-1	.0174	.0155	.0179	.0187
Dummy for married in t-1	.517**	.508**	.518**	.404**
Age	.029**	.022**	.028**	.020**
Race dummy	.014	-.010	.019	-.059
Education	.064*	.063*	.064**	.036*
Baby dummy	-.711**	-.734**	-.702**	-.528**
Young child dummy	-.283*	-.293**	-.280*	-.130*
Number of children younger than 18	.009	.013	.007	
Husband's income	-.025*	-.024*	-.026*	
Change in husband's income	.039**	.039**	.039**	.019*
Dummy for AFDC in t-1	-1.161**	-1.163**	-1.161	-.509*
National unemployment rate	-.491**	-.493*	-.490**	.028
National wage index	-.0388**	-.0388**	-.0388**	.0019
Pseudo R^2 for model	.318	.319	.318	.198

TABLE 5.3
COEFFICIENT ESTIMATES FOR PROBIT INDICES FOR
PROBABILITY OF WORK:
WIVES 47-64 YEARS OF AGE WHO DID NOT WORK IN t-1

	New sample			Old sample
Proportion of years worked since 18	.821**			
Years worked since 18		.021**		
Dummy for never worked since 18	-.121	-.169		
Dummy for married in t-1	-1.083*	-1.110*	-1.241**	-.997**
Age	-.080**	-.089**	-.078**	-.055**
Race dummy	-.038	.010	.270	.014
Education	.051	.054	.071	.038
Number of children younger than 18	-.013	-.018	-.053	.010
Husband's income	-.027*	-.028*	-.031*	-.029*
Negative change in husband's income	.045	.045	.047	.042
Dummy for Social Security in t-1	-.194	-.206	-.152	-.486
National unemployment rate	-.664**	-.663**	-.695**	.033
National wage index	-.0584**	-.0584**	-.0607**	.0041
Pseudo R^2 for model	.256	.254	.228	.076

TABLE 5.4
COEFFICIENT ESTIMATES FOR PROBIT INDICES FOR
PROBABILITY OF WORK:
WIVES 47-64 YEARS OF AGE WHO WORKED IN t-1

	New sample			Old sample
Proportion of years worked since 18	-.567*			
Years worked since 18		-.017*		
Hours in t-1	.00074**	.00074**	.00067**	.00057**
Wage in t-1	.0750*	.0750*	.0649*	.0501*
Dummy for married in t-1	1.820**	1.830**	1.760**	1.443**
Age	-.044**	-.035*	-.042*	-.029*
Race dummy	-.064	.060	-.201	.062
Education	.005	.005	.009	.044
Number of children younger than 18	.030	.030	.037	
Husband's income	-.002	-.002	.001	
Negative change in husband's income	.099**	.098**	.095**	.113**
Dummy for Social Security in t-1	.068	.063	.080	-.373
National unemployment rate	-.470**	-.468**	-.466**	.001
National wage index	-.0372**	-.0371**	-.0367**	.0041
Pseudo R² for model	.317	.318	.310	.189

5 Previous Work Experience

TABLE 5.5
OLS COEFFICIENT ESTIMATES FOR LOG WAGE EQUATIONS:
WORKING WIVES 21-46 YEARS OF AGE WHO DID NOT WORK IN t-1

	New sample			Old sample
Proportion of years worked since 18	.171			
Years worked since 18		.012		
Dummy for never worked since 18	−.021	−.044		
Age	−.009	−.013*	−.010	−.014**
Race dummy	−.132	−.138	−.107	−.066
Education	.102**	.103**	.109**	.141**
National unemployment rate	−.081	−.096	−.090	−.046
National wage index	−.0048	.0060	−.0056	.0002
Selection bias term	.035	.083	.073	.497*
R^2	.084	.085	.081	.099

on previous work experience in addition to information for a single previous year.[2]

To investigate these questions empirically, we have had to eliminate from our pooled data samples for our different demographic groups of women observations that do not include usable information on the number of years a women has worked since turning 18 years of age. We reestimated all the equations for our Inertia Model using these restricted data samples for wives 21-46 and wives 47-64 years of age. In the last column on Tables 5.1 through 5.12 we show again, for convenience, the estimation results for our Inertia Model which were presented for wives 21-46 and wives 47-64 years of age in Chapter 3. These results appear in Tables 5.1 through 5.12 under the column heading "Old sample." In the next to last column of these tables, we show the comparable estimation

TABLE 5.6
OLS COEFFICIENT ESTIMATES FOR LOG WAGE EQUATIONS:
WORKING WIVES 21-46 YEARS OF AGE WHO WORKED IN t-1

	New sample		Old sample	
Proportion of years worked since 18	.286**			
Years worked since 18		.014**		
Hours in t-1	.0001**	.0001**	.0001**	.0001**
Wage in t-1	.055**	.055**	.059**	.067**
Age	.004*	.004*	.002	.001
Race dummy	-.071*	-.080**	-.056*	-.065**
Education	.101**	.102**	.100**	.086**
National unemployment rate	-.018	-.017	-.019	-.024**
National wage index	-.0001	.0000	-.0000	-.0008
Selection bias term	-.167	-.207*	-.167	-.437**
R^2	.269	.269	.256	.253

results for our Inertia Model using our "new" restricted data samples of observations, which include usable information on previous work experience. Thus, the differences between the results presented in the last two columns of these tables are due to differences in the composition of the data samples used in obtaining these results. The only variables for which we find systematic differences in sign depending on the sample used in estimation are the national unemployment rate and national wage index variables. The coefficients of these variables are consistently negative for the new restricted data sample in all of the probit indices and in the wage equations for wives in the younger age group. Without further investigation, it is difficult to judge whether any substantive meaning should be attached to this change in

TABLE 5.7
OLS COEFFICIENT ESTIMATES FOR LOG WAGE EQUATIONS:
WORKING WIVES 47-64 YEARS OF AGE WHO DID NOT WORK IN t-1

	New sample			Old sample
Proportion of years worked since 18	.128			
Years worked since 18		.004		
Dummy for never worked since 18	.669*	.668*		
Age	.013	.011	.010	-.014
Race dummy	.108	.116	.034	.053
Education	.142**	.142**	.113**	.102*
National unemployment rate	.175	.178	.204*	.067
National wage index	.0068	.0068	.0093	-.0038
Selection bias term	-.351	-.352	-.385	-.104
R^2	.224	.222	.190	.143

results. We also note that the coefficient estimates for the own wage variable in the hours equations become somewhat more positive in three out of the four cases for the new restricted samples compared with our results for the old samples.

In the first column of Tables 5.1 through 5.12, we show estimation results for a variation of our Inertia Model incorporating into the probit indices and wage equations a variable for the number of years of work since 18 years of age. In the second column we show estimation results for another variation of our Inertia Model incorporating the proportion of years worked since 18, instead of the number of years worked, into the probit indices and wage equations.[3] Both these variants of our Inertia Model also include a dummy variable set equal to 1 if the woman has never worked since 18 and set equal to 0 otherwise.[4]

TABLE 5.8
OLS COEFFICIENT ESTIMATES FOR LOG WAGE EQUATIONS:
WORKING WIVES 47-64 YEARS OF AGE WHO WORKED IN t-1

	New sample			Old sample
Proportion of years worked since 18	.172*			
Years worked since 18		.005*		
Hours in t-1	.0001**	.0001**	.0002**	.0001*
Wage in t-1	.096**	.096**	.098**	.105**
Age	.002	-.000	.002	.007
Race dummy	-.085*	-.086*	-.056	-.071
Education	.066**	.066**	.064**	.072**
National unemployment rate	.007	.007	.008	.006
National wage index	-.0002	-.0002	-.0000	-.0012
Selection bias term	-.259*	-.268*	-.269*	-.450**
R^2	.377	.377	.374	.365

Comparing the estimation results for the probit indices shown in columns 1, 2 and 3 of Tables 5.1 through 5.4, we find a sign change for the husband's income variable from .001 for the Inertia Model without any experience variable to -.002 for the variants including experience variables for wives 47-64 years of age who worked in the previous years, and we find sign changes for the coefficient estimates for the race dummy, particularly for wives who worked in the previous year.[5] From columns 1, 2 and 3 of Tables 5.5 through 5.9 for the estimated wage equations, we find one apparently trivial sign change for the coefficient of the national wage index, and we find that for both age groups for wives who worked in the previous year, the estimated coefficient of the age variable turns from positive to negative when we introduce our experience variable

5 Previous Work Experience

TABLE 5.9
IV COEFFICIENT ESTIMATES FOR HOURS EQUATIONS:
WORKING WIVES 21-46 YEARS OF AGE WHO DID NOT WORK IN t-1

	New sample			Old sample
Estimated log wage	-325.6	-256.3	-340.4	-397.3*
Dummy for married in t-1	-238.2	-235.9	-238.5	-313.7*
Age	-8.2	-7.9	-8.5	-4.4
Race dummy	193.2*	202.9*	193.4*	252.8**
Baby dummy	-265.6	-272.9*	-268.7*	-135.2
Young child dummy	23.3	17.6	21.4	70.2
Number of children younger than 18	-23.7	-21.7	-22.3	-26.7
Husband's income	-20.5**	-21.8**	-19.8*	-6.3
Change in husband's income	-15.8*	-15.5	-16.0*	-15.4*
Dummy for AFDC in t-1	-313.2	-313.8	-326.7	-204.4
Selection bias term	-80.9	-68.6	-66.9	-187.3
R^2	.129	.128	.129	.109

measured as years of work since 18. From columns 1, 2 and 3 of Tables 5.9 through 5.12 for the hours equations, we find no changes in sign whatever depending on whether or not, or on the manner in which, information concerning years of work since 18 is incorporated.

From the bottom row of Tables 5.1 through 5.4, we see that the addition of an experience variable in the probit indices seems to increase the pseudo R^2 for the model appreciably only for wives 47-64 years of age who did not work in the previous year. From the bottom row of Tables 5.5 through 5.12, we find that this pattern is repeated for the R^2

TABLE 5.10
IV COEFFICIENT ESTIMATES FOR HOURS EQUATIONS: WORKING WIVES 21-46 YEARS OF AGE WHO WORKED IN t-1

	New sample			Old sample
Estimated log wage	156.3**	158.2**	163.5**	85.2*
Hours in t-1	.549**	.550**	.548**	.496**
Dummy for married in t-1	81.1	81.4	84.0	3.9
Age	-3.9*	-3.8*	-3.7*	-5.0**
Race dummy	10.3	10.8	12.4	82.6**
Baby dummy	-67.7	-66.2	-60.7	58.0
Young child dummy	26.1	26.2	28.7	4.0
Number of children younger than 18	-14.5	-14.6	-16.1*	
Husband's income	-7.6*	-7.6*	-7.9**	
Change in husband's income	-3.5	-3.5	-3.3	-10.1**
Dummy for AFDC in t-1	-117.7	-120.7	-131.8	218.0
Selection bias term	-96.4	-86.8	-94.0	-392.0*
R^2	.389	.389	.389	.378

values for our wage and hours equations. Notice also that even the improvements in the pseudo R^2 and R^2 values for wives 47-64 years of age who did not work in the previous year resulting from the addition of an experience variable are modest. However, we find large increases in Tables 5.1 through 5.4 in the pseudo R^2 values for our estimated probit relationships using the new restricted, as opposed to the old, data samples. That is, we are able to predict current work status more accurately within the new restricted samples than

5 Previous Work Experience   289

TABLE 5.11
IV COEFFICIENT ESTIMATES FOR HOURS EQUATIONS:
WORKING WIVES 47-64 YEARS OF AGE WHO DID NOT WORK IN t-1

	New sample			Old sample
Estimated log wage	203.9	182.8	9.5	-106.2
Dummy for married in t-1	-27.5	-38.8	-132.6	219.8
Age	-72.3**	-73.4**	-80.5**	-62.8
Race dummy	-91.7	-94.1	-137.5	-117.3
Number of children younger than 18	-73.2	-75.3	-90.8	-59.9
Husband's income	-79.4**	-79.5**	-79.7**	-57.5*
Negative change in husband's income	-84.2	-82.6	-71.0	-52.7
Dummy for Social Security in t-1	-751.3	-756.7	-800.3	-594.6
Selection bias term	-174.0	-160.7	-63.1	-505.5
R^2	.435	.431	.414	.355

within our old samples, in at least a pooled sense.[6] We do not observe such a difference in Tables 5.5 through 5.12 in the R^2 values for our wage and hours equations.

From the estimates shown in columns 1 and 2 of Tables 5.1 through 5.12 for the coefficients of the experience variables, we see that in the case of the probit results the coefficient estimates for the experience variables are larger in magnitude for wives who did not work in the previous year than for wives who did work in the previous year, while the reverse is true in the case of the results for the wage equations. For both the probit and wage equation results, however, we find very little change due to the addition of an experience variable in the coefficient values for the variables for the wage rate and hours of work in the previous year. From Tables 5.9 through 5.12, we see that the coefficient estimates for the current

TABLE 5.12
IV COEFFICIENT ESTIMATES FOR HOURS EQUATIONS:
WORKING WIVES 47-64 YEARS OF AGE WHO WORKED IN t-1

	New sample			Old sample
Estimated log wage	46.2	46.1	21.4	51.3
Hours in t-1	.654**	.654**	.645**	.650**
Dummy for married in t-1	291.9	289.1	223.8	479.7*
Age	-12.4**	-12.4**	-11.2*	-10.4*
Race dummy	56.8	56.9	53.0	59.9
Number of children younger than 18	-2.5	-2.5	-2.7	
Husband's income	4.7	4.6	4.8	
Negative change in husband's income	12.8	12.7	10.3	9.3
Dummy for Social Security in t-1	38.8	39.4	56.9	101.8
Selection bias term	162.7	160.0	45.4	-2.4
R^2	.476	.476	.475	.483

wage rate variable in the hours equation become somewhat more positive when an experience variable is included in the probit and wage equations of the Inertia Model. The extent of the changes in these coefficient values is modest, except for wives 47-64 years of age who did not work in the previous year, though, and provides no support for the position that the uncompensated wage elasticities of hours of work are substantially in excess of unity for married women.[7] We also note that we are not able to detect any pattern of differences in our coefficient estimates depending on whether the experience variable that is included in the probit indices and wage equations is years of work or the proportion of years of work since 18, except that the estimated coefficient of the age variable is generally more negative in value when the proportion of years, rather than the actual years, of work experience variable is used.

In some published studies, the experience variable is treated as endogenous (see, for example, Heckman, 1981). There are two related motivations for doing this. First, suppose we want to be able to use the estimated coefficient of the experience variable in the wage equation as an estimate of how the current offered wage rate of a woman would differ if, for instance, she had not dropped out of the work force for some number of years while having children. In this case we want to be able to separate out the impacts of additional years of job experience from the impacts on the offered wage of other person-specific unobservable effects, such as basic capabilities and tastes for work, which are embedded in the observed work history of the woman and which may also affect her current work behavior. This is essentially the issue of determining how much of the observed state dependence is due to heterogeneity and how much is due to "true" state dependence.[8] Second, we may be concerned that correlations between the experience variable and the disturbance terms for our relationships for current work behavior will lead to biased and inconsistent estimates of the coefficients of other explanatory variables that are correlated with the experience variable.[9]

In this section, though, we are addressing the more limited question of whether there is any important impact of previous work experience, due to either heterogeneity or true state dependence, on current work behavior, <u>after taking into account work behavior in the previous year</u>. We find some evidence that work experience since 18 is positively related to both the current probability of work and the current wage rate, even after controlling for work behavior in the previous year; but the addition of an experience variable results in very slight increases in the pseudo R^2 and R^2 values for our relationships. Also, the coefficient estimates for our other explanatory variables are largely unchanged in terms of either their signs or their magnitudes.

FOOTNOTES TO CHAPTER 5

1. Starting with the 1974 wave of the PSID, heads of families were asked, "How many years have you worked for money since you were 18?" and, "How many years altogether has your (wife/friend) worked for money since she was 18?" (See Institute for Social Research, 1980, p. 260, variable 6750, and p. 250, variable 6720).)

2. In discussions with officials at Statistics Canada we have come to realize that collecting information on a recall basis pertaining to <u>many years</u> of a person's life, such as information on how many years a person has worked since 18, is much more difficult than collecting recall information for some particular recent year.

3. We used the proportion of years worked since 18 in Nakamura and Nakamura (1983a). In the context of a microanalytic simulation model where values of an experience variable would be generated over the course of the simulation, the proportion of years of experience may have some advantage over the actual years of experience in terms of the potential for distortion of the simulation results for some individuals due to the generation of extreme values of the experience variable. In particular, in the data base used in estimation, as well as in any in-sample or out-of-sample simulations, the computed values for the proportion of years of work experience since 18 years of age will always lie between 0 and 1 inclusive.

4. Such a dummy variable for no previous years of work since turning 18 was found to be important in Nakamura and Nakamura (1983a).

5. Notice that for wives who worked in the previous year there are sign changes for the coefficient estimates for the race dummy depending on the sample or the previous work experience information used. The coefficient signs are negative in all cases for wives 21-46 who did not work in the previous year. The rest of the coefficients are erratic in sign.

6. Since we have not been able to estimate relationships containing an experience variable for unmarried women and since many women change marital status over our simulation time period, we have not been able to assess whether the higher pseudo R^2 values for our probit relationships for married women for whom experience data are available indicate that we could predict the <u>distribution</u> for these women for years of work out of 7 more accurately, too. In Chapter 4 we see that our Inertia Model predicts this distribution quite well for all our demographic groups of women.

7. Killingsworth (1983, p. 192-200) states:

The most striking anomaly, however, is the set of results of Nakamura, Nakamura, and Cullen (1979, for Canadian women) and Nakamura and Nakamura (1981, for both Canadian and U.S. women): In contrast with virtually all other first- <u>and</u> second-generation research, their Procedure VIII results based on Census data imply uncompensated wages elasticities for female hours of work that are <u>negative</u> ....
One possible reason is that Nakamura, Nakamura and

Cullen ... in constrast with most other second-generation work ... do not include a measure of actual work experience in their specification of the wage function or the probability-of-working function.

8. Heterogeneity and true state dependence are differentiated conceptually, for instance, in Heckman (1981).

9. This might be of particular concern in a study in which the objective is to measure long-run response parameters.

CHAPTER 6

SENSITIVITY OF OUR SIMULATION RESULTS FOR WIVES
TO CHANGES IN THEIR CIRCUMSTANCES

In Chapter 4 we determine that among the various models considered in this study, the Inertia Model is probably the best. In Chapter 3 we show the impacts implied by the estimated coefficients of this model on the probability of work, wage rates and hours of work of various hypothetical women for various incremental changes in the explanatory variables included in this model. From these results, however, it may still be difficult to gauge the impact of a change in some explanatory variable on the distributions of interest, such as the distribution of years of work out of 7 or of cumulative earnings. It may also be difficult to see from the material shown in Chapter 3 how different the work behavior implied by our estimated behavioral relationships really is for married versus unmarried women or for women versus men.

In this chapter we first look at how the cumulative distributions for years of work and earnings would be predicted to differ under each of the following sets of circumstances: (1) if none of the women in our in-sample simulation population had any children at home over the simulation period, (2) if all of the husband's income variables were set equal to 0 for the entire simulation period, (3) if all women had an extra year of education, (4) if all women who were married in 1971 were unmarried in 1972, and (5) if all married women behaved according to our estimated relationships for unmarried women over the whole simulation period. We then present the results of three more simulation experiments designed to demonstrate the extent to which the work behavior of wives differs from that of men, as this behavior is summarized by our estimated equations for married women and for men. Finally, we present simulation results that show the extent to which our Inertia Model captures the differences in work behavior between black and nonblack wives, and that show how much of the black-nonblack difference for each of the distributions is estimated to be

6   Sensitivity of Simulation Results

TABLE 6.1

ACTUAL AND SIMULATED PROPORTIONS OF WOMEN BY NUMBER
OF YEARS WORKED OUT OF 7 FOR WOMEN 21-46 YEARS OF
AGE AND MARRIED IN 1971, AND SIMULATED DISTRIBUTIONS
FOR THESE SAME WOMEN GIVEN THE DESIGNATED
EXPERIMENTAL CHANGES IN THEIR CIRCUMSTANCES

Number of years worked out of 7	Actual distribution	Predicted distribution	Predicted distributions for our experiments		
			No children	No husband's income	Extra year of education
0	.17	.13	.12	.07	.09
1-2	.15	.17	.19	.12	.16
3-4	.15	.19	.16	.21	.18
5-6	.23	.21	.21	.28	.25
7	.30	.30	.32	.32	.31
Pseudo chi-square statistic for comparisons with original predicted distribution (n=424)			4	29	9

due to differences in the characteristics of black versus nonblack wives rather than to race-related differences in behavior as summarized by the coefficient estimates for our race dummy variable.[1]

In the first two columns of Tables 6.1 and 6.2, we show the actual and simulated proportions of women by years of work out of 7 and by earned income cumulated over the 7-year simulation period, for women 21-46 years of age and married in 1971.[2] In columns 3 through 5 of these tables, we show the corresponding distributions predicted by our Inertia Model for these same women assuming they had no children at home over the entire simulation period, assuming all of the husband's income variables were set equal to 0 for the whole simulation period, and assuming all of these women had an extra year of education. From these results we see that when these women are assumed to have no children at home over the entire simulation period,[3] there is no clear change in the distribution of years of work out of 7 and only a slight shift from the $0 and under

TABLE 6.2
ACTUAL AND SIMULATED PROPORTIONS OF WOMEN BY EARNED
INCOME CUMULATED OVER 7-YEAR PERIOD FOR WOMEN 21-46
YEARS OF AGE AND MARRIED IN 1971, AND SIMULATED
DISTRIBUTIONS FOR THESE SAME WOMEN GIVEN THE DESIGNATED
EXPERIMENTAL CHANGES IN THEIR CIRCUMSTANCES

Earned income cumulated over 7-year period	Actual distribution	Predicted distribution	No children	No husband's income	Extra year of education
$0	.17	.15	.14	.07	.10
Less than $10,000	.40	.38	.35	.35	.32
$10,000-19,999	.20	.20	.21	.25	.25
$20,000-29,999	.12	.12	.14	.15	.17
$30,000-39,999	.07	.08	.08	.10	.08
Over $39,999	.05	.08	.08	.07	.09
Pseudo chi-square statistic for comparisons with original predicted distribution (n=424)			3	30	26

(Predicted distributions for our experiments)

$10,000 cumulative income categories to the categories in the $10,000 - 29,999 range. Of course, such a drastic alteration of child status is not realistic. What these results demonstrate, however, is that according to our estimated model, once we have accounted for the observed work behavior of these women in the year prior to the start of the simulation period, and after controlling for changes in other explanatory variables over the simulation period, changes in child status over this period have little, if any, effect on work status or cumulative earnings. If this result is correct, it has many implications. For instance, it suggests that it should be possible to make good short- to medium-term forecasts of the work behavior of women, whether or not it is possible to properly forecast their fertility behavior.

We find, however, that there is some responsiveness of

TABLE 6.3
ACTUAL AND SIMULATED PROPORTIONS OF WOMEN BY NUMBER
OF YEARS WORKED OUT OF 7 FOR WOMEN 47-64 YEARS OF AGE
AND MARRIED IN 1971, AND SIMULATED DISTRIBUTIONS
FOR THESE SAME WOMEN GIVEN THE DESIGNATED EXPERIMENTAL
CHANGES IN THEIR CIRCUMSTANCES

Number of years worked out of 7	Actual distribution	Predicted distribution	Predicted distributions for our experiments		
			No children	No husband's income	Extra year of education
0	.38	.36	.36	.28	.35
1-2	.13	.16	.17	.18	.20
3-4	.12	.15	.13	.19	.13
5-6	.19	.12	.13	.11	.11
7	.18	.21	.21	.24	.21
Pseudo chi-square statistic for comparisons with original predicted distribution (n=119)			0	4	2

predicted work behavior to changes in the husband's income
variables, even after taking into account the observed work
behavior of these women in 1970 and changes in the other
explanatory variables. We find that in the extreme case where
all of the husband's income variables are set equal to 0,
there is a clear shift from the 0 and 1-2 years of work
categories to the 3-4, 5-6, and 7 years categories; and there
is also a shift from the categories for no earnings and under
$10,000 of earnings to the cumulative income categories
between $10,000 and $39,999. Thus, when the real earnings of
husbands fall due to illness, unemployment, inflation or any
combination of these causes, we find that there is some
tendency for wives in the 21-46 age bracket to work more and
earn more. The results in Tables 6.1 and 6.2 also tell us that
wives with more education do tend to work more and earn more
than other wives over a period of years, even after
controlling for the observed work behavior of these wives at
the beginning of that period and for changes in other

TABLE 6.4
ACTUAL AND SIMULATED PROPORTIONS OF WOMEN BY EARNED
INCOME CUMULATED OVER 7-YEAR PERIOD FOR WOMEN 47-64
YEARS OF AGE AND MARRIED IN 1971, AND SIMULATED
DISTRIBUTIONS FOR THESE SAME WOMEN GIVEN THE DESIGNATED
EXPERIMENTAL CHANGES IN THEIR CIRCUMSTANCES

			Predicted distributions for our experiments		
Earned income cumulated over 7-year period	Actual distribution	Predicted distribution	No children	No husband's income	Extra year of education
$0	.38	.37	.38	.29	.37
Less than $10,000	.29	.26	.23	.28	.27
$10,000-19,999	.15	.18	.15	.20	.13
$20,000-29,999	.08	.08	.13	.08	.08
$30,000-39,999	.02	.05	.02	.08	.05
Over $39,999	.09	.06	.10	.08	.10
Pseudo chi-square statistic for comparisons with original predicted distribution (n=119)			10	5	5

explanatory variables. The differences are not dramatic for the 21-46-year-old age group, however.

In Tables 6.3 and 6.4, we show the same results for women who were 47-64 years of age and married in 1971 that we show in Tables 6.1 and 6.2 for women who were 21-46 years of age and married in 1971. It is difficult to say if there is any effect at all of our experimental changes in child status, husband's income or educational level for this older group of women.

In column 3 of Tables 6.5 and 6.6 we show, for women 21-46 and married in 1971, the distributions predicted by our Inertia Model for years of work and cumulative income if all of these women were unmarried in 1972.[4] The year 1972 is the second year of our simulation period. We see that substantial shifts are predicted from the 0, 1-2 and 3-4 years of work

TABLE 6.5
ACTUAL AND SIMULATED PROPORTIONS OF WOMEN BY NUMBER
OF YEARS WORKED OUT OF 7 FOR WOMEN 21-46 YEARS OF
AGE AND MARRIED IN 1971, AND SIMULATED DISTRIBUTIONS
FOR THESE SAME WOMEN GIVEN THE DESIGNATED
EXPERIMENTAL CHANGES IN THEIR BEHAVIOR

Number of years worked out of 7	Actual distribution	Predicted distribution	Predicted distributions for our experiments	
			All unmarried in 1972	Behavior same as for unmarried women
0	.17	.13	.03	.00
1-2	.15	.17	.12	.00
3-4	.15	.19	.17	.02
5-6	.23	.21	.36	.09
7	.30	.30	.32	.89
Pseudo chi-square statistic for comparisons with original predicted distribution (n=424)			86	713

categories to the 5-6 and 7 years categories; and from the cumulative income categories for no earnings and under $10,000 to the categories between $10,000 and $79,999. These shifts are all the more impressive since after 1972 the women in our simulation population are again treated according to their actual marital statuses, which for most is married, for the remaining 5 years of the simulation period. Thus, according to our model, an episode of divorce tends to increase a woman's labor supply and earnings for years to come, even if she remarries and even after controlling for her observed work behavior prior to the episode of divorce and for changes over time in other explanatory variables. The behavior of women who have had an episode of divorce and who remarry again is still found to be very different, however, from what it would be if they were single over a prolonged period of time. In the final column of Tables 6.5 and 6.6, we show the predicted distributions for years of work and cumulative earnings for women 21-46 years of age and married in 1971 obtained by

TABLE 6.6
ACTUAL AND SIMULATED PROPORTIONS OF WOMEN BY EARNED
INCOME CUMULATED OVER 7-YEAR PERIOD FOR WOMEN 21-46
YEARS OF AGE AND MARRIED IN 1971, AND SIMULATED
DISTRIBUTIONS FOR THESE SAME WOMEN GIVEN THE DESIGNATED
EXPERIMENTAL CHANGES IN THEIR BEHAVIOR

| | | | Predicted distributions for our experiments ||
Earned income cumulated over 7-year period	Actual distribution	Predicted distribution	All unmarried in 1972	Behavior same as for unmarried women
$0	.17	.15	.04	.01
Less than $10,000	.40	.38	.27	.04
$10,000-19,999	.20	.20	.25	.10
$20,000-29,999	.12	.12	.22	.16
$30,000-39,999	.07	.08	.12	.18
Over $39,999	.05	.08	.10	.50
Pseudo chi-square statistic for comparisons with original predicted distribution (n=424)			99	1199

applying our estimated probability of work, wage rate and
hours of work relationships for unmarried women to these women
over the entire 7-year simulation period. Now 89 percent of
the women are found to work all 7 years, compared with a
predicted 13 percent for our base case; and 50 percent of the
women are found to earn at least $40,000 over the 7-year
period compared with a predicted 8 percent for our base case.

In Tables 6.7 and 6.8, we show the same results for women
who were 47-64 years of age and married in 1971 that we show
in Tables 6.5 and 6.6 for women who were 21-46 years of age
and married in 1971. Again, the effects of treating these
women as unmarried in 1972, or of applying our relationships
for unmarried women to these women for all 7 years of the
simulation period, are dramatic. The effects are not the same,
however, as those predicted for the younger group of women.

6 Sensitivity of Simulation Results

TABLE 6.7
ACTUAL AND SIMULATED PROPORTIONS OF WOMEN BY NUMBER
OF YEARS WORKED OUT OF 7 FOR WOMEN 47-64 YEARS OF AGE
AND MARRIED IN 1971, AND SIMULATED DISTRIBUTIONS
FOR THESE SAME WOMEN GIVEN THE DESIGNATED EXPERIMENTAL
CHANGES IN THEIR BEHAVIOR

Number of years worked out of 7	Actual distribution	Predicted distribution	Predicted distributions for our experiments	
			All unmarried in 1972	Behavior same as for unmarried women
0	.38	.36	.06	.01
1-2	.13	.16	.52	.02
3-4	.12	.15	.22	.08
5-6	.19	.12	.13	.24
7	.18	.21	.07	.65
Pseudo chi-square statistic for comparisons with original predicted distribution (n=119)			141	183

Treating these older women as unmarried in 1972 causes sharp reductions in both the proportion of women predicted not to work at all over the 7-year simulation period <u>and</u> in the proportion simulated to work all 7 years, with substantial increases occuring in the proportions of women simulated to work 1-2 or 3-4 years. There is also a corresponding change in the shape of the cumulative income distribution, with sharp reductions occuring in the proportion of women falling in the no earnings category and in the income categories for over $20,000 in cumulative earnings, and with increases occuring in the categories for under $10,000 and for $10,000 - 19,999. If we instead treat these women as unmarried for all 7 years, most are predicted to work at least 5 out of the 7 years in our simulation period. Thus, the effect of this experimental change on predicted years of work for this older group of women is similar to, though not quite as strong as, the effect observed for our younger group of women. In contrast to our results for younger women, however, we find from Table 6.4

TABLE 6.8
ACTUAL AND SIMULATED PROPORTIONS OF WOMEN BY EARNED
INCOME CUMULATED OVER 7-YEAR PERIOD FOR WOMEN 47-64
YEARS OF AGE AND MARRIED IN 1971, AND SIMULATED
DISTRIBUTIONS FOR THESE SAME WOMEN GIVEN THE DESIGNATED
EXPERIMENTAL CHANGES IN THEIR BEHAVIOR

			Predicted distributions for our experiments	
Earned income cumulated over 7-year period	Actual distribution	Predicted distribution	All unmarried in 1972	Behavior same as for unmarried women
$0	.38	.37	.14	.04
Less than $10,000	.29	.26	.62	.78
$10,000-19,999	.15	.18	.19	.12
$20,000-29,999	.08	.08	.02	.04
$30,000-39,999	.02	.05	.01	.01
Over $39,999	.09	.06	.01	.01
Pseudo chi-square statistic for comparisons with original predicted distribution (n=119)			90	172

that the effect of this experimental change on the cumulative income distribution is a dramatic increase in the proportion of women predicted to have earnings totaling less than $10,000, with decreases in the proportions of women predicted to fall into all other relevant categories. Thus, according to our Inertia Model, if these particular older women were unmarried over the entire 7-year simulation period, most of them would work for most of these years but 94 percent of them would earn less than $20,000 (in constant 1967 dollars) over the _entire_ period.

In Tables 6.9 and 6.10, we show the actual and simulated distributions for years of work out of 7 and cumulative income over this period for women 21-46 and 47-64 years of age and unmarried in 1971. Comparing the appropriate columns in these two tables with the final columns of Tables 6.5 and 6.7 and of

TABLE 6.9
ACTUAL AND SIMULATED PROPORTIONS OF WOMEN IN THE DESIGNATED AGE GROUPS AND UNMARRIED IN 1971 BY NUMBER OF YEARS WORKED OUT OF 7

Number of years worked out of 7	21-46 Actual	Predicted	47-64 Actual	Predicted
0	.11	.04	.28	.19
1-2	.08	.15	.09	.19
3-4	.14	.13	.08	.12
5-6	.17	.21	.16	.13
7	.49	.47	.40	.36

TABLE 6.10
ACTUAL AND SIMULATED PROPORTIONS OF WOMEN IN THE DESIGNATED AGE GROUPS AND UNMARRIED IN 1971 BY EARNED INCOME CUMULATED OVER 7-YEAR PERIOD

Earned income cumulated over 7-year period	21-46 Actual	Predicted	47-64 Actual	Predicted
$0	.12	.04	.28	.23
Less than $10,000	.23	.30	.19	.26
$10,000-19,999	.18	.17	.23	.12
$20,000-29,999	.19	.20	.12	.12
$30,000-39,999	.15	.13	.07	.10
$40,000-59,999	.10	.06	.06	.10
$60,000-79,999	.02	.04	.03	.01
$80,000-99,999	.01	.02	.02	.01
Over $99,999	.00	.03	.00	.03

TABLE 6.11
ACTUAL AND SIMULATED PROPORTIONS OF WOMEN BY NUMBER
OF YEARS WORKED OUT OF 7 FOR WOMEN 21-46 YEARS OF
AGE AND MARRIED IN 1971, AND SIMULATED DISTRIBUTIONS
FOR THESE SAME WOMEN GIVEN THE DESIGNATED EXPERIMENTAL
CHANGES IN THEIR CIRCUMSTANCES OR BEHAVIOR

Number of years worked out of 7	Actual distribution	Predicted distribution	Male mean hours for age group in first year of work	Wage equations for men	Behavior same as for men
0	.17	.13	.13	.13	.00
1-2	.15	.17	.14	.18	.01
3-4	.15	.19	.17	.18	.06
5-6	.23	.21	.28	.22	.28
7	.30	.30	.28	.28	.64
Pseudo chi-square statistic for comparisons with original predicted distribution (n=424)			13	1	330

Tables 6.6 and 6.8, we find that when we apply our estimated relationships for unmarried women to all women in the relevant simulation population of women who were married in 1971, the predicted proportions of women working 5-6 or 7 years are much higher than either the actual or predicted proportions are for our populations of women who were unmarried in 1971. For the younger age group, when we treat married women as unmarried over the entire simulation period, we also predict substantially higher proportions of these women in the cumulative income brackets for over $30,000 than is the case for either the actual or predicted distributions for women who were 21-46 years of age and unmarried in 1971. For the older age group, when we treat married women as unmarried for the entire simulation period, the resulting predicted cumulative income distribution shows 78 percent of the women earning less than $10,000, while the corresponding proportions of women in this category in the actual and predicted cumulative income

TABLE 6.12
ACTUAL AND SIMULATED PROPORTIONS OF WOMEN BY EARNED
INCOME CUMULATED OVER 7 YEAR PERIOD FOR WOMEN 21-46
YEARS OF AGE AND MARRIED IN 1971, AND SIMULATED
DISTRIBUTIONS FOR THESE SAME WOMEN GIVEN THE DESIGNATED
EXPERIMENTAL CHANGES IN THEIR CIRCUMSTANCES OR BEHAVIOR

			Predicted distributions for our experiments		
Earned income cumulated over 7-year period	Actual distribution	Predicted distribution	Male mean hours for age group in first year of work	Wage equations for men	Behavior same as for men
$0	.17	.15	.13	.14	.01
Less than $10,000	.40	.38	.19	.32	.04
$10,000 -19,999	.20	.20	.28	.20	.09
$20,000 -29,999	.12	.12	.20	.12	.16
$30,000 -39,999	.07	.08	.11	.09	.25
Over $39,999	.05	.08	.09	.13	.40
Pseudo chi-square statistic for comparisons with original predicted distribution (n=424)			83	18	1094

distributions for women who were 47-64 years of age and
unmarried in 1971 are 19 and 26 percent, respectively. These
comparisons show, among other things, that the lesser labor
supply and earnings of the married compared with the unmarried
women in our simulation population cannot be fully explained
on the basis of observable characteristics other than marital
status. Thus, current marital status must be serving as a
proxy for unmeasured preferences for home-oriented versus
market-oriented activities and for abilities and circumstances
that have important effects on work behavior that are not

TABLE 6.13
ACTUAL AND SIMULATED PROPORTIONS OF WOMEN BY NUMBER
OF YEARS WORKED OUT OF 7 FOR WOMEN 47-64 YEARS OF
AGE AND MARRIED IN 1971, AND SIMULATED DISTRIBUTIONS
FOR THESE SAME WOMEN GIVEN THE DESIGNATED EXPERIMENTAL
CHANGES IN THEIR CIRCUMSTANCES OR BEHAVIOR

Number of years worked out of 7	Actual distribution	Predicted distribution	Male mean hours for age group in first year of work	Wage equations for men	Behavior same as for men
0	.38	.36	.36	.36	.05
1-2	.13	.16	.17	.17	.14
3-4	.12	.15	.12	.15	.14
5-6	.19	.12	.14	.12	.15
7	.18	.21	.21	.20	.51
Pseudo chi-square statistic for comparisons with original predicted distribution (n=119)			1	0	84

fully reflected, or are reflected differently for married and unmarried women, in the lagged work behavior and other observable characteristics of a woman.

In column 3 of Tables 6.11 and 6.12, we show the results of a simulation experiment for women 21-46 years of age and married in 1971 in which women found to work in the first year of the simulation period are treated as though their hours of work in the previous year were the same as the pooled mean for men in our data base in the appropriate age bracket, and women starting work at any time during the course of the simulation are assigned the appropriate male mean for their age for their first year of work. This experimental change does result in small increases in the predicted proportions of women found to work 3-4 or 5-6 out of 7 years as opposed to 1-2 years. This experimental change also results in an appreciable decrease in the proportion of women predicted to earn under $10,000 and increases in the predicted proportions for the cumulative

TABLE 6.14
ACTUAL AND SIMULATED PROPORTIONS OF WOMEN BY EARNED
INCOME CUMULATED OVER 7-YEAR PERIOD FOR WOMEN 47-64
YEARS OF AGE AND MARRIED IN 1971, AND SIMULATED
DISTRIBUTIONS FOR THESE SAME WOMEN GIVEN THE DESIGNATED
EXPERIMENTAL CHANGES IN THEIR CIRCUMSTANCES OR BEHAVIOR

			Predicted distributions for our experiments		
Earned income cumulated over 7-year period	Actual distribution	Predicted distribution	Male mean hours for age group in first year of work	Wage equations for men	Behavior same as for men
$0	.38	.37	.37	.38	.08
Less than $10,000	.29	.26	.21	.21	.22
$10,000 -19,999	.15	.18	.13	.18	.10
$20,000 -29,999	.08	.08	.16	.04	.11
$30,000 -39,999	.02	.05	.05	.07	.16
Over $39,999	.09	.06	.08	.12	.33
Pseudo chi-square statistic for comparisons with original predicted distribution (n=119)			13	12	207

income categories between $10,000 and $60,000. Thus, our estimated relationships for the Inertia Model imply that women would supply more labor over time and earn substantially more if they started out working with hours of work more similar to those typical for men of the same general age.

The effects of this experiment are much more striking than the effects of our next experiment in which the wage rates for women 21-46 years of age and married in 1971 were generated over the entire simulation period using our estimated wage equations for men. From column 4 in Table 6.11, we see that this experimental treatment produces no systematic

TABLE 6.15
ACTUAL AND SIMULATED PROPORTIONS OF MEN
IN THE DESIGNATED AGE GROUPS AND UNMARRIED IN
1971 BY NUMBER OF YEARS WORKED OUT OF 7

Number of years worked out of 7	21-46 Actual	21-46 Predicted	47-64 Actual	47-64 Predicted
0	.01	.00	.05	.03
1-2	.01	.01	.06	.06
3-4	.01	.02	.08	.11
5-6	.05	.08	.10	.12
7	.92	.89	.71	.68

change in the predicted distribution of women by years of work out of 7. From column 4 of Table 6.12, we find that this wage treatment results in a modest decrease in the predicted proportion of women earning under $10,000 and modest increases in the predicted proportions of women in the cumulative income categories between $30,000 and $80,000. From these results we see that according to our Inertia Model, the increases in the labor supply and earnings of younger married women if they were paid wage rates more in line with those paid to men in the same age bracket would be very modest. Thus, without some change in behavior, due perhaps to changed expectations, equal pay for work of equal value legislation that resulted in substantial wage increases for most women would not be expected to stimulate any major increase in the labor supply of younger married women or to change greatly the earnings profile for these women over time. From the last column of Tables 6.11 and 6.12, however, we see that the predicted distributions for years of work and cumulative income for women 21-46 years of age and married in 1971 are vastly different when our estimated male relationships for the probability of work and the hours of work, as well as for the wage rate, are used to generate the work behavior of these women over the entire simulation period.

In Tables 6.13 and 6.14, we show the same results for women who were 47-64 years of age and married in 1971 that we show in Tables 6.11 and 6.12 for women who were 21-46 years of age and married in 1971. The conclusions to be drawn from

TABLE 6.16
ACTUAL AND SIMULATED PROPORTIONS OF MEN IN THE DESIGNATED AGE GROUPS IN 1971 BY EARNED INCOME CUMULATED OVER 7-YEAR PERIOD

Earned income cumulated over 7-year period	21-46 Actual	21-46 Predicted	47-64 Actual	47-64 Predicted
$0	.01	.00	.05	.03
Less than $10,000	.02	.01	.09	.12
$10,000-19,999	.04	.04	.10	.08
$20,000-29,999	.07	.05	.12	.07
$30,000-39,999	.12	.12	.10	.13
$40,000-59,999	.29	.32	.19	.31
$60,000-79,999	.24	.20	.17	.10
$80,000-99,999	.10	.10	.07	.08
Over $99,999	.11	.14	.10	.08

these results are essentially the same as for the younger group of women.

The predicted distributions presented in the final columns of Tables 6.11 and 6.13 and Tables 6.12 and 6.14 can be compared with the distributions shown for men in Tables 6.15 and 6.16. We see from these tables that even when the male behavioral relationships for our Inertia Model are applied to women, married women are not predicted to work as many years on the average, and higher proportions of them are found in the lower categories of the cumulative income distribution, than is the case for men. These differences are due in part to differences between the women and men in our samples in the distributions of values for our explanatory variables including the values for wage rates and hours of work in the year prior to our simulation period. However, differences between the work behavior simulated for the base line case for married women versus men using our Inertia Model are also due to differences between our sets of estimated behavioral relationships for married women versus men. Thus,

TABLE 6.17

ACTUAL AND SIMULATED PROPORTIONS OF BLACK AND NONBLACK WOMEN WHO WERE 21-46 YEARS OF AGE AND MARRIED IN 1971 BY NUMBER OF YEARS WORKED OUT OF 7, AND SIMULATED DISTRIBUTIONS FOR BLACK WOMEN WITH THE RACE DUMMY VARIABLE SET EQUAL TO ZERO

Number of years worked out of 7	Actual dist. for blacks	Predicted dist. for blacks	Predicted dist. for blacks with race dummy =0	Predicted dist. for non-blacks	Actual dist. for non-blacks
0	.12	.11	.07	.13	.18
1-2	.12	.16	.23	.17	.16
3-4	.15	.15	.15	.20	.16
5-6	.28	.31	.23	.19	.21
7	.33	.28	.33	.30	.29

according to our Inertia Model, married women would not be found to exhibit the same work behavior as men even if they had the same joint distribution of current characteristics as men; just as from our earlier results, according to our Inertia Model, married women would not be found to exhibit the same work behavior as unmarried women even if they had the same joint distribution of observable characteristics as unmarried women.

Finally, in Tables 6.17 and 6.18, we show actual and predicted distributions for years of work out of 7 and for the cumulative income for black and nonblack women who were 21-46 years of age and married in 1971. From these tables we see that higher proportions of the nonblack women are found to have worked less than 5 years or all 7 years, and higher proportions of the nonblack women are found to have earned less than $10,000 or more than $30,000 We also show predicted distributions for black women with our race dummy variable set equal to 0 over the entire simulation period.[5] The upper portion of the predicted distribution for years of work out of 7 for black women is found to be generally more similar to the predicted distribution for nonblack women when our race dummy is set equal to 0 for all women for the entire simulation period, but the lower portions of the distributions can be

6 Sensitivity of Simulation Results

TABLE 6.18
ACTUAL AND SIMULATED PROPORTIONS OF BLACK AND NONBLACK
WOMEN WHO WERE 21-46 YEARS OF AGE AND MARRIED IN 1971
BY EARNED INCOME CUMULATED OVER 7-YEAR PERIOD, AND
SIMULATED DISTRIBUTIONS FOR BLACK WOMEN WITH RACE
DUMMY VARIABLE SET EQUAL TO ZERO

Earned income cumulated over 7-year period	Actual dist. for blacks	Predicted dist. for blacks	Predicted dist. for blacks with race dummy=0	Predicted dist. for non-blacks	Actual dist. for non-blacks
$0	.12	.11	.09	.16	.18
Less than $10,000	.33	.37	.40	.38	.41
$10,000-19,999	.27	.27	.23	.19	.18
$20,000-29,999	.17	.13	.16	.11	.11
$30,000-39,999	.04	.08	.07	.08	.07
$40,000-59,999	.07	.03	.04	.05	.04
$60,000-79,999	.00	.01	.01	.02	.01
Over $79,999	.00	.01	.00	.01	.00

seen to be more dissimilar than for the base case. Also, the differences in the income distributions for the base case are seen, from Table 6.18, to persist, with small alterations, in the experimental setting. The differences between the predicted distributions for black women with the race dummy set equal to 1 in the base case and with this dummy variable set equal to 0 in the experimental case are relatively small. These results are compatible with, but certainly cannot be viewed as "proof" of, the hypothesis that whatever racial discrimination there may be results from, or acts primarily through, the previous work experience of women and differences in persistent ummeasured circumstances, including quality of education and the variability of the income of husbands. From our estimated wage and hours equations, we can also see that one reason the predicted cumulative income distributions are as similar as we find them to be in Table 6.18 for black versus nonblack wives is because the negative effects of our race dummy in our wage equations tend to be offset by positive effects for this dummy in the hours equations.

FOOTNOTES TO CHAPTER 6

1. All of the results in this chapter are obtained using the Inertia Model for which estimation results are presented in Chapter 3 with the $20 wage cutoff explained in section 4.7. The $20 wage cutoff was used because many extreme wage estimates were generated, as might be expected, for some of the simulation experiments for which results are shown in this chapter.

2. Of course, some of these women were unmarried for one or more years over the course of the simulation period.

3. This is implemented by setting all of the child status variables equal to 0 over the entire simulation period.

4. This is implemented by applying our behavioral relationships for unmarried women to these women, most of whom are actually married, in the second simulation year, which corresponds to the calendar year 1972.

5. We have estimated our models with the race dummy set equal to 1 if an individual is black and set equal to 0 if the individual is nonblack. Thus, in this experiment we are treating all black women as though they were nonblack.

CHAPTER 7

UNEMPLOYMENT

In most surveys a person is classified as unemployed if he or she looked for work, but did not work, during some given time period specified by the data collection agency, such as a week. A great deal of confusion can be avoided in interpreting unemployment data by noting that neither those who were underemployed during the given time period nor those who did not look for work because they believed they would not be able to find any are classified as unemployed in most sample surveys. Nor does the period with respect to which the state of unemployment is defined in a particular survey necessarily have anything to do with the planning horizon of individuals. Rather it is part of the definition of the state of unemployment in a given survey. Often, for instance, information is collected on which individuals were unemployed in a given survey "reference week." In the PSID, information is collected on the number of weeks during a given year that a person was unemployed; that is, on the number of weeks in which a person looked for work but did not work at all.

An individual is said to participate in the labor force in a given week if the individual either worked or was unemployed. (From the discussion above it should be clear that a person cannot both work and be unemployed in a week, if the states of work and unemployment are defined with respect to a week.) It is important to notice that those who look for work for awhile in a week and then accept a job offer and begin to work will be classified as employed, not unemployed, for that week. Thus, anyone who finds a job after a search of less than a week will not be counted in a survey with a weekly definition of unemployment as having experienced a spell of unemployment. On the other hand, anyone who looks for work for awhile during a week and then ceases to look without taking a job will be counted as unemployed during the week. The definitions are such that we cannot refer to a person as having looked for work and then having ceased to participate in the labor force during the same week. We can only observe the states of employed (worked during the given time period), unemployed (looked for work but did not work in the given time period), and not in the labor force (did not participate in the labor force in the given time period) for entire units of whatever the time period is with respect to which these states are defined.

There are many economists who view unemployment, and particularly the unemployment of women, as just another aspect of the choice of nonmarket over market activities. Women are viewed by these economists and some politicians as well as casual labor market participants who invest relatively little effort in finding jobs and who accept only jobs with favorable working conditions or with other special conditions such as short or flexible hours. A casual attitude toward labor market participation is particularly attributed to married women whose husbands earn good livings and to women with heavy childcare responsibilities. This view of women is sometimes used as a rationale for policy proposals that would result in limiting the access of women to unemployment benefit coverage through regulations specifying the number of weeks per year or hours per week a person must work to qualify for unemployment benefits.[1] In an important article however, Christopher Flinn and Heckman (1983, p. 38) write: "Our empirical results indicate that unemployed and out of the labor force <u>are</u> behaviorally distinct." Whatever the concern of economists may be, it is clear from a practical perspective that unemployment must be dealt with. For instance, only the unemployed collect unemployment benefits.[2]

This chapter addresses the question of how the unemployment behavior of individuals is related to their work, or employment, behavior. In section 7.1 we generalize a Heckman-type conceptual model of work behavior to include unemployment behavior. In section 7.2 we describe the data base used in our analysis of unemployment behavior and note how the sample mean values for our variables differ for individuals grouped by their unemployment status in the current year and whether or not they worked in the previous year. Finally, in section 7.3 we present empirical results concerning the impacts on the probability of unemployment and the number of weeks of unemployment of essentially the same set of explanatory variables included in our relationships for work behavior.

7.1. Generalizing a Heckman-type Model of Work Behavior to Include Unemployment

In a Heckman-type model of work behavior as described in section 2.2 and in the Addendum to Chapter 2, each individual

7 Unemployment

has an offered wage, w, and also an asking wage, w*, which is an increasing function of hours of work, h. The offered wage is supposed to be the hourly wage the individual will receive if he or she works; while the asking wage evaluated at any given number of hours of work, w*(h), is the amount the individual must receive to be willing to work another hour in the given time interval. Thus, the condition for work in the given time interval is

$$w > w^*(0) . \qquad (7.1.1)$$

Partly, at least, because of the annual nature of suitable data bases, the relevant time interval in such models is typically taken to be a year. Thus, the model is usually designed to account for the fact that some individuals work and some do not work at all within the time interval of a year. In such a model, individuals can be found not to work during a year because of limited market opportunities, characterized by low values of w, or because of the high values of their nonmarket time as measured by w*. Moreover, it is hypothesized that individuals who do work will attempt to choose their hours of work so as to equate their asking wage, evaluated at the actual hours of work, with their offered wage. That is, it is hypothesized that those who work will choose their hours of work so as to satisfy the condition

$$w = w^* . \qquad (7.1.2)$$

A model of this sort is considered to be a static, one-period annual model if no consideration is given to the impacts on current work behavior of past work behavior or of future expectations through the introduction of either lagged or future considerations into the underlying utility function or budget constraint. (See the Addendum to Chapter 2 for the relationship of conditions such as (7.1.1) and (7.1.2) to the utility and budget functions for a Heckman-type model of work behavior). The question of whether the model is to be considered a static, one-period model or a dynamic model rests, in an operational sense, on the specification of the variables entered into the functions defining w and w* (that is, on whether lagged or future or expectational variables are included) and on the specification of the behavior of the error terms for these relationships. Much of the basic structure of the behavioral model, and of the equations to be estimated, is not altered by whether the model is considered to be static or dynamic. For instance, we can incorporate the phenomenon of a person turning down a good wage offer in this time period because the person believes a better wage offer will be received next period by specifying the person's asking wage in the current period as a function of the wage offer(s) the person expects to receive in the next time period. We can also incorporate into the asking wage function a person's preferences for income in the present period versus income, with some degree of uncertainty attached to it, in future periods. Modifications of the basic model along these lines may lead to model specifications that contain key variables on which we have no data or that are intractable from an econometric or computational perspective. Yet, in principle, problems of introducing dynamic elements into a Heckman-type model of work behavior are not the fundamental barrier to introducing unemployment behavior into such a model.

The real problem is the customary annual time frame, which is not an essential element of such a model, at least at the conceptual level. The state of unemployment is most commonly defined in survey questions with respect to the time interval of a week. It would be possible to define the state of unemployment with respect to a longer time interval, such as a year. However, there are relatively few individuals who look for work but never work during a year. If we use a weekly definition for the state of unemployment, we see that in the space of a year, individuals can have weeks of work, weeks of unemployment and weeks when the person is not in the labor force. Such an event set cannot be accommodated by annual comparisons of offered and asking wage rates, no matter how they are defined.

A Heckman-type model of work behavior can easily be generalized to include unemployment behavior, however, if it is formulated at the conceptual level around the basic time interval of a week. Let AW denote the anticipated real hourly return to work in a week net of the costs of participating in the labor force in the given week. Note that conceptually a person must decide whether to participate in the labor force in a week before he can receive, and hence before he can know the value of, his wage offer, or offers, for the week. Even a person who has been working and who plans to continue at the same job might receive a new wage offer or might unexpectedly be laid off or fired in any given week of labor force participation. Thus, in principle, it is an anticipated, rather than a known, wage offer on the basis of which a person must decide whether or not to participate in the labor force in any given week. (Of course, for many the difference between the anticipated wage, AW, and the actual wage offer received in the week, w, may be small. This will be true, for instance, for those continuing on from one week to the next at a contractually determined wage and for whom the costs associated with participating in the labor force for an additional week are small.) We will also let $w^*(0,0)$

7 Unemployment

denote the person's asking wage evaluated for nonparticipation (and hence, no hours of work) in the given week, where the second 0 in the parentheses following w^* indicates that w^* is being evaluated for nonparticipation in the week and the first indicates that w^* is being evaluated for 0 hours of work. The person will participate in the week if the condition

$$AW > w^*(0,0) \qquad (7.1.3)$$

is satisfied. Otherwise, the person will not participate in the labor force and hence, will not work or be unemployed in that week.

A person who participates in the labor force in a week will work, according to the specification of this model, if the condition

$$w > w^*(0,+) \qquad (7.1.4)$$

is satisfied, where w is the person's offered wage for the week and $w^*(0,+)$ is the person's asking wage evaluated for participation in the week. We note that $w^*(0,0)$ and $w^*(0,+)$ will not be equal if there are monetary, time or psychological costs associated with the decision to participate in the week that become sunk, or fixed, costs to those who do participate the asking wage evaluated for participation will be lower than the asking wage evaluated for nonparticipation, for instance, if some of the income available to the individual for the week from sources other than the labor of the individual ("other" income) has been expended to defray monetary costs of participation. Moreover, the higher the costs of participation in a week are for an individual, the lower we would expect $w^*(0,+)$ to be in relationship to $w^*(0,0)$. For many, of course, the difference between $w^*(0,0)$ and $w^*(0,+)$ in any given week may also be small. If condition (7.1.3) is satisfied but condition (7.1.4) is not satisfied, then according to this model, the person will be observed to be unemployed in the given week.

The model is completed by the condition that those who work in a week will choose their hours of work, h, which are now defined with respect to the time interval of a week, so that the condition

$$w = w^*(h,+) \qquad (7.1.5)$$

is satisfied, where $w^*(h,+)$ is the person's asking wage evaluated for the actual number of hours of work during the week.[3] Conditions (7.1.4) and (7.1.5) are directly analogous to the condition for an individual to work and the equilibrium condition determining hours of work for those who do work, respectively, in the standard Heckman-type model described in greater detail in the Addendum to Chapter 2. We note that the anticipated offered wage, AW, need not be the expectation of w in a mathematical sense. Certain types of individuals might tend to base their wage anticipations on outdated, incomplete or inappropriate information, such as on information about the wage rates received by those around them who have jobs or the wage rates received on the jobs from which they themselves were laid off or fired.[4]

As in the case of the standard Heckman-type model of work behavior, such a model of employment and unemployment behavior can be specified to incorporate dynamic considerations through the incorporation of lagged variables and future variables and through the specification of the error processes. In fact, given weekly data on the employment status, hours of work, earnings and other appropriate explanatory variables for a sample of individuals, such a model could be used as the basis for an empirical study of questions related to the dynamic determinants of the length of spells of unemployment, including the question of how the asking wage rates of individuals change over spells of unemployment (see, for instance, Kiefer and Neumann, 1979).

Our present study is based on annual PSID data that includes information about the number of weeks of work and the number of weeks of unemployment during the year. Since we have no information on when these weeks of employment and unemployment occurred during the year, we are unable to consider questions related to the week-to-week dynamics of unemployment behavior. Nevertheless, the simple model that has been developed can be useful in thinking about how various factors might affect the probability that an individual will report at least one week of unemployment during the time period of a year and how these factors might affect the number of weeks of unemployment experienced in a year by those unemployed for at least one week during the year.

Even if AW is not the mathematical expectation of w and even if $w^*(0,0)$ cannot be related to $w^*(0,+)$ in a precise manner because we no not observe the factors that cause these different wage rates to differ, it seems reasonable to assume that many of the same factors that increase or decrease AW will also increase or decrease w and that many of the factors that increase or decrease $w^*(0,0)$ will have an impact in the same direction on $w^*(0,+)$. In the model outlined above, a person will be found to be unemployed in a week if AW exceeds $w^*(0,0)$ but w, the wage drawing actually obtained, falls short of $w^*(0,+)$. We see, therefore, that factors that increase both AW and w will act to increase the probability of unemployment through

7 Unemployment 319

the increase in AW, leading to an increase in the probability of participation; and at the same time these factors will act to decrease the probability of unemployment in the week through the increase in w , leading to an increase in the probability of employment. Likewise, factors that increase w*(0,0) and w*(0,+) will act to decrease the probability of unemployment through the increase in w*(0,0), leading to a decrease in the probability of participation; and at the same time they will act to increase the probability of unemployment due to the increase in w*(0,+), leading to a decrease in the probability the individual will work during the week.

Ideally, we would like to be able to separate out the impacts of our explanatory variables on AW versus w and on w*(0,0) versus w*(0,+). To do so, we would have to treat separately the decision to participate and the decision to work in any given week. It is difficult, though perhaps not impossible, to carry out such an analysis using annual data of the sort available in the PSID. Such an analysis also inherently involves problems of multiple sample selection.[5] We do not attempt such an analysis in this study.

In this study we simply examine the impacts of the explanatory variables included in our study of work behavior on the probability that a person will have at least one week of unemployment in a year, and on the expected weeks of unemployment in a year for those individuals who have experienced at least one week of unemployment in the year. The analysis is unsophisticated also in the sense that we make no effort to compensate for any selection biases that may be present in our regression results for the expected weeks of unemployment for those individuals who have experienced at least one week of unemployment.

If a variable such as education, which is presumed to primarily affect AW and w , is demonstrated in Chapter 3 to have an impact on the probability of work and if it is demonstrated in the empirical portion of this chapter to have impacts of the same sign on the incidence of unemployment as well, we might interpret these findings as weak evidence that the variable has a stronger impact on AW than on w. On the other hand, if this variable is found to have impacts of the opposite sign on the incidence of unemployment, we might interpret this finding as evidence that the variable has a stronger impact on w than on AW. Likewise, if a variable such as our baby dummy, which is presumed to primarily affect w*(0,0) and w*(0,+), is demonstrated in Chapter 3 to have an impact on the probability of employment and if this variable is demonstrated in this chapter to have impacts of the same sign on the incidence of unemployment, we might interpret this as evidence that the variable has a greater impact on w*(0,0) than on w*(0,+), while we might reach the opposite conclusion if this variable is found to have impacts on the incidence of unemployment of the opposite sign compared with the impact of this variable on the probability of employment. If a variable is demonstrated in Chapter 3 to have an impact on the probability of employment but is demonstrated in this chapter to have no impact on the incidence of unemployment, we might interpret this as evidence that the impacts of the variable on AW and w, or on $w^*(0,0)$ and $w^*(0,+)$, are roughly the same in terms of both sign and magnitude. In particular, if AW is the <u>mathematical expectation</u> of w and if $w^*(0,0)$ equals $w^*(0,+)$, we would expect the impact of all of our explanatory variables on the incidence of unemployment to be essentially 0. Suppose, finally, that a variable is found to have an impact on the incidence of unemployment that is found in Chapter 3 to have no impact on the probability of employment. This could mean that the variable affects AW or $w^*(0,0)$, but not w or $w^*(0,+)$, respectively. It could also mean that the variable has impacts of opposite sign on AW and w, or on $w^*(0,0)$ and $w^*(0,+)$. For instance, a woman with many small children might have a high value for $w^*(0,0)$ because of the high value she places on caring for her children herself, and she might have a low value of AW because of the high costs for her of participating in the labor force during a week. However, if she does participate and the child-related costs of participation become sunken or fixed costs, the net impact of her child status on $w^*(0,+)$ could conceivably turn out to be negative.

    The descriptive tables presented in section 2.2 and the probit and regression results presented in section 2.3 may be of interest, of course, even to readers who do not fully accept the model presented in this section or the behavioral inferences we draw from it.

7 Unemployment

7.2. The Data Base for Our Analysis of Unemployment

No information is available in the PSID on the weeks of unemployment for married women prior to 1974. We wish to include a lagged unemployment variable on the right-hand side of our probit indices for the probability of unemployment in a year, and in our regression equations for the number of weeks of unemployment in a year for those found to be unemployed for at least one week during the year. Thus, our unemployment behavioral relationships are estimated using pooled data for 1975 through 1978 from the 1974 through 1979 waves of the PSID. We will refer to this data set as our unemployment data base.

We have carried out our analysis of unemployment behavior using the same ten demographic groups used in our analysis of employment behavior. Moreover, for estimation purposes we have again split the observations in all six groups of women and our youngest group of men depending on whether or not the individual worked in the previous year. It seemed to us that the information available to the individual on labor market conditions, the realism of job expectations, and the basic motivation to find a job might be quite different, due to a variety of unobservable factors, for those who worked last year versus those without a job for at least a year prior to the current year.

In Tables 7.2.1 through 7.2.3, we show point estimates for the probability of unemployment in the current year. We see that the estimated probabilities of unemployment are much lower for those who did not work in the previous year than for those who worked in the previous year. This is mostly because those who did not work in the previous year are much less likely than those who did to participate in the labor force in the current year, and participation in the labor force is a precondition for unemployment. From Tables 7.2.1 and 7.2.2, we see that the unemployment probabilities are consistently higher for unmarried than for married women. We find also from Tables 7.2.2 and 7.2.3 that the unemployment probabilities for men are roughly comparable in magnitude to those for women who worked in the previous year. The figures shown in Tables 7.2.1 through 7.2.3 are not to be confused with unemployment rates, since these are the probabilities of unemployment for individuals without regard for whether these individuals participated in the labor force.

In Tables 7.2.4 through 7.2.6, we show the mean weeks of unemployment in a year for individuals found to be unemployed for at least one week during a year. From these tables we see that those individuals who did not work in the previous year but who did experience unemployment in the current year were unemployed for substantially more weeks on the average than

TABLE 7.2.1
POINT ESTIMATES OF THE PROBABILITY OF UNEMPLOYMENT: WOMEN WHO DID NOT WORK IN t-1

Marital status	Age 14-20	21-46	47-64	65+
Married		.04 (836)	.01 (429)	
	.09 (236)			.00 (444)
Unmarried		.15 (430)	.02 (310)	

TABLE 7.2.2
POINT ESTIMATES OF THE PROBABILITY OF UNEMPLOYMENT: WOMEN WHO WORKED IN t-1

Marital status	Age 14-20	21-46	47-64	65+
Married		.11 (1436)	.09 (436)	
	.13 (207)			.04 (113)
Unmarried		.19 (880)	.10 (503)	

TABLE 7.2.3
POINT ESTIMATES OF THE PROBABILITY OF UNEMPLOYMENT: MEN

Work status in t-1	Age 14-20	21-46	47-64	65+
Did not work	.04 (147)			
		.16 (3915)	.07 (2018)	.00 (573)
Worked	.23 (266)			

7 Unemployment

TABLE 7.2.4
SAMPLE MEANS FOR ANNUAL WEEKS OF UNEMPLOYMENT:
WOMEN EXPERIENCING UNEMPLOYMENT WHO DID NOT WORK IN t-1

Marital status	Age			
	14-20	21-46	47-64	65+
Married		23.0 (31)	14.0 (3)	
	19.1 (21)			----- (0)
Unmarried		25.5 (65)	24.9 (5)	

TABLE 7.2.5
SAMPLE MEANS FOR ANNUAL WEEKS OF UNEMPLOYMENT:
WOMEN EXPERIENCING UNEMPLOYMENT WHO WORKED IN t-1

Marital status	Age			
	14-20	21-46	47-64	65+
Married		14.0 (165)	11.2 (40)	
	18.2 (28)			23.3 (5)
Unmarried		17.1 (164)	16.2 (53)	

TABLE 7.2.6
SAMPLE MEANS FOR ANNUAL WEEKS OF UNEMPLOYMENT:
MEN EXPERIENCING UNEMPLOYMENT

Work status in t-1	Age			
	14-20	21-46	47-64	65+
Did not work	19.7 (6)			
		13.5 (629)	11.5 (143)	22.3 (1)
Worked	14.4 (61)			

TABLE 7.2.7
MEAN VALUES FOR MARITAL STATUS VARIABLES FOR WOMEN
WHO EXPERIENCED UNEMPLOYMENT IN THE CURRENT YEAR
WHO DID NOT WORK IN THE PREVIOUS YEAR AND WHO
WORKED IN THE PREVIOUS YEAR, RESPECTIVELY

Group	Dummy for currently married	Dummy for married in t-1	Dummy for currently widowed	Dummy for currently divorced
Women 14-20	.26	.17		
	.50	.27		
Wives 21-46		.94		
		.94		
Unmarried women 21-46		.17		
		.01		
Wives 47-64		.67		
		1.00		
Unmarried women 47-64		.00	.40	.60
		.02	.47	.49
Women 65+	---	---	---	---
		.20	.80	.00

were those experiencing unemployment who worked in the previous year. We find that unmarried women who experienced unemployment had more weeks of unemployment on the average than married women who experienced unemployment, just as unmarried women were more likely than married women to experience unemployment. Also from Tables 7.2.5 and 7.2.6, we find that men who experienced unemployment had roughly as many weeks of unemployment on the average as women who experienced unemployment in the current year and who also worked in the previous year.

We have already shown in section 2.7 that women who worked in the previous year have systematically different mean values for many of our explanatory variables compared with the mean values for women who did not work in the previous year. In the following tables, we show mean values calculated using our unemployment data base. These tables are for women who experienced unemployment in the current year, divided into those who did not and those who did work in the previous year;

7   Unemployment

TABLE 7.2.8
MEAN VALUES FOR MARITAL STATUS VARIABLES FOR WOMEN
WHO DID NOT EXPERIENCE UNEMPLOYMENT IN THE CURRENT
YEAR WHO DID NOT WORK IN THE PREVIOUS YEAR AND WHO
WORKED IN THE PREVIOUS YEAR, RESPECTIVELY

Group	Dummy for currently married	Dummy for married in t-1	Dummy for currently widowed	Dummy for currently divorced
Women 14-20	.15	.15		
	.29	.13		
Wives 21-46		.98		
		.93		
Unmarried women 21-46		.13		
		.00		
Wives 47-64		.99		
		.98		
Unmarried women 47-64		.04	.40	.50
		.00	.38	.51
Women 65+		.26	.57	.05
		.11	.58	.12

for women who did not experience unemployment in the current year, divided into those who did not and those who did work in the previous year; and for our groups of men, divided into those who did and those who did not experience unemployment in the current year.

In Tables 7.2.7 through 7.2.9, we show the mean values for our marital status variables. The top number in each pair of numbers in Tables 7.2.7, 7.2.8 and all similar tables for women that follow is for those women who did not work in the previous year, while the bottom number is for those who did work in the previous year. The top figure in each pair of numbers in Table 7.2.9 and all similar tables for men is for men who experienced unemployment in the year, while the bottom figure is for men who did not experience unemployment. In section 2.7 we show that, except for the youngest age group, the proportions of women married in the current or previous year are consistently lower for women who worked in the previous year than for women who did not work in the previous

TABLE 7.2.9
MEAN VALUES FOR DUMMY VARIABLE FOR CURRENTLY MARRIED FOR MEN WHO DID AND FOR MEN WHO DID NOT EXPERIENCE UNEMPLOYMENT IN THE CURRENT YEAR

Work status in t-1	14-20	Age 21-46	47-64
Did not work	.00 .01	.68 .77	.84 .93
Worked	.35 .18		

TABLE 7.2.10
MEAN VALUES FOR AGE, RACE DUMMY AND EDUCATION VARIABLES FOR WOMEN WHO EXPERIENCED UNEMPLOYMENT IN THE CURRENT YEAR WHO DID NOT WORK IN THE PREVIOUS YEAR AND WHO WORKED IN THE PREVIOUS YEAR, RESPECTIVELY

Group	Age	Race dummy	Education
Women 14-20	19.2	.48	11.2
	19.4	.20	11.7
Wives 21-46	30.2	.29	11.6
	32.6	.27	11.7
Unmarried women 21-46	28.0	.33	11.6
	28.8	.51	11.8
Wives 47-64	53.7	.60	10.3
	52.4	.10	11.0
Unmarried women 47-64	54.4	.00	10.6
	54.6	.43	10.2
Women 65+	----	---	----
	69.4	.00	12.0

7 Unemployment

TABLE 7.2.11
MEAN VALUES FOR AGE, RACE DUMMY AND EDUCATION
VARIABLES FOR ALL WOMEN WHO DID NOT EXPERIENCE
UNEMPLOYMENT IN THE CURRENT YEAR WHO DID NOT
WORK IN THE PREVIOUS YEAR AND WHO WORKED IN THE
PREVIOUS YEAR, RESPECTIVELY

Group	Age	Race dummy	Education
Women 14-20	18.7	.55	11.6
	19.0	.40	11.9
Wives 21-46	33.0	.18	11.9
	32.9	.21	12.4
Unmarried women 21-46	31.3	.68	11.3
	32.6	.53	12.2
Wives 47-64	54.6	.12	11.2
	52.1	.14	11.7
Unmarried women 47-64	55.3	.63	9.8
	54.6	.45	11.5
Women 65+	72.7	.16	10.1
	68.2	.11	12.0

year. Also, we show the proportions of currently divorced women to be higher for those who worked in the previous year than for those who did not. We show, too, that in our youngest age group, higher proportions of women than men are currently married. From Table 7.2.8 we find that for women who did not experience unemployment in the current year and who are at least 21 years of age, the proportions who were married in the previous year are lower for those who worked in the previous year than for those who did not. For those women who experienced unemployment in the current year, however, we find this pattern only for currently unmarried women 21-46 years of age. Comparing the means for our dummy for married in the previous year for women who experienced unemployment in the current year with the means for those who did not experience this, we find that the means are lower for those who did not experience unemployment for the subgroups of women who worked in the previous year while the reverse tends to be true for the subgroups of women who did not work in the previous year.

TABLE 7.2.12
MEAN VALUES FOR AGE, RACE DUMMY AND EDUCATION
VARIABLES FOR MEN WHO DID AND FOR MEN WHO
DID NOT EXPERIENCE UNEMPLOYMENT IN CURRENT YEAR

Group	Age	Race dummy	Education
Men 14-20 who did not work in t-1	18.5	.67	11.0
	18.9	.58	11.0
Men 14-20 who worked in t-1	19.2	.26	11.5
	18.9	.34	11.5
Men 21-46	31.3	.35	11.7
	33.7	.23	12.8
Men 47-64	52.8	.27	10.2
	54.0	.17	12.1

For men the proportions married in the current year are lower for the subgroups of men who experienced unemployment in the previous year than for the subgroups for men who did not experience unemployment in the current year, except for men 14-20 years of age who worked in the previous year.

In section 2.7 we show that there is no clear age pattern depending on whether a woman worked in the previous year. In Tables 7.2.10 and 7.2.11, this result is reiterated for both women who did and women who did not experience unemployment in the current year. We find, however, that except for the youngest and oldest age groups, those who did compared with those who did not experience unemployment in each demographic and lagged work status grouping are generally younger on the average. We do not find this average age pattern repeated in Table 7.2.12 for men grouped by whether or not they experienced unemployment, however.

In section 2.7 we show that black women make up much higher proportions of our samples of unmarried, compared with our samples of married, women. We find also that within our age and marital status groupings there is a higher representation of black women in the subgroups of women who did not work in the previous year compared with the corresponding subgroups for women who did work in the previous year, except for our two age groupings of married women where this pattern is reversed. This same set of patterns is also

TABLE 7.2.13
MEAN VALUES FOR DISABILITY AND RETIREMENT AGE DUMMIES FOR MEN WHO DID AND FOR MEN WHO DID NOT EXPERIENCE UNEMPLOYMENT IN CURRENT YEAR

Group	Disability dummy	Dummy for 60-62 years of age	Dummy for 63-64 years of age
Men 14-20	.13		
	.10		
Men 47-64	.17	.07	.03
	.22	.12	.07

TABLE 7.2.14
MEAN VALUES FOR DUMMY VARIABLE FOR STUDENT IN PREVIOUS YEAR AND FOR DUMMY VARIABLE FOR LIVING WITH PARENTS FOR WOMEN 14-20 WHO EXPERIENCED UNEMPLOYMENT IN THE CURRENT YEAR WHO DID NOT WORK IN THE PREVIOUS YEAR AND WHO WORKED IN THE PREVIOUS YEAR, RESPECTIVELY

Dummy for student in t-1	Dummy for living with parents
.22	.48
.07	.30

TABLE 7.2.15
MEAN VALUES FOR DUMMY VARIABLE FOR STUDENT IN PREVIOUS YEAR AND FOR DUMMY VARIABLE FOR LIVING WITH PARENTS FOR WOMEN 14-20 WHO DID NOT EXPERIENCE UNEMPLOYMENT IN THE CURRENT YEAR WHO DID NOT WORK IN THE PREVIOUS YEAR AND WHO WORKED IN THE PREVIOUS YEAR, RESPECTIVELY

Dummy student in t-1	Dummy for living with parents
.14	.72
.09	.60

TABLE 7.2.16
MEAN VALUES FOR DUMMY VARIABLE FOR STUDENT IN
PREVIOUS YEAR AND FOR DUMMY VARIABLE FOR LIVING
WITH PARENTS FOR MEN 14-20 WHO DID AND FOR MEN
WHO DID NOT EXPERIENCE UNEMPLOYMENT IN CURRENT YEAR

Group	Dummy for students in t-1	Dummy for living with parents
Men 14-20 who did not work	.17 .11	1.00 .92
Men 14-20 who worked in t-1	.08 .09	.45 .71

TABLE 7.2.17
MEAN VALUES FOR CHILD STATUS VARIABLES FOR WOMEN
WHO EXPERIENCED UNEMPLOYMENT IN THE CURRENT YEAR
WHO DID NOT WORK IN THE PREVIOUS YEAR AND WHO
WORKED IN THE PREVIOUS YEAR, RESPECTIVELY

Group	Baby dummy	Young child dummy	Number of children younger than 18
Women 14-20	.09 .07	.39 .20	1.22 .83
Wives 21-46	.19 .07	.35 .25	1.65 1.70
Unmarried women 21-46	.08 .04	.38 .20	1.86 1.30
Wives 47-64			.67 .80
Unmarried women 47-64			1.00 .49
Women 65+			--- .00

7 Unemployment   331

TABLE 7.2.18
MEAN VALUES FOR CHILD STATUS VARIABLES FOR WOMEN
WHO DID NOT EXPERIENCE UNEMPLOYMENT IN THE
CURRENT YEAR WHO DID NOT WORK IN THE PREVIOUS
YEAR AND WORKED IN THE PREVIOUS YEAR, RESPECTIVELY

Group	Baby dummy	Young child dummy	Number of children younger than 18
Women 14-20	.11	.20	2.05
	.05	.21	1.82
Wives 21-46	.09	.43	2.27
	.07	.25	1.73
Unmarried women 21-46	.05	.28	2.25
	.02	.17	1.31
Wives 47-64			.60
			.68
Unmarried women 47-64			.74
			.49
Women 65+			.10
			.09

TABLE 7.2.19
MEAN VALUES FOR VARIABLE FOR NUMBER OF CHILDREN
YOUNGER THAN 18 FOR MEN WHO DID AND FOR
MEN WHO DID NOT EXPERIENCE UNEMPLOYMENT IN CURRENT YEAR

Men 21-46	Men 47-64
1.65	1.15
1.72	.97

evident in Table 7.2.11 for women who did not experience
unemployment in the current year, but does not seem to hold in
Table 7.2.10 for women who experienced unemployment. From
Table 7.2.12 we see that for men as for married women, blacks
are more heavily represented among those who experienced
unemployment in the current year than among those who did not.
   In section 2.7 we show that those who worked in the

TABLE 7.2.20
MEAN VALUES OF OTHER INCOME VARIABLES FOR WOMEN WHO
EXPERIENCED UNEMPLOYMENT IN THE CURRENT YEAR WHO DID
NOT WORK IN THE PREVIOUS YEAR AND WHO WORKED IN THE
PREVIOUS YEAR, RESPECTIVELY

Group	Husband's income	Change in husband's income	Negative change in husband's income	Dummy for AFDC in t-1	Dummy for Social Security in t-1
Women 14-20	.9	.01			
	3.3	.35			
Wives 21-46	6.2	.14		.03	
	7.1	.32		.02	
Unmarried women 21-46				.20	
				.11	
Wives 47-64	3.5		-.8	.00	
	5.4		-1.0	.05	
Unmarried women 47-64				.00	
				.04	
Women 65+				---	
				.20	

previous year have more education on the average than those who did not. On the whole we find this pattern repeated in Tables 7.2.10 and 7.2.11. We also find in these tables a clear tendency for those women who experienced unemployment to have less education than those women who did not experience unemployment. This pattern is replicated in Table 7.2.12 for men at least 21 years of age. In Table 7.2.13 we do not find that men who are disabled or who are in the retirement age brackets of 60-62 or 63-64 years are disproportionately represented among those who experienced unemployment. This is undoubtedly because the disabled and those in the older age categories are less likely than other men to participate in the labor force.

We show in section 2.7 that those who worked in the previous year are less likely to have been students in the previous year and considerably less likely to be living with parents. We find this same pattern for both women and men aged

TABLE 7.2.21
MEAN VALUES FOR OTHER INCOME VARIABLES FOR WOMEN WHO
DID NOT EXPERIENCE UNEMPLOYMENT IN THE CURRENT
YEAR WHO DID NOT WORK IN THE PREVIOUS YEAR AND WHO
WORKED IN THE PREVIOUS YEAR, RESPECTIVELY

Group	Husband's income	Change in husband's income	Negative change in husband's income	Dummy for AFDC in t-1	Dummy for Social Security in t-1
Women 14-20	.7	-.01			
	1.4	-.08			
Wives 21-46	9.6	-.13		.02	
	8.0	.10		.01	
Unmarried women 21-46				.30	
				.08	
Wives 47-64	6.6		-1.16	.06	
	8.1		-.86	.02	
Unmarried women 47-64				.20	
				.05	
Women 65+	.2				.24
	---				.19

14-20 in Tables 7.2.14 through 7.2.16. We also find for women and men who did not work in the previous year that those who were students in the previous year are more heavily represented among those who experienced unemployment in the current year than those who were not, with the reverse being true for women and men who did work in the previous year. For both men and women, we also find that the proportions of those who experienced unemployment and who are living with parents are lower than the corresponding proportions for those who did not experience unemployment, except for men 14-20 years of age who did not work in the previous year.

In section 2.7 we show that women who worked in the previous year are less likely to have a baby or young child, and have fewer children younger than 18 on the average than women who did not work in the previous year. We find from Tables 7.2.17 and 7.2.18 that even after sorting women into those who did and those who did not experience unemployment in

TABLE 7.2.22
MEAN VALUES FOR OTHER INCOME VARIABLES FOR MEN
WHO DID AND FOR MEN WHO DID NOT EXPERIENCE
UNEMPLOYMENT IN CURRENT YEAR

Group	Wife's income in t-1	Dummy for AFDC in t-1	Dummy for Social Security in t-1
Men 14-20 who did not work in t-1	.0 .0	.00 .02	
Men 14-20 who worked in t-1	.1 .1	.05 .03	
Men 21-46	1.1 1.4	.02 .02	
Men 47-64	1.2 1.7		.00 .03

the current year, it is still generally the case that those women who worked in the previous year, on the average, are less likely to have a baby or young child and have fewer children younger than 18 than those women who did not work in the previous year. We also find from these tables that those who experienced unemployment are somewhat more likely in general to have a baby or young child than those who did not experience unemployment. Those younger than 47 years of age who experienced unemployment, however, have substantially fewer children younger than 18, on the average, than their counterparts who did not experience unemployment. From Table 7.2.19 we find no systematic differences in the mean number of children younger than 18 for men divided according to whether or not they experienced unemployment in the current year.

The mean values for our other income variables are shown in Tables 7.2.20 through 7.2.22. In line with our findings in section 2.7, we see that both women who experienced unemployment and women who did not experience unemployment are less likely to have received AFDC or Social Security benefits in the previous year if they worked in the previous year, except for our two groups of women 47-64 years of age who experienced unemployment. However, the subsamples of women in this age group who did not work in the previous year are very

TABLE 7.2.23
MEAN VALUES FOR MACROECONOMIC VARIABLES FOR WOMEN WHO EXPERIENCED UNEMPLOYMENT IN THE CURRENT YEAR WHO DID NOT WORK IN THE PREVIOUS YEAR AND WHO WORKED IN THE PREVIOUS YEAR, RESPECTIVELY

Group	National unemployment rate	National wage index
Women 14-20	7.3	97.2
	7.8	92.5
Wives 21-46	7.1	100.3
	6.8	103.4
Unmarried women 21-46	6.9	103.4
	7.0	101.7
Wives 47-64	7.6	95.1
	6.9	102.9
Unmarried women 47-64	7.3	98.3
	7.2	99.4
Women 65+	---	-----
	6.9	102.5

small. We find no patterns for either women or men in the mean values of our AFDC and Social Security dummy variables depending on whether or not an individual experienced unemployment in the current year. The mean values for the change in the husband's income variable are more negative for women who did not experience unemployment in the current year than for those who did. We are not sure what meaning, if any, is conveyed by this pattern. We find also that for wives 21-46 and for wives 47-64 years of age, those who experienced unemployment in the current year are married to men with much lower earned incomes, on the average, than are those who did not experience unemployment in the current year, after controlling for work status in the previous year. In fact, the wives whose husbands have the lowest earned incomes of all, on the average, are the wives who did not work in the previous year and who experienced unemployment in the current year. These are the wives who are entering the labor force for the first time or after an extended period of not working and who cannot find a job. If it is true that these wives are marginal

TABLE 7.2.24
MEAN VALUES FOR MACROECONOMIC VARIABLES FOR
WOMEN WHO DID NOT EXPERIENCE UNEMPLOYMENT
IN THE CURRENT YEAR WHO DID NOT WORK IN THE PREVIOUS
YEAR AND WHO WORKED IN THE PREVIOUS YEAR, RESPECTIVELY

Group	National unemployment rate	National wage index
Women 14-20	7.7	93.3
	7.7	93.0
Wives 21-46	7.1	100.6
	7.0	101.7
Unmarried women 21-46	7.0	101.5
	7.0	101.5
Wives 47-64	7.0	101.9
	6.9	102.8
Unmarried women 47-64	7.0	101.6
	7.0	101.5
Women 65+	6.9	103.3
	6.9	102.2

TABLE 7.2.25
MEAN VALUES FOR MACROECONOMIC VARIABLES FOR MEN WHO DID AND
FOR MEN WHO DID NOT EXPERIENCE UNEMPLOYMENT IN CURRENT YEAR

Group	National unemployment rate	National wage index
Men 14-20 who did not work in t-1	7.7	94.0
	7.8	92.7
Men 14-20 who worked in t-1	7.6	94.5
	7.7	93.3
Men 21-46	7.1	100.0
	7.0	101.5
Men 47-64	7.0	101.7
	7.0	102.0

7 Unemployment   337

labor force participants in the sense that they look less hard
for work or place more constraints on what they would consider
to be a reasonable job offer than other labor force
participants, they are certainly not marginal participants in
terms of the need their families have for the additional
income they might earn. From Table 7.2.22 we find also that
men at least 21 years of age who experienced unemployment were
able to count on less, on the average, in the way of earnings
from a wife. This is probably mostly because smaller
proportions of the men who experienced unemployment are
married, however.

We do not find any consistent patterns of interest in the
mean values displayed in Tables 7.2.23 through 7.2.25 for our
macroeconomic variables. Certainly there is no tendency for
the mean values of the unemployment variable to be higher for
women or men in our sample for years in which they experienced
unemployment themselves.

7.3. Determinants of the Probability and Duration of Unemployment

We have used probit analysis to estimate the parameters
of indices for the probability that an individual will
experience at least one week of unemployment in a given year.
Thus, the dependent variable for the probit models is set
equal to 1 if an individual experienced at least a week of
unemployment in the given year and is set equal to 0
otherwise. Ordinary least squares regression has then been
used to estimate the parameters of equations for the number of
weeks of unemployment in a year for those found to experience
unemployment in the year. The pooled data base used in
estimating these relationships is described in section 7.2.
The estimation of these relationships has been carried out
separately for the ten demographic groups used in our analysis
of work behavior, with our groups of women and our youngest
group of men being further divided depending on whether or not
an individual worked in the previous year. The variables
included in our relationships for the incidence of
unemployment are essentially the same as those that are listed
at the beginning of Chapter 3 and that are included in our
analysis of work behavior.

The results presented in this section can be thought of
within the context of the behavioral model outlined in section
7.1. We make no effort, however, to justify our choice of a
probit model for the probability of unemployment or of a
linear relationship for weeks of unemployment for those found
to experience unemployment in a year. We do not have the a

TABLE 7.3.1
COEFFICIENT ESTIMATES FOR MARITAL STATUS
VARIABLES IN PROBIT INDICES FOR PROBABILITY
OF UNEMPLOYMENT: WOMEN

Group	Dummy for currently married	Dummy for married in t-1	Dummy for currently widowed	Dummy for currently divorced
Women who did not work in t-1				
Wives 21-46		.145		
Unmarried women 21-46		.200		
Unmarried women 47-64		-1.147	1.011	1.037
Women who worked in t-1				
Wives 21-46		.056		
Unmarried women 21-46		.210		
Wives 47-64		1.515		
Ummarried women 47-64		.842	.335	.196
Women 65+	2.655*		1.816	.672

priori understanding of unemployment behavior, in either a theoretical or empirical sense, on which to base any such justification. In discussing the estimation results presented in this section, we make frequent reference to the corresponding results for our relationships for the probability of work, wage rates and hours of work in a year presented in Chapter 3.

For women who did not work in the previous year, we show in Chapter 3 that a change in marital status increases both the probability of starting work and the expected starting hours of work if the woman does work. The positive effects of

TABLE 7.3.2
COEFFICIENT ESTIMATES FOR DUMMY VARIABLE FOR
CURRENTLY MARRIED IN PROBIT INDICES FOR
PROBABILITY OF UNEMPLOYMENT: MEN

Work status in t-1	Age 14-20	21-46	47-64
Did not work	.202	-.087	-.256*
Worked	-.045		

TABLE 7.3.3
OLS COEFFICIENT ESTIMATES FOR MARITAL STATUS
VARIABLES IN WEEKS OF UNEMPLOYMENT EQUATIONS:
WOMEN EXPERIENCING UNEMPLOYMENT WHO WORKED IN t-1

Group	Dummy for married in t-1	Dummy for currently widowed	Dummy for currently divorced
Women who did not work in t-1			
Wives 21-46	4.2		
Unmarried women 21-46	-12.9**		
Women who worked in t-1			
Wives 21-46	-4.5		
Unmarried women 21-46	-1.9		
Wives 47-64			
Unmarried women 47-64	27.4*	-7.6	-11.0

TABLE 7.3.4
OLS COEFFICIENT ESTIMATES FOR DUMMY VARIABLE FOR CURRENTLY MARRIED IN WEEKS OF UNEMPLOYMENT EQUATIONS: MEN EXPERIENCING UNEMPLOYMENT

Work status in t-1	Age 14-20	21-46	47-64	65+
Did not work	---	-3.4**	-4.2*	
Worked	2.8			

TABLE 7.3.5
COEFFICIENT ESTIMATES FOR AGE VARIABLE IN PROBIT INDICES FOR PROBABILITY OF UNEMPLOYMENT: WOMEN

Marital status	Age 14-20	21-46	47-64	65+
Women who did not work in t-1				
Married		-.007	----	
	.029			
Unmarried		-.020*	-.017	
Women who worked in t-1				
Married		-.005	.018	
	.274**			.091
Unmarried		-.027**	-.022	

a change in marital status from being married in the previous year to unmarried in the current year are shown to be much larger in magnitude than the positive effects of a change in marital status from being unmarried in the previous year to married in the current year. Women who worked in the previous year are shown to be more likely to continue working if they were married rather than unmarried in the previous year, with the positive effects being greatest for those who are

TABLE 7.3.6
OLS COEFFICIENT ESTIMATES FOR AGE VARIABLE
IN WEEKS OF UNEMPLOYMENT EQUATIONS:
WOMEN EXPERIENCING UNEMPLOYMENT

Marital status	Age 14-20	Age 21-46	Age 47-64
	Women who did not work in t-1		
Married	-8.9**	-.2	
Unmarried		-.4*	
	Women who worked in t-1		
Married	-2.5	.2*	
Unmarried		-.1	-.0

TABLE 7.3.7
COEFFICIENT ESTIMATES FOR AGE VARIABLE AND FOR DISABILITY
AND RETIREMENT AGE DUMMIES IN PROBIT INDICES
FOR PROBABILITY OF UNEMPLOYMENT: MEN

Variable	14-20 Did not work in t-1	14-20 Worked in t-1	21-46	47-64
Age	-.305	.089	-.016**	-.011
Disability dummy			-.030	-.210*
Dummy for 60-62 years of age				-.334*
Dummy for 63-64 years of age				-.307

TABLE 7.3.8
OLS COEFFICIENT ESTIMATES FOR AGE VARIABLE AND FOR
DISABILITY AND RETIREMENT AGE DUMMIES IN WEEKS OF
UNEMPLOYMENT EQUATIONS: MEN EXPERIENCING UNEMPLOYMENT

	Age		
Dummy variable	14-20 Worked in t-1	21-46	47-64
Age	4.2**	.1	.1
Disability dummy		1.5	-.9
Dummy for 60-62 years of age			-5.9*
Dummy for 63-64 years of age			1.4

TABLE 7.3.9
COEFFICIENT ESTIMATES FOR BLACK DUMMY IN PROBIT
INDICES FOR PROBABILITY OF UNEMPLOYMENT:
WOMEN

	Age			
Marital status	14-20	21-46	47-64	65+
Women who did not work in t-1
Married		.217		
	-.500*			
Unmarried		.436**	-.112	
Women who worked in t-1
Married		-.047	-.359	
	-.563*			-1.560
Unmarried		-.146	-.234	

7 Unemployment 343

TABLE 7.2.10
OLS COEFFICIENT ESTIMATES FOR RACE DUMMY
IN WEEKS OF UNEMPLOYMENT EQUATIONS:
WOMEN EXPERIENCING UNEMPLOYMENT

Marital status	Age 14-20	Age 21-46	Age 47-64
Women who did not work in t-1			
Married		4.7	
	4.1		
Unmarried		6.3	
Women who worked in t-1			
Married		2.0	6.4
	19.2**		
Unmarried		.4	-1.8

TABLE 7.3.11
COEFFICIENT ESTIMATES FOR RACE DUMMY IN PROBIT
INDICES FOR PROBABILITY OF UNEMPLOYMENT: MEN

Work status in t-1	Age 14-20	Age 21-46	Age 47-64
Did not work	.163		
		.044	-.062
Worked	-.203		

currently unmarried. We have also found that, in general, women who are currently married supply less labor and men who are currently married supply more labor than otherwise identical unmarried men and women.

From Tables 7.3.1 and 7.3.2, we see that in general being, or having been, married increases the probability of unemployment for women regardless of work status in the previous year, and it decreases the probability of unemployment for men. However, from Tables 7.3.3 and 7.3.4,

TABLE 7.3.12
OLS COEFFICIENT ESTIMATES FOR RACE DUMMY
IN WEEKS OF UNEMPLOYMENT EQUATIONS:
MEN EXPERIENCING UNEMPLOYMENT

Work status in t-1	Age 14-20	Age 21-46	Age 47-64
Did not work	---	.3	-1.1
Worked	5.8		

TABLE 7.3.13
COEFFICIENT ESTIMATES FOR EDUCATION VARIABLE IN
PROBIT INDICES FOR PROBABILITY OF UNEMPLOYMENT:
WOMEN

Marital status	14-20	21-46	47-64	65+
Women who did not work in t-1				
Married	-.074	.025	----	
Unmarried		.021	.069	
Women who worked in t-1				
Married		-.108**	-.042	-.008
Unmarried		-.035	-.085**	

the balance of the evidence suggests that being, or having been, married tends to decrease the weeks of unemployment during a year for those experiencing unemployment.

We have found that the probability of starting to work and the starting hours of work, as well as the probability of continuing to work and the continuing hours, rise steeply with increasing age for women over the 14-20 age interval. From Table 7.3.5 we see that the probability of unemployment also

7 Unemployment   345

TABLE 7.3.14
OLS COEFFICIENT ESTIMATES FOR EDUCATION VARIABLE
IN WEEKS OF UNEMPLOYMENT EQUATIONS:
WOMEN EXPERIENCING UNEMPLOYMENT

Marital status	Age 14-20	Age 21-46	Age 65+
Women who did not work in t-1			
Married		-5.6**	
	-.7		
Unmarried		-.2	
Women who worked in t-1			
Married		-.8	-.2
	-2.6		
Unmarried		-.6	-.1

TABLE 7.3.15
COEFFICIENT ESTIMATES FOR EDUCATION VARIABLE IN
PROBIT INDICES FOR PROBABILITY OF UNEMPLOYMENT: MEN

Work status in t-1	Age 14-20	Age 21-46	Age 47-64	Age 65+
Did not work	.011			
		-.073**	-.087**	-.356*
Worked	.017			

rises for women over this age interval, though the rise is slight for women who did not work in the previous year. We have found that for women over 20, the probability of work and hours of work for those who do work tend to fall with increasing age, except for prime-aged women who worked in the previous year. The results displayed in Table 7.3.5 suggest that the probability of unemployment also falls with increasing age for women over age 20. The results in Table 7.3.6 suggest that the number of weeks of unemployment for

TABLE 7.3.16
OLS COEFFICIENT ESTIMATES FOR EDUCATION VARIABLE
IN WEEKS OF UNEMPLOYMENT EQUATIONS:
MEN EXPERIENCING UNEMPLOYMENT

Work status in t-1	Age 14-20	Age 21-46	Age 47-64
Did not work	---	-.3	-1.1
Worked	1.4		

TABLE 7.3.17
COEFFICIENT ESTIMATES IN PROBIT INDICES FOR
PROBABILITY OF UNEMPLOYMENT, AND OLS COEFFICIENT
ESTIMATES IN WEEKS OF UNEMPLOYMENT EQUATIONS,
FOR DUMMY VARIABLE FOR HAVING BEEN A STUDENT IN
t-1 AND FOR DUMMY VARIABLE FOR LIVING WITH PARENTS

Dummy variable	Women 14-20 Worked in t-1	Women 14-20 Did not work in t-1	Men 14-20 Worked in t-1	Men 14-20 Did not work in t-1
Probit indices for probability of unemployment				
Dummy for student in t-1	-.029	.583*	.047	.078
Dummy for living with parents			-.499*	1.693
Weeks of unemployment equations				
Dummy for student in t-1	.3	-12.5*	-.4	
Dummy for living with parents			7.3*	

TABLE 7.3.18
COEFFICIENT ESTIMATES FOR CHILD STATUS VARIABLES IN PROBIT INDICES FOR PROBABILITY OF UNEMPLOYMENT: WOMEN

Group	Baby dummy	Young child dummy	Number of children younger than 18
Women who did not work in t-1			
Women 14-20	.345	.443*	
Wives 21-46	.240	-.157	-.172**
Unmarried women 21-46	.397	.254*	-.077*
Wives 47-64			.010
Unmarried women 47-64			.031
Women 65+			.210*
Women who worked in t-1			
Women 14-20	.200	-.037	
Wives 21-46	-.008	-.081	
Unmarried women 21-46	.333	-.091	

women experiencing unemployment falls steeply with increasing age over the 14-20 age group and falls more gradually with increasing age for women over 20 years of age.

For men we find from Table 7.3.7 that the probability of unemployment seems to fall with increasing age for all groups, except men 14-20 who worked in the previous year. In contrast to our results for women, however, from Table 7.3.8 we see that the number of weeks of unemployment for men experiencing unemployment shows some tendency to rise with age. We show in Chapter 3 that our disability and retirement age dummies act to depress both the probability of work and the hours of work for men. From Table 7.3.7 we see that these dummies also act

TABLE 7.3.19
OLS COEFFICIENT ESTIMATES FOR CHILD STATUS
VARIABLES IN WEEKS OF UNEMPLOYMENT EQUATIONS:
WOMEN EXPERIENCING UNEMPLOYMENT

Group	Baby dummy	Young child dummy	Number of children younger than 18
Women who did not work in t-1			
Women 14-20	-22.3*	10.3*	
Wives 21-46	-1.0	-10.7	-2.3
Unmarried women 21-46	-4.4	3.2	.5
Women who worked in t-1			
Women 14-20	2.3	7.9	
Wives 21-46	.4	3.9	
Unmarried women 21-46	-2.6	5.3*	

to depress the probability of unemployment. From Table 7.3.8 we see, however, that the impact of these dummies on the number of weeks of unemployment for those men experiencing unemployment is unclear.

After controlling for other factors, including work status in the previous year, we find that for women, being black is generally associated with lower probabilities of starting to work and of continuing to work. From Table 7.3.9 we see that after controlling for work status in the previous year, for women, being black also lowers the probability of unemployment, except for women 21-46 years of age who did not work in the previous year.

We do not find any consistent pattern of impacts of being black on the starting and continuing hours of work of women. From Table 7.3.10, however, we find that even after controlling for work behavior in the previous year, being black seems to increase the number of weeks of unemployment for women experiencing unemployment.

7 Unemployment   349

TABLE 7.3.20
COEFFICIENT ESTIMATES FOR VARIABLE FOR NUMBER
OF CHILDREN YOUNGER THAN 18 IN PROBIT
INDICES FOR PROBABILITY OF UNEMPLOYMENT
AND WEEKS OF UNEMPLOYMENT EQUATIONS:
MEN AND MEN EXPERIENCING UNEMPLOYMENT, RESPECTIVELY

| | Age | |
Equation	21-46	47-64
Probit index	-.011	-.005
Weeks of unemployment equation	.3	-1.3**

We find no consistent pattern of impacts of being black on the probability of work for men, though black men are found generally to work somewhat fewer hours in the year than otherwise-similar nonblack men. From Tables 7.3.11 and 7.3.12, we find no consistent evidence of any impact of being black on either the probability or duration of unemployment for men, after controlling for work behavior in the previous year.

For women we find that increased education raises the probabilities of starting and of continuing to work. From Table 7.3.13 we see that increased education also raises the probability of unemployment for women who did not work in the previous year. However, for women who did work in the previous year we see that increased education consistently decreases the probability of unemployment. We see from Table 7.3.14 that increased education also consistently tends to decrease the number of weeks of unemployment for women experiencing unemployment.

Education is not found to have any consistent impact on the probability of work for men, after controlling for work behavior in the previous year. From Tables 7.3.15 and 7.3.16, however, we see that increased education acts to decrease both the probability and duration of unemployment for men even after controlling for work behavior in the previous year.

We find that having been a student in the previous year or living at home has an important impact on the starting and continuing work behavior of both young women and men in the 14-20 age group. However, from Table 7.3.17 we see that we are not able to identify any consistent pattern of impacts of these factors on the probability or duration of unemployment for young women or for young men.

Child status variables are found to have little, if any,

TABLE 7.3.21
COEFFICIENT ESTIMATES FOR OTHER INCOME VARIABLES
IN PROBIT INDICES FOR PROBABILITY OF UNEMPLOYMENT:
WOMEN WHO DID NOT WORK IN t-1

Group	Husband's income	Change in husband's income	Negative change in income	Dummy for AFDC in t-1	Dummy for Social Security in t-1
Women who did not work in t-1					
Women 14-20	-.026	.039			
Wives 21-46	-.068**	.053*		.075	
Unmarried women 21-46				-.339**	
Unmarried women 47-64					-1.000
Women who worked in t-1					
Wives 21-46	.010			.336	
Unmarried women 21-46				-.052	
Wives 47-64			-.039		
Unmarried women 47-64				-.670*	
Women 65+			.843	.491	

effect on the starting or continuing work behavior of women, after controlling for work behavior in the previous year. Likewise from Tables 7.3.18 and 7.3.19, we find that after controlling for a woman's work behavior in the previous year there is no systematic evidence that child status affects either the probability of a woman becoming unemployed or the duration of her unemployment if she does become unemployed. The presence of children younger than 18 is shown in Chapter 3

7 Unemployment

TABLE 7.3.22
OLS COEFFICIENT ESTIMATES FOR OTHER INCOME VARIABLES IN WEEKS OF UNEMPLOYMENT EQUATIONS: WOMEN EXPERIENCING UNEMPLOYMENT

Group	Husband's income	Change in husband's income	Negative change in husband's income
Women who did not work in t-1			
Women 14-20	-5.3**	-8.6	
Wives 21-46	1.0	-1.9	
Women who worked in t-1			
Wives 21-46		.0	
Wives 47-64			-2.3**

TABLE 7.3.23
COEFFICIENT ESTIMATES FOR OTHER INCOME VARIABLES IN PROBIT INDICES FOR PROBABILITY OF UNEMPLOYMENT: MEN

Group	Dummy for AFDC in t-1	Dummy for Social Security in t-1	Dummy for Unemployment Compensation in t-1
Men 14-20 who did not work in t-1	-1.710		.817*
Men 14-20 who worked in t-1	.607*		.074
Men 21-46	.110		.180*
Men 47-64		-2.130*	-.421**

TABLE 7.3.24
OLS COEFFICIENT ESTIMATES FOR OTHER INCOME
VARIABLES IN WEEKS OF UNEMPLOYMENT EQUATIONS:
MEN EXPERIENCING UNEMPLOYMENT

Group	Dummy for Unemployment Compensation in t-1
Men 14-20 who worked in t-1	-2.7
Men 21-46	-.8
Men 47-64	3.6

TABLE 7.3.25
COEFFICIENT ESTIMATES FOR NATIONAL UNEMPLOYMENT
RATE VARIABLE IN PROBIT INDICES FOR PROBABILITY
OF UNEMPLOYMENT: WOMEN

Marital status	Age 14-20	21-46	47-64	65+
Women who did not work in t-1				
Married		.021	----	
	-.401**			
Unmarried		-.164*	.115	
Women who worked in t-1				
Married		-.064*	.073	
	.135			-.142
Unmarried		.018	.138*	

to depress the labor supply of men. From Table 7.3.20 we find that prime-aged men are slightly less likely to be unemployed the more children they have and that men 47-64 who become unemployed may experience somewhat fewer weeks of unemployment

7 Unemployment

TABLE 7.3.26
COEFFICIENT ESTIMATES FOR NATIONAL UNEMPLOYMENT
RATE VARIABLE IN PROBIT INDICES FOR PROBABILITY
OF UNEMPLOYMENT: MEN

Work status in t-1	Age 14-20	Age 21-46	Age 47-64
Did not work	-.404	.118**	-.016
Worked	.087		

TABLE 7.3.27
OLS COEFFICIENT ESTIMATES FOR NATIONAL UNEMPLOYMENT
RATE VARIABLE IN WEEKS OF UNEMPLOYMENT EQUATIONS:
WOMEN EXPERIENCING UNEMPLOYMENT

Marital status	Age 14-20	Age 21-46	Age 47-64
Women who did not work in t-1			
Married	10.2**	.4	
Unmarried		-1.5	
Women who worked in t-1			
Married	4.9	.3	-2.2
Unmarried		.3	2.4

the more children they have.

We find weak negative relationships between the probability of a wife younger than 47 starting work and the level of her husband's income and between such a wife's starting hours of work and the level of her husband's income. Also, for these wives we find a positive relationship between the probability of starting to work and the <u>change</u> in the husband's income from the previous to the current year. From

TABLE 7.3.28
OLS COEFFICIENT ESTIMATES FOR NATIONAL UNEMPLOYMENT
RATE VARIABLE IN WEEKS OF UNEMPLOYMENT EQUATIONS:
MEN EXPERIENCING UNEMPLOYMENT

Work status in t-1	Age 14-20	Age 21-46	Age 47-64
Did not work	---	.3	.5
Worked	3.3		

Table 7.3.21 we see that for women 14-20 and wives 21-46 years of age who did not work in the previous year there is a negative relationship between the level of the husband's income and the probability of unemployment and a positive relationship between the <u>change</u> in the husband's income and the probability of unemployment. In Chapter 3 we present weak evidence, too, that women in families that received AFDC or Social Security benefits in the previous year are less likely to work in the present year. From Table 7.3.21 it appears that unmarried women who received AFDC or Social Security benefits in the previous year may also be less likely to be unemployed in the current year. From Table 7.3.22 we find weak evidence that among women who experienced unemployment, those with higher income husbands or with husbands whose income has increased since the previous year tend to be unemployed fewer weeks than otherwise-similar women.

We find no evidence that other income has any impact on the probability or hours of work of men. From Tables 7.3.23 and 7.3.24, we see that after controlling for work behavior in the previous year, there is also no evidence from this study that men whose families received AFDC benefits or who received Social Security or Unemployment Compensation in the previous year are any more or less likely than otherwise-similar men to be unemployed, or to be unemployed for more weeks if they are unemployed, in the current year.

We show in Chapter 3 that increases in our national unemployment rate variable decrease the labor supply of men and unmarried women but increase the labor supply of married women, both in terms of the probability of work and the expected hours of work for those individuals who do work. From Tables 7.3.25 and 7.3.26 we see that increases in the national unemployment rate decrease the probability of unemployment for young men and women who did not work in the previous year and

7 Unemployment

TABLE 7.3.29
COEFFICIENT ESTIMATES FOR LAGGED UNEMPLOYMENT
VARIABLES IN PROBIT INDICES FOR PROBABILITY
OF UNEMPLOYMENT: WOMEN

Group	Dummy for unemployed in t-1	Weeks of unemployment in t-1
Women who did not work in t-1		
Women 14-20	1.662**	
Wives 21-46	.257	.027
Unmarried women 21-46	3.160	-.037
Unmarried women 47-64	2.451	-.073
Women who worked in t-1		
Women 14-20	.252	
Wives 21-46	.709**	-.013*
Unmarried women 21-46	1.114**	-.024**
Wives 47-64	1.041**	-.007
Unmarried women 47-64	1.190**	.015
Women 65+	2.673**	-.146

may also decrease the probability of unemployment for wives 21-46 years of age who did work in the previous year and for older women and men. On the other hand, increases in the national unemployment rate appear to increase the probability of unemployment for women younger than 65 who worked in the previous year, with the exception of 21-46-year-old wives; and also increase the probability of unemployment for men younger

TABLE 7.3.30
COEFFICIENT ESTIMATES FOR LAGGED UNEMPLOYMENT
VARIABLES IN PROBIT INDICES FOR PROBABILITY
OF UNEMPLOYMENT: MEN

Group	Dummy for unemployed in t-1	Weeks of unemployment in t-1
Men 14-20 who worked in t-1	.707*	.010
Men 21-46	1.101**	.008*
Men 47-64	1.315**	.010

than 47, excluding men 14-20 who did not work in the previous year. In other words, increases in the national unemployment rate seem to decrease the probability of unemployment for those entering and those more loosely attached to the labor force while they increase the probability of unemployment for everyone else. From Tables 7.3.27 and 7.3.28 we see that increases in the national unemployment rate seem to systematically increase the weeks of unemployment for individuals experiencing unemployment during a year, with the greatest impacts being observed for young women and men in the 14-20 age group.

Lagged unemployment variables are not included in our probit indices for the probability of work, our wage rate equations or our hours of work equations. A dummy variable set equal to 1 if an individual was unemployed in the previous year and set equal to 0 otherwise, and a variable for the number of weeks an individual was unemployed in the previous year are included, however, in our probit indices for the probability of unemployment and in our weeks of unemployment equations. From Tables 7.3.29 and 7.3.30, we see that women and men who were unemployed in the previous year are found to have a consistently higher probability of being unemployed in the current year, even after controlling for whether or not the individual worked in the previous year. After controlling for whether a woman experienced unemployment in the previous year, we find that there is an inverse relationship between the number of weeks of unemployment in the previous year and the probability of unemployment in the present year. On the other hand, we find that men are more likely to be unemployed in the current year the more weeks they were unemployed in the previous year, even after controlling for whether unemployment

TABLE 7.3.31
OLS COEFFICIENT ESTIMATES FOR LAGGED UNEMPLOYMENT VARIABLES IN WEEKS OF UNEMPLOYMENT EQUATIONS: WOMEN EXPERIENCING UNEMPLOYMENT WHO WORKED IN t-1

Group	Dummy for unemployed in t-1	Weeks of unemployment in t-1
Women who did not work in t-1		
Women 14-20	.4	--
Wives 21-46	2.4	.2
Unmarried women 21-46	-5.6	.4
Women who worked in t-1		
Women 14-20	-3.6	--
Wives 21-46	-4.1*	.1
Unmarried women 21-46	-3.6	.1
Wives 47-64	-2.9	.2
Unmarried women 47-64	-7.9	.4*

was experienced in the previous year.

From Tables 7.2.31 through 7.3.32, it appears that women and men who experienced unemployment in the current year tend to be unemployed for fewer weeks if they were also unemployed in the previous year, with the evidence being most convincing for women who worked in the previous year. Having taken this effect into account, however, we find that those women and men who experienced unemployment in the current year and who were unemployed for more weeks in the previous year tend also to be unemployed for more weeks in the current year.

TABLE 7.3.32
OLS COEFFICIENT ESTIMATES FOR LAGGED UNEMPLOYMENT
VARIABLES IN WEEKS OF UNEMPLOYMENT EQUATIONS:
MEN EXPERIENCING UNEMPLOYMENT

Group	Dummy for unemployed in t-1	Weeks of unemployment in t-1
Men 14-20 who worked in t-1	3.8	-.1
Men 21-46	-1.9*	.2**
Men 47-64	1.0	.1

FOOTNOTES TO CHAPTER 7

1. Ehrenberg and Smith (1982, pp. 450-451) write:

White female adult unemployment rates are high because of proportionately large flows of women from employment to out-of-labor-force status, which suggests that some of their higher labor turnover (and unemployment) may be voluntary in nature. In contrast, the major cause of high nonwhite adult male unemployment rates is ... members of that group leaving or losing their jobs to become unemployed; the fact that they remain attached to the labor force suggests that their unemployment problem is serious and that the case for government intervention is strong.

2. Thus, the state of unemployment must be simulated for individuals in a microanalytic simulation model like the one in which our labor force behavioral relationships will be used.

3. This model is developed and related to the literature on unemployment behavior, including the literature on "reservation wage" models of unemployment, in Nakamura and Nakamura (1983b).

4. The closest relative of this conceptual model of unemployment of which we are aware is a multistate model of labor force dynamics presented by Flinn and Heckman (1982, pp. 155-163). A key difference between the two models is that in the Flinn-Heckman model, the labor market state of

7 Unemployment

unemployment is defined as "that state in which the rate of arrival of job offers is higher than in the other labor force states" (p. 156). Thus unemployment is an economically viable choice under appropriate conditions not only with respect to the state of not in the labor force, but also with respect to the employed state. In our model an individual enters the labor force in the <u>belief</u> that he or she will be better off than if he or she does not participate in the labor force, and unemployment is a transient state that occurs when the wage drawing obtained in a given week is less than what the individual expected and is furthermore below the relevant asking wage for the individual. In our model, if the individual knew prior to entering the labor force that his or her offered wage that week would fall below his or her asking wage, the individual would not choose to enter the labor force and hence, would not be observed to be unemployed. We suspect that relatively few of those who report themselves to be unemployed in the current economic climate would say that the reason they are unemployed is that if they accepted a job and became employed, then they would not get as many job offers. See also Toikka (1976) for a model in which unemployment is treated together with the states of employed and not in the labor force.

    5. See Dagenais, Nakamura and Nakamura (1984) for a theoretical discussion of this econometric problem.

CHAPTER 8

CONCLUSIONS

In the first section of this chapter we summarize the main behavioral findings of this study. In section 8.2 we outline what we believe to be the main contributions of this study to the formulation of models for the employment and earnings behavior, as well as the unemployment behavior, of individuals. Section 8.3 consists of a review of distinguishing features of this study in terms of our methods for establishing our behavioral results and choosing among and exploring potential weaknesses of our models, and in terms of our methods for presenting our empirical results.

In examining individual records from the Michigan Panel Study of Income Dynamics data and in reading the literature, as well as through carrying out the formal analyses presented in this book, we have come to believe that working wives can be meaningfully classified into three basic groups. In section 8.4 we describe what we believe are the distinguishing behavioral and attitudinal features of these different groups, and we indicate the potential importance of these groups for understanding and forecasting the employment and earnings behavior of married women. Finally, in section 8.5 we discuss the implications of the findings of this study for future data collection efforts.

8.1. Behavioral Results

Several of our empirical findings differ from, or add to, the findings of other researchers. We find that a woman's child status has little impact on her current work behavior after controlling for her work behavior in the previous year. We find that black women are less, not more, likely to work than nonblack women after controlling for other observable factors including work behavior in the previous year. We find that changes in marital status dramatically affect the work behavior of women. Effects of marital instability cannot be detected in cross-sectional studies. Nor can these effects be detected in panel data studies based on continuously married women.

Our results suggest that selection bias is important for men as well as women. That is, the expected hours of work and wage rates for men as well as women appear to vary systematically depending on the probability of work for the individual. Also, our estimates for women for the uncompensated wage elasticity of hours of work are all small in magnitude and lie in roughly the same range as our estimates for men. Using nonexperimental data, most other researchers have estimated this elasticity to be close to 0 or negative for men but positive and large in magnitude for women. We note, however, that our estimates for the uncompensated wage elasticity of hours of work are in basic agreement with the results of some of the more recent studies based on experimental data. Thus, we find more similarity between the labor force behavioral responses of women and men than most other researchers have found. Our results also carry the implication that in the future, anyone who claims to have discovered behavioral responses for women that differ drastically from the general consensus concerning the behavior of men should be required to show empirical results for both women and men based on the same data source and utilizing the same methodology in so far as this is possible.

8.2. Modeling Contributions

In recent years there has been a great flowering of model building and econometric methodology related to studies of the labor force behavior of married women. There have been suggestions that some of these innovations in modeling and estimation might also be relevant to the analysis of the work behavior of other groups sometimes loosely grouped under the heading of the secondary work force: the young and the old. In this study, however, we find the models and estimation techniques developed for analyzing the work behavior of married women to be appropriate for analyzing the work behavior of all individuals, including prime-aged men. As already mentioned, we find that a Heckman-style selection bias term plays essentially the same role in estimated relationships for the hours of work and wage rates of working men as in the corresponding estimated relationships for married and for unmarried women. We also find evidence that the errors-in-the-variables problem for a wage rate variable created by dividing earned income by a measure of hours of work has similar consequences in estimated relationships for both men and women.

Person-specific effects have posed a special problem in models incorporating inequality decision rules, since first difference or Cochrane-Orcutt-type transformations are not possible, in general, for models of this sort. In the Addendum to Chapter 2 we show, however, that differencing can be carried out for relationships based on inequality decision rules if we have available to us some measure of the extent to which the inequality decision rule was satisfied, or failed to be satisfied, in the previous time period. In a Heckman-style model of the work behavior of individuals, an individual will work in the current year if the wage offer that the individual receives exceeds the individual's asking wage evaluated at 0 hours of work. We have shown in the Addendum to Chapter 2 that a measure of the extent to which this decision rule was satisfied, or failed to be satisfied, in the previous year can be formed as a function of the number of hours the person worked and the person's wage rate in the previous year. This measure can be viewed as a measure of the attachment of the person to the work force in the previous year. Thus, we can rewrite an inequality decision rule for work in the current year to state that a person will work if the change in the person's offered wage from the previous to the current year exceeds the change in the person's asking wage evaluated at 0 hours of work minus our measure of the attachment of the person to the work force in the previous year. Using this line of reasoning, we argue that unobservable fixed or persistent factors that affect the work behavior of individuals year after year will be embedded in the lagged hours of work and wage rate variables. This insight is used in a conceptual sense in the formulation of our Inertia Model. Since we do not observe lagged hours of work and wage rates for those who did not work in the previous year, we estimate separate sets of behavioral relationships for those who did and those who did not work in the previous year.

In estimating separate sets of relationships for those who did and those who did not work in the previous year, we may be introducing additional problems of sample selection. The trade-offs we face in making these modeling and estimation choices are of the same nature as those that applied researchers have long faced, for instance, between bias and multicollinearity problems. That is, in alleviating one estimation problem, we often worsen some other problem, hoping that the estimation results will be improved in some overall sense.[1]

In the literature on fixed effects, the fixed or persistent unobservables, like tastes for work, are usually thought of as characteristics of the individual. There may also be important unobservable factors that are characteristics of the region in which the person lives or of

8 Conclusions

the person's job, however. For instance, a person may have acquired job-specific seniority or training leading to a wage advantage that will be retained so long as the person keeps the same job. There are other unobservable factors, too, which may differ in a systematic manner for those who did and for those who did not work in the previous year. Search costs involved in obtaining a job offer would be expected to be much lower, on the average, for those who are able to keep working at the same job they held in the previous year. These are additional reasons for estimating separate sets of relationships for those who did and for those who did not work in the previous year and for including lagged hours work and wage rate variables in the appropriate relationships for those who did work in the previous year.[2]

One class of unobservable factors that has received attention in recent years are the future expectations of individuals. Future expectations about family size and fertility may be an integral component of the child status variables that we observe, just as a wife's future expectations about the income of her husband may be partially reflected in a variable for his current income. To the extent that these future expectations persist and affect the work behavior of an individual year after year, the effects of these expectations will be embedded in the person's work behavior in the previous year. On the other hand, to the extent that these future expectations change in response to or together with observable events, such as the birth of a baby or marital dissolution, the impacts of these expectations on work behavior will be reflected in the estimated responses to the variables for these events. Variables for child status, educational level, race and so forth are all composite variables reflecting a variety of socioeconomic, life cycle, expectational and institutional factors. The objective of this study has been to identify variables that have an impact on either starting or continuing work behavior after controlling for work behavior in the previous year. No attempt has been made to disentangle expectational and other components of the _current_ impacts of our explanatory variables on work behavior. The research presented in this book is thus not structural research in the sense in which this term is often used, although we believe it is a good deal more than just an ad hoc forecasting exercise.[3]

Models of the work behavior of individuals in the tradition established by Heckman allow for the states of working and not working, but they provide no basis for splitting the state of not working into the states of not in the labor force and unemployed. In this modeling tradition, a person who is unemployed is someone who chooses not to work because the person's wage offer is less than his or her asking wage, and such a person is observationally indistinguishable from someone who has no interest in working at any wage rate. Thus, within this modeling framework it is difficult to utilize information on the number of weeks in a year when a person looked for work but did not work; that is, on weeks of unemployment. In Chapter 7 we extend a Heckman-style model of work behavior to allow for the three distinct states of employed, unemployed and not in the labor force.

8.3. Inference

The purpose of tests of significance of the sort for which results are routinely reported in empirical studies is to establish whether the observed relationships are stronger than expected by chance. We do not make use of conventional tests of significance in this study. Rather, we adopt a courtroom-style approach to hypothesis testing.

We have estimated all of our behavioral relationships for six demographic groups of women further divided into subgroups of those who worked in the previous year and those who did not, and for four demographic groups of men where the men in the youngest group have been divided into those who worked in the previous year and those who did not. Thus, we have estimated our behavioral relationships for 17 different demographic-lagged work status groups. We look first to see if a result, such as the estimated sign for the coefficient of some variable, is replicated for several or all of our groups. If a result is only replicated for a few groups, we consider whether there is some relationship among these groups. For instance, is the result replicated for most of the groups of women who worked in the previous year or for women and men at least 47 years of age?

All of our explanatory variables appear in more than one of our behavioral relationships. For instance, our child status variables appear in both our probit indices for the probability of work and in our equations for the number of hours of work in the year for those who work. Moreover, for many of our explanatory variables certain sign patterns for the associated coefficients of these variables in our various behavioral relationships would be expected on the basis of the theoretical specification of the given model. For instance, we expect the coefficient signs for variables appearing in our probit indices for the probability of work and in our hours equations, but not in our wage equations, to be the same in the probit index and hours equation for any given demographic-work status group. We look to see, therefore, if the signs of the estimated coefficients of our explanatory variables match these expected patterns.

8 Conclusions

If the estimated coefficients for some variable have the same sign for most of our groups, or for most of the groups of some type, we conclude that the observed relationship is probably stronger than we would expect by chance. This conclusion is further supported if the observed sign patterns for the coefficients of this variable in different behavioral relationships of the model match the patterns logically implied by the specification of our model.

Our behavioral conclusions all rest on the accumulation of circumstantial evidence of these sorts. Moreover, the issue of when the weight of accumulated evidence is sufficient to warrant a particular conclusion is treated as a matter of judgment.[4] In a courtroom proceeding, eyewitness reports, expert testimony and various sorts of circumstantial evidence may all be brought before the court, but it is the ultimate responsibility of a judge or jury to weight this evidence and reach a verdict. In a study like the present one in which there is uncertainty about the proper specification of the functional forms of the behavioral relationships, about the distributions of the disturbance terms, and so forth, we do not believe that better conclusions will necessarily be reached by avoiding the degree of arbitrariness inherent in judgmental decision making by appeals to mathematical statistics predicated on assumptions that cannot be checked. One advantage to this courtroom-style approach to hypothesis testing[5] is that it allows us to work with models that are attractive on the basis of our a priori knowledge, or with estimation methods that are attractive on a priori grounds, even though estimates of the appropriate standard errors have not been derived or have not been shown to be consistent. This approach may appear to some to be lacking in rigor. We suggest, however, that some of the empirical results that are presented in the literature with full mathematical rigor, but that are based on a single data sample, would not stand up to the sort of testing on which the results presented in this book are based.

In an effort to detect misspecifications in our estimated relationships, we perform extensive simulation checks on these relationships. If an estimated model, including the estimated parametric specification of the joint distribution of the disturbance terms of the model, is a proper representation of the behavior of the particular sample of individuals whose data were used in estimating the model, then the model should be able to reproduce features of the joint distribution of the dependent variables of interest that were not taken into account in the estimation of the model. For instance, most of the behavioral relationships for which empirical results are presented in this book were estimated using pooled data where the only information used about a person's past work behavior is for the previous year. We look at the ability of these estimated relationships to reproduce various distributional characteristics concerning the employment and earnings histories of the individuals in our data set over a period of 7 years. We also examine the ability of our estimated relationships to reproduce various aspects of the employment and earnings behavior of subsets of individuals, such as women with babies or small children.

The mix of direct and proxy effects on work behavior of our explanatory variables, such as our variable for years of schooling, may be different in different time periods for the same individuals or for different individuals or groups of individuals. Thus, a model that appears to adequately describe the in-sample behavior of the individuals whose data were used in estimating the model may fail to describe the behavior of these same individuals in another time period or may not provide a good representation of the behavior of a different group of individuals. Thus, in addition to performing in-sample simulation checks on our estimated relationships, we also perform and report selected results for out-of-sample simulation checks on these estimated relationships.

Simulation checks of the sort for which summary results are presented in this book are possible because of the richness of our panel data set. It has long been standard practice to try to validate macroeconomic simulation models by making comparisons between actual and simulated time series for key variables. Because of the autoregressive nature of macro time series, however, even out-of-sample simulation results for such models are largely the reflection of information directly used in the estimation of the model. And it is not possible in a macro time series environment to make comparisons at different levels of aggregation or to make distributional comparisons. The difference between the sort of simulation checks possible in a micro data, compared with an aggregate data, environment is one of degree. In a micro data environment, we are likely to have used a much smaller fraction of the total information in a data set in the estimation of a model. Thus, there is more latitude for carrying out meaningful in-sample checks on the ability of the model to simulate observed behavior. Out-of-sample data are usually more readily available in a micro data setting too.

The failure of a model to stand up to simulation checks of the sort for which results are shown in this book probably implies some sort of specification problem. For instance, the specification of the distribution of the disturbance terms of the model may be incorrect, which in turn would throw into question all hypothesis tests for the model utilizing estimated standard errors. If a model passes simulation checks of this sort, however, we cannot jump to the conclusion that the estimated coefficients of the explanatory variables of the model reflect the changes we would expect to observe in the appropriate dependent variables given exogenous unit changes of any nature in each of the explanatory variables. Rather, what we have accomplished is to isolate a set of explanatory variables that seem to have important effects of particular sorts on certain other variables of interest. This information might be used as the basis for informed conjectures about how proposed policy changes, or exogenous changes in circumstances, might affect behavior. This information might also form a basis for seeking out or collecting data that could help us in isolating certain impacts of a composite variable. This is the way data collection activities have frequently proceeded in medical science. For instance, once an apparent link was established between the intake of cholesteral and cardiovascular disease, a massive effort was launched to collect data in which various genetic, environmental or other circumstantial factors that might be associated with cholesterol intake and cardiovascular disease in a proxy sense were held constant, or controlled for, by the way in which the data were collected. Information of this sort could also form the basis for the design of social experiments. Thus, we believe that estimation results of the sort presented in this book can be useful and can advance our basic understanding of the employment and earnings behavior of women, even though we do not claim that the estimated coefficients of our behavioral relationships are unbiased or consistent in a structural sense.

A final methodological contribution of this book is the presentation of our estimation results in the form of model outputs, as well as in the more conventional form of coefficient estimates and derivatives of these coefficient estimates such as elasticities. In a model incorporating simple linear relationships with few, or no, feedbacks, reported coefficient estimates for the explanatory variables of the model can easily be translated in a reader's mind into expected impacts on, or expected values for, the explanatory variable or variables of interest. How many readers, though, can readily translate probit coefficient estimates into impacts on, or values for, the expected probabilities of work for women of different types, given specified changes in, or values for, the explanatory variables? Feedbacks from one equation of a model to another through endogenous variables included on the right-hand sides of equations, selection bias corrections, and the inclusion of lagged endogenous variables as explanatory variables make it even harder for a reader to ascertain the relative or absolute sensitivity of the dependent variables of an estimated model to each of the explanatory variables. Presentations of estimation results in the form of model outputs for various hypothetical cases or changes, such as those we provide in this book, are lacking in generality by their case-specific nature. We believe, however,

that presentations of this sort can be valuable aids to
readers in gaining an intuitive understanding of the nature
and meaning of estimation results for models incorporating
nonlinearities and feedbacks. Presentations of this sort can
also be important aids in comparing the estimation results for
models with and without selection bias terms, with log-linear
versus linear wage equations, with and without certain lagged
endogenous variables included as explanatory variables, and so
forth. Such comparisons should be based, at least in part, on
comparisons of the <u>total</u> impacts of the various explanatory
variables on the dependent variables for the alternative
models of interest.

We believe that an approach to econometrics of the sort
adopted in this study can make econometrics more doable by
those with genuine behavioral, policy and other substantive
interests. Certainly such an approach should make the <u>findings</u>
of econometric studies more accessible to those whose
substantive interests or range of abilities prevent them from
devoting most of their time to understanding and keeping up
with new developments in econometric methodology. It is not
the use of sophisticated estimation methods that renders the
findings of econometric studies inaccessible to many of those
with substantive interest in these findings. It is rather the
mathematical and statistical material related to the
validation of the model and estimation results and the manner
in which the results of econometric studies are customarily
presented that appear to be the real limiting factors. In this
study we present an alternative, or complementary, approach to
dealing with these problems of hypothesis testing and the
presentation of results, which we hope will make our findings
accessible to those who are interested in the work behavior of
women and have some training in econometrics, but who may not
be specialists in, or up-to-date on many aspects of,
econometric methodology.

8.4. A Conjecture Loosely Related to Our Behavioral Results

One of the main findings to emerge from this study is
that observable factors such as age, education and child
status explain relatively little of the variation in the
current work behavior of wives after controlling for work
behavior in the previous year. This does not mean it is
unimportant or uninteresting to determine the existence and
nature of responses to these observable factors. But it does
suggest that the work behavior of wives is determined
primarily by unobservable conditions. Moreover, since very

8 Conclusions

little of the observed continuity in work behavior can be accounted for by observable variables, this suggests that many of these unobservable factors persist over periods of years. Determining the nature of these persistent conditions may be difficult. Suppose it is true, for instance, that more wives are contemplating careers now because with the rising divorce rates, they are more uncertain about the long-run prospects for their marriages. This would be an unobservable, persistent condition. How would we go about testing empirically for the existence, or measuring the strength, of the labor supply response to such a condition, however? We have no answer to this question. Nevertheless, if we could determine what some of these conditions might be, our ability to foresee long-run changes in the labor supply of married women might be greatly improved. What follows in this section are our speculations on what some of these persistent conditions are and how they may relate to various aspects of observed behavior.

In the course of carrying out this study, we have come to believe that working wives can be classified meaningfully into three basic groups: those who see themselves as working for only a short time to meet the current economic needs of their families, those who see themselves as working on a long-term or career basis to meet the economic needs of their families, and those whose work activities are not primarily motivated by the economic needs of their families. Moreover, we suggest that the wives within each of these three broad groupings tend to share certain characteristics concerning the nature of their preparation for work and their interest in increasing their job skills, their interest in trade union activities, their preferences for the manner in which they are remunerated for their work, and the degree to which their work activities are predicated on the belief that their current marriages will endure. We will sketch what we believe to be the distinguishing average characteristics of the working wives in each of our three broad groupings.

We begin with wives who see themselves as working for only a short time to meet the current economic needs of their families. For instance, the husband may still be in training for the career that both he and his wife believe will allow him to eventually assume sole responsibility for the economic welfare of his family. Or the family may need additional income on a short-term basis to cover the expense of some major purchase, such as a home, or to cover the costs of sending older children to college. Other possible reasons why the family may be short of funds on what the family views as a temporary basis might include a career change by the husband, the husband's unemployment or illness; or perhaps economic loss in financial markets, through the collapse of a family company or other business deals, or through disaster such as a fire or theft. These wives did not originally plan on working.

They planned instead to devote themselves to home-oriented activities. On the basis of the human capital literature, we would not expect them to have invested heavily in occupational education or training even though they may have spent substantial numbers of years in school developing personal interests, acquiring other sorts of skills, and perhaps searching for a husband with suitable future earnings prospects.[6] Due to the economic needs that have brought these women into the labor market, they are not in a position to afford on-the-job or other employer-supplied training at the expense of current earnings. Nor is it in their interests to make substantial current investments in job skills, because they could not recoup these expenses in working for only a short period. At the same time, to the extent that employers are aware of the short-term employment interests of these women, it will not be in the best interests of employers to make substantial investments in training these women either, because employers could not recoup these expenses over a short period of work.

Women who see themselves as short-term workers would not be expected to show much interest in joining or participating in the organization or running of trade unions and would be expected to be hostile on the whole to strike actions or any other sort of political or legal activity that might result in the disruption of their employment situation. Wage or other sorts of gains in the future are not going to interest a woman who needs money right now so she can solve her family's current economic problems and return to her life as a homemaker. Nor are wives who see themselves as short-term workers likely to be interested in what really amount to deferred forms of remuneration, which may have tax advantages from the point of view of long-term workers, such as dental and health benefits, life insurance plans, pension benefits and so forth. Finally, the work behavior of these wives would appear to presume that their current marriage situations will endure. How else could they live their lives in a way that makes them so economically dependent on their current husbands?[7]

We next consider wives who see themselves as working on a long-term or career basis to meet the economic needs of their families. That is, these are women who would not work if they found themselves in more affluent circumstances, but as things are they see themselves as having a long-term commitment to the world of work. Wives of low income husbands probably make up the largest component of this group, with the low incomes of the husbands tending to be related to chronic unemployment or underemployment either due to problems of disability or ill health, low educational levels, low skills levels, or other personality or behavioral factors or due to the decline of some particular occupation or industry or to special regional economic problems. Even if the income levels of the husbands are higher for occasional stretches of as much as a year or so, the wives may continue working because they feel the long-run earnings prospects for their husbands are poor.

Because of the nature of the factors that tend to result in men having chronically low earnings and because of observed patterns of marital sorting, we would expect many of the wives in this group to have been relatively underprivileged in their access to good quality education and occupational training. Because they begin work out of economic necessity, they may not feel they can sacrifice any portion of their low potential earnings in order to take special training in preparation for work. For a variety of reasons, employers are believed to be less willing to invest in employees with low initial levels of education and occupational skills. This may be particularly true in the case of married women, since employers may be unable or unwilling to differentiate between those who have long-term commitments to the labor force and those who do not. Thus, even though these women have reason to be interested in employer-funded training programs or on-the-job training, they may have few such opportunities.[8]

Because of their long-term commitment to the labor force, their economic needs, and some of the special problems they may face in the work place, these women might appear to be ideal candidates for union membership and activism. They might also be expected to be particularly interested in promoting legislative or legal measures that would improve conditions for women in the work place. One barrier to the unionization of these women, however, is that relatively uneducated, unskilled women tend to be disproportionately employed in very small establishments; and unions have not been successful on the whole in organizing this sort of a fragmented workforce.[9] Because these women are working out of economic necessitiy and because many fill job slots where they are readily replaceable, they would also be expected to be at least as concerned as men in similar circumstances about union or political activities that might result in a loss of income or loss of job.

Unlike wives with short-term work aspirations, we would expect these long-term working wives to have some interest in deferred forms of remuneration for work, such as medical and dental plans and pensions. The concentration of these women in small establishments and their lack of job security, resulting for many in frequent job changes, may be significant factors, however, in curtailing the access of these wives to such benefit programs. These wives may also find themselves working alongside, and perhaps being outnumbered by other women who have short-term employment objectives and who are uninterested in, or are against, any program that might be seen as reducing their current level of remuneration through wages or salaries.

Wives in this group are working because they lack income security through marriage, as opposed to working to help the family through a period of short-term disequilibrium between the family's income requirements and the earnings of the husband. In some cases, in fact, these wives may have little or no economic stake in holding their marriages together.

The last group of working wives is made up of those whose work activities are not strongly motivated by economic needs within their families. Among them we consider the subgroups of those who do not and those who do display career-oriented behavior. In both cases, however, these women tend to be better educated, married to better educated and higher income men, and to have relatively fewer children.

Among these wives, the work activities of those who are not career oriented might be considered an extension of volunteer or hobby activities. That is, these women appear to work for personal fulfillment with little or no regard for the extent to which they are financially remunerated for these services. These wives can be found in all sorts of poorly paid but innately interesting positions in community and social service organizations, churches, political organizations, special interest movements, amateur sports organizations and universities. Because this subgroup of working wives is not very concerned with the financial remuneration they receive and because they work by choice in job circumstances that are usually flexible and otherwise desirable, they will have little interest in trade unions or in legislative or legal measures to improve the lot of working women, except to the extent that they have taken on some issue related to the conditions or opportunities of working women as a personal cause to fight for. Nor are they likely to be interested in deferred forms of remuneration like pension benefits.

These non-career-oriented wives can afford to behave as they do because of the high incomes of their husbands. Thus, marital stability is a precondition for their lifestyles. Moreover, since they are so dependent on the earnings capabilities of their husbands, one might expect that in some cases these non-career-oriented working wives would oppose, if only as members of a silent but voting public, measures that might be seen as enhancing the employment and earnings prospects of working women at the expense of working men.

The rest of the wives who are not working primarily because of the economic needs of their families, can be described as career motivated. Many of these wives have had interests in pursuing careers that predate their marriages, and they may have invested heavily in education and other sorts of training in preparation for these intended careers. Because of the observed dynamics of marital sorting, we would expect to find these women married to better educated, career-oriented men who could support their families if their

8 Conclusions

wives were not working. Nevertheless, because these women are professionally ambitious and because power and pay are so closely linked in large organizational structures, these women would be expected to be interested in being paid what their work is worth and in enhancing their job classifications and salary levels through opportunities for further training. We would also expect these women to receive relatively favorable consideration from employers for employer-supplied training programs and on-the-job training opportunities because of their initial educational and skill levels and because of their generally identifiable career orientations. These women may also be some of the main beneficiaries of legislative, legal and public-opinion efforts to expand the access of women to education and to occupation-related training and career opportunities.

Because of their long-term job commitments, we would expect these women to be interested in deferred forms of remuneration, such as pension benefits. We would also expect them to be interested in issues relating to job security and the treatment of women in the workplace. The extent to which these women belong to or are active in trade unions may be limited, however, by the general reluctance of those in professional and management positions to become involved in trade unions, since many of these women will be found in, or will aspire to, professional and management positions.

Although the income of these career-oriented women may be a large and important component of family income, particularly as the lifestyle of a family evolves to match the family's income level, by definition these women are not working because of their families. It is more likely, in fact, that family-related responsibilities and the career decisions of their husbands will act as a constraint on the time and energy these women can devote to their careers and as a constraint on their career-related needs for geographic mobility. Thus, not only is it the case that the work activities of these wives are not predicted on the preservation of their marriages, but, in fact, their marriages may hamper these wives to some extent in the pursuit of their work activities.[10]

We suggest that in their late teens and early twenties, most young women deliberately pursue or make a series of inadvertent choices that, together with circumstance, lead them to a lifestyle as primarily a wife and homemaker or to a lifetime on the job. Those who head toward lifestyles as full-time wives and homemakers will, primarily by preference, have more children and will invest less in general education and in occupation-oriented training than their work-oriented counterparts. Some of these home-oriented women may also end up working on short- or long-term bases over the course of their adult lives, due to the economic troubles of their families. That is, some of these women will end up working because their husbands do not earn enough to support their families. Also, some of these women whose husbands are closer to the more affluent end of the income spectrum may take jobs that might be viewed, in some senses, as extensions of volunteer activities. On the other hand, many of those who head toward lifetimes on the job will marry and have families. There will also be shifts among our categories of working wives over time. For instance, a woman may start working on what she believes to be a short-term basis in response to family budget problems and may come eventually to view these problems as chronic and her attachment to the workforce as semipermanent. Or she may come to like her job, become career oriented to some degree, and go on working long after the economic necessity that originally motivated her work has passed. (See Juster and Stafford, 1984, for interesting theoretical work and empirical evidence relating to this last point.)

Much of the growth in employment in recent years has taken place in occupations and industries in which women have always made up substantial proportions of the workforces.[11] The hypothesis has been advanced in the literature that the increase in the demand for women workers resulting from this occupational and industrial pattern of economic growth caused the wage rates of women to rise, which in turn led to increases in the labor supply of women. What may have happened instead, though, is that these increases in female job opportunities have served to offset what otherwise would have been decreases in the wage rates of women as more and more women have joined the competition, due to supply side phenomena, for those sorts of jobs that have traditionally been held by women (see Bergmann and Adelman, 1973). In other words, the historical growth in job opportunities for women may have facilitated or permitted, as opposed to or in addition to having directly caused, the observed increase in the employment and earnings of wives. It may also have been a factor affecting the formation of tastes for work by very young women, contributing in a delayed way to the observed rise in the labor supply of women.

8.5. Implications for Further Research

If our behavioral findings are essentially correct, and if there is some truth to the conjectural picture drawn in the previous section, certain implications emerge with regard to the direction and nature of future research efforts. If we are to understand what has caused the dramatic upswing in recent years in the labor supply of married women we must look for factors that could have caused a major shift in the proportions of very young women heading toward lifestyles as full-time, or would-be full-time, wives and homemakers versus lifestyles with a career orientation. Could rising divorce rates have changed the ideas of successive cohorts of young women, for instance, concerning the stability that they can expect in future marriages and the wisdom of choosing or preparing for adult lifestyles involving economic dependency on still unknown future husbands? We feel that more research should be concentrated on the formation of attitudes toward work and on the decisions to obtain occupation- or work-oriented training by young women who are not yet married. We must also look for factors that could have caused large changes in the proportions of would-be full-time homemakers who decide to go to work on a short-term or long-term basis.

The identification of factors of these sorts might allow us to anticipate future major changes in the work behavior of wives by allowing us to more accurately read the early signs of future behavioral patterns. For instance, do the current record levels of enrolment of young women in business schools, medical and dentistry programs, law schools, and in a whole range of occupational training programs mean that more young women than ever are now preparing to work on a career basis in their adult lives? Will such a future increase in the proportion of adult women who are career oriented bring with it future increases in the participation of women in trade unions, continuing pressure for legislative and legal changes to improve the labor market conditions of women, and continuing pressure for the extension to larger numbers of women of benefit programs, which are of interest to long-term workers? The answers to some of the questions of policy makers and others involved in long-term planning concerning the future work behavior of married women, or of women in general, may hinge as much on anticipating the way in which women in future years will view work and the extent to which they will seek to acquire occupation-related training as on simply anticipating how many women will work or how many hours of work they will want to supply.

We need to ask whether much of the information carried in variables describing the earnings of the husbands of married women is expectational in nature. We have found, as other researchers have, that women married to higher income men are less likely to work, and can be expected to work fewer hours if they do work, than otherwise-similar women married to lower income husbands. Yet we have been unable to demonstrate that changes from the previous to the current year in the earnings of husbands are negatively related to the likelihood of work or hours of work for their wives. Perhaps this is because information about the expectations of wives concerning the future earnings capacities of their husbands is primarily embedded in the levels, as opposed to the first differences, of our variable for the earnings of the husband; and perhaps it is their future or longer term expectations, as opposed to year-to-year fluctuations in the earnings of the husband, that primarily determine whether a wife will work and how much she will work if she does.

We have found heterogeneity, or differences in behavior due to persistent unobservable factors, to be important in this study. We suspect that heterogeneity may be more than a matter of persistent person-specific unobservable variables that can be treated as individual fixed effects. Heterogeneity may also involve systematic differences in behavioral responses to observable variables for women classified according to differences in circumstances or other characteristics that are unknown or unobservable to the econometrician. For instance, wives of higher income husbands who are working by choice at jobs that pay token wages may have to curtail their work if their husbands' incomes fall and they no longer can afford babysitting and other household help that they feel they require to be able to spend time working outside their homes. On the other hand, wives of lower income husbands may be compelled to work to pay their families' bills when their husbands' incomes fall. What we would like, of course, is to find ways of improving our strategies for identifying groups of women who have homogeneous work responses to our observable explanatory variables. We could then estimate separate sets of behavioral relationships for these different groups of women. If possible, however, we would like to avoid grouping by a variable like race, where the essence of our policy interests in the variable lies in trying to determine why women in different racial groups display different work behavior.

The behavioral relationships we have estimated contain a number of endogenous and lagged endogenous feedbacks. For instance, all of our equations for hours of work contain the wage rate, or the log wage rate, of the individual as an explanatory variable. All of these feedbacks are with respect to aspects of work behavior, however. The importance of changes in marital status in our estimated relationships suggests that feedbacks involving other sorts of variables may also be important. Sociological studies of family formation and dissolution indicate that as unemployment rates rise and families are subjected to more economic stress, more couples fall to quarrelling and ultimately separate or divorce. Women whose marriages have recently broken down have been found in this study to be much more likely than otherwise-similar women to start, or continue, working. Perhaps an important impact of macro unemployment conditions on the work behavior of women, therefore, comes via the impact of these unemployment conditions on rates of marital dissolution.

8.6. Implications for Further Data Collection

Most of the models of the work behavior of women developed by other researchers to account for fixed effects or heterogeneity really require panel data over a period of many years for a large sample of women. Data of this sort are not available for research purposes in most countries other than the United States. Nor is it appropriate for those in other countries to simply rely on behavioral findings from studies based on U.S. panel data as a basis for understanding and forecasting the work behavior of women in their own countries. There are too many differences in customs, institutional factors such as tax laws, industrial structure, the sensitivity of the domestic economy to problems in foreign labor and product markets, and so forth that may affect domestic labor markets in ways that are not well understood. Yet even if countries like Canada and Japan made the decision tommorrow to begin collecting panel data, these data would not be available over any reasonable time period for years to come.

On the other hand, all of the behavioral relationships for which estimation results are presented in this study, with the exception of those presented in Chapter 5, can be estimated using lagged information from only the immediately preceding year. Information of this sort could easily be collected on a recall basis as part of national population censuses or other surveys. In fact, the key information required for the estimation of two of our model variants could be collected by rewording a single question on the 1981 or 1971 form for the Census of Canada (see Chap. 4. fn. 4).

Even in the United States there might be advantages to collecting information of the sort required to estimate the behavioral relationships presented in this book as part, say, of the next U.S. Census (see Chap. 4, fn. 5). By their nature, census data do not entail the same sorts of weighting and attrition problems associated with, for instance, data from the Panel Study of Income Dynamics. With census data there is less of a problem of obtaining samples of reasonable sizes for minority individuals of various types, such as women with five or more children or older women who are working full-time. Also, recent political events in the United States suggest that public funding may not always be forthcoming to support major panel studies like the Panel Study of Income Dynamics.

In Chapter 5 we show that after controlling for work behavior in the previous year, variables for the number or proportion of years worked since 18 years of age explain very little of the remaining variability in the work behavior of married women. This finding suggests that if only a few items of information about previous work behavior are going to be collected on a recall basis as part of a cross-sectional survey, it is the information about work behavior in the previous year, as opposed to summary information about work experience over some longer period, that would be most useful to us for explaining current work behavior. This is fortunate since the response rate and accuracy of information collected on a recall basis about the previous year are likely to be much better than for recall information about, for instance, the number of years of work since 18.

Our results also demonstrate the potential importance of event- or change-oriented data. For instance, among our child status variables, it is only the variable for the presence of a new baby that seems to be of some importance in explaining current work behavior after controlling for work behavior in the previous year. Likewise, it is the estimated responses to our variables for the change in the income of the husband from the previous to the current year that throw doubt on our a priori theories of how the earnings of husbands affect the work behavior of their wives. Even when event- or change-oriented data are present in the raw version of a data set, it is often difficult to recover this information from the data set in the form in which it is released to researchers. For instance, in the version of the Panel Study of Income Dynamics that we used in this study, there is no variable indicating the presence of a new baby. Rather, we infer that there must be a new baby if a woman has a child younger than two years of age and if the number of children younger than 18 years of age living at home has increased by one from the previous to the current year. Thus, although some of this event information is present in existing panel data sets like the Panel Study of Income Dynamics, recovering this information from these data sets often requires manipulations of the data that are costly, that demand both knowledge of the data set and certain skills in computer programming and that may frequently be subject to errors that are difficult for either the researcher or others to detect. If event data about, for instance, whether a women has a new baby, whether a person is newly married, divorced or widowed, and whether a person is newly disabled or has changed or lost his or her job in the preceding year were readily available as part of each individual's current year's information in cross-sectional and panel data sets, we believe researchers would quickly find valuable ways of utilizing this information.

8   Conclusions

FOOTNOTES TO CHAPTER 8

1. Griliches (1977, p. 13) writes:

It is a sad fact that in doing empirical work we must continuously search for the passage between the Syclla of biased inferences due to left-out and confounded influences and the Charybdis of overzealously purging our data of most of their identifying variance, being left largely with noise and error in our hands. In a sense, we run into a kind of uncertainty principle: The amount of information contained in any one specific data set is finite and, therefore, as we keep asking finer and finer questions, our answers become more and more uncertain.

2. Zellner (1979, p. 635) quotes Tukey as stating:

When Fisher introduced the formalities of the analysis of variance in the early 1920's, its most important function was to conceal the fact that the data was being adjusted for block means, an important step forward which if openly visible would have been considered by too many wiseacres of the time to be "cooking the data". If so, let up hope the day will soon come when the role of "decent concealment" can be freely admitted.

The recent work on fixed effects makes it clear that we must use information on past work behavior, in one way or another, if it is available to us. From this work we can see, for instance, that there is little hope of obtaining unbiased or consistent parameter estimates without controlling for the persistent unobservable effects embedded in this past behavior. Of course, it has been clear for some time to many of those trying to predict the future work behavior of individuals that we ought to be making use of available information on past work behavior. See, for instance, the work of Wertheimer on labor force behavior in Orcutt, Caldwell and Wertheimer (1976).

3. In a different context Nerlove (1983, p. 1253) writes:

I do not believe that there is a sharp dichotomy between "data analysis" and "structural estimation" .... Rather there is a continuum of approaches, ranging from simple techniques designed to uncover bivariate associations to elaborate multivariate models .... While there are situations and bodies of

> data for which a "hardline" structural approach may
> be both desirable and appropriate, it is more useful
> in this context to allow the data to speak more
> fully and to reveal associations.

We believe these words apply as well to the subject area and data on which this book is based.

4. Zellner (1979, p. 635) quotes Tukey as stating:

> It is my impression that rather generally, not just
> in econometrics, it is considered decent to use
> judgment in choosing a functional form, but indecent
> to use judgment in choosing a coefficient. If
> judgment about important things is quite all right,
> why should it not be used for less important ones as
> well?

5. One could also think of this as a judgmental, as opposed to a formal statistical, Bayesian approach. In contrast to the style (though not, perhaps, the practice) that has come to dominate much of the econometric literature, the term _judgmental_ figures prominently in the writings of a Bayesian like Zellner. In discussing the procedure for evaluating and reformulating a model Zellner (1979, p. 629) writes:

> A good deal of judgment or prior information is
> employed, usually informally. For example, the
> algebraic signs and magnitudes of parameter
> estimates are reviewed to ascertain whether they
> are compatible with results provided by economic
> theory, by previous studies, and by judgmental
> information.

6. Typical estimates of the average money rate of return for white males in the United States are 11 to 13 percent on a college education, with higher rates of return on a high school education and still higher rates of return on an elementary school education. Rates of return on education at all levels are consistently estimated to be lower for women than for men, however. Also, while business investments may often pay off within 5 to 10 years, the pay-off period for a college education may be much longer than this. (See Becker, 1975. See also Wachtel, 1975, for some estimates of the rate of return to schooling when the costs are more carefully considered.) Thus, women who do not expect to work much outside their homes as adults will expect a low money-rate of return on career-oriented investments in education or training and thus, would not be expected to make substantial investments of this sort (Mincer and Polachek, 1974). They

8   Conclusions   381

may, however, be interested in educational opportunities that they believe will make them better homemakers, better citizens, more interesting conversationalists, or that will enhance the value of their leisure time in years to come. Thus, they may attend college but will be unlikely to select career- or job-oriented courses. On the other hand, young women who expect to work most of their adult lives may exhibit behavior with regard to investment in human capital through education and training that is similar to the behavior of young men, adjusting for lower rates of return and taking into account perceived barriers to the entry or promotion of women in various lines of work and barriers due to anticipated responsibilities for a home or children.

7. See Bergmann (1981) for an interesting consideration of the economic risks associated with being a housewife.

8. For statistical theories of discrimination that might, at least partially, explain the reluctance of employers to make human capital investments in workers with less formal education or in women workers in general, see, for instance, Phelps (1972) and Arrow (1973).

9. For references on the history and problem of organizing fragmented workforces see, for instance, Sen (1984), White (1980) and Lowe (1978).

10. For instance, Susan Fraker (1984, p. 44) writes:

Motherhood clearly slows the progress of women who decided to take long maternity leave or who choose to work part-time. But even those committed to working full-time on their return believe they are sometimes held back.

11. See Oppenheimer (1970), Gunderson (1976), Gross (1968), Nakamura et al. (1979), Nakamura, Nakamura and Cullen (1979), Merrilees (1982) and Cullen and Nakamura (1984) for further discussion and evidence on the occupational segregation of women.

Appendix A. Year by Year Average Simulation Results for the Standard, Dummy, Split and Inertia Models

TABLE A.1
PROPORTIONS OF INDIVIDUALS OBSERVED TO AND SIMULATED TO WORK IN EACH YEAR

		Model variant			
Year	Actual	Standard	Dummy	Split	Inertia
1971	.71	.71	.71	.70	.70
1972	.72	.71	.73	.70	.70
1973	.74	.72	.74	.72	.72
1974	.73	.73	.74	.73	.72
1975	.73	.73	.74	.74	.72
1976	.72	.73	.74	.73	.72
1977	.73	.75	.74	.74	.73
Average percentage point deviation		0.0	.8	.3	−1.0

TABLE A.2
PROPORTIONS OF WOMEN 14-20 YEARS OF AGE IN 1971 OBSERVED TO AND SIMULATED TO WORK IN EACH YEAR

		Model variant			
Year	Actual	Standard	Dummy	Split	Inertia
1971	.41	.44	.44	.42	.46
1972	.50	.51	.53	.47	.42
1973	.53	.44	.51	.54	.48
1974	.56	.53	.50	.52	.54
1975	.49	.55	.53	.56	.54
1976	.44	.53	.58	.58	.54
1977	.60	.58	.52	.61	.51
Average percentage point deviation		.7	1.1	2.4	−.6

Appendix A

TABLE A.3
PROPORTIONS OF WOMEN 21-46 YEARS OF AGE AND
MARRIED IN 1971 OBSERVED TO AND SIMULATED
TO WORK IN EACH YEAR

		Model variant			
Year	Actual	Standard	Dummy	Split	Inertia
1971	.54	.51	.53	.53	.51
1972	.53	.49	.55	.46	.52
1973	.55	.56	.56	.49	.51
1974	.58	.58	.57	.55	.55
1975	.64	.58	.61	.57	.57
1976	.63	.65	.62	.58	.62
1977	.64	.67	.65	.58	.65
Average percentage point deviation		-1.0	-.3	-5.0	-2.6

TABLE A.4
PROPORTIONS OF WOMEN 21-46 YEARS OF AGE AND
UNMARRIED IN 1971 OBSERVED TO AND SIMULATED
TO WORK IN EACH YEAR

		Model variant			
Year	Actual	Standard	Dummy	Split	Inertia
1971	.75	.72	.73	.74	.73
1972	.69	.70	.74	.71	.75
1973	.74	.71	.76	.76	.78
1974	.75	.75	.80	.78	.78
1975	.74	.80	.78	.76	.78
1976	.72	.72	.74	.73	.76
1977	.75	.71	.77	.74	.80
Average percentage point deviation		-.4	2.6	1.1	3.4

TABLE A.5
PROPORTIONS OF WOMEN 47-64 YEARS OF AGE AND
MARRIED IN 1971 OBSERVED TO AND SIMULATED
TO WORK IN EACH YEAR

		Model variant			
Year	Actual	Standard	Dummy	Split	Inertia
1971	.45	.49	.47	.48	.45
1972	.50	.44	.48	.48	.40
1973	.48	.46	.44	.39	.46
1974	.46	.45	.46	.44	.47
1975	.45	.48	.39	.45	.46
1976	.51	.42	.41	.49	.45
1977	.48	.52	.39	.47	.45
Average percentage point deviation		−1.0	−4.1	−1.8	−2.7

TABLE A.6
PROPORTIONS OF WOMEN 47-64 YEARS OF AGE AND
UNMARRIED IN 1971 OBSERVED TO AND SIMULATED
TO WORK IN EACH YEAR

		Model variant			
Year	Actual	Standard	Dummy	Split	Inertia
1971	.66	.66	.63	.68	.63
1972	.65	.62	.66	.62	.63
1973	.66	.68	.69	.67	.63
1974	.62	.61	.66	.65	.61
1975	.60	.62	.65	.65	.62
1976	.60	.61	.65	.64	.60
1977	.59	.68	.62	.68	.64
Average percentage point deviation		1.4	2.6	3.0	−.3

TABLE A.7
PROPORTIONS OF WOMEN 65+ YEARS OF AGE IN 1971
OBSERVED TO AND SIMULATED TO WORK IN EACH YEAR

		Model variant			
Year	Actual	Standard	Dummy	Split	Inertia
1971	.32	.40	.21	.27	.25
1972	.28	.28	.32	.31	.32
1973	.21	.25	.29	.26	.31
1974	.19	.23	.31	.24	.21
1975	.19	.19	.28	.26	.18
1976	.23	.20	.31	.25	.19
1977	.18	.20	.28	.26	.16
Average percentage point deviation		2.1	5.7	3.6	.3

TABLE A.8
ACTUAL AND SIMULATED AVERAGE WAGE RATES OF
INDIVIDUALS FOUND TO WORK IN EACH YEAR

		Model variant			
Year	Actual	Standard	Dummy	Split	Inertia
1971	$3.20	$3.23	$3.18	$3.24	$2.92
1972	3.31	3.28	3.33	3.25	2.95
1973	3.37	3.30	3.19	3.26	2.93
1974	3.37	3.31	3.33	3.30	2.93
1975	3.33	3.25	3.43	3.40	3.06
1976	3.47	3.35	3.35	3.44	3.08
1977	3.49	3.44	3.46	3.38	3.09
Average deviation		−.05	−.04	−.04	−.37

TABLE A.9
ACTUAL AND SIMULATED AVERAGE WAGE RATES OF
WOMEN FOUND TO WORK IN EACH YEAR WHO WERE
14-20 YEARS OF AGE IN 1971

		Model variant			
Year	Actual	Standard	Dummy	Split	Inertia
1971	$2.10	$1.73	$1.66	$1.63	$1.69
1972	1.85	1.73	1.92	1.94	1.74
1973	1.66	1.87	1.76	1.78	1.86
1974	1.84	2.08	1.66	2.03	1.71
1975	2.04	1.73	2.21	2.06	1.95
1976	2.30	2.00	2.20	1.91	2.19
1977	1.76	2.00	2.48	2.04	2.05
Average deviation		-.06	.04	-.02	-.05

TABLE A.10
ACTUAL AND SIMULATED AVERAGE WAGE RATES OF
WOMEN FOUND TO WORK IN EACH YEAR WHO WERE
21-46 YEARS OF AGE AND MARRIED IN 1971

		Model variant			
Year	Actual	Standard	Dummy	Split	Inertia
1971	$2.42	$2.63	$2.40	$2.45	$2.34
1972	2.42	2.33	2.55	2.53	2.37
1973	2.76	2.48	2.60	2.44	2.23
1974	2.33	2.35	2.33	2.47	2.21
1975	2.54	2.35	2.49	2.44	2.46
1976	2.66	2.54	2.45	2.46	2.37
1977	2.54	2.71	2.48	2.39	2.44
Average deviation		-.04	-.05	-.07	-.18

TABLE A.11
ACTUAL AND SIMULATED AVERAGE WAGE RATES OF WOMEN FOUND TO WORK IN EACH YEAR WHO WERE 21-46 YEARS OF AGE AND UNMARRIED IN 1971

		Model variant			
Year	Actual	Standard	Dummy	Split	Inertia
1971	$2.24	$2.23	$2.23	$2.36	$2.15
1972	2.47	2.42	2.31	2.43	2.23
1973	2.44	2.30	2.28	2.62	2.27
1974	2.68	2.79	2.82	2.54	2.35
1975	2.55	2.48	2.91	2.82	2.41
1976	2.66	2.61	2.60	2.64	2.38
1977	2.53	2.61	2.63	2.52	2.51
Average deviation		-.02	.03	.05	-.18

TABLE A.12
ACTUAL AND SIMULATED AVERAGE WAGE RATES OF WOMEN FOUND TO WORK IN EACH YEAR WHO WERE 47-64 YEARS OF AGE AND MARRIED IN 1971

		Model variant			
Year	Actual	Standard	Dummy	Split	Inertia
1971	$2.62	$2.32	$2.44	$2.88	$2.39
1972	2.60	2.57	2.90	2.33	2.78
1973	2.70	2.69	3.07	2.78	2.64
1974	2.94	2.29	2.74	2.32	2.51
1975	2.38	2.13	2.86	2.60	2.39
1976	2.59	2.36	2.68	2.52	2.40
1977	2.71	2.75	2.44	2.18	2.56
Average deviation		-.20	.08	-.13	-.12

TABLE A.13
ACTUAL AND SIMULATED AVERAGE WAGE RATES OF
WOMEN FOUND TO WORK IN EACH YEAR WHO WERE
47-64 YEARS OF AGE AND UNMARRIED IN 1971

		Model variant			
Year	Actual	Standard	Dummy	Split	Inertia
1971	$2.35	$2.31	$2.39	$2.78	$2.14
1972	2.31	2.44	2.19	2.55	2.22
1973	2.41	2.48	2.39	2.26	2.28
1974	2.55	2.53	2.58	3.05	2.38
1975	2.61	2.32	2.56	2.66	2.61
1976	2.65	2.54	2.80	2.68	2.44
1977	2.38	2.48	2.35	2.42	2.37
Average deviation		-.02	-.00	.17	-.12

TABLE A.14
ACTUAL AND SIMULATED AVERAGE WAGE RATES OF
WOMEN FOUND TO WORK IN EACH YEAR WHO WERE
65+ YEARS OF AGE IN 1971

		Model variant			
Year	Actual	Standard	Dummy	Split	Inertia
1971	$1.72	$1.58	$1.84	$2.30	$1.75
1972	.94	1.46	1.42	1.37	1.55
1973	1.67	2.03	1.86	2.82	1.00
1974	1.03	1.33	1.13	1.64	1.60
1975	1.71	1.24	1.81	1.63	1.43
1976	1.52	1.83	2.13	1.92	1.94
1977	1.94	1.47	1.45	2.15	1.83
Average deviation		.06	.16	.47	.08

Appendix A

TABLE A.15
ACTUAL AND SIMULATED AVERAGE HOURS OF WORK
OF INDIVIDUALS FOUND TO WORK IN EACH YEAR

		Model variant			
Year	Actual	Standard	Dummy	Split	Inertia
1971	1762	1726	1770	1773	1727
1972	1794	1766	1771	1802	1727
1973	1809	1826	1789	1789	1748
1974	1798	1815	1833	1851	1771
1975	1803	1845	1839	1844	1793
1976	1830	1816	1809	1825	1800
1977	1832	1857	1851	1834	1814
Average deviation		3	5	13	-35

TABLE A.16
ACTUAL AND SIMULATED AVERAGE HOURS OF WORK
OF WOMEN FOUND TO WORK IN EACH YEAR WHO WERE
14-20 YEARS OF AGE IN 1971

		Model variant			
Year	Actual	Standard	Dummy	Split	Inertia
1971	707	804	698	988	784
1972	769	877	879	1293	1051
1973	1045	1038	998	1159	1089
1974	1077	1179	1104	1244	1034
1975	1002	1115	936	1324	965
1976	1295	1291	1045	1247	1350
1977	1287	1453	1353	1475	1328
Average deviation		83	-24	221	60

TABLE A.17
ACTUAL AND SIMULATED AVERAGE HOURS OF WORK
OF WOMEN FOUND TO WORK IN EACH YEAR WHO WERE
21-46 YEARS OF AGE AND MARRIED IN 1971

		Model variant			
Year	Actual	Standard	Dummy	Split	Inertia
1971	1201	1139	1232	1270	1183
1972	1276	1177	1202	1207	1151
1973	1307	1264	1277	1127	1180
1974	1271	1263	1267	1258	1250
1975	1297	1313	1273	1388	1298
1976	1328	1361	1262	1287	1222
1977	1330	1327	1304	1328	1325
Average deviation		−24	−27	−21	−57

TABLE A.18
ACTUAL AND SIMULATED AVERAGE HOURS OF WORK
OF WOMEN FOUND TO WORK IN EACH YEAR WHO WERE
21-46 YEARS OF AGE AND UNMARRIED IN 1971

		Model variant			
Year	Actual	Standard	Dummy	Split	Inertia
1971	1576	1447	1584	1586	1536
1972	1638	1561	1676	1582	1541
1973	1568	1517	1589	1501	1555
1974	1585	1634	1688	1626	1577
1975	1553	1592	1646	1676	1587
1976	1543	1570	1599	1555	1541
1977	1502	1562	1612	1477	1515
Average deviation		−12	61	5	−16

Appendix A

TABLE A.19
ACTUAL AND SIMULATED AVERAGE HOURS OF WORK
OF WOMEN FOUND TO WORK IN EACH YEAR WHO WERE
47-64 YEARS OF AGE AND MARRIED IN 1971

		Model variant			
Year	Actual	Standard	Dummy	Split	Inertia
1971	1336	1292	1471	1312	1376
1972	1358	1431	1370	1437	1453
1973	1412	1505	1423	1490	1363
1974	1272	1268	1396	1293	1192
1975	1416	1466	1265	1138	1226
1976	1283	1401	1389	1186	1274
1977	1299	1283	1578	1208	1319
Average deviation		39	74	-44	-25

TABLE A.20
ACTUAL AND SIMULATED AVERAGE HOURS OF WORK
OF WOMEN FOUND TO WORK IN EACH YEAR WHO WERE
47-64 YEARS OF AGE AND UNMARRIED IN 1971

		Model variant			
Year	Actual	Standard	Dummy	Split	Inertia
1971	1684	1751	1644	1681	1674
1972	1731	1616	1640	1664	1618
1973	1650	1820	1755	1583	1561
1974	1651	1698	1598	1596	1557
1975	1615	1526	1643	1522	1539
1976	1588	1707	1584	1589	1668
1977	1681	1607	1751	1607	1716
Average deviation		18	2	-51	-38

TABLE A.21
ACTUAL AND SIMULATED AVERAGE HOURS OF WORK
OF WOMEN FOUND TO WORK IN EACH YEAR WHO WERE
65+ YEARS OF AGE IN 1971

		Model variant			
Year	Actual	Standard	Dummy	Split	Inertia
1971	676	1013	1063	671	985
1972	581	760	884	881	886
1973	915	955	1067	825	931
1974	970	923	943	1067	1116
1975	857	909	1007	1099	930
1976	987	1082	752	1082	1022
1977	849	1156	813	908	1156
Average deviation		137	99	100	170

TABLE A.22
ACTUAL AND SIMULATED AVERAGE INCOMES OF
INDIVIDUALS FOUND TO WORK IN EACH YEAR

		Model variant			
Year	Actual	Standard	Dummy	Split	Inertia
1971	$5933	$6225	$6360	$6372	$5593
1972	6276	6517	6651	6462	5643
1973	6378	6668	6273	6475	5658
1974	6312	6537	6761	6625	5752
1975	6203	6527	6920	6902	6021
1976	6457	6562	6646	6843	5961
1977	6589	6942	7011	6749	6013
Average deviation		261	353	326	−501

Appendix A

TABLE A.23
ACTUAL AND SIMULATED AVERAGE INCOMES OF
WOMEN FOUND TO WORK IN EACH YEAR WHO WERE
14-20 YEARS OF AGE IN 1971

		Model variant			
Year	Actual	Standard	Dummy	Split	Inertia
1971	$1261	$1453	$1342	$2342	$1703
1972	1217	1918	1940	3707	2513
1973	1691	2165	1920	2997	2565
1974	1920	2779	1984	3458	2207
1975	1718	2217	2341	4060	2648
1976	2322	2709	2537	3471	3619
1977	2272	2636	3419	4440	3553
Average deviation		496	440	1725	915

TABLE A.24
ACTUAL AND SIMULATED AVERAGE INCOMES OF
WOMEN FOUND TO WORK IN EACH YEAR WHO WERE
21-46 YEARS OF AGE AND MARRIED IN 1971

		Model variant			
Year	Actual	Standard	Dummy	Split	Inertia
1971	$2662	$2905	$3100	$3115	$3057
1972	2988	2681	3131	3023	2858
1973	2994	2996	3383	2711	2738
1974	2837	2794	2996	3144	2946
1975	2873	2940	3098	3507	3323
1976	3210	3293	3247	3193	2993
1977	3257	3411	3324	3047	3253
Average deviation		28	208	131	49

TABLE A.25
ACTUAL AND SIMULATED AVERAGE INCOMES OF
WOMEN FOUND TO WORK IN EACH YEAR WHO WERE
21-46 YEARS OF AGE AND UNMARRIED IN 1971

		Model variant			
Year	Actual	Standard	Dummy	Split	Inertia
1971	$3657	$3238	$3549	$3603	$3525
1972	4001	3928	3871	3763	3682
1973	3925	3571	3714	3882	3900
1974	4146	4601	4702	4167	4029
1975	3969	3987	4856	4675	4151
1976	4138	4005	4213	4049	4007
1977	3958	4123	4252	3773	4061
Average deviation		-49	195	17	-63

TABLE A.26
ACTUAL AND SIMULATED AVERAGE INCOMES OF
WOMEN FOUND TO WORK IN EACH YEAR WHO WERE
47-64 YEARS OF AGE AND MARRIED IN 1971

		Model variant			
Year	Actual	Standard	Dummy	Split	Inertia
1971	$3419	$3000	$3641	$3967	$3444
1972	3501	3384	4074	3167	4059
1973	3629	4249	4646	4301	3790
1974	3217	2790	3897	3109	3282
1975	3393	3031	3682	3152	3053
1976	3118	3228	3789	3037	3105
1977	3358	3327	3807	2482	3354
Average deviation		-89	557	-60	-64

Appendix A

TABLE A.27
ACTUAL AND SIMULATED AVERAGE INCOMES OF
WOMEN FOUND TO WORK IN EACH YEAR WHO WERE
47-64 YEARS OF AGE AND UNMARRIED IN 1971

		Model variant			
Year	Actual	Standard	Dummy	Split	Inertia
1971	$3873	$3688	$3759	$4716	$3686
1972	4198	3757	3667	4282	3725
1973	4071	4240	4005	3493	3740
1974	4237	4228	4030	4790	3805
1975	4327	3341	4439	3747	4076
1976	3926	4083	4735	4089	3979
1977	4143	3786	4143	3468	4233
Average deviation		-223	0	-27	-219

TABLE A.28
ACTUAL AND SIMULATED AVERAGE INCOMES OF
WOMEN FOUND TO WORK IN EACH YEAR WHO WERE
65+ YEARS OF AGE IN 1971

		Model variant			
Year	Actual	Standard	Dummy	Split	Inertia
1971	$1303	$1572	$2419	$ 807	$2042
1972	760	944	1589	732	1551
1973	1574	1867	3258	815	1171
1974	1001	1206	1120	1114	2128
1975	1704	935	1880	1093	1245
1976	1627	1782	2200	1336	1828
1977	1381	1732	1041	1168	2486
Average deviation		98	594	-326	443

Appendix B. Distributional Comparisons for Our Simulation
Results for the Standard, Dummy, Split and Inertia Models

TABLE B.1
ACTUAL AND SIMULATED DISTRIBUTIONS OF ANNUAL HOURS
OF WORK OF INDIVIDUALS POOLED OVER 7-YEAR PERIOD

Annual hours of work	Actual	Standard	Dummy	Split	Inertia
0	.27	.29	.28	.30	.30
1-600	.09	.04	.04	.04	.05
601-1,200	.08	.11	.11	.10	.11
1,201-1,400	.03	.06	.05	.05	.06
1,401-1,800	.09	.13	.13	.12	.13
1,801-2,200	.25	.13	.14	.14	.13
2,201 +	.20	.24	.24	.25	.22
Pseudo chi-square statistic (n=18,599)		2862	2360	2238	2599

Appendix B

TABLE B.2
ACTUAL AND SIMULATED DISTRIBUTIONS OF ANNUAL HOURS OF WORK OF
WOMEN 14-20 YEARS OF AGE IN 1971 POOLED OVER 7-YEAR PERIOD

Annual hours of work	Actual	Standard	Dummy	Split	Inertia
0	.44	.46	.46	.50	.49
1-600	.19	.08	.08	.09	.09
601-1,200	.12	.16	.18	.13	.14
1,201-1,400	.03	.07	.06	.05	.06
1,401-1,800	.07	.10	.11	.08	.10
1,801-2,200	.13	.07	.05	.06	.06
2,201 +	.02	.05	.05	.09	.05
Pseudo chi-square statistic (n=1,904)		413	460	684	356

TABLE B.3
ACTUAL AND SIMULATED DISTRIBUTIONS OF ANNUAL
HOURS OF WORK OF WOMEN 21-46 YEARS OF AGE
AND MARRIED IN 1971 POOLED OVER 7-YEAR PERIOD

Annual hours of work	Actual	Standard	Dummy	Split	Inertia
0	.40	.44	.45	.47	.46
1-600	.15	.08	.07	.07	.08
601-1,200	.12	.17	.17	.15	.16
1,201-1,400	.03	.07	.06	.06	.07
1,401-1,800	.10	.11	.11	.11	.11
1,801-2,200	.17	.07	.08	.08	.07
2,201 +	.02	.06	.05	.05	.05
Pseudo chi-square statistic (n=2,968)		744	574	552	633

TABLE B.4
ACTUAL AND SIMULATED DISTRIBUTIONS OF ANNUAL HOURS OF WORK OF WOMEN 21-46 YEARS OF AGE AND UNMARRIED IN 1971 POOLED OVER 7-YEAR PERIOD

Annual hours of work	Actual	Standard	Dummy	Split	Inertia
0	.28	.30	.26	.29	.27
1-600	.07	.05	.04	.04	.05
601-1,200	.10	.14	.17	.15	.16
1,201-1,400	.04	.08	.07	.08	.09
1,401-1,800	.13	.16	.16	.16	.16
1,801-2,200	.30	.14	.15	.15	.13
2,201 +	.07	.12	.14	.13	.14
Pseudo chi-square statistic (n=1,729)		330	411	366	480

TABLE B.5
ACTUAL AND SIMULATED DISTRIBUTIONS OF ANNUAL HOURS OF WORK OF WOMEN 47-64 YEARS OF AGE AND MARRIED IN 1971 POOLED OVER 7-YEAR PERIOD

Annual hours of work	Actual	Standard	Dummy	Split	Inertia
0	.56	.62	.61	.62	.63
1-600	.11	.04	.04	.06	.05
601-1,200	.09	.11	.10	.11	.11
1,201-1,400	.03	.05	.04	.03	.04
1,401-1,800	.08	.08	.09	.08	.09
1,801-2,200	.11	.05	.06	.06	.06
2,201 +	.02	.04	.05	.04	.02
Pseudo chi-square statistic (n=833)		101	102	63	61

Appendix B

TABLE B.6
ACTUAL AND SIMULATED DISTRIBUTIONS OF ANNUAL
HOURS OF WORK OF WOMEN 47-64 YEARS OF AGE
AND UNMARRIED IN 1971 POOLED OVER 7-YEAR PERIOD

Annual hours of work	Actual	Standard	Dummy	Split	Inertia
0	.43	.41	.41	.41	.47
1-600	.05	.04	.03	.05	.03
601-1,200	.09	.13	.12	.10	.10
1,201-1,400	.04	.06	.06	.05	.06
1,401-1,800	.11	.13	.14	.14	.13
1,801-2,200	.22	.10	.12	.13	.10
2,201 +	.07	.13	.12	.11	.11
Pseudo chi-square statistic (n=1,015)		153	120	73	116

TABLE B.7
ACTUAL AND SIMULATED DISTRIBUTIONS OF ANNUAL
HOURS OF WORK OF WOMEN 65+ YEARS OF AGE
IN 1971 POOLED OVER 7-YEAR PERIOD

Annual hours of work	Actual	Standard	Dummy	Split	Inertia
0	.87	.85	.81	.86	.82
1-600	.07	.04	.06	.05	.07
601-1,200	.02	.05	.07	.03	.04
1,201-1,400	.00	.02	.01	.01	.01
1,401-1,800	.01	.02	.04	.02	.03
1,801-2,200	.01	.01	.01	.02	.02
2,201 +	.01	.00	.00	.01	.01
Pseudo chi-square statistic (n=399)		28	64	16	30

TABLE B.8
ACTUAL AND SIMULATED DISTRIBUTIONS OF ANNUAL
INCOMES OF INDIVIDUALS POOLED OVER
7-YEAR PERIOD

Annual income	Actual	Standard	Dummy	Split	Inertia
$0	.28	.29	.28	.30	.30
$1–1,000	.09	.05	.05	.05	.06
$2,001–5,000	.19	.23	.23	.22	.22
$5,001–10,000	.24	.19	.19	.19	.21
$10,001–20,000	.11	.11	.11	.12	.10
$20,001 +	.02	.03	.03	.03	.01
Pseudo chi-square statistic (n=18,599)		1060	1053	873	604

TABLE B.9
ACTUAL AND SIMULATED DISTRIBUTIONS
OF INCOMES OF WOMEN 14–20 YEARS OF AGE
IN 1971 POOLED OVER 7-YEAR PERIOD

Annual income	Actual	Standard	Dummy	Split	Inertia
$0	.46	.46	.46	.50	.49
$1–1,000	.20	.12	.12	.12	.13
$1,001–2,000	.09	.12	.14	.10	.11
$2,001–5,000	.18	.21	.19	.17	.17
$5,001–10,000	.06	.08	.07	.07	.07
$10,001–20,000	.00	.01	.01	.03	.03
$20,001 +	.00	.00	.00	.01	.00
Pseudo chi-square statistic (n=1,904)		118	127	150	111

Appendix B

TABLE B.10
ACTUAL AND SIMULATED DISTRIBUTIONS OF ANNUAL
INCOMES OF WOMEN 21-46 YEARS OF AGE
AND MARRIED IN 1971 POOLED OVER 7-YEAR PERIOD

Annual income	Actual	Standard	Model variant Dummy	Split	Inertia
$0	.41	.44	.45	.47	.46
$1-1,000	.14	.08	.08	.09	.10
$1,001-2,000	.10	.14	.13	.12	.13
$2,001-5,000	.24	.24	.22	.20	.20
$5,001-10,000	.11	.08	.09	.09	.08
$10,001-20,000	.00	.01	.02	.02	.02
$20,001 +	.00	.00	.00	.00	.00
Pseudo chi-square statistic (n=2,968)		133	119	111	101

TABLE B.11
ACTUAL AND SIMULATED DISTRIBUTIONS OF ANNUAL
INCOMES OF WOMEN 21-46 YEARS OF AGE
AND UNMARRIED IN 1971 POOLED OVER 7-YEAR PERIOD

Annual income	Actual	Standard	Model variant Dummy	Split	Inertia
$0	.29	.30	.26	.29	.27
$1-1,000	.08	.07	.06	.06	.08
$1,001-2,000	.08	.15	.14	.12	.15
$2,001-5,000	.31	.32	.32	.34	.30
$5,001-10,000	.21	.12	.17	.14	.15
$10,001-20,000	.02	.04	.03	.04	.04
$20,001 +	.00	.00	.00	.00	.00
Pseudo chi-square statistic (n=1,729)		210	114	123	173

TABLE B.12
ACTUAL AND SIMULATED DISTRIBUTIONS OF ANNUAL
INCOMES OF WOMEN 47-64 YEARS OF AGE
AND MARRIED IN 1971 POOLED OVER 7-YEAR PERIOD

Annual income	Actual	Standard	Dummy	Split	Inertia
$0	.57	.62	.61	.62	.63
$1-1,000	.10	.04	.04	.07	.06
$1,001-2,000	.07	.10	.08	.08	.07
$2,001-5,000	.15	.16	.17	.16	.17
$5,001-10,000	.10	.05	.08	.05	.06
$10,001-20,000	.01	.02	.02	.02	.01
$20,001 +	.00	.00	.00	.00	.00
Pseudo chi-square statistic (n=833)		74	47	42	34

TABLE B.13
ACTUAL AND SIMULATED DISTRIBUTIONS OF ANNUAL
INCOMES OF WOMEN 47-64 YEARS OF AGE
AND UNMARRIED IN 1971 POOLED OVER 7-YEAR PERIOD

Annual income	Actual	Standard	Dummy	Split	Inertia
$0	.43	.41	.41	.41	.47
$1-1,000	.08	.06	.06	.07	.06
$1,001-2,000	.09	.12	.12	.13	.11
$2,001-5,000	.23	.26	.25	.23	.22
$5,001-10,000	.13	.12	.11	.11	.12
$10,001-20,000	.03	.03	.03	.04	.02
$20,001 +	.00	.00	.00	.00	.00
Pseudo chi-square statistic (n=1,015)		21	21	27	18

Appendix B

TABLE B.14
ACTUAL AND SIMULATED DISTRIBUTIONS OF ANNUAL INCOMES OF WOMEN 65+ YEARS OF AGE IN 1971 POOLED OVER 7-YEAR PERIOD

Annual income	Actual	Standard	Model variant Dummy	Split	Inertia
$0	.87	.85	.81	.86	.82
$1-1,000	.09	.06	.11	.08	.09
$1,001-2,000	.01	.04	.04	.03	.05
$2,001-5,000	.01	.04	.04	.03	.02
$5,001-10,000	.01	.00	.00	.00	.01
$10,001-20,000	.00	.00	.00	.00	.00
$20,001 +	.00	.00	.00	.00	.00
Pseudo chi-square statistic (n=399)		80	79	37	69

TABLE B.15
ACTUAL AND SIMULATED PROPORTIONS OF INDIVIDUALS BY NUMBER OF YEARS WORKED OUT OF 7

Number of years worked out of 7	Actual	Standard	Model variant Dummy	Split	Inertia
0	.11	.01	.09	.09	.08
1-2	.09	.11	.09	.11	.12
3-4	.12	.23	.13	.14	.15
5-6	.15	.29	.18	.18	.17
7	.52	.35	.50	.49	.48
Pseudo chi-square statistic (n=2657)		1016	30	51	83

TABLE B.16
ACTUAL AND SIMULATED PROPORTIONS OF WOMEN
14-20 YEARS OF AGE IN 1971 BY NUMBER OF
YEARS WORKED OUT OF 7

Number of years worked out of 7	Actual	Standard	Dummy	Split	Inertia
0	.07	.01	.06	.04	.05
1-2	.23	.17	.23	.23	.21
3-4	.28	.43	.25	.31	.32
5-6	.31	.34	.30	.28	.30
7	.13	.05	.17	.13	.12
Pseudo chi-square statistic (n=272)		54	5	5	4

TABLE B.17
ACTUAL AND SIMULATED PROPORTIONS OF WOMEN
21-46 YEARS OF AGE AND MARRIED IN 1971 BY
NUMBER OF YEARS WORKED OUT OF 7

Number of years worked out of 7	Actual	Standard	Dummy	Split	Inertia
0	.17	.00	.15	.13	.13
1-2	.15	.16	.16	.20	.16
3-4	.15	.42	.21	.22	.27
5-6	.22	.38	.23	.24	.20
7	.30	.03	.25	.21	.23
Pseudo chi-square statistic (n=424)		431	15	37	53

Appendix B

TABLE B.18
ACTUAL AND SIMULATED PROPORTIONS OF WOMEN
21-46 YEARS OF AGE AND UNMARRIED IN 1971
BY NUMBER OF YEARS WORKED OUT OF 7

Number of years worked out of 7	Actual	Standard	Dummy	Split	Inertia
0	.11	.00	.05	.05	.05
1-2	.08	.05	.09	.13	.12
3-4	.14	.31	.15	.16	.15
5-6	.17	.48	.25	.24	.18
7	.47	.16	.46	.42	.48
Pseudo chi-square statistic (n=247)		271	18	25	13

TABLE B.19
ACTUAL AND SIMULATED PROPORTIONS OF WOMEN
47-64 YEARS OF AGE AND MARRIED IN 1971
BY NUMBER OF YEARS WORKED OUT OF 7

Number of years worked out of 7	Actual	Standard	Dummy	Split	Inertia
0	.38	.09	.36	.34	.32
1-2	.13	.39	.19	.15	.19
3-4	.12	.33	.13	.23	.18
5-6	.19	.18	.15	.15	.15
7	.18	.00	.17	.14	.14
Pseudo chi-square statistic (n=247)		318	9	31	21

TABLE B.20
ACTUAL AND SIMULATED PROPORTIONS OF WOMEN
47-64 YEARS OF AGE AND UNMARRIED IN 1971
BY NUMBER OF YEARS WORKED OUT OF 7

Number of years worked out of 7	Actual	Standard	Dummy	Split	Inertia
0	.28	.03	.17	.18	.22
1-2	.08	.17	.15	.12	.16
3-4	.08	.31	.12	.13	.17
5-6	.16	.41	.24	.22	.11
7	.40	.07	.31	.35	.30
Pseudo chi-square statistic (n=145)		239	27	17	34

Model variant

TABLE B.21
ACTUAL AND SIMULATED PROPORTIONS OF WOMEN
65+ YEARS OF AGE IN 1971 BY NUMBER OF YEARS
WORKED OUT OF 7

Number of years worked out of 7	Actual	Standard	Dummy	Split	Inertia
0	.60	.32	.52	.60	.58
1-2	.21	.54	.20	.16	.13
3-4	.14	.14	.14	.13	.18
5-6	.02	.00	.09	.05	.06
7	.03	.00	.05	.05	.05
Pseudo chi-square statistic (n=57)		40	15	4	8

Model variant

Appendix B

TABLE B.22
ACTUAL AND SIMULATED PROPORTIONS OF INDIVIDUALS
BY NUMBERS OF YEARS OUT OF 7 OF FULL-TIME
(OVER 1,400 HOURS) AND PART-TIME
(1 to 1,400 HOURS) WORK

Number of years with over 1,400 hours	Number of years with 1 to 1,400 hours			
	0	1-3	4-6	7
0	.11	.10	.04	.02
	.02	.08	.02	.00
	.10	.07	.01	.00
	.09	.08	.01	.00
	.10	.11	.04	.05
1-3	.01	.10	.07	
	.04	.31	.05	
	.03	.19	.09	
	.04	.21	.07	
	.02	.17	.08	
4-6	.01	.20		
	.06	.27		
	.03	.32		
	.03	.31		
	.02	.23		
7	.33			
	.15			
	.16			
	.17			
	.22			

Model	Standard	Dummy	Split	Inertia
Pseudo chi-square statistic (n=2647)	2289	894	1012	446

TABLE B.23
ACTUAL AND SIMULATED PROPORTIONS OF WOMEN 14-20
YEARS OF AGE IN 1971 BY NUMBERS OF YEARS
OUT OF 7 OF FULL-TIME (OVER 1,400 HOURS) AND
PART-TIME (1 to 1,400 HOURS) WORK

Number of years with over 1,400 hours	\multicolumn{4}{c}{Number of years with 1 to 1,400 hours}
	0	1-3	4-6	7
0	.07	.28	.09	.01
	.01	.15	.04	.00
	.09	.19	.04	.00
	.05	.21	.01	.00
	.07	.25	.07	.00
1-3	.02	.22	.11	
	.05	.55	.12	
	.03	.36	.16	
	.05	.47	.08	
	.03	.35	.09	
4-6	.01	.15		
	.00	.06		
	.01	.11		
	.01	.10		
	.02	.10		
7	.01			
	.00			
	.00			
	.00			
	.01			

Model	Standard	Dummy	Split	Inertia
Pseudo chi-square statistic (n=272)	204	58	122	34

Appendix B

TABLE B.24
ACTUAL AND SIMULATED PROPORTIONS OF WOMEN 21-46
YEARS OF AGE AND MARRIED IN 1971 BY NUMBERS OF YEARS
OUT OF 7 OF FULL-TIME (OVER 1,400 HOURS) AND
PART-TIME (1 to 1,400 HOURS) WORK

Number of years with over 1,400 hours	Number of years with 1 to 1,400 hours			
	0	1-3	4-6	7
0	.16	.18	.07	.05
	.00	.14	.05	.00
	.16	.13	.02	.00
	.15	.15	.02	.00
	.15	.18	.08	.01
1-3	.01	.12	.12	
	.06	.54	.12	
	.03	.32	.19	
	.05	.31	.17	
	.03	.24	.13	
4-6	.00	.18		
	.02	.05		
	.01	.14		
	.01	.14		
	.01	.14		
7	.10			
	.00			
	.00			
	.00			
	.02			

Model	Standard	Dummy	Split	Inertia
Pseudo chi-square statistic (n=424)	877	251	264	106

TABLE B.25
ACTUAL AND SIMULATED PROPORTIONS OF WOMEN 21-46
YEARS OF AGE AND UNMARRIED IN 1971 BY NUMBERS OF
YEARS OUT OF 7 OF FULL-TIME (OVER 1,400 HOURS) AND
PART-TIME (1 to 1,400 HOURS) WORK

Number of years with over 1,400 hours	\multicolumn{4}{c}{Number of years with 1 to 1,400 hours}			
	0	1-3	4-6	7
0	.12	.10	.07	.01
	.00	.03	.02	.00
	.05	.07	.01	.00
	.05	.08	.01	.00
	.06	.11	.04	.01
1-3	.01	.11	.07	
	.04	.45	.09	
	.02	.27	.12	
	.06	.24	.13	
	.03	.17	.18	
4-6	.02	.22		
	.08	.29		
	.02	.39		
	.02	.37		
	.01	.31		
7	.26			
	.00			
	.03			
	.03			
	.08			

Model	Standard	Dummy	Split	Inertia
Pseudo chi-square statistic (n=247)	451	175	196	100

TABLE B.26
ACTUAL AND SIMULATED PROPORTIONS OF WOMEN 47-64
YEARS OF AGE AND MARRIED IN 1971 BY NUMBERS OF
YEARS OUT OF 7 OF FULL-TIME (OVER 1,400 HOURS) AND
PART-TIME (1 to 1,400 HOURS) WORK

Number of years with over 1,400 hours	Number of years with 1 to 1,400 hours			
	0	1-3	4-6	7
0	.36	.13	.08	.04
	.10	.17	.00	.00
	.36	.11	.00	.00
	.34	.12	.02	.00
	.37	.10	.11	.01
1-3	.01	.10	.06	
	.11	.56	.03	
	.03	.28	.09	
	.03	.27	.10	
	.07	.11	.08	
4-6	.03	.13		
	.01	.01		
	.03	.09		
	.01	.10		
	.02	.11		
7	.06			
	.00			
	.00			
	.00			
	.03			

Model	Standard	Dummy	Split	Inertia
Pseudo chi-square statistic (n=119)	466	67	62	58

TABLE B.27
ACTUAL AND SIMULATED PROPORTIONS OF WOMEN 47-64
YEARS OF AGE AND UNMARRIED IN 1971 BY NUMBERS OF
YEARS OUT OF 7 OF FULL-TIME (OVER 1,400 HOURS) AND
PART-TIME (1 to 1,400 HOURS) WORK

Number of years with over 1,400 hours	Number of years with 1 to 1,400 hours			
	0	1-3	4-6	7
0	.28	.07	.01	.02
	.03	.06	.01	.00
	.17	.14	.00	.00
	.18	.08	.01	.00
	.24	.11	.02	.01
1-3	.03	.08	.09	
	.10	.43	.06	
	.06	.19	.08	
	.06	.20	.08	
	.04	.17	.06	
4-6	.03	.21		
	.09	.21		
	.03	.29		
	.04	.29		
	.02	.23		
7	.03			
	.00			
	.04			
	.04			
	.08			

Model	Standard	Dummy	Split	Inertia
Pseudo chi-square statistic (n=145)	280	48	42	39

Appendix B

TABLE B.28
ACTUAL AND SIMULATED PROPORTIONS OF WOMEN 65+
YEARS OF AGE IN 1971 BY NUMBERS OF YEARS OUT
OF 7 OF FULL-TIME (OVER 1,400 HOURS) AND PART-TIME
(1 to 1,400 HOURS) WORK

Number of years with over 1,400 hours	\multicolumn{4}{c}{Number of years with 1 to 1,400 hours}
	0	1-3	4-6	7
0	.68	.17	.03	.00
	.38	.40	.00	.00
	.59	.20	.02	.00
	.67	.18	.00	.00
	.58	.25	.00	.00
1-3	.02	.05	.02	
	.07	.14	.00	
	.05	.09	.05	
	.02	.09	.02	
	.02	.05	.02	
4-6	.00	.02		
	.00	.00		
	.00	.00		
	.01	.02		
	.00	.02		
7	.00			
	.00			
	.00			
	.00			
	.00			

Model	Standard	Dummy	Split	Inertia
Pseudo chi-square statistic (n=57)	46	11	3	4

TABLE B.29
ACTUAL AND SIMULATED PROPORTIONS OF
INDIVIDUALS BY EARNED INCOME CUMULATED
OVER 7-YEAR PERIOD

Earned income cumulated over 7-year period	Actual	Standard	Dummy	Split	Inertia
$0	.12	.02	.10	.09	.10
Less than $10,000	.23	.25	.18	.21	.25
$10,000-19,999	.14	.22	.16	.15	.14
$20,000-29,999	.11	.10	.13	.12	.11
$30,000-39,999	.09	.08	.09	.08	.10
$40,000-59,999	.14	.14	.14	.14	.15
$60,000-79,999	.10	.10	.10	.10	.09
$80,000-99,999	.04	.05	.05	.05	.03
$100,000-119,999	.02	.02	.03	.03	.02
$120,000-139,999	.01	.01	.01	.01	.00
Over $139,999	.01	.01	.01	.00	.00
Pseudo chi-square statistic (n=2657)		329	75	79	79

Appendix B

TABLE B.30
ACTUAL AND SIMULATED PROPORTIONS OF
WOMEN 14-20 YEARS OF AGE IN 1971 BY EARNED
INCOME CUMULATED OVER 7-YEAR PERIOD

Earned income cumulated over 7-year period	Actual	Model variant			
		Standard	Dummy	Split	Inertia
$0	.08	.01	.09	.05	.07
Less than $10,000	.57	.50	.44	.47	.52
$10,000-19,999	.23	.37	.29	.23	.23
$20,000-29,999	.08	.10	.13	.15	.10
Over $29,999	.04	.01	.05	.11	.08
Pseudo chi-square statistic (n=272)		50	21	57	14

TABLE B.31
ACTUAL AND SIMULATED PROPORTIONS OF WOMEN 21-46
YEARS OF AGE AND MARRIED IN 1971 BY EARNED
INCOME CUMULATED OVER 7-YEAR PERIOD

Earned income cumulated over 7-year period	Actual	Model variant			
		Standard	Dummy	Split	Inertia
$0	.17	.00	.16	.15	.15
Less than $10,000	.40	.44	.29	.35	.44
$10,000-19,999	.20	.42	.29	.27	.18
$20,000-29,999	.12	.10	.15	.13	.12
$30,000-39,999	.07	.02	.08	.07	.06
Over $39,999	.05	.01	.03	.02	.05
Pseudo chi-square statistic (n=424)		207	37	22	4

TABLE B.32
ACTUAL AND SIMULATED PROPORTIONS OF WOMEN 21-46
YEARS OF AGE AND UNMARRIED IN 1971 BY EARNED
INCOME CUMULATED OVER 7-YEAR PERIOD

Earned income cumulated over 7-year period	Actual	Standard	Dummy	Split	Inertia
$0	.12	.00	.05	.05	.06
Less than $10,000	.23	.22	.18	.23	.26
$10,000-19,999	.18	.42	.23	.25	.21
$20,000-29,999	.19	.20	.30	.26	.21
$30,000-39,999	.15	.11	.12	.12	.15
$40,000-59,999	.10	.05	.10	.08	.08
Over $59,999	.03	.01	.00	.00	.03
Pseudo chi-square statistic (n=247)		125	41	34	12

TABLE B.33
ACTUAL AND SIMULATED PROPORTIONS OF WOMEN 47-64
YEARS OF AGE AND MARRIED IN 1971 BY EARNED
INCOME CUMULATED OVER 7-YEAR PERIOD

Earned income cumulated over 7-year period	Actual	Standard	Dummy	Split	Inertia
$0	.38	.10	.36	.34	.37
Less than $10,000	.29	.53	.22	.34	.31
$10,000-19,999	.15	.25	.19	.15	.15
$20,000-29,999	.08	.09	.15	.12	.09
Over $29,999	.11	.02	.08	.05	.08
Pseudo chi-square statistic (n=119)		366	13	8	1

TABLE B.34
ACTUAL AND SIMULATED PROPORTIONS OF WOMEN 47-64 OF AGE AND UNMARRIED BY 1971 BY EARNED INCOME CUMULATED OVER 7-YEAR PERIOD

Earned income cumulated over 7-year period	Actual	Standard	Dummy	Split	Inertia
$0	.28	.03	.17	.18	.24
Less than $10,000	.19	.33	.23	.24	.29
$10,000-19,999	.23	.34	.22	.20	.14
$20,000-29,999	.12	.20	.20	.22	.16
$30,000-39,999	.07	.07	.11	.09	.08
Over $39,999	.11	.03	.06	.07	.09
Pseudo chi-square statistic (n=145)		77	24	26	17

TABLE B.35
ACTUAL AND SIMULATED PROPORTIONS OF WOMEN 65+ YEARS OF AGE IN 1971 BY EARNED INCOME CUMULATED OVER 7-YEAR PERIOD

Earned income cumulated over 7-year period	Actual	Standard	Dummy	Split	Inertia
$0	.68	.39	.59	.67	.58
Less than $10,000	.30	.61	.36	.31	.36
$10,000-19,999	.02	.00	.05	.02	.04
Over $19,999	.00	.00	.00	.00	.02
Pseudo chi-square statistic (n=57)		23	2	1	2

Appendix C. Distributional Comparisons for Our Simulation
Results for the Inertia Model and Models A, B and C

TABLE C.1
ACTUAL AND SIMULATED DISTRIBUTIONS OF ANNUAL HOURS
OF WORK OF INDIVIDUALS POOLED OVER 7-YEAR PERIOD

Annual hours of work	Actual	Model variant Inertia	A	B	C
0	.27	.30	.30	.30	.29
1-600	.09	.05	.05	.05	.05
601-1,200	.08	.11	.10	.11	.11
1,201-1,400	.03	.06	.05	.05	.05
1,401-1,800	.09	.13	.13	.13	.12
1,801-2,200	.25	.13	.14	.13	.14
2,201 +	.20	.22	.24	.23	.24
Pseudo chi-square statistic (n=18,599)		2599	2113	2336	2050

Appendix C

TABLE C.2
ACTUAL AND SIMULATED DISTRIBUTIONS OF ANNUAL HOURS OF WORK
OF WOMEN 14-20 YEARS OF AGE IN 1971 POOLED OVER 7-YEAR PERIOD

Annual hours of work	Actual	Inertia	A	B	C
0	.44	.49	.50	.45	.46
1-600	.19	.09	.10	.11	.10
601-1,200	.12	.14	.13	.15	.16
1,201-1,400	.03	.06	.04	.04	.05
1,401-1,800	.07	.10	.08	.10	.08
1,801-2,200	.13	.06	.06	.07	.07
2,201 +	.02	.05	.08	.08	.08
Pseudo chi-square statistic (n=1,904)		356	521	505	532

TABLE C.3
ACTUAL AND SIMULATED DISTRIBUTIONS OF ANNUAL
HOURS OF WORK OF WOMEN 21-46 YEARS OF AGE
AND MARRIED IN 1971 POOLED OVER 7-YEAR PERIOD

Annual hours of work	Actual	Inertia	A	B	C
0	.40	.46	.43	.45	.44
1-600	.15	.08	.07	.07	.07
601-1,200	.12	.16	.15	.17	.16
1,201-1,400	.03	.07	.07	.06	.06
1,401-1,800	.10	.11	.13	.12	.12
1,801-2,200	.17	.07	.08	.08	.08
2,201 +	.02	.05	.05	.05	.06
Pseudo chi-square statistic (n=2,968)		633	617	583	660

TABLE C.4
ACTUAL AND SIMULATED DISTRIBUTIONS OF ANNUAL
HOURS OF WORK OF WOMEN 21-46 YEARS OF AGE
AND UNMARRIED IN 1971 POOLED OVER 7-YEAR PERIOD

Annual hours of work	Actual	Model variant Inertia	A	B	C
0	.28	.27	.30	.28	.28
1-600	.07	.05	.04	.04	.05
601-1,200	.10	.16	.12	.16	.15
1,201-1,400	.04	.09	.08	.08	.07
1,401-1,800	.13	.16	.18	.18	.17
1,801-2,200	.30	.13	.15	.14	.15
2,201 +	.07	.14	.13	.12	.13
Pseudo chi-square statistic (n=1,729)		480	353	396	333

TABLE C.5
ACTUAL AND SIMULATED DISTRIBUTIONS OF ANNUAL
HOURS OF WORK OF WOMEN 47-64 YEARS OF AGE
AND MARRIED IN 1971 POOLED OVER 7-YEAR PERIOD

Annual hours of work	Actual	Model variant Inertia	A	B	C
0	.56	.63	.61	.61	.60
1-600	.11	.05	.06	.05	.05
601-1,200	.09	.11	.11	.11	.11
1,201-1,400	.03	.04	.04	.05	.04
1,401-1,800	.08	.09	.09	.07	.07
1,801-2,200	.11	.06	.05	.06	.07
2,201 +	.02	.02	.03	.04	.05
Pseudo chi-square statistic (n=833)		61	61	82	87

Appendix C

TABLE C.6
ACTUAL AND SIMULATED DISTRIBUTIONS OF ANNUAL
HOURS OF WORK OF WOMEN 47-64 YEARS OF AGE
AND UNMARRIED IN 1971 POOLED OVER 7-YEAR PERIOD

Annual hours of work	Actual	Inertia	A	B	C
0	.43	.47	.47	.45	.44
1-600	.05	.03	.04	.04	.04
601-1,200	.09	.10	.09	.11	.11
1,201-1,400	.04	.06	.06	.07	.07
1,401-1,800	.11	.13	.12	.11	.12
1,801-2,200	.22	.10	.12	.10	.11
2,201 +	.07	.11	.09	.12	.10
Pseudo chi-square statistic (n=1,015)		116	68	133	98

TABLE C.7
ACTUAL AND SIMULATED DISTRIBUTIONS OF ANNUAL
HOURS OF WORK OF WOMEN 65+ YEARS OF AGE
IN 1971 POOLED OVER 7-YEAR PERIOD

Annual hours of work	Actual	Inertia	A	B	C
0	.87	.82	.90	.76	.85
1-600	.07	.07	.06	.09	.05
601-1,200	.02	.04	.02	.07	.06
1,201-1,400	.00	.01	.00	.03	.00
1,401-1,800	.01	.03	.01	.03	.02
1,801-2,200	.01	.02	.00	.01	.01
2,201 +	.01	.01	.00	.00	.00
Pseudo chi-square statistic (n=399)		30	6	79	34

TABLE C.8
ACTUAL AND SIMULATED DISTRIBUTIONS OF ANNUAL
INCOMES OF INDIVIDUALS POOLED OVER
7-YEAR PERIOD

Annual income	Actual	Model variant Inertia	A	B	C
$0	.28	.30	.30	.30	.29
$1–1,000	.09	.06	.06	.07	.11
$1,001–2,000	.06	.08	.07	.08	.05
$2,001–5,000	.19	.22	.23	.23	.16
$5,001–10,000	.24	.21	.22	.21	.19
$10,001–20,000	.11	.10	.10	.10	.16
$20,001 +	.02	.01	.01	.01	.03
Pseudo chi-square statistic (n=18,599)		604	541	569	918

TABLE C.9
ACTUAL AND SIMULATED DISTRIBUTIONS OF ANNUAL
INCOMES OF WOMEN 14–20 YEARS OF AGE
IN 1971 POOLED OVER 7-YEAR PERIOD

Annual income	Actual	Model variant Inertia	A	B	C
$0	.46	.49	.50	.45	.46
$1–1,000	.20	.13	.14	.15	.16
$1,001–2,000	.09	.11	.09	.11	.06
$2,001–5,000	.18	.17	.16	.18	.15
$5,001–10,000	.06	.07	.07	.08	.11
$10,001–20,000	.00	.03	.03	.02	.05
$20,001 +	.00	.00	.01	.00	.00
Pseudo chi-square statistic (n=18,599)		111	125	83	360

Appendix C

TABLE C.10
ACTUAL AND SIMULATED DISTRIBUTIONS OF ANNUAL
INCOMES OF WOMEN 21-46 YEARS OF AGE
AND MARRIED IN 1971 POOLED OVER 7-YEAR PERIOD

Annual income	Actual	Inertia	A	B	C
$0	.41	.46	.43	.45	.44
$1-1,000	.14	.10	.09	.10	.13
$1,001-2,000	.10	.13	.12	.13	.08
$2,001-5,000	.24	.20	.24	.21	.18
$5,001-10,000	.11	.08	.10	.08	.13
$10,001-20,000	.00	.02	.01	.02	.04
$20,001 +	.00	.00	.00	.00	.00
Pseudo chi-square statistic (n=2,968)		101	67	86	163

TABLE C.11
ACTUAL AND SIMULATED DISTRIBUTIONS OF ANNUAL
INCOMES OF WOMEN 21-46 YEARS OF AGE
AND UNMARRIED IN 1971 POOLED OVER 7-YEAR PERIOD

Annual income	Actual	Inertia	A	B	C
$0	.29	.27	.30	.28	.28
$1-1,000	.08	.08	.06	.07	.14
$1,001-2,000	.08	.15	.12	.14	.08
$2,001-5,000	.31	.30	.32	.35	.23
$5,001-10,000	.21	.15	.17	.13	.20
$10,001-20,000	.02	.04	.03	.02	.07
$20,001 +	.00	.00	.00	.00	.00
Pseudo chi-square statistic (n=1,729)		173	67	142	338

TABLE C.12
ACTUAL AND SIMULATED DISTRIBUTIONS OF ANNUAL
INCOMES OF WOMEN 47-64 YEARS OF AGE
AND MARRIED IN 1971 POOLED OVER 7-YEAR PERIOD

Annual income	Actual	Inertia	A	B	C
$0	.57	.63	.61	.61	.60
$1-1,000	.10	.06	.07	.06	.09
$1,001-2,000	.07	.07	.08	.07	.03
$2,001-5,000	.15	.17	.16	.14	.12
$5,001-10,000	.10	.06	.06	.08	.11
$10,001-20,000	.01	.01	.02	.02	.04
$20,001 +	.00	.00	.00	.00	.01
Pseudo chi-square statistic (n=833)		34	35	29	163

TABLE C.13
ACTUAL AND SIMULATED DISTRIBUTIONS OF ANNUAL
INCOMES OF WOMEN 47-64 YEARS OF AGE
AND UNMARRIED IN 1971 POOLED OVER 7-YEAR PERIOD

Annual income	Actual	Inertia	A	B	C
$0	.43	.47	.47	.45	.44
$1-1,000	.08	.06	.05	.09	.12
$1,001-2,000	.09	.11	.10	.10	.06
$2,001-5,000	.23	.22	.25	.23	.20
$5,001-10,000	.13	.12	.11	.10	.16
$10,001-20,000	.03	.02	.02	.02	.03
$20,001 +	.00	.00	.00	.00	.00
Pseudo chi-square statistic (n=1,015)		18	24	14	42

TABLE C.14
ACTUAL AND SIMULATED DISTRIBUTIONS OF ANNUAL
INCOMES OF WOMEN 65+ YEARS OF AGE
IN 1971 POOLED OVER 7-YEAR PERIOD

Annual income	Actual	Model variant			
		Inertia	A	B	C
$0	.87	.82	.90	.76	.85
$1-1,000	.09	.09	.07	.17	.09
$1,001-2,000	.01	.05	.02	.04	.01
$2,001-5,000	.01	.02	.02	.03	.02
$5,001-10,000	.01	.01	.00	.00	.01
$10,001-20,000	.00	.00	.00	.00	.00
$20,001 +	.00	.00	.00	.00	.00
Pseudo chi-square statistic (n=399)		69	14	90	4

TABLE C.15
ACTUAL AND SIMULATED PROPORTIONS OF
INDIVIDUALS BY NUMBER OF YEARS WORKED OUT OF 7

Number of years worked out of 7	Actual	Model variant			
		Inertia	A	B	C
0	.11	.08	.09	.08	.08
1-2	.09	.12	.10	.11	.10
3-4	.12	.15	.14	.15	.14
5-6	.15	.17	.17	.16	.16
7	.52	.48	.49	.49	.51
Pseudo chi-square statistic (n=2657)		84	33	60	36

TABLE C.16
ACTUAL AND SIMULATED PROPORTIONS OF WOMEN
14-20 YEARS OF AGE IN 1971 BY NUMBER
OF YEARS WORKED OUT OF 7

Number of years worked out of 7	Actual	Inertia	A	B	C
0	.07	.05	.06	.04	.04
1-2	.23	.21	.21	.20	.19
3-4	.28	.32	.29	.30	.32
5-6	.31	.30	.30	.27	.31
7	.13	.12	.15	.18	.13
Pseudo chi-square statistic (n=272)		4	2	12	7

TABLE C.17
ACTUAL AND SIMULATED PROPORTIONS OF WOMEN
21-46 YEARS OF AGE AND MARRIED IN 1971
BY NUMBER OF YEARS WORKED OUT OF 7

Number of years worked out of 7	Actual	Inertia	A	B	C
0	.17	.13	.14	.12	.13
1-2	.15	.16	.15	.19	.18
3-4	.15	.27	.19	.22	.18
5-6	.22	.20	.25	.20	.22
7	.30	.23	.27	.26	.29
Pseudo chi-square statistic (n=424)		53	9	26	10

Appendix C

TABLE C.18
ACTUAL AND SIMULATED PROPORTIONS OF WOMEN
21-46 YEARS OF AGE AND UNMARRIED IN 1971
BY NUMBER OF YEARS WORKED OUT OF 7

Number of years worked out of 7	Actual	Inertia	A	B	C
0	.11	.05	.08	.06	.04
1-2	.08	.12	.10	.13	.12
3-4	.14	.15	.18	.16	.17
5-6	.17	.18	.20	.18	.20
7	.47	.48	.44	.48	.46
Pseudo chi-square statistic (n=247)		13	8	13	19

TABLE C.19
ACTUAL AND SIMULATED PROPORTIONS OF WOMEN
47-64 YEARS OF AGE AND MARRIED IN 1971
BY NUMBER OF YEARS WORKED OUT OF 7

Number of years worked out of 7	Actual	Inertia	A	B	C
0	.38	.32	.28	.36	.36
1-2	.13	.19	.25	.17	.19
3-4	.12	.18	.16	.16	.12
5-6	.19	.15	.11	.11	.10
7	.18	.14	.20	.21	.22
Pseudo chi-square statistic (n=119)		21	25	9	11

TABLE C.20
ACTUAL AND SIMULATED PROPORTIONS OF WOMEN
47-64 YEARS OF AGE AND UNMARRIED IN 1971
BY NUMBER OF YEARS WORKED OUT OF 7

Number of years worked out of 7	Actual	Inertia	A	B	C
0	.28	.22	.27	.22	.19
1-2	.08	.16	.11	.15	.15
3-4	.08	.17	.11	.13	.14
5-6	.16	.11	.18	.16	.16
7	.40	.30	.32	.35	.34
Pseudo chi-square statistic (n=145)		34	6	15	20

Model variant

TABLE C.21
ACTUAL AND SIMULATED PROPORTIONS OF WOMEN
65+ YEARS OF AGE IN 1971 BY NUMBER
OF YEARS WORKED OUT OF 7

Number of years worked out of 7	Actual	Inertia	A	B	C
0	.60	.58	.59	.51	.60
1-2	.21	.13	.27	.09	.10
3-4	.14	.18	.11	.28	.19
5-6	.02	.06	.00	.06	.12
7	.03	.05	.02	.05	.02
Pseudo chi-square statistic (n=57)		8	3	17	41

Model variant

Appendix C   429

TABLE C.22
ACTUAL AND SIMULATED PROPORTIONS OF INDIVIDUALS
BY NUMBERS OF YEARS OUT OF 7 OF FULL-TIME
(OVER 1,400 HOURS) AND PART-TIME
(1 to 1,400 HOURS) WORK

Number of years with over 1,400 hours	Number of years with 1 to 1,400 hours			
	0	1-3	4-6	7
0	.11	.10	.04	.02
	.10	.11	.04	.05
	.10	.11	.02	.00
	.09	.12	.03	.00
	.09	.12	.03	.01
1-3	.01	.10	.07	
	.02	.17	.08	
	.03	.16	.07	
	.02	.15	.08	
	.02	.14	.07	
4-6	.01	.20		
	.02	.23		
	.02	.30		
	.02	.24		
	.01	.25		
7	.33			
	.22			
	.19			
	.23			
	.25			

Model	Inertia	A	B	C
Pseudo chi-square statistic (n=2647)	446	541	264	184

TABLE C.23
ACTUAL AND SIMULATED PROPORTIONS OF WOMEN 14-20
YEARS OF AGE IN 1971 BY NUMBERS OF YEARS OUT OF
7 OF FULL-TIME (OVER 1,400 HOURS) AND PART-TIME
(1 to 1,400 HOURS) WORK

Number of years with over 1,400 hours	\multicolumn{4}{c}{Number of years with 1 to 1,400 hours}
	0	1-3	4-6	7
0	.07	.28	.09	.01
	.07	.25	.07	.00
	.08	.22	.06	.00
	.05	.25	.07	.00
	.05	.27	.07	.00
1-3	.02	.22	.11	
	.03	.35	.09	
	.05	.36	.08	
	.05	.25	.11	
	.04	.30	.09	
4-6	.01	.15		
	.02	.10		
	.00	.13		
	.03	.18		
	.01	.14		
7	.01			
	.01			
	.01			
	.01			
	.02			

Model	Inertia	A	B	C
Pseudo chi-square statistic (n=272)	34	47	26	18

TABLE C.24
ACTUAL AND SIMULATED PROPORTIONS OF WOMEN 21-46 YEARS OF AGE AND MARRIED IN 1971 BY NUMBERS OF YEARS OUT OF 7 OF FULL-TIME (OVER 1,400 HOURS) AND PART-TIME (1 to 1,400 HOURS) WORK

Number of years with over 1,400 hours	Number of years with 1 to 1,400 hours			
	0	1-3	4-6	7
0	.16	.18	.07	.05
	.15	.18	.08	.01
	.14	.17	.04	.00
	.14	.19	.06	.02
	.15	.19	.07	.01
1-3	.01	.12	.12	
	.03	.24	.13	
	.05	.22	.15	
	.02	.23	.11	
	.03	.15	.14	
4-6	.00	.18		
	.01	.14		
	.02	.18		
	.02	.17		
	.01	.19		
7	.10			
	.02			
	.01			
	.03			
	.04			

Model	Inertia	A	B	C
Pseudo chi-square statistic (n=424)	106	165	89	47

TABLE C.25
ACTUAL AND SIMULATED PROPORTIONS OF WOMEN 21-46
YEARS OF AGE AND UNMARRIED IN 1971 BY NUMBERS OF
YEARS OUT OF 7 OF FULL-TIME (OVER 1,400 HOURS) AND
PART-TIME (1 to 1,400 HOURS) WORK

Number of years with over 1,400 hours	\multicolumn{4}{c}{Number of years with 1 to 1,400 hours}			
	0	1-3	4-6	7
0	.12	.10	.07	.01
	.06	.11	.04	.01
	.09	.10	.01	.00
	.07	.11	.03	.00
	.06	.15	.02	.01
1-3	.01	.11	.07	
	.03	.17	.18	
	.03	.22	.08	
	.03	.18	.15	
	.01	.17	.12	
4-6	.02	.22		
	.01	.31		
	.03	.35		
	.03	.32		
	.03	.35		
7	.26			
	.08			
	.07			
	.08			
	.08			

Model	Inertia	A	B	C
Pseudo chi-square statistic (n=247)	100	102	92	89

Appendix C

TABLE C.26
ACTUAL AND SIMULATED PROPORTIONS OF WOMEN 47-64
YEARS OF AGE AND MARRIED IN 1971 BY NUMBERS OF
YEARS OUT OF 7 OF FULL-TIME (OVER 1,400 HOURS) AND
PART-TIME (1 to 1,400 HOURS) WORK

Number of years with over 1,400 hours	Number of years with 1 to 1,400 hours			
	0	1-3	4-6	7
0	.36	.13	.08	.04
	.37	.10	.11	.01
	.31	.22	.04	.00
	.37	.19	.05	.01
	.36	.17	.03	.02
1-3	.01	.10	.06	
	.07	.11	.08	
	.04	.12	.13	
	.03	.11	.09	
	.03	.12	.11	
4-6	.03	.13		
	.02	.11		
	.00	.13		
	.01	.09		
	.02	.11		
7	.06			
	.03			
	.01			
	.04			
	.03			

Model	Inertia	A	B	C
Pseudo chi-square statistic (n=119)	58	51	19	24

TABLE C.27
ACTUAL AND SIMULATED PROPORTIONS OF WOMEN 47-64
YEARS OF AGE AND UNMARRIED IN 1971 BY NUMBERS OF
YEARS OUT OF 7 OF FULL-TIME (OVER 1,400 HOURS) AND
PART-TIME (1 to 1,400 HOURS) WORK

Number of years with over 1,400 hours	Number of years with 1 to 1,400 hours			
	0	1-3	4-6	7
0	.28	.07	.01	.02
	.24	.11	.02	.01
	.29	.10	.03	.00
	.23	.13	.03	.01
	.23	.11	.06	.01
1-3	.03	.08	.09	
	.04	.17	.06	
	.02	.11	.07	
	.04	.15	.13	
	.03	.13	.08	
4-6	.03	.21		
	.02	.23		
	.00	.31		
	.03	.15		
	.02	.23		
7	.03			
	.08			
	.06			
	.10			
	.07			

Model	Inertia	A	B	C
Pseudo chi-square statistic (n=145)	39	27	52	47

Appendix C

TABLE C.28
ACTUAL AND SIMULATED PROPORTIONS OF WOMEN 65+
YEARS OF AGE IN 1971 BY NUMBERS OF YEARS OUT OF
7 OF FULL-TIME (OVER 1,400 HOURS) AND PART-TIME
(1 to 1,400 HOURS) WORK

Number of years with over 1,400 hours	Number of years with 1 to 1,400 hours			
	0	1-3	4-6	7
0	.68	.17	.03	.00
	.58	.25	.00	.00
	.63	.30	.02	.00
	.51	.27	.04	.02
	.65	.17	.07	.00
1-3	.02	.05	.02	
	.02	.05	.02	
	.00	.04	.00	
	.00	.11	.04	
	.00	.09	.00	
4-6	.00	.02		
	.00	.02		
	.00	.02		
	.00	.02		
	.00	.02		
7	.00			
	.00			
	.00			
	.00			
	.00			
Model	Inertia	A	B	C
Pseudo chi-square statistic (n=57)	4	8	11	5

TABLE C.29
ACTUAL AND SIMULATED PROPORTIONS OF
INDIVIDUALS BY EARNED INCOME
CUMULATED OVER 7-YEAR PERIOD

Earned income cumulated over 7-year period	Actual	Inertia	A	B	C
$0	.12	.10	.10	.09	.09
Less than $10,000	.23	.25	.21	.24	.23
$10,000-19,999	.14	.14	.14	.15	.13
$20,000-29,999	.11	.11	.11	.11	.10
$30,000-39,999	.09	.10	.11	.10	.09
$40,000-59,999	.14	.15	.18	.15	.13
$60,000-79,999	.10	.09	.10	.09	.09
$80,000-99,999	.04	.03	.03	.04	.06
$100,100-119,999	.02	.02	.01	.01	.03
$120,000-139,999	.01	.00	.00	.00	.02
Over $139,999	.01	.00	.00	.00	.02
Pseudo chi-square statistic (n=2657)		79	127	70	99

Appendix C

TABLE C.30
ACTUAL AND SIMULATED PROPORTIONS OF WOMEN 14-20
YEARS OF AGE IN 1971 BY EARNED INCOME
CUMULATED OVER 7-YEAR PERIOD

Earned income cumulated over 7-year period	Actual	Inertia	A	B	C
$0	.08	.07	.08	.05	.05
Less than $10,000	.57	.52	.52	.50	.44
$10,000-19,999	.23	.23	.19	.23	.23
$20,000-29,999	.08	.10	.08	.13	.11
Over $29,999	.04	.08	.13	.08	.16
Pseudo chi-square statistic (n=272)		14	55	22	14

TABLE C.31
ACTUAL AND SIMULATED PROPORTIONS OF WOMEN 21-46
YEARS OF AGE AND MARRIED IN 1971 BY EARNED INCOME
CUMULATED OVER 7-YEAR PERIOD

Earned income cumulated over 7-year period	Actual	Inertia	A	B	C
$0	.17	.15	.14	.15	.15
Less than $10,000	.40	.44	.34	.40	.35
$10,000-19,999	.20	.18	.25	.22	.19
$20,000-29,999	.12	.12	.18	.11	.12
$30,000-39,999	.07	.06	.05	.07	.10
Over $39,999	.05	.05	.04	.06	.09
Pseudo chi-square statistic (n=424)		4	27	3	23

TABLE C.32
ACTUAL AND SIMULATED PROPORTIONS OF WOMEN 21-46 YEARS OF AGE AND UNMARRIED IN 1971 BY EARNED INCOME CUMULATED OVER 7-YEAR PERIOD

Earned income cumulated over 7-year period	Actual	Inertia	A	B	C
$0	.12	.06	.09	.07	.06
Less than $10,000	.23	.26	.21	.24	.32
$10,000-19,999	.18	.21	.23	.30	.16
$20,000-29,999	.19	.21	.22	.23	.15
$30,000-39,999	.15	.15	.16	.09	.11
$40,000-59,999	.10	.08	.08	.06	.15
Over $59,999	.03	.03	.00	.01	.05
Pseudo chi-square statistic (n=247)		12	16	42	31

TABLE C.33
ACTUAL AND SIMULATED PROPORTIONS OF WOMEN 47-64 YEARS OF AGE AND MARRIED IN 1971 BY EARNED INCOME CUMULATED OVER 7-YEAR PERIOD

Earned income cumulated over 7-year period	Actual	Inertia	A	B	C
$0	.38	.37	.31	.37	.36
Less than $10,000	.29	.31	.34	.31	.26
$10,000-19,999	.15	.15	.19	.15	.13
$20,000-29,999	.08	.09	.09	.05	.10
Over $29,999	.11	.08	.06	.11	.14
Pseudo chi-square statistic (n=119)		1	6	1	3

Appendix C

TABLE C.34
ACTUAL AND SIMULATED PROPORTIONS OF WOMEN 47-64 YEARS
OF AGE AND UNMARRIED IN 1971 BY EARNED INCOME
CUMULATED OVER 7-YEAR PERIOD

Earned income cumulated over 7-year period	Actual	Model variant			
		Inertia	A	B	C
$0	.28	.24	.29	.23	.23
Less than $10,000	.19	.29	.20	.27	.28
$10,000-19,999	.23	.14	.18	.19	.16
$20,000-29,999	.12	.16	.17	.18	.10
$30,000-39,999	.07	.08	.10	.05	.12
Over $39,999	.11	.09	.06	.06	.10
Pseudo chi-square statistic (n=145)		17	10	18	17

TABLE C.35
ACTUAL AND SIMULATED PROPORTIONS OF WOMEN 65+
YEARS OF AGE IN 1971 BY EARNED INCOME
CUMULATED OVER 7-YEAR PERIOD

Earned income cumulated over 7-year period	Actual	Model variant			
		Inertia	A	B	C
$0	.68	.58	.63	.51	.65
Less than $10,000	.30	.36	.35	.47	.30
$10,000-19,999	.02	.04	.02	.02	.03
Over $19,999	.00	.00	.00	.00	.00
Pseudo chi-square statistic (n=57)		2	1	8	0

Appendix D. Actual and Simulated Distributions for Years of Work Out of 7 and Individual Income Cumulated Over 7 Years for Various Partitions of Our Simulation Population

TABLE D.1
ACTUAL AND SIMULATED PROPORTIONS BY YEARS WORKED: WOMEN 14-20 IN 1971 WHO HAD A BABY OR YOUNG CHILD IN 7-YEAR PERIOD

Years worked out of 7	Actual	Inertia	Dummy	Split	A	B	C
0	.07	.06	.07	.07	.08	.04	.04
1-2	.26	.21	.27	.26	.20	.23	.23
3-4	.30	.31	.26	.32	.29	.32	.32
5-6	.27	.32	.26	.23	.28	.29	.30
7	.10	.10	.14	.12	.14	.11	.11
Pseudo chi-square statistic (n=161)		3	4	2	5	3	4

TABLE D.2
ACTUAL AND SIMULATED PROPORTIONS BY YEARS WORKED: WOMEN 14-20 IN 1971 WHO DID NOT HAVE A BABY OR YOUNG CHILD IN 7-YEAR PERIOD

Years worked out of 7	Actual	Inertia	Dummy	Split	A	B	C
0	.06	.04	.03	.01	.03	.03	.03
1-2	.19	.20	.17	.17	.22	.14	.15
3-4	.22	.35	.23	.30	.28	.29	.31
5-6	.36	.26	.36	.37	.31	.26	.34
7	.17	.15	.21	.15	.15	.28	.16
Pseudo chi-square statistic (n=111)		13	3	8	5	17	7

Appendix D

TABLE D.3
ACTUAL AND SIMULATED PROPORTIONS OF WOMEN
BY NUMBER OF YEARS WORKED OUT OF 7:
WOMEN 21-46 YEARS OF AGE AND MARRIED IN 1971 WHO
HAD A BABY OR YOUNG CHILD IN 7-YEAR PERIOD

Number of years worked out of 7	Actual	Inertia	Dummy	Split	A	B	C
0	.16	.14	.16	.15	.15	.12	.12
1-2	.22	.19	.20	.22	.14	.22	.21
3-4	.16	.31	.23	.24	.25	.25	.22
5-6	.23	.19	.22	.25	.25	.21	.23
7	.23	.17	.18	.13	.21	.20	.22
Pseudo chi-square statistic (n=255)		43	11	22	21	17	8

TABLE D.4
ACTUAL AND SIMULATED PROPORTIONS OF WOMEN
BY NUMBER OF YEARS WORKED OUT OF 7:
WOMEN 21-46 YEARS OF AGE AND MARRIED IN 1971 WHO
DID NOT HAVE A BABY OR YOUNG CHILD IN 7-YEAR PERIOD

Number of years worked out of 7	Actual	Inertia	Dummy	Split	A	B	C
0	.18	.12	.13	.10	.12	.11	.14
1-2	.06	.12	.10	.17	.17	.14	.14
3-4	.14	.21	.17	.18	.11	.20	.12
5-6	.21	.21	.24	.21	.24	.19	.19
7	.40	.34	.35	.33	.36	.35	.41
Pseudo chi-square statistic (n=169)		21	10	44	40	28	20

TABLE D.5
ACTUAL AND SIMULATED PROPORTIONS OF WOMEN BY NUMBER OF YEARS WORKED OUT OF 7: WOMEN 21-46 YEARS OF AGE AND UNMARRIED IN 1971 WHO HAD A BABY OR YOUNG CHILD IN 7-YEAR PERIOD

Number of years worked out of 7	Actual	Inertia	Dummy	Split	A	B	C
0	.14	.07	.08	.07	.08	.08	.05
1-2	.14	.11	.14	.17	.17	.17	.18
3-4	.20	.24	.17	.18	.20	.17	.21
5-6	.20	.16	.28	.26	.18	.21	.21
7	.31	.42	.32	.32	.36	.36	.34
Pseudo chi-square statistic (n=112)		11	7	7	5	5	8

TABLE D.6
ACTUAL AND SIMULATED PROPORTIONS OF WOMEN BY NUMBER OF YEARS WORKED OUT OF 7: WOMEN 21-46 YEARS OF AGE AND UNMARRIED IN 1971 WHO DID NOT HAVE A BABY OR YOUNG CHILD IN 7-YEAR PERIOD

Number of years worked out of 7	Actual	Inertia	Dummy	Split	A	B	C
0	.09	.04	.02	.03	.08	.04	.03
1-2	.04	.13	.06	.09	.05	.09	.08
3-4	.10	.08	.13	.15	.15	.14	.13
5-6	.14	.22	.22	.23	.21	.16	.19
7	.64	.53	.57	.50	.52	.57	.56
Pseudo chi-square statistic (n=135)		40	17	29	12	16	16

Appendix D

TABLE D.7
ACTUAL AND SIMULATED PROPORTIONS OF WOMEN
BY EARNED INCOME CUMULATED OVER 7-YEAR PERIOD:
WOMEN 14-20 YEARS OF AGE IN 1971 WHO HAD
A BABY OR YOUNG CHILD IN 7-YEAR PERIOD

Earned income cumulated over 7-year period	Actual	Inertia	Dummy	Split	A	B	C
$0	.09	.08	.13	.07	.09	.06	.06
Less than $10,000	.66	.53	.46	.53	.55	.53	.47
$10,000 - 19,999	.19	.23	.29	.23	.19	.24	.22
$20,000 - 29,999	.03	.09	.09	.11	.08	.10	.11
Over $29,999	.03	.06	.03	.05	.08	.07	.15
Pseudo chi-square statistic (n=161)		30	41	43	30	43	123

TABLE D.8
ACTUAL AND SIMULATED PROPORTIONS OF WOMEN
BY EARNED INCOME CUMULATED OVER 7-YEAR PERIOD:
WOMEN 14-20 YEARS OF AGE IN 1971 WHO DID
NOT HAVE A BABY OR YOUNG CHILD IN 7-YEAR PERIOD

Earned income cumulated over 7-year period	Actual	Inertia	Dummy	Split	A	B	C
$0	.06	.06	.04	.01	.06	.04	.04
Less than $10,000	.45	.50	.40	.37	.48	.46	.40
$10,000 - 19,999	.28	.22	.29	.24	.18	.21	.26
$20,000 - 29,999	.14	.11	.19	.19	.09	.18	.13
Over $29,999	.06	.11	.08	.19	.19	.12	.18
Pseudo chi-square statistic (n=111)		7	4	40	37	11	28

TABLE D.9
ACTUAL AND SIMULATED PROPORTIONS OF WOMEN BY EARNED INCOME CUMULATED OVER 7-YEAR PERIOD: WOMEN 21-46 YEARS OF AGE AND MARRIED IN 1971 WHO HAD A BABY OR YOUNG CHILD IN 7-YEAR PERIOD

Earned income cumulated over 7-year period	Actual	Inertia	Dummy	Split	A	B	C
$0	.16	.16	.18	.18	.16	.14	.16
Less than $10,000	.46	.51	.34	.41	.37	.45	.40
$10,000 - 19,999	.20	.14	.29	.25	.26	.22	.18
$20,000 - 29,999	.09	.10	.11	.10	.14	.08	.12
$30,000 - 39,999	.05	.05	.06	.04	.04	.05	.07
Over $39,999	.04	.05	.01	.02	.04	.05	.06
Pseudo chi-square statistic (n=255)		7	26	8	17	2	10

TABLE D.10
ACTUAL AND SIMULATED PROPORTIONS OF WOMEN BY EARNED INCOME CUMULATED OVER 7-YEAR PERIOD: WOMEN 21-46 YEARS OF AGE AND MARRIED IN 1971 WHO DID NOT HAVE A BABY OR YOUNG CHILD IN 7-YEAR PERIOD

Earned income cumulated over 7-year period	Actual	Inertia	Dummy	Split	A	B	C
$0	.18	.14	.14	.11	.12	.15	.15
Less than $10,000	.30	.32	.20	.27	.29	.32	.27
$10,000 - 19,999	.19	.23	.30	.30	.23	.21	.19
$20,000 - 29,999	.17	.14	.20	.18	.23	.16	.11
$30,000 - 39,999	.10	.08	.10	.12	.07	.09	.13
Over $39,999	.06	.07	.06	.03	.06	.07	.14
Pseudo chi-square statistic (n=169)		5	19	19	10	2	24

Appendix D

TABLE D.11
ACTUAL AND SIMULATED PROPORTIONS OF WOMEN BY EARNED INCOME
CUMULATED OVER 7-YEAR PERIOD: WOMEN 21-46 AND UNMARRIED
IN 1971 WHO HAD A BABY OR YOUNG CHILD IN 7-YEAR PERIOD

Earned income cumulated over 7-year period	Actual	Inertia	Dummy	Split	A	B	C
$0	.15	.07	.08	.07	.11	.09	.06
Less than $10,000	.34	.34	.27	.29	.28	.31	.43
$10,000 - 19,999	.20	.21	.26	.30	.22	.32	.16
$20,000 - 29,999	.17	.19	.26	.26	.19	.20	.12
$30,000 - 39,999	.09	.13	.09	.07	.14	.04	.12
Over $39,999	.05	.06	.02	.02	.06	.04	.11
Pseudo chi-square statistic (n=112)		7	15	19	6	15	20

TABLE D.12
ACTUAL AND SIMULATED PROPORTIONS OF WOMEN BY EARNED INCOME
CUMULATED OVER 7-YEAR PERIOD: WOMEN 21-46 AND UNMARRIED IN
1971 WHO DID NOT HAVE A BABY OR YOUNG CHILD IN 7-YEAR PERIOD

Earned income cumulated over 7-year period	Actual	Inertia	Dummy	Split	A	B	C
$0	.10	.05	.02	.04	.08	.05	.05
Less than $10,000	.14	.18	.11	.19	.14	.17	.23
$10,000 - 19,999	.17	.22	.21	.20	.23	.28	.16
$20,000 - 29,999	.20	.23	.32	.26	.24	.26	.18
$30,000 - 39,999	.19	.17	.15	.17	.19	.14	.11
$40,000 - 59,999	.14	.10	.17	.14	.11	.08	.20
Over $59,999	.06	.05	.02	.01	.01	.02	.07
Pseudo chi-square statistic (n=135)		10	26	16	11	25	20

TABLE D.13
ACTUAL AND SIMULATED PROPORTIONS OF WOMEN
BY NUMBER OF YEARS WORKED OUT OF 7:
WOMEN 21-33 YEARS OF AGE AND MARRIED IN 1971

Number of years worked out of 7	Actual	Inertia	Dummy	Split	A	B	C
0	.13	.12	.14	.14	.14	.13	.09
1-2	.19	.19	.20	.21	.12	.21	.19
3-4	.18	.34	.24	.23	.25	.23	.21
5-6	.23	.17	.20	.25	.23	.20	.23
7	.27	.19	.22	.16	.26	.22	.28
Pseudo chi-square statistic (n=228)		42	8	14	12	7	4

TABLE D.14
ACTUAL AND SIMULATED PROPORTIONS OF WOMEN
BY NUMBER OF YEARS WORKED OUT OF 7:
WOMEN 34-46 YEARS OF AGE AND MARRIED IN 1971

Number of years worked out of 7	Actual	Inertia	Dummy	Split	A	B	C
0	.21	.15	.16	.12	.14	.10	.17
1-2	.11	.14	.12	.18	.19	.16	.17
3-4	.12	.19	.17	.20	.13	.22	.14
5-6	.22	.23	.26	.21	.25	.20	.20
7	.33	.29	.28	.28	.28	.31	.32
Pseudo chi-square statistic (n=196)		14	9	28	18	33	9

Appendix D

TABLE D.15
ACTUAL AND SIMULATED PROPORTIONS OF WOMEN
BY NUMBER OF YEARS WORKED OUT OF 7:
WOMEN 21-33 YEARS OF AGE AND UNMARRIED IN 1971

Number of years worked out of 7	Actual	Inertia	Dummy	Split	A	B	C
0	.08	.02	.04	.02	.05	.03	.03
1-2	.09	.14	.08	.16	.08	.13	.13
3-4	.18	.21	.16	.20	.22	.22	.21
5-6	.17	.21	.27	.29	.23	.23	.21
7	.48	.43	.45	.33	.41	.40	.41
Pseudo chi-square statistic (n=117)		11	10	27	6	11	9

TABLE D.16
ACTUAL AND SIMULATED PROPORTIONS OF WOMEN
BY NUMBER OF YEARS WORKED OUT OF 7:
WOMEN 34-46 YEARS OF AGE AND UNMARRIED IN 1971

Number of years worked out of 7	Actual	Inertia	Dummy	Split	A	B	C
0	.15	.08	.06	.08	.11	.08	.05
1-2	.08	.11	.11	.09	.10	.13	.12
3-4	.11	.11	.13	.13	.13	.10	.13
5-6	.17	.18	.23	.19	.16	.14	.19
7	.50	.52	.46	.50	.47	.55	.51
Pseudo chi-square statistic (n=130)		6	12	5	3	10	12

TABLE D.17
ACTUAL AND SIMULATED PROPORTIONS OF WOMEN
BY NUMBER OF YEARS WORKED OUT OF 7:
WOMEN 47-55 YEARS OF AGE AND MARRIED IN 1971

Number of years worked out of 7	Actual	Inertia	Dummy	Split	A	B	C
0	.30	.18	.22	.27	.22	.28	.27
1-2	.12	.22	.22	.09	.18	.18	.18
3-4	.13	.22	.17	.26	.18	.15	.11
5-6	.21	.19	.17	.18	.15	.11	.12
7	.23	.20	.22	.20	.28	.27	.31
Pseudo chi-square statistic (n=81)		16	10	12	8	7	8

TABLE D.18
ACTUAL AND SIMULATED PROPORTIONS OF WOMEN
BY NUMBER OF YEARS WORKED OUT OF 7:
WOMEN 56-64 YEARS OF AGE AND MARRIED IN 1971

Number of years worked out of 7	Actual	Inertia	Dummy	Split	A	B	C
0	.55	.62	.63	.49	.42	.53	.55
1-2	.13	.16	.13	.27	.39	.13	.21
3-4	.08	.11	.05	.16	.14	.16	.13
5-6	.16	.08	.11	.08	.03	.10	.05
7	.08	.03	.08	.00	.03	.00	.05
Pseudo chi-square statistic (n=38)		4	1	14	28	7	6

Appendix D

TABLE D.19
ACTUAL AND SIMULATED PROPORTIONS OF WOMEN
BY NUMBER OF YEARS WORKED OUT OF 7:
WOMEN 47-55 YEARS OF AGE AND UNMARRIED IN 1971

Number of years worked out of 7	Actual	Inertia	Dummy	Split	A	B	C
0	.26	.20	.15	.12	.25	.21	.15
1-2	.08	.17	.14	.13	.09	.16	.14
3-4	.04	.14	.09	.08	.09	.10	.15
5-6	.11	.08	.25	.28	.11	.16	.13
7	.51	.41	.37	.39	.45	.37	.42
Pseudo chi-square statistic (n=78)		31	29	34	5	19	32

TABLE D.20
ACTUAL AND SIMULATED PROPORTIONS OF WOMEN
BY NUMBER OF YEARS WORKED OUT OF 7:
WOMEN 56-64 YEARS OF AGE AND UNMARRIED IN 1971

Number of years worked out of 7	Actual	Inertia	Dummy	Split	A	B	C
0	.30	.25	.20	.24	.30	.23	.24
1-2	.10	.15	.17	.10	.13	.13	.18
3-4	.12	.20	.15	.18	.13	.16	.13
5-6	.21	.13	.23	.16	.25	.16	.19
7	.27	.27	.25	.31	.18	.32	.25
Pseudo chi-square statistic (n=67)		8	6	4	3	4	5

TABLE D.21
ACTUAL AND SIMULATED PROPORTIONS OF WOMEN
BY EARNED INCOME CUMULATED OVER 7-YEAR PERIOD:
WOMEN 21-33 YEARS OF AGE AND MARRIED IN 1971

Earned income cumulated over 7-year period	Actual	Inertia	Dummy	Split	A	B	C
$0	.13	.14	.15	.17	.14	.17	.11
Less than $10,000	.43	.49	.33	.38	.35	.42	.39
$10,000 - 19,999	.19	.16	.30	.25	.25	.22	.17
$20,000 - 29,999	.11	.11	.11	.11	.17	.06	.14
$30,000 - 39,999	.06	.05	.08	.07	.05	.07	.09
Over $39,999	.07	.04	.02	.02	.04	.05	.10
Pseudo chi-square statistic (n=228)		6	30	17	19	11	10

TABLE D.22
ACTUAL AND SIMULATED PROPORTIONS OF WOMEN
BY EARNED INCOME CUMULATED OVER 7-YEAR PERIOD:
WOMEN 34-46 YEARS OF AGE AND MARRIED IN 1971

Earned income cumulated over 7-year period	Actual	Inertia	Dummy	Split	A	B	C
$0	.21	.17	.18	.13	.14	.12	.20
Less than $10,000	.35	.37	.24	.32	.33	.37	.31
$10,000 - 19,999	.20	.19	.28	.29	.24	.21	.21
$20,000 - 29,999	.13	.12	.18	.16	.19	.17	.10
$30,000 - 39,999	.08	.07	.07	.07	.05	.07	.10
Over $39,999	.03	.07	.04	.02	.05	.05	.08
Pseudo chi-square statistic (n=196)		13	18	17	17	13	20

Appendix D

TABLE D.23
ACTUAL AND SIMULATED PROPORTIONS OF WOMEN BY EARNED INCOME
CUMULATED OVER 7-YEARS: WOMEN 21-33 AND UNMARRIED IN 1971

Earned income cumulated over 7-year period	Actual	Inertia	Dummy	Split	A	B	C
$0	.08	.03	.04	.02	.06	.04	.04
Less than $10,000	.26	.30	.18	.31	.23	.26	.34
$10,000 - 19,999	.16	.25	.24	.28	.24	.30	.21
$20,000 - 29,999	.21	.21	.34	.23	.19	.25	.13
$30,000 - 39,999	.16	.11	.09	.10	.20	.07	.09
$40,000 - 59,999	.11	.08	.10	.04	.07	.06	.14
Over $59,999	.02	.02	.01	.01	.01	.01	.04
Pseudo chi-square statistic (n=117)		13	24	26	9	27	24

TABLE D.24
ACTUAL AND SIMULATED PROPORTIONS OF WOMEN BY EARNED INCOME
CUMULATED OVER 7-YEARS: WOMEN 34-46 AND UNMARRIED IN 1971

Earned income cumulated over 7-year period	Actual	Inertia	Dummy	Split	A	B	C
$0	.16	.08	.06	.09	.13	.09	.07
Less than $10,000	.21	.22	.19	.16	.19	.21	.30
$10,000 - 19,999	.20	.18	.23	.21	.21	.29	.11
$20,000 - 29,999	.16	.22	.26	.28	.25	.21	.18
$30,000 - 39,999	.13	.19	.15	.14	.14	.11	.13
$40,000 - 59,999	.09	.08	.10	.12	.09	.07	.15
Over $59,999	.04	.03	.01	.00	.00	.02	.06
Pseudo chi-square statistic (n=130)		12	20	24	13	13	24

TABLE D.25
ACTUAL AND SIMULATED PROPORTIONS OF WOMEN BY EARNED INCOME CUMULATED OVER 7-YEAR PERIOD: WOMEN 47-55 YEARS OF AGE AND MARRIED IN 1971

Earned income cumulated over 7-year period	Actual	Inertia	Dummy	Split	A	B	C
$0	.30	.23	.23	.27	.26	.29	.27
Less than $10,000	.28	.35	.25	.31	.27	.32	.26
$10,000 - 19,999	.20	.18	.21	.19	.26	.18	.12
$20,000 - 29,999	.07	.12	.21	.17	.12	.06	.14
Over $29,999	.15	.12	.10	.06	.10	.14	.20
Pseudo chi-square statistic (n=81)		6	26	16	6	1	10

TABLE D.26
ACTUAL AND SIMULATED PROPORTIONS OF WOMEN BY EARNED INCOME CUMULATED OVER 7-YEAR PERIOD: WOMEN 56-64 YEARS OF AGE AND MARRIED IN 1971

Earned income cumulated over 7-year period	Actual	Inertia	Dummy	Split	A	B	C
$0	.55	.65	.63	.49	.42	.53	.55
Less than $10,000	.29	.22	.16	.40	.50	.29	.26
$10,000 - 19,999	.05	.11	.16	.05	.06	.10	.16
$20,000 - 29,999	.08	.03	.03	.03	.03	.03	.03
Over $29,999	.03	.00	.03	.03	.00	.05	.00
Pseudo chi-square statistic (n=38)		6	13	3	9	4	12

TABLE D.27
ACTUAL AND SIMULATED PROPORTIONS OF WOMEN
BY EARNED INCOME CUMULATED OVER 7-YEAR PERIOD:
WOMEN 47-55 YEARS OF AGE AND UNMARRIED IN 1971

Earned income cumulated over 7-year period	Actual	Inertia	Dummy	Split	A	B	C
$0	.26	.21	.15	.13	.27	.23	.19
Less than $10,000	.18	.31	.18	.16	.17	.30	.27
$10,000 - 19,999	.19	.13	.23	.27	.11	.14	.18
$20,000 - 29,999	.13	.18	.25	.23	.22	.14	.08
$30,000 - 39,999	.11	.08	.11	.15	.14	.10	.18
Over $39,999	.14	.08	.08	.06	.09	.08	.10
Pseudo chi-square statistic (n=78)		14	15	19	10	10	11

TABLE D.28
ACTUAL AND SIMULATED PROPORTIONS OF WOMEN
BY EARNED INCOME CUMULATED OVER 7-YEAR PERIOD:
WOMEN 56-64 YEARS OF AGE AND UNMARRIED IN 1971

Earned income cumulated over 7-year period	Actual	Inertia	Dummy	Split	A	B	C
$0	.31	.28	.20	.24	.32	.24	.28
Less than $10,000	.19	.27	.29	.33	.23	.24	.30
$10,000 - 19,999	.27	.17	.21	.12	.27	.24	.13
$20,000 - 29,999	.12	.13	.14	.22	.12	.23	.13
$30,000 - 39,999	.01	.07	.11	.03	.05	.00	.06
Over $39,999	.08	.08	.04	.06	.02	.06	.08
Pseudo chi-square statistic (n=67)		29	76	22	14	10	26

TABLE D.29
ACTUAL AND SIMULATED PROPORTIONS OF WOMEN BY NUMBER OF YEARS WORKED OUT OF 7: WOMEN 21-46 YEARS OF AGE AND MARRIED IN 1971 WHO WERE ALSO MARRIED IN ALL YEARS FROM 1972 THROUGH 1977

Number of years worked out of 7	Actual	Inertia	Dummy	Split	A	B	C
0	.18	.15	.16	.15	.14	.13	.13
1-2	.16	.17	.17	.20	.16	.21	.19
3-4	.15	.26	.21	.21	.19	.24	.17
5-6	.18	.19	.21	.23	.24	.18	.22
7	.33	.22	.24	.21	.27	.24	.28
Pseudo chi-square statistic (n=381)		47	21	37	19	41	15

TABLE D.30
ACTUAL AND SIMULATED PROPORTIONS OF WOMEN BY NUMBER OF YEARS WORKED OUT OF 7: WOMEN 21-46 YEARS OF AGE AND MARRIED IN 1971 WHO WERE NOT MARRIED IN AT LEAST ONE YEAR FROM 1972 THROUGH 1977

Number of years worked out of 7	Actual	Inertia	Dummy	Split	A	B	C
0	.05	.00	.05	.00	.08	.02	.09
1-2	.12	.05	.05	.15	.03	.02	.12
3-4	.21	.36	.22	.27	.29	.12	.21
5-6	.63	.26	.37	.30	.29	.29	.19
7	.00	.33	.30	.27	.32	.44	.39
Pseudo chi-square statistic (n=43)		9	2	3	5	9	1

TABLE D.31
ACTUAL AND SIMULATED PROPORTIONS OF WOMEN BY NUMBER
OF YEARS WORKED OUT OF 7: WOMEN 47-64 YEARS OF AGE
AND MARRIED IN 1971 WHO WERE ALSO MARRIED IN ALL
YEARS FROM 1972 THROUGH 1977

Number of years worked out of 7	Actual	Inertia	Dummy	Split	A	B	C
0	.40	.35	.38	.37	.32	.40	.39
1-2	.10	.18	.20	.15	.23	.17	.17
3-4	.10	.17	.14	.21	.14	.13	.09
5-6	.18	.15	.12	.13	.09	.10	.10
7	.21	.14	.17	.15	.21	.21	.25
Pseudo chi-square statistic (n=105)		15	15	19	26	10	10

TABLE D.32
ACTUAL AND SIMULATED PROPORTIONS OF WOMEN BY NUMBER
OF YEARS WORKED OUT OF 7: WOMEN 21-46 YEARS OF AGE
UNMARRIED IN 1971 WHO WERE ALSO UNMARRIED IN ALL
YEARS FROM 1972 THROUGH 1977

Number of years worked out of 7	Actual	Inertia	Dummy	Split	A	B	C
0	.15	.07	.06	.07	.10	.07	.04
1-2	.09	.11	.10	.13	.12	.13	.14
3-4	.12	.15	.13	.13	.16	.16	.15
5-6	.12	.19	.23	.24	.18	.14	.19
7	.52	.48	.46	.44	.45	.50	.48
Pseudo chi-square statistic (n=181)		18	30	35	14	14	29

TABLE D.33
ACTUAL AND SIMULATED PROPORTIONS OF WOMEN BY NUMBER OF YEARS WORKED OUT OF 7: WOMEN 21-46 YEARS OF AGE AND UNMARRIED IN 1971 WHO WERE ALSO MARRIED IN AT LEAST ONE YEAR FROM 1972 THROUGH 1977

Number of years worked out of 7	Actual	Inertia	Dummy	Split	A	B	C
0	.00	.02	.02	.00	.03	.03	.03
1-2	.08	.15	.06	.12	.07	.11	.09
3-4	.21	.17	.18	.26	.22	.14	.23
5-6	.32	.18	.29	.26	.25	.29	.24
7	.39	.48	.44	.36	.43	.42	.41
Pseudo chi-square statistic (n=66)		12	1	3	2	5	3

TABLE D.34
ACTUAL AND SIMULATED PROPORTIONS OF WOMEN BY NUMBER OF YEARS WORKED OUT OF 7: WOMEN 47-64 YEARS OF AGE AND UNMARRIED IN 1971 WHO WERE ALSO UNMARRIED IN ALL YEARS FROM 1972 THROUGH 1977

Number of years worked out of 7	Actual	Inertia	Dummy	Split	A	B	C
0	.27	.23	.17	.18	.28	.22	.20
1-2	.09	.15	.15	.12	.11	.13	.15
3-4	.06	.16	.12	.13	.11	.13	.14
5-6	.14	.09	.24	.22	.18	.15	.14
7	.42	.36	.31	.35	.33	.37	.35
Pseudo chi-square statistic (n=138)		33	33	25	11	16	24

Appendix D

TABLE D.35
ACTUAL AND SIMULATED PROPORTIONS OF WOMEN BY EARNED
INCOME CUMULATED OVER 7-YEAR PERIOD: WOMEN 21-46 YEARS
OF AGE AND MARRIED IN 1971 WHO WERE ALSO MARRIED
IN ALL YEARS FROM 1972 THROUGH 1977

Earned income cumulated over 7-year period	Actual	Inertia	Dummy	Split	A	B	C
$0	.18	.17	.18	.17	.15	.16	.16
Less than $10,000	.41	.44	.29	.36	.36	.42	.36
$10,000 - 19,999	.19	.17	.31	.26	.23	.20	.19
$20,000 - 29,999	.10	.11	.14	.13	.17	.10	.12
$30,000 - 39,999	.07	.06	.06	.06	.05	.06	.09
Over $39,999	.05	.05	.03	.02	.04	.05	.08
Pseudo chi-square statistic (n=381)		3	52	23	29	2	14

TABLE D.36
ACTUAL AND SIMULATED PROPORTIONS OF WOMEN BY EARNED
INCOME CUMULATED OVER 7-YEAR PERIOD: WOMEN 21-46 YEARS
OF AGE AND MARRIED IN 1971 WHO WERE NOT MARRIED IN
AT LEAST ONE YEAR FROM 1972 THROUGH 1977

Earned income cumulated over 7-year period	Actual	Inertia	Dummy	Split	A	B	C
$0	.05	.00	.05	.00	.08	.02	.09
Less than $10,000	.30	.36	.22	.25	.13	.17	.28
$10,000 - 19,999	.23	.23	.15	.40	.37	.37	.19
$20,000 - 29,999	.28	.20	.25	.15	.26	.19	.14
$30,000 - 39,999	.09	.08	.27	.15	.10	.15	.12
Over $39,999	.05	.13	.05	.05	.05	.09	.18
Pseudo chi-square statistic (n=43)		9	18	12	9	11	20

TABLE D.37
ACTUAL AND SIMULATED PROPORTIONS OF WOMEN BY EARNED INCOME CUMULATED OVER 7-YEARS: WOMEN 47-64 AND MARRIED IN 1971 WHO WERE ALSO MARRIED IN ALL YEARS FROM 1972 THROUGH 1977

Earned income cumulated over 7-year period	Actual	Inertia	Dummy	Split	A	B	C
$0	.40	.39	.39	.37	.35	.41	.39
Less than $10,000	.25	.28	.22	.33	.31	.30	.22
$10,000 - 19,999	.15	.15	.18	.15	.18	.11	.12
$20,000 - 29,999	.09	.09	.13	.11	.09	.06	.11
Over $29,999	.12	.09	.09	.05	.07	.12	.15
Pseudo chi-square statistic (n=105)		1	4	8	5	3	3

TABLE D.38
ACTUAL AND SIMULATED PROPORTIONS OF WOMEN BY EARNED INCOME CUMULATED OVER 7-YEARS: WOMEN 21-46 AND UNMARRIED IN 1971 WHO WERE ALSO UNMARRIED IN ALL YEARS FROM 1972 THROUGH 1977

Earned income cumulated over 7-year period	Actual	Inertia	Dummy	Split	A	B	C
$0	.16	.07	.06	.07	.11	.08	.07
Less than $10,000	.22	.24	.18	.20	.19	.24	.33
$10,000 - 19,999	.19	.20	.22	.22	.22	.28	.12
$20,000 - 29,999	.17	.20	.27	.27	.24	.23	.17
$30,000 - 39,999	.13	.17	.13	.12	.15	.10	.13
$40,000 - 59,999	.09	.07	.12	.10	.08	.06	.13
Over $59,999	.05	.04	.02	.01	.00	.02	.06
Pseudo chi-square statistic (n=181)		14	29	27	19	25	27

TABLE D.39
ACTUAL AND SIMULATED PROPORTIONS OF WOMEN BY EARNED INCOME CUMULATED OVER 7-YEAR PERIOD: WOMEN 21-46 YEARS OF AGE AND UNMARRIED IN 1971 WHO WERE MARRIED IN AT LEAST ONE YEAR FROM 1972 THROUGH 1977

Earned income cumulated over 7-year period	Actual	Inertia	Dummy	Split	A	B	C
$0	.01	.03	.02	.00	.03	.03	.03
Less than $10,000	.26	.30	.20	.32	.25	.21	.30
$10,000 - 19,999	.17	.23	.26	.32	.25	.35	.26
$20,000 - 29,999	.23	.23	.38	.21	.15	.24	.11
$30,000 - 39,999	.20	.10	.10	.12	.20	.08	.08
Over $39,999	.14	.10	.05	.03	.12	.08	.21
Pseudo chi-square statistic (n=66)		8	18	18	7	22	17

TABLE D.40
ACTUAL AND SIMULATED PROPORTIONS OF WOMEN BY EARNED INCOME CUMULATED OVER 7-YEAR PERIOD: WOMEN 47-64 YEARS OF AGE AND UNMARRIED IN 1971 WHO WERE ALSO UNMARRIED IN ALL YEARS FROM 1972 THROUGH 1977

Earned income cumulated over 7-year period	Actual	Inertia	Dummy	Split	A	B	C
$0	.28	.26	.17	.19	.29	.24	.24
Less than $10,000	.17	.25	.23	.24	.19	.26	.27
$10,000 - 19,999	.24	.15	.22	.18	.19	.19	.15
$20,000 - 29,999	.12	.17	.20	.22	.17	.18	.11
$30,000 - 39,999	.07	.08	.11	.10	.10	.06	.13
Over $39,999	.11	.09	.06	.07	.05	.08	.10
Pseudo chi-square statistic (n=138)		14	23	25	11	14	21

TABLE D.41
ACTUAL AND SIMULATED PROPORTIONS OF WOMEN BY NUMBER
OF YEARS WORKED OUT OF 7: WOMEN 47-64 YEARS OF AGE
AND MARRIED IN 1971 WITH HUSBANDS WHO NEVER HAD A DROP
IN EARNINGS AS LARGE AS $3,000 OVER 7-YEAR PERIOD

Number of years worked out of 7	Actual	Inertia	Dummy	Split	A	B	C
0	.38	.33	.38	.32	.32	.34	.36
1-2	.13	.20	.15	.17	.20	.21	.18
3-4	.09	.16	.15	.23	.08	.17	.07
5-6	.20	.16	.15	.11	.12	.11	.04
7	.20	.16	.15	.17	.28	.17	.34
Pseudo chi-square statistic (n=55)		6	4	16	6	9	14

TABLE D.42
ACTUAL AND SIMULATED PROPORTIONS OF WOMEN BY NUMBER
OF YEARS WORKED OUT OF 7: WOMEN 47-64 YEARS OF AGE
AND MARRIED IN 1971 WITH HUSBANDS WHO HAD A DROP
IN EARNINGS OF AT LEAST $3,000 SOMETIME DURING 7-YEAR PERIOD

Number of years worked out of 7	Actual	Inertia	Dummy	Split	A	B	C
0	.37	.32	.33	.35	.25	.38	.36
1-2	.12	.20	.22	.13	.28	.13	.20
3-4	.14	.20	.11	.23	.23	.14	.16
5-6	.19	.15	.14	.18	.10	.11	.16
7	.17	.13	.19	.11	.13	.24	.12
Pseudo chi-square statistic (n=64)		7	7	5	23	4	5

Appendix D

TABLE D.43
ACTUAL AND SIMULATED PROPORTIONS OF WOMEN
BY EARNED INCOME CUMULATED OVER 7-YEAR PERIOD:
WOMEN 47-64 YEARS OF AGE AND MARRIED IN 1971
WITH HUSBANDS WHO NEVER HAD A DROP IN EARNINGS
AS LARGE AS $3,000 OVER 7-YEAR PERIOD

Earned income cumulated over 7-year period	Actual	Model variant					
		Inertia	Dummy	Split	A	B	C
$0	.38	.37	.40	.32	.32	.34	.36
Less than $10,000	.31	.33	.13	.36	.28	.41	.20
$10,000 - 19,999	.16	.16	.27	.11	.24	.13	.18
$20,000 - 29,999	.04	.08	.10	.13	.10	.06	.07
Over $29,999	.11	.06	.10	.08	.06	.06	.19
Pseudo chi-square statistic (n=55)		3	15	13	9	4	7

TABLE D.44
ACTUAL AND SIMULATED PROPORTIONS OF WOMEN
BY EARNED INCOME CUMULATED OVER 7-YEAR PERIOD:
WOMEN 47-64 YEARS OF AGE AND MARRIED IN 1971 WITH
HUSBANDS WHO HAD A DROP IN EARNINGS OF AT LEAST
$3,000 SOMETIME DURING 7-YEAR PERIOD

Earned income cumulated over 7-year period	Actual	Model variant					
		Inertia	Dummy	Split	A	B	C
$0	.37	.37	.33	.35	.30	.40	.36
Less than $10,000	.27	.28	.29	.32	.40	.22	.31
$10,000 - 19,999	.14	.15	.13	.18	.15	.17	.09
$20,000 - 29,999	.11	.10	.19	.11	.08	.05	.12
Over $29,999	.12	.10	.06	.04	.07	.16	.10
Pseudo chi-square statistic (n=64)		0	6	5	7	4	2

TABLE D.45
ACTUAL AND SIMULATED PROPORTIONS OF WOMEN
BY NUMBER OF YEARS WORKED OUT OF 7:
BLACK WOMEN 21-46 YEARS OF AGE AND MARRIED IN 1971

Number of years worked out of 7	Actual	Inertia	Dummy	Split	A	B	C
0	.12	.08	.17	.23	.10	.10	.11
1-2	.12	.18	.21	.22	.14	.19	.16
3-4	.15	.36	.17	.15	.24	.22	.15
5-6	.28	.18	.25	.18	.24	.22	.29
7	.33	.19	.20	.22	.27	.27	.29
Pseudo chi-square statistic (n=75)		32	11	19	6	7	1

TABLE D.46
ACTUAL AND SIMULATED PROPORTIONS OF WOMEN
BY NUMBER OF YEARS WORKED OUT OF 7:
NONBLACK WOMEN 21-46 YEARS OF AGE AND MARRIED IN 1971

Number of years worked out of 7	Actual	Inertia	Dummy	Split	A	B	C
0	.18	.14	.15	.11	.15	.12	.13
1-2	.16	.16	.15	.20	.15	.19	.19
3-4	.16	.25	.22	.23	.19	.23	.18
5-6	.21	.20	.22	.25	.24	.20	.20
7	.29	.24	.26	.21	.27	.26	.29
Pseudo chi-square statistic (n=349)		24	11	34	6	21	8

TABLE D.47
ACTUAL AND SIMULATED PROPORTIONS OF WOMEN BY NUMBER OF YEARS WORKED OUT OF 7: BLACK WOMEN 21-46 YEARS OF AGE AND UNMARRIED IN 1971

Number of years worked out of 7	Actual	Inertia	Dummy	Split	A	B	C
0	.15	.07	.07	.06	.12	.08	.03
1-2	.12	.14	.13	.15	.15	.19	.15
3-4	.17	.14	.17	.17	.17	.16	.20
5-6	.21	.20	.22	.25	.24	.20	.20
7	.43	.45	.33	.36	.39	.39	.41
Pseudo chi-square statistic (n=144)		10	33	25	4	13	20

TABLE D.48
ACTUAL AND SIMULATED PROPORTIONS OF WOMEN BY NUMBER OF YEARS WORKED OUT OF 7: NONBLACK WOMEN 21-46 YEARS OF AGE AND UNMARRIED IN 1971

Number of years worked out of 7	Actual	Inertia	Dummy	Split	A	B	C
0	.07	.02	.02	.04	.02	.02	.05
1-2	.04	.09	.04	.09	.05	.04	.09
3-4	.11	.17	.11	.15	.18	.15	.13
5-6	.21	.19	.20	.22	.22	.18	.20
7	.57	.52	.63	.50	.53	.60	.53
Pseudo chi-square statistic (n=103)		14	4	10	9	6	8

TABLE D.49
ACTUAL AND SIMULATED PROPORTIONS OF WOMEN
BY NUMBER OF YEARS WORKED OUT OF 7:
NONBLACK WOMEN 47-64 YEARS OF AGE AND MARRIED IN 1971

Number of years worked out of 7	Actual	Inertia	Dummy	Split	A	B	C
0	.39	.33	.38	.32	.29	.36	.36
1-2	.13	.19	.20	.16	.27	.16	.20
3-4	.13	.09	.12	.25	.15	.16	.11
5-6	.18	.16	.13	.12	.11	.11	.11
7	.17	.14	.16	.14	.18	.21	.22
Pseudo chi-square statistic (n=108)		6	6	17	22	6	9

TABLE D.50
ACTUAL AND SIMULATED PROPORTIONS OF WOMEN
BY NUMBER OF YEARS WORKED OUT OF 7:
BLACK WOMEN 47-64 YEARS OF AGE AND UNMARRIED IN 1971

Number of years worked out of 7	Actual	Inertia	Dummy	Split	A	B	C
0	.36	.27	.24	.29	.29	.25	.23
1-2	.15	.24	.17	.20	.11	.16	.15
3-4	.08	.19	.12	.07	.15	.13	.18
5-6	.06	.03	.22	.19	.10	.16	.13
7	.34	.27	.24	.25	.35	.29	.31
Pseudo chi-square statistic (n=61)		16	32	20	7	15	16

TABLE D.51
ACTUAL AND SIMULATED PROPORTIONS OF WOMEN
BY NUMBER OF YEARS WORKED OUT OF 7:
NONBLACK WOMEN 47-64 YEARS OF AGE AND UNMARRIED IN 1971

Number of years worked out of 7	Actual	Inertia	Dummy	Split	A	B	C
0	.21	.18	.12	.10	.26	.20	.17
1-2	.05	.10	.14	.06	.11	.13	.17
3-4	.07	.15	.12	.17	.08	.13	.12
5-6	.23	.17	.25	.25	.24	.15	.18
7	.44	.40	.36	.42	.31	.39	.37
Pseudo chi-square statistic (n=84)		14	21	17	10	8	30

TABLE D.52
ACTUAL AND SIMULATED PROPORTIONS OF WOMEN
BY EARNED INCOME CUMULATED OVER 7-YEAR PERIOD:
BLACK WOMEN 21-46 YEARS OF AGE AND MARRIED IN 1971

Earned income cumulated over 7-year period	Actual	Inertia	Dummy	Split	A	B	C
$0	.12	.08	.17	.26	.10	.11	.11
Less than $10,000	.33	.51	.34	.31	.34	.42	.33
$10,000 - 19,999	.27	.18	.32	.22	.33	.27	.21
$20,000 - 29,999	.17	.14	.10	.10	.13	.10	.09
$30,000 - 39,999	.04	.04	.07	.10	.06	.07	.13
Over $39,999	.07	.04	.00	.01	.04	.02	.12
Pseudo chi-square statistic (n=75)		12	11	26	4	8	22

TABLE D.53
ACTUAL AND SIMULATED PROPORTIONS OF WOMEN
BY EARNED INCOME CUMULATED OVER 7-YEAR PERIOD:
NONBLACK WOMEN 21-46 YEARS OF AGE AND MARRIED IN 1971

Earned income cumulated over 7-year period	Actual	Inertia	Dummy	Split	A	B	C
$0	.18	.17	.16	.13	.15	.15	.16
Less than $10,000	.41	.42	.28	.36	.34	.39	.35
$10,000 - 19,999	.18	.17	.29	.28	.23	.20	.18
$20,000 - 29,999	.12	.11	.16	.14	.19	.11	.10
Over $29,999	.12	.13	.12	.09	.09	.13	.17
Pseudo chi-square statistic (n=349)		1	43	30	28	3	12

TABLE D.54
ACTUAL AND SIMULATED PROPORTIONS OF WOMEN
BY EARNED INCOME CUMULATED OVER 7-YEAR PERIOD:
BLACK WOMEN 21-46 YEARS OF AGE AND UNMARRIED IN 1971

Earned income cumulated over 7-year period	Actual	Inertia	Dummy	Split	A	B	C
$0	.15	.07	.07	.06	.14	.10	.06
Less than $10,000	.30	.27	.24	.28	.26	.32	.42
$10,000 - 19,999	.22	.22	.28	.27	.23	.29	.15
$20,000 - 29,999	.17	.19	.27	.24	.20	.16	.16
$30,000 - 39,999	.10	.19	.11	.11	.14	.07	.11
Over $39,999	.07	.05	.02	.03	.04	.06	.11
Pseudo chi-square statistic (n=144)		19	24	17	6	7	21

Appendix D

TABLE D.55
ACTUAL AND SIMULATED PROPORTIONS OF WOMEN BY EARNED INCOME CUMULATED OVER 7-YEAR PERIOD: NONBLACK WOMEN 21-46 YEARS OF AGE AND UNMARRIED IN 1971

Earned income cumulated over 7-year period	Actual	Inertia	Dummy	Split	A	B	C
$0	.09	.03	.02	.04	.02	.02	.06
Less than $10,000	.14	.24	.11	.17	.12	.11	.18
$10,000 - 19,999	.13	.19	.16	.21	.23	.31	.17
$20,000 - 29,999	.21	.24	.33	.28	.25	.33	.15
$30,000 - 39,999	.20	.09	.14	.14	.20	.12	.12
$40,000 - 59,999	.16	.14	.21	.15	.16	.10	.22
Over $59,999	.07	.06	.02	.01	.01	.01	.10
Pseudo chi-square statistic (n=103)		21	21	18	20	50	12

TABLE D.56
ACTUAL AND SIMULATED PROPORTIONS OF WOMEN BY EARNED INCOME CUMULATED OVER 7-YEAR PERIOD: NONBLACK WOMEN 47-64 YEARS OF AGE AND MARRIED IN 1971

Earned income cumulated over 7-year period	Actual	Inertia	Dummy	Split	A	B	C
$0	.39	.37	.39	.32	.32	.37	.36
Less than $10,000	.30	.31	.23	.36	.35	.30	.27
$10,000 - 19,999	.14	.16	.17	.15	.17	.16	.11
$20,000 - 29,999	.07	.08	.14	.12	.09	.06	.11
$30,000 - 39,999	.03	.06	.04	.03	.02	.06	.03
Over $39,999	.07	.03	.03	.01	.05	.06	.12
Pseudo chi-square statistic (n=108)		1	11	10	4	1	6

TABLE D.57
ACTUAL AND SIMULATED PROPORTIONS OF WOMEN
BY EARNED INCOME CUMULATED OVER 7-YEAR PERIOD:
BLACK WOMEN 47-64 YEARS OF AGE AND UNMARRIED IN 1971

Earned income cumulated over 7-year period	Actual	Inertia	Dummy	Split	A	B	C
$0	.36	.29	.24	.29	.31	.25	.26
Less than $10,000	.23	.41	.31	.25	.23	.33	.34
$10,000 - 19,999	.23	.12	.17	.19	.13	.23	.15
$20,000 - 29,999	.08	.10	.22	.19	.21	.08	.10
$30,000 - 39,999	.07	.05	.05	.08	.08	.05	.13
Over $39,999	.03	.03	.00	.00	.04	.07	.02
Pseudo chi-square statistic (n=61)		13	22	12	16	8	10

TABLE D.58
ACTUAL AND SIMULATED PROPORTIONS OF WOMEN
BY EARNED INCOME CUMULATED OVER 7-YEAR PERIOD:
NONBLACK WOMEN 21-46 YEARS OF AGE AND UNMARRIED IN 1971

Earned income cumulated over 7-year period	Actual	Inertia	Dummy	Split	A	B	C
$0	.23	.21	.12	.11	.28	.22	.21
Less than $10,000	.15	.19	.17	.23	.18	.22	.24
$10,000 - 19,999	.23	.17	.26	.20	.22	.15	.17
$20,000 - 29,999	.15	.21	.17	.25	.14	.27	.11
$30,000 - 39,999	.07	.10	.15	.10	.11	.06	.12
Over $39,999	.17	.12	.11	.11	.07	.06	.14
Pseudo chi-square statistic (n=84)		7	15	18	8	19	10

TABLE D.59
ACTUAL AND SIMULATED PROPORTIONS OF WOMEN
BY NUMBER OF YEARS WORKED OUT OF 7:
WOMEN 21-46 YEARS OF AGE AND UNMARRIED IN 1971
WHO RECEIVED AFDC SOMETIME DURING 7-YEAR PERIOD

Number of years worked out of 7	Actual	Inertia	Dummy	Split	A	B	C
0	.29	.09	.13	.09	.14	.12	.07
1-2	.21	.17	.13	.18	.17	.18	.25
3-4	.21	.25	.19	.22	.23	.21	.22
5-6	.15	.20	.27	.32	.20	.14	.22
7	.15	.28	.29	.19	.26	.34	.23
Pseudo chi-square statistic (n=68)		19	24	23	12	23	17

TABLE D.60
ACTUAL AND SIMULATED PROPORTIONS OF WOMEN
BY NUMBER OF YEARS WORKED OUT OF 7:
WOMEN 21-46 YEARS OF AGE AND UNMARRIED IN 1971
WHO DID NOT RECEIVE AFDC DURING 7-YEAR PERIOD

Number of years worked out of 7	Actual	Inertia	Dummy	Split	A	B	C
0	.04	.04	.02	.03	.06	.03	.03
1-2	.04	.10	.08	.11	.08	.11	.08
3-4	.12	.11	.13	.14	.15	.13	.15
5-6	.18	.18	.24	.21	.19	.20	.19
7	.62	.56	.52	.51	.52	.53	.55
Pseudo chi-square statistic (n=179)		17	15	27	13	25	10

TABLE D.61
ACTUAL AND SIMULATED PROPORTIONS OF WOMEN
BY NUMBER OF YEARS WORKED OUT OF 7:
WOMEN 47-64 YEARS OF AGE AND UNMARRIED IN 1971 WHO
RECEIVED SOCIAL SECURITY SOMETIME DURING 7-YEAR PERIOD

Number of years worked out of 7	Actual	Inertia	Dummy	Split	A	B	C
0	.72	.47	.28	.35	.38	.44	.41
1-2	.19	.22	.17	.19	.15	.16	.19
3-4	.03	.13	.24	.10	.11	.09	.12
5-6	.06	.06	.14	.13	.15	.19	.16
7	.00	.12	.17	.23	.19	.12	.12
Pseudo chi-square statistic (n=32)		21	89	59	54	41	39

TABLE D.62
ACTUAL AND SIMULATED PROPORTIONS OF WOMEN
BY NUMBER OF YEARS WORKED OUT OF 7:
WOMEN 47-64 YEARS OF AGE AND UNMARRIED IN 1971 WHO
DID NOT RECEIVE SOCIAL SECURITY DURING 7-YEAR PERIOD

Number of years worked out of 7	Actual	Inertia	Dummy	Split	A	B	C
0	.15	.14	.15	.13	.24	.15	.13
1-2	.06	.14	.15	.10	.10	.14	.15
3-4	.09	.18	.09	.13	.11	.14	.15
5-6	.19	.12	.27	.25	.18	.15	.16
7	.51	.41	.35	.39	.36	.42	.41
Pseudo chi-square statistic (n=113)		27	25	11	15	18	23

Appendix D

TABLE D.63
ACTUAL AND SIMULATED PROPORTIONS OF WOMEN BY EARNED INCOME
CUMULATED OVER 7-YEAR PERIOD: WOMEN 21-46 AND UNMARRIED IN
1971 WHO RECEIVED AFDC SOMETIME DURING 7-YEAR PERIOD

Earned income cumulated over 7-year period	Actual	Inertia	Dummy	Split	A	B	C
$0	.29	.09	.13	.10	.17	.14	.07
Less than $10,000	.43	.39	.25	.35	.34	.34	.54
$10,000 - 19,999	.13	.22	.29	.28	.21	.21	.15
$20,000 - 29,999	.09	.16	.24	.18	.12	.20	.09
Over $29,999	.06	.14	.10	.09	.15	.11	.14
Pseudo chi-square statistic (n=68)		25	43	28	18	22	21

TABLE D.64
ACTUAL AND SIMULATED PROPORTIONS OF WOMEN BY EARNED INCOME
CUMULATED OVER 7-YEAR PERIOD: WOMEN 21-46 AND UNMARRIED IN
1971 WHO DID NOT RECEIVE AFDC DURING 7-YEAR PERIOD

Earned income cumulated over 7-year period	Actual	Inertia	Dummy	Split	A	B	C
$0	.06	.04	.02	.03	.06	.04	.05
Less than $10,000	.16	.20	.16	.19	.16	.19	.23
$10,000 - 19,999	.20	.21	.21	.23	.23	.33	.16
$20,000 - 29,999	.22	.24	.32	.29	.26	.24	.18
$30,000 - 39,999	.18	.18	.14	.14	.17	.10	.13
$40,000 - 59,999	.14	.08	.13	.11	.11	.07	.19
Over $59,999	.05	.04	.02	.01	.01	.02	.06
Pseudo chi-square statistic (n=179)		8	18	17	9	33	14

TABLE D.65
ACTUAL AND SIMULATED PROPORTIONS OF WOMEN BY EARNED INCOME CUMULATED OVER 7-YEAR PERIOD: WOMEN 47-64 YEARS OF AGE AND UNMARRIED IN 1971 WHO RECEIVED SOCIAL SECURITY SOMETIME DURING 7-YEAR PERIOD

Earned income cumulated over 7-year period	Actual	Inertia	Dummy	Split	A	B	C
$0	.72	.50	.28	.35	.42	.47	.44
Less than $10,000	.28	.37	.41	.29	.27	.31	.37
$10,000 - 19,999	.00	.06	.17	.13	.15	.12	.06
Over $19,999	.00	.06	.14	.22	.16	.09	.12
Pseudo chi-square statistic (n=32)		7	31	21	14	9	12

TABLE D.66
ACTUAL AND SIMULATED PROPORTIONS OF WOMEN BY EARNED INCOME CUMULATED OVER 7-YEAR PERIOD: WOMEN 47-64 YEARS OF AGE AND UNMARRIED IN 1971 WHO DID NOT RECEIVE SOCIAL SECURITY DURING 7-YEAR PERIOD

Earned income cumulated over 7-year period	Actual	Inertia	Dummy	Split	A	B	C
$0	.16	.16	.15	.13	.25	.16	.18
Less than $10,000	.16	.26	.18	.22	.18	.26	.26
$10,000 - 19,999	.29	.17	.24	.22	.19	.21	.19
$20,000 - 29,999	.16	.20	.23	.23	.19	.23	.11
$30,000 - 39,999	.09	.10	.12	.11	.10	.06	.15
Over $39,999	.14	.10	.08	.08	.07	.08	.12
Pseudo chi-square statistic (n=113)		15	9	12	15	17	18

Appendix E

Appendix E. Out-of-Sample Simulation Results for All Models

TABLE E.1
ACTUAL AND SIMULATED PROPORTIONS OF INDIVIDUALS
BY EARNED INCOME CUMULATED OVER 2-YEAR PERIOD

Earned income cumulated over 2-year period	Actual	Standard	Dummy	Split	A	B	C	Inertia
$0	.26	.24	.30	.32	.30	.29	.29	.30
Less than $1,000	.10	.05	.03	.04	.05	.06	.09	.06
$1,000-2,499	.07	.09	.06	.06	.07	.07	.07	.07
$2,500-4,999	.10	.14	.11	.11	.09	.10	.09	.10
$5,000-7,499	.10	.11	.11	.10	.10	.10	.08	.10
$7,500-9,999	.09	.08	.09	.09	.10	.09	.07	.09
$10,000-14,999	.13	.12	.13	.13	.15	.14	.11	.14
$15,000-19,999	.08	.07	.07	.07	.07	.07	.07	.07
$20,000-29,999	.05	.06	.06	.06	.05	.06	.08	.06
$30,000-49,999	.01	.03	.02	.03	.02	.02	.03	.02
Over $49,999	.00	.00	.00	.00	.00	.00	.01	.00
Pseudo chi-square statistic (n=9747)		657	648	668	383	274	762	300

TABLE E.2
ACTUAL AND SIMULATED PROPORTIONS OF WOMEN 14-20 YEARS OF
AGE IN 1981 BY EARNED INCOME CUMULATED OVER 2-YEAR PERIOD

Earned income cumulated over 2-year period	Actual	Standard	Dummy	Split	A	B	C	Inertia
$0	.44	.65	.61	.68	.65	.66	.67	.65
Less than $1,000	.25	.07	.07	.07	.09	.10	.11	.08
$1,000-2,499	.11	.09	.09	.07	.09	.05	.05	.08
$2,500-4,999	.10	.10	.09	.08	.06	.07	.04	.07
$5,000-7,499	.05	.05	.07	.03	.02	.03	.03	.04
Over $7,499	.04	.04	.08	.08	.08	.07	.10	.09
Pseudo chi-square statistic (n=840)		196	208	275	1235	229	307	250

TABLE E.3
ACTUAL AND SIMULATED PROPORTIONS OF WOMEN 21-46 AND MARRIED
IN 1981 BY EARNED INCOME CUMULATED OVER 2-YEAR PERIOD

Earned income cumulated over 2-year period	Actual	Standard	Dummy	Split	A	B	C	Inertia
$0	.22	.11	.22	.23	.21	.21	.21	.21
Less than $1,000	.13	.07	.05	.05	.08	.10	.13	.09
$1,000-2,499	.11	.18	.11	.10	.12	.10	.12	.13
$2,500-4,999	.15	.27	.21	.21	.18	.19	.16	.19
$5,000-7,499	.13	.18	.17	.18	.16	.15	.11	.15
$7,500-9,999	.11	.09	.10	.11	.11	.10	.09	.09
$10,000-14,999	.10	.08	.09	.09	.09	.10	.11	.08
Over $14,999	.04	.02	.05	.03	.04	.04	.06	.04
Pseudo chi-square statistic (n=1724)		448	155	168	59	39	34	65

Appendix E

TABLE E.4
ACTUAL AND SIMULATED PROPORTIONS OF WOMEN 21-46 AND UNMARRIED
IN 1981 BY EARNED INCOME CUMULATED OVER 2-YEAR PERIOD

Earned income over 2 years	Actual	Standard	Dummy	Split	A	B	C	Inertia
$0	.16	.05	.10	.12	.12	.13	.12	.14
Less than $1,000	.09	.03	.02	.05	.06	.05	.09	.05
$1,000-2,499	.06	.13	.07	.05	.06	.08	.09	.08
$2,500-4,999	.14	.22	.16	.14	.14	.19	.13	.16
$5,000-7,499	.18	.20	.20	.22	.19	.15	.13	.14
$7,500-9,999	.15	.14	.15	.16	.15	.15	.12	.12
$10,000-14,999	.16	.15	.18	.16	.19	.14	.17	.19
Over $14,999	.05	.06	.10	.09	.09	.09	.14	.12
Pseudo chi-square (n=9747)	233	120	63	51	77	184	131	

TABLE E.5
ACTUAL AND SIMULATED PROPORTIONS OF WOMEN 47-64 AND MARRIED
IN 1981 BY EARNED INCOME CUMULATED OVER 2-YEAR PERIOD

Earned income over 2 years	Actual	Standard	Dummy	Split	A	B	C	Inertia
$0	.45	.37	.49	.46	.49	.51	.50	.52
Less than $1,000	.09	.07	.03	.05	.07	.06	.09	.06
$1,000-2,499	.10	.15	.06	.09	.08	.11	.08	.10
$2,500-4,999	.11	.19	.15	.15	.10	.14	.10	.11
$5,000-7,499	.08	.12	.10	.09	.08	.06	.07	.08
$7,500-9,999	.07	.04	.07	.06	.07	.05	.05	.05
$10,000-14,999	.06	.04	.06	.06	.07	.04	.06	.04
Over $14,999	.05	.00	.03	.04	.03	.02	.05	.02
Pseudo chi-square (n=594)	114	52	23	13	37	10	30	

TABLE E.6
ACTUAL AND SIMULATED PROPORTIONS OF WOMEN 46-64
YEARS OF AGE AND UNMARRIED IN 1981 BY EARNED
INCOME CUMULATED OVER 2-YEAR PERIOD

Earned income cumulated over 2-year period	Actual	Standard	Dummy	Split	A	B	C	Inertia
$0	.40	.25	.39	.40	.40	.41	.42	.41
Less than $1,000	.09	.05	.03	.02	.04	.04	.06	.05
$1,000-2,499	.06	.17	.07	.06	.06	.09	.08	.07
$2,500-4,999	.12	.20	.14	.15	.10	.12	.10	.13
$5,000-7,499	.11	.15	.13	.16	.13	.13	.10	.10
$7,500-9,999	.08	.07	.10	.09	.09	.09	.07	.06
$10,000-14,999	.11	.09	.08	.08	.12	.08	.11	.11
Over $14,999	.02	.03	.04	.04	.07	.04	.05	.05
Pseudo chi-square statistic (n=388)		137	32	43	63	29	26	28

TABLE E.7
ACTUAL AND SIMULATED PROPORTIONS OF
WOMEN 65+ YEARS OF AGE IN 1981 BY EARNED
INCOME CUMULATED OVER 2-YEAR PERIOD

Earned income cumulated over 2-year period	Actual	Standard	Dummy	Split	A	B	C	Inertia
$0	.84	.88	.90	.91	.91	.90	.89	.88
Less than $1,000	.08	.04	.04	.03	.02	.03	.04	.04
$1,000-2,499	.03	.04	.03	.03	.03	.03	.02	.03
Over $2,499	.04	.03	.02	.04	.02	.03	.05	.04
Pseudo chi-square statistic (n=468)		13	16	17	28	18	13	10

Appendix F. Simulation Populations for Models
with Log-Linear Wage Equations, and Results
Using $20 Wage Cutoff

TABLE F.1
ACTUAL PROPORTIONS OF INDIVIDUALS BY NUMBER
OF YEARS WORKED OUT OF 7

Number of years worked out of 7	Whole sample	Samples used for model variants with log-linear wage equations					
		Standard	Dummy	Split	A	B	Inertia
0	.11	.11	.11	.11	.11	.12	.11
1-2	.09	.09	.09	.09	.09	.10	.09
3-4	.12	.12	.12	.12	.12	.12	.12
5-6	.15	.16	.16	.16	.15	.16	.16
7	.52	.52	.52	.52	.51	.50	.50
n	2657	2525	2530	2552	2377	2406	2391
Chi-square statistic		2	2	2	0	9	4

TABLE F.2
ACTUAL PROPORTIONS OF WOMEN 14-20 YEARS OF AGE
IN 1971 BY NUMBER OF YEARS WORKED OUT OF 7

Number of years worked out of 7	Whole sample	Standard	Dummy	Split	A	B	Inertia
0	.07	.06	.07	.07	.06	.06	.07
1-2	.23	.23	.23	.23	.24	.24	.23
3-4	.28	.25	.26	.27	.27	.27	.27
5-6	.31	.32	.31	.31	.30	.31	.32
7	.13	.13	.13	.13	.13	.12	.12
n	272	262	266	268	258	263	265
Chi-square statistic		1	0	0	1	1	0

Columns 3–8: Samples used for model variants with log-linear wage equations

TABLE F.3
ACTUAL PROPORTIONS OF WOMEN 21-46 YEARS OF AGE AND
MARRIED IN 1971 BY NUMBER OF YEARS WORKED OUT OF 7

Number of years worked out of 7	Whole sample	Standard	Dummy	Split	A	B	Inertia
0	.17	.17	.16	.17	.17	.17	.17
1-2	.15	.16	.16	.15	.16	.15	.15
3-4	.15	.15	.16	.16	.16	.15	.16
5-6	.22	.22	.23	.22	.21	.23	.22
7	.30	.30	.29	.29	.29	.30	.30
n	424	412	409	411	403	411	411
Chi-square statistic		0	1	0	1	0	0

Columns 3–8: Samples used for model variants with log-linear wage equations

TABLE F.4
ACTUAL PROPORTIONS OF WOMEN 21-46 YEARS OF AGE AND
UNMARRIED IN 1971 BY NUMBER OF YEARS WORKED OUT OF 7

Number of years worked out of 7	Whole sample	Samples used for model variants with log-linear wage equations					
		Standard	Dummy	Split	A	B	Inertia
0	.11	.12	.11	.11	.12	.12	.12
1-2	.08	.09	.09	.09	.09	.09	.09
3-4	.14	.14	.14	.14	.15	.14	.15
5-6	.17	.17	.16	.17	.17	.16	.18
7	.47	.49	.50	.48	.47	.48	.47
n	247	232	232	244	225	225	221
Chi-square statistic		1	1	0	1	1	1

TABLE F.5
ACTUAL PROPORTIONS OF WOMEN 47-64 YEARS OF AGE AND
MARRIED IN 1971 BY NUMBER OF YEARS WORKED OUT OF 7

Number of years worked out of 7	Whole sample	Samples used for model variants with log-linear wage equations					
		Standard	Dummy	Split	A	B	Inertia
0	.38	.39	.38	.38	.38	.39	.38
1-2	.13	.12	.13	.13	.14	.13	.13
3-4	.12	.12	.12	.11	.13	.12	.13
5-6	.19	.19	.18	.19	.19	.20	.20
7	.18	.17	.18	.18	.16	.16	.17
n	119	114	115	115	110	116	111
Chi-square statistic	0	0	0	0	0	0	0

TABLE F.6
ACTUAL PROPORTIONS OF WOMEN 47-64 YEARS OF AGE AND
UNMARRIED IN 1971 BY NUMBER OF YEARS WORKED OUT OF 7

Number of years worked out of 7	Whole sample	Standard	Dummy	Split	A	B	Inertia
0	.28	.27	.26	.27	.27	.30	.30
1-2	.08	.09	.09	.09	.10	.10	.09
3-4	.08	.08	.07	.08	.08	.07	.06
5-6	.16	.16	.16	.16	.14	.16	.15
7	.40	.40	.41	.39	.40	.36	.39
n	145	140	138	142	124	132	131
Chi-square statistic	0	1	0	1	2	1

TABLE F.7
ACTUAL PROPORTIONS OF WOMEN 65+ YEARS OF AGE
IN 1971 BY NUMBER OF YEARS WORKED OUT OF 7

Number of years worked out of 7	Whole sample	Standard	Dummy	Split	A	B	Inertia
0	.60	.60	.61	.62	.63	.62	.62
1-2	.21	.21	.21	.22	.20	.22	.18
3-4	.14	.14	.12	.13	.11	.11	.15
5-6	.02	.02	.02	.00	.02	.02	.02
7	.03	.03	.04	.04	.04	.04	.04
n	57	57	56	55	54	55	55
Chi-square statistic	0	0	1	1	1	0

Appendix F

TABLE F.8
ACTUAL PROPORTIONS OF INDIVIDUALS BY EARNED INCOME CUMULATED OVER 7-YEAR PERIOD

Earned income cumulated over 7-year period	Whole sample	Stand.	Dummy	Split	A	B	Inertia
$0	.12	.12	.11	.12	.12	.12	.12
Less than $10,000	.23	.23	.24	.24	.24	.24	.25
$10,000-19,999	.14	.14	.14	.14	.14	.14	.14
$20,000-29,999	.11	.11	.11	.11	.11	.11	.10
$30,000-39,999	.09	.09	.09	.09	.09	.09	.09
$40,000-59,999	.14	.14	.13	.14	.14	.13	.14
$60,000-79,999	.10	.09	.10	.09	.09	.09	.09
$80,000-99,999	.04	.04	.04	.04	.03	.04	.04
$100,000-119,999	.02	.02	.02	.02	.02	.01	.01
$120,000-139,999	.01	.01	.01	.01	.01	.01	.01
Over $139,999	.01	.01	.01	.01	.01	.01	.01
n	2657	2525	2530	2552	2377	2406	2391
Chi-square statistic		3	5	4	10	19	23

Samples used for model variants with log-linear wage equations

TABLE F.9
ACTUAL PROPORTIONS OF WOMEN 14-20 YEARS OF AGE
IN 1971 BY EARNED INCOME CUMULATED OVER 7-YEAR PERIOD

Earned income cumulated over 7-year period	Whole sample	Stand.	Dummy	Split	A	B	Inertia
$0	.08	.08	.08	.08	.08	.07	.08
Less than $10,000	.57	.57	.57	.58	.59	.58	.58
$10,000-19,999	.23	.23	.23	.23	.22	.23	.23
$20,000-29,999	.08	.08	.08	.07	.07	.08	.07
$30,000-39,999	.04	.04	.04	.04	.04	.03	.04
Over $39,999	.00	.00	.00	.00	.00	.00	.00
n	272	262	266	268	258	263	265
Chi-square statistic		0	0	0	1	1	0

Samples used for model variants with log-linear wage equations

TABLE F.10
ACTUAL PROPORTIONS OF WOMEN 21-46 YEARS OF AGE AND MARRIED
IN 1971 BY EARNED INCOME CUMULATED OVER 7-YEAR PERIOD

Earned income cumulated over 7-year period	Whole sample	Stand.	Dummy	Split	A	B	Inertia
$0	.17	.17	.16	.17	.17	.17	.17
Less than $10,000	.40	.39	.41	.40	.40	.39	.40
$10,000-19,999	.20	.20	.20	.20	.19	.20	.19
$20,000-29,999	.12	.12	.11	.12	.12	.12	.11
$30,000-39,999	.07	.07	.07	.07	.07	.07	.07
$40,000-59,999	.05	.05	.04	.05	.04	.04	.05
Over $59,999	.00	.00	.00	.00	.00	.00	.00
n	424	412	409	411	403	411	411
Chi-square statistic		0	1	0	1	1	0

Samples used for model variants with log-linear wage equations

Appendix F

TABLE F.11
ACTUAL PROPORTIONS OF WOMEN 21-46 YEARS OF AGE AND UNMARRIED
IN 1971 BY EARNED INCOME CUMULATED OVER 7-YEAR PERIOD

Earned income cumulated over 7-year period	Whole sample	Stand.	Dummy	Split	A	B	Inertia
$0	.12	.12	.12	.12	.12	.13	.12
Less than $10,000	.23	.23	.23	.23	.24	.24	.24
$10,000-19,999	.18	.18	.18	.18	.19	.18	.19
$20,000-29,999	.19	.19	.19	.18	.19	.19	.19
$30,000-39,999	.15	.15	.14	.15	.14	.15	.13
$40,000-59,999	.10	.10	.11	.10	.09	.09	.11
$60,000-79,999	.02	.02	.02	.02	.01	.01	.01
$80,000-99,999	.01	.00	.01	.01	.00	.01	.00
Over $99,999	.00	.00	.00	.00	.00	.00	.00
n	247	232	232	244	225	225	221
Chi-square statistic		2	0	0	4	2	5

Samples used for model variants with log-linear wage equations

TABLE F.12
ACTUAL PROPORTIONS OF WOMEN 47-64 YEARS OF AGE AND MARRIED
IN 1971 BY EARNED INCOME CUMULATED OVER 7-YEAR PERIOD

Earned income cumulated over 7-year period	Whole sample	Stand.	Dummy	Split	A	B	Inertia
$0	.38	.39	.38	.38	.38	.39	.38
Less than $10,000	.29	.29	.30	.30	.29	.28	.30
$10,000-19,999	.15	.16	.16	.16	.15	.15	.15
$20,000-29,999	.08	.07	.08	.06	.08	.08	.07
$30,000-39,999	.02	.03	.02	.03	.02	.03	.02
$40,000-59,999	.07	.05	.05	.06	.05	.06	.06
$60,000-79,999	.02	.02	.02	.02	.02	.01	.02
Over $79,999	.00	.00	.00	.00	.00	.00	.00
n	119	114	115	115	110	116	111
Chi-square statistic		1	1	1	1	1	0

Samples used for model variants with log-linear wage equations

TABLE F.13
ACTUAL PROPORTIONS OF WOMEN 47-64 YEARS OF AGE AND UNMARRIED
IN 1971 BY EARNED INCOME CUMULATED OVER 7-YEAR PERIOD

Earned income cumulated over 7-year period	Whole sample	Stand.	Dummy	Split	A	B	Inertia
$0	.28	.28	.27	.28	.28	.31	.31
Less than $10,000	.19	.18	.19	.19	.20	.20	.18
$10,000-19,999	.23	.24	.24	.23	.25	.20	.24
$20,000-29,999	.12	.13	.12	.12	.11	.14	.10
$30,000-39,999	.07	.07	.07	.07	.07	.07	.08
$40,000-59,999	.06	.06	.06	.06	.05	.06	.06
$60,000-79,999	.03	.03	.03	.03	.03	.01	.02
$80,000-99,999	.02	.01	.02	.02	.00	.01	.01
Over $99,999	.00	.00	.00	.00	.00	.00	.00
n	145	140	138	142	124	132	131
Chi-square statistic		1	0	0	3	4	9

TABLE F.14
ACTUAL PROPORTIONS OF WOMEN 65+ YEARS OF AGE
IN 1971 BY EARNED INCOME CUMULATED OVER 7-YEAR PERIOD

Earned income cumulated over 7-year period	Whole sample	Stand.	Dummy	Split	A	B	Inertia
$0	.68	.68	.68	.69	.70	.69	.71
Less than $10,000	.30	.30	.30	.29	.28	.31	.27
$10,000-19,999	.02	.02	.02	.02	.02	.00	.02
Over $19,999	.00	.00	.00	.00	.00	.00	.00
n	57	57	56	55	54	55	55
Chi-square statistic		0	0	0	0	1	0

TABLE F.15
ACTUAL AND SIMULATED PROPORTIONS OF WOMEN 21-46 YEARS OF AGE AND MARRIED IN 1971 BY EARNED INCOME CUMULATED OVER 7-YEAR PERIOD

Earned income cumulated over 7-year period	Actual	Stand.	Dummy	Split	A	B	C	Inertia
$0	.17	.01	.12	.17	.16	.14	.15	.15
Less than $10,000	.40	.43	.32	.32	.37	.37	.35	.38
$10,000-19,999	.20	.37	.32	.28	.23	.18	.19	.20
$20,000-29,999	.12	.13	.13	.14	.11	.14	.12	.12
$30,000-39,999	.07	.03	.07	.06	.08	.09	.10	.08
Over $39,999	.05	.02	.04	.03	.05	.07	.09	.08
Pseudo chi-square statistic (n=424)		144	45	26	4	11	23	10

Model variants with $20 wage cut-off

TABLE F.16
ACTUAL AND SIMULATED PROPORTIONS OF WOMEN 47-64 YEARS OF AGE AND MARRIED IN 1971 BY EARNED INCOME CUMULATED OVER 7-YEAR PERIOD

Earned income cumulated over 7-year period	Actual	Stand.	Dummy	Split	A	B	C	Inertia
$0	.38	.10	.34	.36	.40	.39	.36	.37
Less than $10,000	.29	.45	.26	.23	.29	.27	.26	.26
$10,000-19,999	.15	.34	.16	.23	.15	.18	.13	.18
$20,000-29,999	.08	.05	.15	.13	.07	.10	.10	.08
Over $29,999	.11	.06	.09	.05	.08	.06	.14	.11
Pseudo chi-square statistic (n=119)		68	9	14	1	4	2	1

Model variants with $20 wage cut-off

Appendix F

TABLE F.17
ACTUAL AND SIMULATED PROPORTIONS OF WOMEN 21-46 AND MARRIED
IN 1971 BY EARNED INCOME CUMULATED OVER 2-YEAR PERIOD

Earned income over 2 years	Actual	Stand.	Dummy	Split	A	B	C	Inertia
$0	.22	.10	.22	.22	.21	.21	.21	.21
Less than $1,000	.13	.05	.05	.06	.08	.08	.13	.08
$1,000-2,499	.11	.20	.09	.09	.10	.13	.12	.13
$2,500-4,999	.15	.30	.21	.23	.18	.20	.16	.20
$5,000-7,499	.13	.16	.18	.19	.16	.12	.11	.13
$7,500-9,999	.11	.09	.11	.10	.10	.10	.09	.10
$10,000-14,999	.10	.06	.09	.07	.10	.08	.11	.09
Over $14,999	.04	.03	.04	.03	.04	.06	.06	.05
Pseu.chi-sq.stat.(n=1724)	633	167	214	59	96	34	76

Model variants with $20 wage cut-off

TABLE F.18
ACTUAL AND SIMULATED PROPORTIONS OF WOMEN 47-64 AND MARRIED
IN 1971 BY EARNED INCOME CUMULATED OVER 2-YEAR PERIOD

Earned income over 2 years	Actual	Stand.	Dummy	Split	A	B	C	Inertia
$0	.45	.33	.45	.47	.48	.50	.50	.49
Less than $1,000	.09	.09	.05	.06	.07	.06	.09	.08
$1,000-2,499	.10	.17	.09	.09	.07	.11	.08	.10
$2,500-4,999	.11	.20	.14	.14	.09	.12	.10	.11
$5,000-7,499	.08	.10	.12	.09	.10	.09	.07	.09
$7,500-9,999	.07	.04	.07	.06	.07	.05	.05	.04
$10,000-14,999	.06	.03	.05	.05	.07	.05	.06	.05
Over $14,999	.05	.02	.04	.03	.04	.02	.05	.04
Pseu.chi-sq.stat.(n=882)	181	45	28	24	39	15	20

Model variants with $20 wage cut-off

References

Amemiya, T. "Regression Analysis when the Dependent Variable Is Truncated Normal." Econometrica, 1973, 997-1016.
Amemiya, T. "Tobit Models: A Survey." Journal of Econometrics, 1984, 3-61.
Arabmazar, A. and B. Schmidt. "An Investigation of the Robustness of the Tobit Estimator to Non-Normality." Econometrica, 1982, 1055-1063.
Arrow, K. "The Theory of Discrimination." In O. Ashenfelter and A. Rees (Eds.), Discrimination in Labor Markets, Princeton University Press, 1973, 3-33.
Ashenfelter, O. "Estimating the Effect of Training Programs on Earnings." Review of Economics and Statistics, 1978, 47-57.
de Beauvoir, Simone. The Second Sex. Translated and edited by H.M. Parshley, Bantam Books, 1952.
Becker, G. Human Capital. University of Chicago Press, 1964, Second Edition 1975.
Becker, G. "A Theory of the Allocation of Time." Economic Journal, 1965, 493-517.
Becker, G. A Treatise on the Family. Harvard University Press, 1981.
Becker, G., Landes, E.M. and R.T. Michael. "An Economic Analysis of Marital Instability." Journal of Political Economy, 1977, 1141-1187.
Ben-Porath. "Labor-Force Participation and the Supply of Labor." Journal of Political Economy, 1973, 697-704.
Bergmann, B. "The Economic Risks of Being a Housewife." American Economic Review, Papers and Proceedings, 1981, 81-86.
Bergmann, B. and I. Adelman. "The 1973 Report of the President's Council of Economic Advisers: The Economic Role of Women." American Economic Review, 1973, 509-514.
Bowen, W.G. and T.A. Finegan. The Economics of Labor Force Participation. Princeton University Press, 1969.
Cain, G.G. Married Women in the Labor Force. University of Chicago Press, 1966.
Cain G.G. "The Economic Analysis of Labor Supply: An Essay on Developments Since Mincer." Paper presented at a Social Science Research Council conference on labor supply, December 3, 1982.
Cain, G.G. and M. Dooley. "Estimation of a Model of Labor Supply, Fertility, and Wages of Married Women." Journal of Political Economy, 1976, S179-S199.
Cain, G.G. and H.W. Watts (Eds.). Income Maintenance and Labor Supply. Academic Press, 1973.
Caldwell, S.B. "Microanalytic Modeling of Household Energy Demand." In M. Mickle and W. Voyt (Eds.), Modeling and Simulation, Vol. 10, No. 3, 1979, 1279-1287.
Caldwell, S.B. "Modeling Demographic-Economic Interactions: Micro, Macro and Linked Micro/Macro Strategies." Socio-Economic Planning Science, 1983, 365-372.
Carliner, G., C. Robinson and N. Tomes. "Female Labor Supply and Fertility in Canada." Canadian Journal of Economics, 1980, 46-64. 1980, 371-378.
Christ, C.F. Econometric Models and Methods. John Wiley and Sons, Inc., 1966.
Cogan, J. "Labor Supply with Costs of Labor Market Entry." In J.P. Smith (Ed.), Female Labor Supply: Theory and Estimation, Princeton University Press, 1980, 327-359.
Cogan, J. "Fixed Costs and Labor Supply." Econometrica, 1981, 945-964.

Conway, D.A. and H.V. Roberts. "Reverse Regression, Fairness, and Employment Discrimination." Journal of Business and Economic Statistics, 1983, 75-85.

Conway, D.A. and H.V. Roberts. "Rejoinder to Comments on 'Reverse Regression, Fairness, and Employment Discrimination'." Journal of Business and Economic Statistics, 1984, 126-139.

Corcoran, M. "The Employment and Wage Consequences of Teenage Women's Nonemployment." In R.B. Freeman and D.A. Wise (Eds.), The Youth Labor Market Problem: Its Nature, Causes, and Consequences, University of Chicago Press, 1982, 391-419.

Cullen, D. and A. Nakamura. "U.S. - Canadian Historical Comparison: The Impact of Differing Occupational and Industrial Structures on Woman's Labour Force Participation." Paper presented at the Canadian Sociology and Anthropology Association Meeting, Fredericton, N.B., June, 1977, revised and updated 1984.

Dagenais, M.G., A. Nakamura and M. Nakamura. "Estimating Transition Probabilities from Panel Data." Discussion paper, Department of Economics, University of Montreal, 1985.

DaVanzo, J., D.N. De Tray and D.H. Greenberg. "The Sensitivity of Male Labor Supply Estimates to Choice of Assumptions." Review of Economics and Statistics, 1976, 313-325.

Deaton, A. and J. Muellbauer. Economics and Consumer Behavior. Cambridge University Press, 1980.

Dooley, M.D. "Labor Supply and Fertility of Married Women: An Analysis with Grouped and Individual Data from the 1970 U.S. Census." Journal of Human Resources, 1982, 499-532.

Durbin, J. "Errors in Variables." Review of the International Statistical Institute, 1954, 23-32.

Ehrenberg, R.G. and R.S. Smith. Modern Labor Economics. Scott, Foresman and Co., 1982.

Eliasson, G. (Ed.). A Micro-to-Macro Model of the Swedish Economy. IUI Conferences Reports, Utgivna Publication, 1978.

Fama, E.F. and H. Babiak. "Dividend Policy: An Empirical Analysis." Journal of the American Statistical Association, 1968, 1132-1161.

Feldstein, M. "Errors in Variables." Review of the International Statistical Institute, 1974, 23-32.

Feldstein, M. and D.T. Ellwood. "Teenage Unemployment: What Is the Problem?" In R.B. Freeman and D.A. Wise (Eds.), The Youth Labor Market Problem: Its Nature, Causes, and Consequences, University of Chicago Press, 1982, 17-33.

Ferris, A. Indicators of Trends in the Status of American Women. Russell Sage Foundation, New York, 1971.

Flinn, C. and J.J. Heckman. "New Methods for Analyzing Structural Models of Labor Force Dynamics." Journal of Econometrics, 1982, 115-168.

Flinn, C. and J.J. Heckman. "Are Unemployment and Out of the Labor Force Behaviorally Distinct Labor Force States?" Journal of Labor Economics, 1983, 28-42.

Fraker, S. "Why Women Aren't Getting to the Top." FORTUNE, April 16, 1984, 40-45.

Freeman, R.B. and J.L. Medoff. "The Youth Labor Market Problem in the United States: An Overview." In R.B. Freeman and D.A. Wise (Eds.), The Youth Labor Market Problem: Its Nature, Causes, and Consequences, University of Chicago Press, 1982, 35-74.

Fuller, W.A. "Some Properties of a Modification of the Limited Information Estimator." Econometrica, 1977, 939-953.

Fuchs, V.R. How We Live: An Economic Perspective on Americans from Birth to Death. Harvard University Press, 1983.

Garfinkel, I. "On Estimating the Labor-Supply Effects of a Negative Income Tax." In G.G. Cain and H.W. Watts (Eds.), Income Maintenance and Labor Supply,

References

Rand-McNally, 1973.
Gintis, H. "Education, Technology, and Characteristics of Worker Productivity." American Economic Review, 1971, 266-279.
Glick, P. and A. Norton. "Perspectives on the Recent Upturn in Divorce and Remarriage." Demography, August 1973.
Goldberger, A.S. "Linear Regression After Selection." Journal of Econometrics, 1981, 357-366.
Goldberger, A.S. "Abnormal Selection Bias." In Studies in Econometrics, Time Series, and Multivariate Statistics, Academic Press, 1983, 67-84.
Goldberger, A.S. "Reverse Regression and Salary Discrimination." Paper presented at the winter meetings of the Econometric Society, San Francisco, December 28-30, 1983, revised January 1984.
Goldberger, A.S. "Redirecting Reverse Regression." Journal of Business and Economic Statistics, 1984, 114-116.
Gould, S.J. "Sex, Drugs, Disasters, and the Extinction of Dinosaurs." Discover, March 1984, 67-72.
Gramm, W.I. "Household Utility Maximization and the Working Wife." American Economic Review, 1975, 90-100.
Greene, W.H. "Sample Selection Bias as a Specification Error: Comment." Econometrica, 1981, 795-798.
Griliches, Z. "Estimating the Returns to Schooling: Some Econometric Problems." Econometrica, 1977, 1-22.
Gronau, R. "Wage Comparisons - A Selectivity Bias." Journal of Political Economy 82, 1974, 1119-1143.
Gross, E. "Plus ca Change ...? The Sexual Structure of Occupations Over Time." Social Problems, 1968, 198-208.
Gunderson, M. "Work Patterns." In C.G.A. Cook (Ed.), Opportunity for Choice, Statistics Canada in association with the C.D. Howe Research Institute, Ottawa, 1976, 93-142.
Hall, R.E. "Wages, Income, and Hours of Work in the U.S. Labor Force." In G.G. Cain and H.W. Watts (Eds.), Income Maintenance and Labor Supply, 1973, 102-162.
Hausman, J. "The Effect of Wages, Taxes, and Fixed Costs on Women's Labor Force Participation." Journal of Public Economics, 1980, 161-194.
Heckman, J.J. "Shadow Prices, Market Wages and Labor Supply." Econometrica, 1974, 679-694.
Heckman, J.J. "The Common Structure of Statistical Models of Truncation, Sample Selection and Limited Dependent Variables and a Simple Estimator for Such Models." Annals of Economic and Social Measurement, 1976, 475-492.
Heckman, J.J. "A Partial Survey of Recent Research on the Labor Supply of Women." American Economic Review, 1978, 200-207.
Heckman, J.J. "New Evidence on the Dynamics of Female Labor Supply." Working paper, University of Chicago, 1978a.
Heckman, J.J. "The Sample Selection Bias as a Specification Error," Econometrica 47, 1979, 153-162.
Heckman, J.J. "The Sample Selection Bias as a Specification Error with an Application to the Estimation of Labor Supply Functions." In J.P. Smith (Ed.), Female Labor Supply: Theory and Estimation, Princeton University Press, 1980, 206-248.
Heckman, J.J. "Heterogeneity and State Dependence." In S. Rosen, (Ed.), Studies in Labor Markets, University of Chicago Press, 1981, 91-139.
Heckman, J.J. "Statistical Models for Discrete Panel Data." In C. Manski and D. McFadden (Eds.), The Structural Analysis of Discrete Data, C. Manski MIT Press, 1981a.
Heckman, J.J. "The Incidental Parameters Problem and the Problem of Initial Conditions in Estimating a Discrete Time-Discrete Data Stochastic Process." In

C. Manski and D. McFadden (Eds.), Structural Analysis of Discrete Data, MIT Press, 1981b.

Heckman, J.J. and T. Macurdy. "A Dynamic Model of Female Labor Supply." Review of Economic Studies, 1979, 41-74.

Heckman, J.J. and S. Polachek. "Empirical Evidence on the Functional Form of the Earnings - Schooling Relationship." Journal of the American Statistical Association, 1974, 350-354.

Heckman, J. and B. Singer. "A Method for Minimizing the Impact of Distributional Assumptions in Econometric Models for Duration Data." Econometrica, 1984, 271-230.

Heckman, J.J. and R.J. Willis. "A Beta Logistic Model for the Analysis of Sequential Labor Force Participation of Married Women." Journal of Political Economy, 1977, 27-58.

Heckman, J.J. and R.J. Willis. "Reply to Mincer and Ofek." Journal of Political Economy 87, 1979, 203-211.

Institute for Social Research. A Panel Study of Income Dynamics: 1978 Interviewing Year, Wave XI, University of Michigan, 1979.

Institute for Social Research. A Panel Study of Income Dynamics: Procedures and Tape Codes, 1979 Interviewing Year, University of Michigan, 1980.

Johnson, N.L. and S. Kotz. Distributions in Statistics, Vols. 1 and 4, Wiley, 1970, 1972.

Johnson, T.R. and J.H. Pencavel. "Dynamic Hours of Work Functions for Husbands, Wives and Single Females." Econometrica, 1984, 363-389.

Johnston, J. Econometric Methods, 2nd Edition, McGraw-Hill Book Company, 1972.

Juster, F.T. and F.P. Stafford. Time, Goods and Well-Being. Institute for Social Research, University of Michigan, 1984.

Kalachek, E.D., F.Q. Raines, and D. Larson. "The Determination of Labor Supply: A Dynamic Model." Industrial and Labor Relations Review, 1979, 367-377.

Kamalich, R.F., R. Fand and S.W. Polachek. "Discrimination: Fact or Fiction? An Examination Using an Alternative Approach." Southern Economic Journal, 1982, 450-461.

Kiefer, N. and G. Neumann. "An Empirical Job-Search Model with a Test of the Constant Reservation-Wage Hypothesis." Journal of Political Economy, 1979, 89-107.

Killingsworth, M. Labor Supply. Cambridge University Press, 1983.

Kmenta, J. Elements of Econometrics. Macmillan Company, 1971.

Kreps, J. and R. Clark. Sex, Age and Work: The Changing Composition of the Labor Force. Johns Hopkins University Press, 1975.

Kuznets, S. Economic Growth and Structure. Norton, New York, 1965.

Lazear, E. "Age, Experience, and Wage Growth." American Economic Review, 1976, 548-558.

Lewis, H.G. "Interes del Empleador en las Horas de Trabajo del Empleado." Cuadernos de Economia, 1969, 38-54.

Lewis, H.G. "Comments on Selectivity Biases in Wage Comparisons." Journal of Political Economy, 1974, 1145-1155.

Lin, K. and J. Kmenta. "Ridge Regression Under Alternative Loss Criteria." The Review of Economics and Statistics, 1982, 488-494.

Long, C.D. The Labor Force under Changing Income and Employment, Princeton University Press, 1958.

Long, J.E. and E.B. Jones. "Labor Force Entry and Exit by Married Women: A Longitudinal Analysis." The Review of Economics and Statistics, 1980, 1-6.

Lowe, G. The Canadian Union of Bank Employees: A Case Study, University of Toronto Press, 1978.

Malinvaud, E. "Estimation et Prevision dans les Modeles Economiques Autoregressifs." Review of the International Statistical Institute, 1961, 1-32.

Malinvaud, E. Statistical Methods of Econometrics, Rand McNally and Company, 1966.

References

Mangasarian, O.L. Nonlinear Programming, McGraw-Hill, 1969.

Massy, W.F., D.B. Montgomery and D.G. Morrison. Stochastic Models of Buying Behavior, MIT Press, 1970.

McDonald, G. and C. Robinson. "Cautionary Tales in Estimating Variance Components (Or: Throwing the Variance Out with the Bath Water)." Forthcoming in Journal of Labor Economics, 1984.

Merrilees, W.J. "Labour Market Segmentation in Canada: an Econometric Approach." Canadian Journal of Economics, 1982, 458-473.

Meyer, R.H. and D.A. Wise. "High School Preparation and Early Labor Force Experience." In R.B. Freeman and D.A. Wise (Eds.), The Youth Labor Market Problem: Its Nature, Causes, and Consequences, University of Chicago Press, 1982, 277-339.

Michael, R.T. "Education in Nonmarket Production." Journal of Political Economy, 1973, 306-327.

Mincer, J. "Labor Force Participation of Married Women: A Study of Labor Supply." In H.G. Lewis (Ed.), Aspects of Labor Economics, Princeton University Press, 1962, 63-97.

Mincer, J. "Schooling, Experience, and Earnings." National Bureau of Economic Research, 1974.

Mincer, J. and H. Ofek. "The Distribution of Lifetime Labor Force Participation of Married Women: Comment." Journal of Political Economy, 1979, 197-201.

Mincer, J. and S. Polachek. "Family Investments in Human Capital: Earnings of Women." In T.W. Schultz (Ed.), Economics of the Family, The University of Chicago Press, 1974, p. 397-429.

Morimune, K. "Improving the Limited-Information Maximum Likelihood Estimator When the Disturbances are Small." Journal of the American Statistical Association, 1978, 867-871.

Nagar, A.L. "The Bias and Moment Matrix of General k-class Estimators of the Parameters in Structural Equations." Econometrica, 1959, 575-595.

Nakamura, A. and M. Nakamura. "On Microanalytic Simulation and Its Applications in Population Projection." Journal of the Operational Research Society, 1978, 349-360.

Nakamura, A. and M. Nakamura. "A Comparison of the Labor Force Behavior of Married Women in the United States and Canada, with Special Attention to the Impact of Income Taxes." Econometrica, 1981, 451-489.

Nakamura, A. and M. Nakamura. "On the Relationships among Several Specification Error Tests Presented by Durbin, Wu and Hausman," Econometrica, 1981a, 1583-1588.

Nakamura, A. and M. Nakakmura. "Part-time and Full-time Work Behavior of Married Women: a Model with a Doubly Truncated Dependent Variable." Canadian Journal of Economics, 1983, 229-257.

Nakamura, A. and M. Nakamura. "Dynamic Models of the Labor Force Behavior of Married Women Which Can Be Estimated Using Limited Amounts of Past Information." Forthcoming in Journal of Econometrics, 1983a.

Nakamura, A. and M. Nakamura. "Modeling and Simulation of the Participation, Employment and Earnings Behavior of Married Women: An Application Using Sequential Heckit Analysis." Paper presented at the Econometric Society Meetings in San Francisco, December, 1983b.

Nakamura, A. and M. Nakamura. "On the Performance of Tests by Wu and by Hausman for Detecting the Ordinary Least Squares Bias Problem." Paper presented at an Econometrics Workshop at the University of Chicago and at the Econometric Society Meetings in New York, December 1982, forthcoming in Journal of Econometrics, March 1983c.

Nakamura, A. and M. Nakamura. "On the Continuity Over Time and the Cross-sectional Distributions of Employment, Hours of Work and Earnings." Paper presented at the Canadian Economic Association Meetings in Vancouver,

June, 1983, revised 1984.

Nakamura, A., M. Nakamura, D. Cullen, D. Grant and H. Orcutt. Employment and Earnings of Married Females. Statistics Canada, 1979.

Nakamura, A., M. Nakamura and D. Cullen. "Job Opportunities, the Offered Wage, and the Labor Supply of Married Women." American Economic Review, 1979, 787-805.

Nelson, R.R. and S.G. Winter. "Neoclassical vs. Evolutionary Theories of Economic Growth: Critique and Prospectives." Institute of Public Policy Studies Discussion Paper No. 46, University of Michigan, 1973.

Nerlove, M. "Expectations, Plans, and Realizations in Theory and Practice." Econometrica, 1983, 1251-1279.

Nerlove, M. and T.P. Schultz. Love and Life Between the Censuses: A Model of Family Decision Making in Puerto Rico, 1950-1960. RM6322-AID, RAND Corp., Calif., 1970.

Oppenheimer, V. The Female Labor Force in the United States: Demographic and Economic Factors Governing Its Growth and Changing Composition. Berkeley, 1970.

Orcutt, G.H. "A New Type of Socio-Economic System." Review of Economics and Statistics, 1957, 773-797.

Orcutt, G.H. "Simulation of Economic Systems." American Economic Review, 1960.

Orcutt, G.H. "Structural Modeling, Joint Conditional Probability Functions and Recursive Regressions." Forthcoming in M.L. King and D.E.A. Giles (Eds.), Specification Analysis in the Linear Model, 1982.

Orcutt, G.H., S. Caldwell and R. Wertheimer II. Policy Exploration Through Microanalytic Simulation. Urban Institute, Washington, D.C., 1976.

Orcutt, G.H. and J. Edwards. "Should Aggregation Prior to Estimation Be the Rule." The Review of Economics and Statistics, 1969.

Orcutt, G.H. and A. Glazer. "Microanalytical Modeling and Simulation." In B. Bergmann, G. Eliasson and G.H. Orcutt (Eds.), Micro Simulation-Models, Methods and Applications, IUI Conference reports, 1980:1, Stockholm: Almquist and Wilksell International, 1980.

Orcutt, G., M. Greenberger, J. Korbel, and A. Rivlin. Microanalysis of Socioeconomic Systems: A Simulation Study. Harper & Brothers, 1961.

Orcutt, G.H., A. Nakamura and M. Nakamura. "Poverty Research on Family Determination of Labor Income." In Poverty and Public Policy: An Evaluation of Social Science Research, Schenkman Publishing Co., 1980.

Orcutt, G.H., H. Watts and J. Edwards. "Data Aggregation and Information Loss." The American Economic Review, 1968.

Park, S.B. "Some Sampling Properties of Minimum Expected Loss Estimators of Structural Coefficients." Journal of Econometrics, 1982, 295-311.

Parnes, H., J. Shea, R. Spitz and F. Zeller. Dual Careers. Vol. 1, Manpower Research Monograph No. 21, U.S. Department of Labor, 1970.

Perlman, R. Labor Theory. Wiley, 1969.

Phelps, E.S. "The Statistical Theory of Racism and Sexism." American Economic Review, 1972, 659-661.

Polacheck, S.W. "Occupational Self-Selection: A Human Capital Approach to Sex Differences in Occupational Structure." Review of Economics and Statistics, 1981, 60-69.

Research Seminar in Quantitative Economics. Malthus 1.05: The Michigan Annual Model of the U.S. Economy. University of Michigan, June 1982.

Reynolds, R.A. "Posterior Odds for the Hypothesis of Independence Between Stochastic Regressors and Disturbances." International Economic Review, 1982, 479-490.

Roberts, H.V. "Statistical Biases in the Measurement of Employment Discrimination." In E.R. Livernash (Ed.), Comparable Worth: Issues and Alternatives, Equal Employment Advisory Council, Washington, D.C., 1980, 173-195.

References

Robinson, C. and N. Tomes. "Family Labor Supply and Fertility: A Two-Regime Model." Canadian Journal of Economics, 1982, 706-734.
Robinson, C. and N. Tomes. "More on the Labor Supply of Canadian Women." Canadian Journal of Economics, forthcoming, 1985.
Rosen, H.S. "Taxes in a Labor Supply Model with Joint Wage-Hours Determination." Econometrica, 1976, 485-507.
Rosenzweig, M. and K. Wolpin. "Life-Cycle Labor Supply and Fertility: Causal Inferences from Household Models." Journal of Political Economy, 1980, 328-348.
Ross, H.L. and I. Sawhill. Time of Transition: The Growth of Families Headed by Women. Urban Institute, Washington, D.C., 1975.
Sadowsky, G. MASH: A Computer System for Microanalytic Simulation for Policy Exploration. Urban Institute, Washington, D.C., 1977.
Sawa, T. "The Mean Square Error of a Combined Estimator and Numerical Comparison with the 2SLS Estimator." Journal of Econometrics, 1973, 115-132.
Sawa, T. "Almost Unbiased Estimators in Simultaneous Equations Systems." International Economics Review, 1973a, 97-106.
Schulz, J. et al. Private Pension Policy Simulation. U.S. Department of Labor, 1980.
Schultz, T.P. "Birth Rate Changes over Space and Time: A Study of Taiwan." In T.W. Schultz (Ed.), Economics of the Family: Marriage, Children, and Human Capital, University of Chicago Press, 1973.
Schultz, T.P. "The Influence of Fertility on Labor Supply of Married Women: Simultaneous Equation Estimates." Research in Labor Economics, 1978, 273-351.
Schultz, T.P. "Estimating Labor Supply Functions for Married Women." In J.P. Smith (Ed.), Female Labor Supply: Theory and Estimation, Princeton University Press, 1980, 25-89.
Schultz, T.W. "Investment in Human Capital." American Economic Review, 1961, 1-17.
Schultz, T.W. "Investment in Human Beings." Journal of Political Economy, 1962, 1-157.
Schultz, T.W. (Ed.). Economics of the Family: Marriage, Children and Human Capital. University of Chicago Press, 1974.
Sen, J. Women's Participation in the Canadian Labour Market and Barriers to Their Unionization. Ph.D. dissertation, University of Toronto, 1984.
Sharir, S. "The Income-Leisure Model: A Diagrammatic Extension." Economic Record, 1975, 93-98.
Silk, L. Economics in Plain English: All You Need to Know About Economics - in Language Anyone Can Understand. Simon and Schuster, 1978.
Smith, J.P. (Ed.). Female Labor Supply: Theory and Estimation. Princeton University Press, 1980.
Social Security Administration. "A Model for the Analysis and Simulation of Social Securitiy (MODASS)." U.S. Department of Health and Human Services, Washington, D.C., 1980.
Spence, M. Market Signaling: Informational Transfer in Hiring and Related Screening Processes. Harvard University Press, 1974.
Statistics Canada. Public Use Sample Tapes User Documentation. March 1975.
Sweet, J.A. Women in the Labor Force. Seminar Press, Inc., 1973.
Swidinsky, R. "Minimum Wages and Teenage Unemployment." Canadian Journal of Economics, 1980, 158-171.
Taubman, P. and T. Wales. "Education as an Investment and a Screening Device." In F.T. Juster (Ed.), Education, Income and Human Behavior, McGraw-Hill, 1975, 95-121.
Thurow, L.C. "The Changing Structure of Unemployment: An Econometric Study." Review of Economics and Statistics, 1965, 137-149.
Thurow, L.C. "Education and Economic Inequality." The Public Interest, Summer 1972, 66-81.
Thurow, L.C. Generating Inequality. Basic Books, 1975.
Toikka, R.S. "A Markovian Model of Labor Market Decisions by Workers." American

Economic Review, 1976, 821-834.
U.S. Department of Commerce. Public Use Samples of Basic Records from the 1970 Census. Bureau of the Census, 1972.
U.S. Department of Commerce. Statistical Abstract of the United States 1982-83. Bureau of Census, 1983.
U.S. Department of Health, Education and Welfare. User's Manual for POPSIM. National Center for Health Statistics, 1973.
Viscusi, W.K. "Sex Differences in Worker Quitting." Review of Economics and Statistics, 1980, 388-398.
Wachtel, P. "The Returns to Investment in Higher Education: Another View." In F.T. Juster (Ed.), Education, Income and Human Behavior, McGraw-Hill, 1975, 151-170.
Wales, T.J. and A.D. Woodland. "Sample Selectivity and the Estimation of Labor Supply Functions." International Economic Review, 1980, 437-468.
White, J. Women and Unions. Canadian Advisory Council on the Status of Women, Ottawa, 1980, pp. 46-49.
Zedlewski, S. Simulation of Social Security. Urban Urban Institute Working Paper No. 980-4, Washington, D.C., 1974.
Zellner, A. An Introduction to Bayesian Inference in Econometrics. Wiley, 1971.
Zellner, A. "Estimation of Functions of Population Means and Regression Coefficients Including Structural Coefficients: A Minimum Expected Loss (MELO) Approach." Journal of Econometrics, 1978, 127-158.
Zellner, A. "Statistical Analysis of Econometric Models." Journal of the American Statistical Association , 1979, 628-643.
Zellner, A. "A Note on the Relationship of Minimum Expected Loss and Other Structural Coefficient Estimators." Review of Economics and Statistics, 1980, 482-484.
Zellner, A. "Bayesian Econometrics." Forthcoming in Econometrica, August, 1983.
Zellner, A., and S.B. Park. "Minimum Expected Loss (MELO) Estimators for Functions of Parameters and Structural Coefficients of Econometric Models." Journal of the American Statistical Association, 1979, 185-193.

Author Index

Adelman, I., 374
Amemiya, T., 3, 59
Arabmazar, A., 275
Arrow, K., 381
Ashenfelter, O., 65
Babiak, H., 65
Becker, G., 3, 11, 191, 380
Ben-Porath, Y., 181
Bergmann,B., 374, 380
Bowen, W.G., 11, 12, 194
Cain, G., 3, 11, 12, 42, 66, 83, 86, 99, 193
Caldwell, S., 13, 379
Carliner, 193
Christ, C.F., 64
Clark, R., 5
Cogan, J., 3, 61
Cole, K.C., 23, 24
Conway, D.A., 66
Corcoran, M., 191, 278
Cullen, D., 12, 59, 81, 181, 191, 192, 193, 194, 276, 292, 293, 381
Dagenais, M.G., 359
DaVanzo, J., 196
Deaton, A., 23, 195
de Beavoir, S., 1
De Tray, D.N., 196
Dooley, M.D., 59, 193
Duleep, H. (see H. Orcutt)
Duncan, G., 68
Durbin, J., 61, 65
Edwards, J., 8
Ehrenberg, R.G., 195, 358
Einstein, A., 197
Eliasson, G., 13
Ellwood, D.T., 192
Fama, E.F., 65
Fand, R., 66
Feldstein, M., 67,192
Finegan, T.A., 11, 12, 194
Fisher, R.A., 379
Flinn, C., 314, 358
Fraker, S., 61, 191, 381
Freeman, R.B., 192

Friedman, M., 3
Fuchs, V., 1
Fuller, W.A., 67
Garfinkel, I., 196
Gintis, H., 5, 61, 191
Glazer, A., 13, 277
Glick, P., 5
Goldberger, A.S., 3, 66, 274
Gould, S.J., 5
Gramm, W.I., 145
Grant, D., 12
Greenberg, D.H., 196
Greenberger, M. 13
Greene, W.H., 66
Griliches, Z., 65, 66, 379
Gronau, R., 3
Gross, E., 381
Gunderson, M., 381
Hall, R.E., 12, 61, 190, 191
Hausman, J., 61
Heckman, J.J., 3, 11, 12, 16, 17, 18, 20, 37, 59, 60, 66, 67, 72, 73, 81, 82, 191, 193, 194, 197, 199, 274, 275, 276, 278, 291, 293, 314, 358, 363
Institute for Social Research, 61, 62, 63, 68, 277, 291
Johnson, N.L., 81
Johnson, T.R., 12, 61
Johnston, J., 64
Jones, E.B., 60
Juster, F.T., 374
Kalachek, E.D., 61
Kamalich, R.F., 66
Kiefer, N., 318
Killingsworth, M., 133, 181, 182, 196, 292
Kmenta, J., 64, 67
Korbel, J., 13
Kotz, S., 81
Kreps, J., 5
Kuznets, S., 67
Landes, E.M., 11
Larson, 61
Lazear, E., 129

Lewis, H.G., 3
Lin, K., 67
Long, C.D., 11, 60
Lowe, 381
Macurdy, T., 73, 191, 192
Malinvaud, E., 64, 65, 66
Mangasarian, O.L., 81
Massy, W.F., 276
McDonald, G., 67
Medoff, J.L., 192
Merrilees, W.J., 381
Meyer, R.H., 192
Michael, R.T., 11, 191
Mincer, J., 3, 11, 83, 191, 192, 193, 195, 275, 380
Montgomery, D.B., 276
Morgan, J., 68
Morimune, K., 67
Morrison, D.G., 276
Muellbauer, J., 23, 195
Nagar, A.L., 67
Nakamura, A., 11, 12, 13, 17, 18, 19, 59, 60, 61, 67, 68, 80, 81, 82, 181, 191, 192, 193, 194, 195, 275, 276, 292, 358, 359, 381
Nakamura, M., 11, 12, 13, 17, 18, 19, 59, 60, 61, 67, 68, 80, 81, 82, 181, 191, 192, 193, 194, 195, 275, 276, 292, 358, 359, 381
Nerlove, M., 379
Neumann, G., 318
Newton, I., 24
Norton, A., 5
Ofek, H., 11
Oppenheimer, V., 381
Orcutt, G.H., 8, 13, 66, 277, 379
Orcutt, H. (now H. Duleep), 12
Park, S.B., 67
Parnes, H., 68
Pencavel, J.H., 12, 61
Perlman, 195
Phelps, 381
Polachek, S., 66, 191, 275, 380
Raines, F.Q., 61
Research Seminar in Quantitative Economics, 62
Reynolds, R.A., 67
Rivlin, A., 13
Roberts, H.V., 66
Robinson, C., 67, 183, 193
Rosen, H.S., 3, 59, 60
Rosenzweig, M., 193
Ross, H.L., 190

Sadowsky, G., 13
Sawa, T., 67
Sawhill, I., 190
Schmidt, P., 285
Schulz, J.H., 9
Schultz, T.P., 3, 4, 11, 12, 192, 193, 196
Schultz, T.W., 3, 11
Sen, J., 381
Sharir, S., 195
Shea, J., 68
Silk, L., 68
Singer, B., 67
Smith, J.D., 13
Smith, J.P., 2, 66, 81
Smith, R.S., 195, 358
Social Security Administration, 13
Spence, M., 12
Spitz, R., 68
Stafford, F., 374
Sweet, J.A., 100, 190
Taubman, P., 5
Thurow, L.C., 5, 61, 191
Toikka, R.S., 359
Tomes, N., 183, 193
Tukey, J., 379, 380
U.S. Department of Commerce, 11, 276
U.S. Department of Health, Education and Welfare, 13
Wachtel, P., 191, 380
Wales, T., 5, 275
Watts, H., 8
Wertheimer II, R., 13, 379
White, J., 381
Willis, R.J., 11
Winter, S., 20
Wise, D.A., 192
Wolpin, K., 193
Woodland, A., 275
Zedlewski, S., 13
Zeller, F., 68
Zellner, A., 8, 65, 66, 67, 379, 380

Subject Index

Added worker effect, 159
AFDC, see Aid to Families with Dependent Children
Age dummies, see Retirement Age dummies
Age variable, 28, 85, 86, 101-115, 229-234
  coefficient estimates
    for Dummy Split and Inertia Models, 202-204
    for men, 104-108
    for Models A, B, C and Inertia Model, 229-230
  conclusions for, 114-115
  impacts
    for hypothetical women for Models A, B, C and Inertia Model of, 230-234
    on probability of and duration of unemployment, 344-348
  Inertia Model
    coefficient estimates for women, 101-104
    impacts for hypothetical women of, 108-114
    with work experience variables, 286-287
  as proxy for, 190
  sample means for, 48, 328
  simulation results for partition based on, 255-257
Aid to Families with Dependent Children, see also Other income variables
  dummy for receipt of benefits from, 29, 87
Annual hours
  means for, 56
  other studies including lagged, 61
  variables in PSID for, 61
Anticipated real hourly return to work, 316
  relationship to offered wage, 316-317, 318

Asking wage, 17-18, 25, 70
  deflation of, 71
  dependence on offered wage of, 81
  estimation of equations for, 72
  evaluated for nonparticipation, 317
  evaluation at equilibrium hours of, 72
  indifference version of Standard Model, 73, 74
  in Inertia Model, 25
  in Standard Model, 71
Attachment to labor force
  measure of strength of, 79, 164
Autoregressive
  parameters, 74, 76
  processes, 74, 76, 82
Autonomy, 64
Auxiliary equation, 33, 38
Average differences for actual and simulated annual averages
  definition for, 215
  example of, 215
AW, 316, see also Anticipated real hourly return to work

Baby dummy, 28, 86, see also Child status variables
  definition for, 62
Bayesian approach, 380
Bias, 30-40, 269
  corrections in this study for, 34-40
  costs of, 33
  costs of remedies for, 30
  judging the seriousness of, 33-34
  meaning of corrections for, 38-40
  problems of, 7
  in reduced form sense, 32
  in structural sense, 35-36
  tradeoffs with variance, 30
  types of remedies for, 36
  use of simulation methods for detecting, 34
  versus errors of measurement

499

problems, 66
weight in mean square error of, 65
Bias correction
  of first type, 36-37
  of second type, 36-37
Biased predictions, relationship to coefficient biases, 65

Censored population, 79
Censored sample, 71, 72, 73
  estimation results for men with, 196
Censoring, 44
  on basis of lagged work behavior, 76
Changed circumstances, see Structural change
Change in husband's income, 29, 87, see also Other income variables
  unanticipated, 152
Child status, multidimensional nature of, 143
Child status variables, 28, 86, 141-152, 237-243
  attempts to capture child status more fully with, 144-145, 192
  coefficient estimates
    for Dummy, Split and Inertia Models for, 204-205
    for men for, 151
    for Models A, B, C and Inertia Models for, 237-241
  conclusions for, 151-152
  end-point problems in defining, 143-144
  impacts
    for hypothetical women for Models A, B, C and Inertia Model of, 241-243
    on probability of and duration of unemployment of, 349-353
  Inertia Model
    coefficient estimates for women for, 146, 147-148
    impacts for hypothetical women of, 146-147, 148-151
  linearity problems in defining, 143-144
  sample means for, 51, 333-334
  sensitivity of simulation results to, 295-298
  simulation results for partition based on, 255
Chi-square statistic for goodness-of-fit, 220, see also Pseudo

chi-square statistic
  for comparing fit of alternative models, 276
  Heckman's usage of, 276
Cochrane-Orcutt autoregressive transformations, 74
Combined estimator, 67
Compensation per manhour, 62
Condition labor supply function, 181
Condition
  for participation in week, 317
  for unemployed, 317
  for work in week, 317
  for work in year in difference version of Standard Model, 74-75, 79-80
  for work in year in Inertia Model, 26-27
  for work in year in Standard Model, 70-71
Confidence intervals, 41
Consistent, see also Bias; Unbiased estimator
  estimation, 74
  estimator, 31
Continuing hours
  definition for, 56, 84
  effects of wage change on, 183-186
  sample means for, 56
Continuing wage rates
  definition, 56, 84
  means for, 56
Costs
  fixed, 3
  of participation, 317
  unobservable, 61
  variable, 61
Cross-sectional data
  augmented by recall information, 7, 18
  definition of, 43
  results based on, 59
Current wage variable, 87
  alternative sets of coefficient estimates for women and men for, 186-189
  coefficient estimates
    for Dummy, Split and Inertia Models, 210
    for men, 183
  conclusions for, 189, 190
  Inertia Model
    coefficient estimates for women, 183
    estimated with restricted samples, 285

Subject Index

impacts for hypothetical women, 183-186
Cutoff value, 273-274, 312

Data
  advantages of recall, 224
  deficiencies of, 23
  suggestions for collection of, 7, 377-378
Data base for this study, 42-45
Demographic categories
  definitions for, 44
  examples for, 44-45
Disability dummy, 29, 86, 104-108
  coefficient estimates for men, 104-108
  conclusions for, 114
  impacts on probability of and duration of unemployment of, 347-348
  sample means for, 50, 331
Disaggregated data, see Micro data
Discouraged worker effect, 158-159, 163
Discouraged workers, 313
Doubly censored population, 77, 79
Dummy for currently married, 29, 85, see also Marital status variables
  definition for, 63
Dummy for divorced or separated, 29, 85, see also Marital status variables
Dummy for living with parents, 29, 86, 133-141
  coefficient estimates for men, 139-140
  conclusions, 140-141
  impacts on probability of and duration of unemployment, 349
  Inertia Model
    coefficient estimates for women, 136
    impacts for hypothetical women, 137-139
  as proxy for financial assistance from parents, 63
  sample means for, 51, 332-333
Dummy for married in previous year, 29, 85, see also Marital status variables
Dummy Model, 199-200
  definition of, 199-200
  data requirements for, 200, 210
Dummy for never worked since 18 years of age, 285, 292, see also Marital status variables
Dummy for student status, 29, 86, 133-141
  coefficient estimates for men, 139-140
  conclusions, 140-141
  impacts on probability of and duration of unemployment, 349
  Inertia Model
    coefficient estimates for women, 135-136
    impacts for hypothetical women, 137-139
  reason for lagging, 63
  sample means for, 51, 332-333
Dummy for unemployed in previous year
  definition of, 356
  impacts on probability of and duration of unemployment in current year, 356-357
Dummy for widowed, 29, 85, see also Marital status variables
Dynamic versus static models, 315-316
DYNASIM, 13, see also Microanalytic simulation model

E, 24, 71, see also Macroeconomic variables
  variables included in, 28
Economics as a science, weakness of, 68
Education, 35
  effects on tastes of, 191
  multicollinearity problems associated with inclusion in hours equations of variable for, 191
  reasons for including in hours equations variable for, 191
  as screening factor, 4, 61, 129, 191
Education variable, 28, 86, 124-133, 237
  coefficient estimates
    for Dummy, Split and Inertia Models, 202-204
    for men, 127-129
    for Models A, B, C and Inertia Model, 237
  conclusions for, 132-133
  impacts
    for hypothetical women for Models A, B, C and Inertia Model of, 237
    on probability of and duration of

unemployment of, 349
Inertia Model
  coefficient estimates for women, 125-127
  impacts for hypothetical women of, 129-132
  sample means for, 48-50, 331
Effects of explanatory variables, 83-84, 85-87
  cumulative, 36-37, 193
  current, 36-37
  direct, 37, 88
  indirect, 88
  in lifetime context, 193
  long-run, 192, 193
  proxy, 32-33, 35-38, 275
  secondary, 88
  short-run, 192-193
Employment behavior
  continuity of, 18
  definition of, 18
Employment rates, Canadian and U.S., 12
Equilibrium position, 20
Errors of measurement problem, 66
Evolutionary theories, 20-22, 27
Expected loss, 65
Explanatory variables, 85-87, see also Effects of explanatory variables
  composite nature of, 35-36, 269
Extreme wage estimates
  implications of not dropping, 277
  problem of, 245-246

Feminist issues, 4
First difference transformations, 74
First difference version of Standard model, 17-19
Fixed
  costs, 3
  effects models, 60
  effects terms, 75, see also Person-specific terms; Unobservables
Forecasts of work behavior of women, importance of fertility forecasting for, 296
Full-time work
  accumulation of Social Security benefits over years of, 218
  definition for, 218
  wage response of hours for, 59
Future
  expectations, 73

offered wage distributions, 134

Goodness-of-fit of simulated to actual distributions, 40

h, see Hours of work
Heckman model, 17
Heckman-type conceptual model of work behavior, 314-315, see also Standard Model
Heterogeneity, 291, 293
Heteroscedastic error term, 81
Hicksian composite good, 69
Hourly wage rates
  means for, 56
  variables in PSID for, 61
Hours of work
  annual, 28
  as choice variable, 22
  determination of, 18, 71, 78, 317
  reduced form expression for, 81
  response to wage change depending on hours worked of, 195
  variable
    in difference version of Standard model, 79, 80
    in Inertia Model, 26
    in Standard Model, 73
Human capital, 3, 35, 65
Husband's income, 29, 87, see also Other income variables
  permanent, 193
  transitory component of, 193
Hypothesis testing
  unsuitability of ridge regression for, 67
  use of specification error tests in, 67
Hypothetical women, 84-91
  calculation of impacts for, 88-89
  characteristics of, 89-90
  continuing work behavior of, 90
  starting work behavior of, 88

I, see also Other income variables
  variables included in, 28, 69
Imputed wages, see also Wage variable, instrumental
  for men, 196
Income constraints, 69
Income effects, 3, 181, 195, 196
Income of wife, 64, 87, see also Other income variables

reason for including value for
    previous year of, 63-64
variable for, 29
Index for probability of work
    in difference version of Standard
        Model, 76, 80
    in Inertia Model, 26
    in Standard Model, 71
Inequality decision rule, 74, 76
Inertia Model, 15, 17-27
    coefficient estimates for, 83-190
    data for, 43, 200, 210
    formal statement of, 24-27
    inadequacy of, for men, 222-223
    pseudo R^2 and R^2 values for, 287-288
    reestimated
        including work experience variables, 283-291
        with restricted sample, 283-291
    unique features of, 197
Inference, 364-368
    as carried out in this study, 41-42, 84
    a priori information needed for, 66
    role of replication in, 7
    use of simulation in, 7
    using traditional tests of significance, 7, 9
In-sample data, 43-44
    subgroups of, 44
In-sample period, years for, 35
Instrumental wage equations, see also
    Wage variable, instrumental
    low R^2 values for, 186
Instrumental variable, loss of efficiency
    with, 65, see also Bias; wage
    variable, instrumental
Intertemporal trade-offs, 134

JCMH, 62
Job opportunities
    Canadian and U.S., 12
    indices, 194

Labor force, female participation in, 2
Labor force behavior, 3
    multistate models of, 358-359
Labor markets, 7
    women as casual participants in, 314
Labor supply curve, 195
    backward sloping, 195
    negatively sloped, 195
Lagged hours of work variable, 87, 164-166
coefficient estimates
    for men, 164-166
    conclusions, 171-173
Inertia model
    coefficient estimates for women, 164
    impacts for hypothetical women, 166-171
Lagged wage variable, 87, 164-173
coefficient estimates
    for men, 164-166
    conclusions, 171-173
Inertia model
    coefficient estimates for women, 164
    impacts for hypothetical women, 166-171
Lagged unemployment variables, 356
Leisure time, 69, 181, 195
Life cycle, approach to research, 23
Limits to choice, 23
ln w, see Offered wage
ln w*, see Asking wage
Logit models, 82
Log wage variable, see Wage variable

Macroeconomic variables, 158-164, 243
coefficient estimates
    for Dummy, Split and Inertia
        Models for, 208
    for men for, 163
    for Models A, B, C and Inertia
        Model for, 243
conclusions for, 163-164
first differences of, 19, 60
impacts
    for hypothetical women for
        Models A, B, C and Inertia
        Model of, 243
    on probability of and duration of
        unemployment of, 354-356
Inertia model
    coefficient estimates for women
        for, 159-162
    estimated with restricted samples, 284-285
    impacts for hypothetical women
        of, 163
    with work experience variables, 286
measured
    at national level, 19
    at state or provincial level, 60
multicollinearity problems with, 19

sample means for, 54-55, 337
Marginal wage rate, see also Wage
variable
concept of, 21-22
effect of hours of work on, 22
relationship to average wage, 22
Marital sorting, effects of, 152
Marital status, collection of recall
information for, 190
Marital status variables, 29, 85-86,
91-100, 225-229
coefficient estimates
for Dummy, Split and Inertia
Models for, 200-202
for men for, 100
for Models A, B, C and Inertia
Model for, 225
conclusions, 100
impacts
for hypothetical women for
Models A, B, C and Inertia
Model, 225-229
on probability of and duration of
unemployment of, 338-344
Inertia model
coefficient estimates for women
for, 91-93
impacts for hypothetical women
of, 93-99
sample means for, 45-48, 325-328
sensitivity of simulation results to,
298-306
simulation results for partition based
on, 257-259
Maximizing behavior, 27
Mean square error, 65
Meal values of variables, 45-59
in unemployment data base, 324-337
Michigan Panel Study of Income
Dynamics, 42-44, 68
weights for, 43-44, 68
Microanalytic simulation
approach to forecasting, 9
research strategy, 8-9
distributional comparisons and, 8
Microanalytic simulation model, 9, 277
AFDC benefits in, 63
auxiliary models for, 9
generation of earnings of husbands
and wives in, 64
initial population for, 9
labor force module for, 9, 246-247
macroeconomic variables in, 60
modules of, 9
operating characteristics for, 9
original, 12-13

simulation population for, 9
Social Security benefits in, 63
taxes in, 19
welfare income in, 63
work experience variables in, 292
Micro data, 6, 12
consideration of bias problems using,
31
MICROSIM, 13
MODASS, 13
Model A, 245
coefficient estimates for, 224-244
definition for, 224
impacts on hypothetical women for,
224-244
Model B, 245
coefficient estimates for, 224-244
definition for, 224
impacts on hypothetical women for,
224-244
Model C, 246-247
coefficient estimates for, 224-244
definition for, 224
impacts on hypothetical women for,
224-244
as new labor force module, 246-247

National Longitudinal Survey of Work
Experience, 68
National unemployment rate, 28, 87,
see also Macroeconomic
variables
definition for, 62
problems with variable for, 275
National wage index, see also
Macroeconomic variables
definition for, 62
Natural experiments, 65
Negative change in husband's income,
29, 87, see also Other income
variables
Neoclassical theory, 20
Nonmarket time, 69, 181, 195
Not in labor force, definition of, 314
Number of children in age brackets,
62
Number of children younger than 18
variable, 28, 86
source for, 62
Number of years of work since 18
variable, 79, 285, see also
Work experience

Offered wage, 17-18, 24, 69, 70, see

Subject Index

also Wage variable
  dependence on hours of work of, 21-22, 59, 60
  full impact of change in, 181
Old sample, 283
One-period models, 134
Other income variables, 25, 29, 87, 243
  coefficient estimates
    for Dummy, Split and Inertia Models for, 206-207
    for men for, 57
    for Models A, B, C and Inertia Model for, 243
  conclusions for, 157-158
  deflation of, 63, 71
  impacts
    for hypothetical women for Models A, B, C and Inertia Model of, 243
    on probability of and duration of unemployment of, 353-354
  Inertia model
    coefficient estimates for women for, 153-154
    impacts for hypothetical women of, 154
    with work experience variables, 286
  omitted from this study, 63
  sample means for, 53-54, 334-337
  sensitivity of simulation results to, 296-298
  simulation results for partitions based on, 259-261, 265-268
Out-of sample period, years for, 270
Own log wage variable, see Current log wage variable

Panel data, 18, 42
  definition of, 6, 43
Participation in labor force, definition of, 313
Participation rates, 11
Partitions of demographic groups, 254-255
Part-time work
  definition for, 218
  wage response of hours for, 59
Pooled data
  definition of, 43
Prediction checks, 34, see also Simulation checks
Preferences, 23, see also Tastes and preferences

Pretesting, 67
Price variables, 21
Probabilities of continuing work, 84
Probabilities of starting work, 84
Probabilities of work, point estimates for, 45
Probit analysis, 27
Probit index, 27
Proportion of years worked since 18 variable, 79, 285, 295, see also Work experience
Proxy, 32-33
  for heterogeneity, 275
Pseudo chi-square statistic, definition for, 220
PSID, see Michigan Panel Study of Income Dynamics

Race dummy, 28, 86, 115-124, 234-236
  coefficient estimates
    for Dummy, Split and Inertia Models for, 202-204
    for men, 118
    for Models A, B, C and Inertia Model, 234
  conclusions for, 123-124
  impacts
    for hypothetical women for Models A, B, C and Inertia Model, 234-236
    on probability of and duration of unemployment of, 348-349
  Inertia model
    coefficient estimates for women, 115-118
    impacts for hypothetical women of, 118-123
    with work experience variables, 286
  sample means for, 48, 328-331
  sensitivity of simulation results to, 310-312
  source for, 62-63
  simulation results for partition based on, 261-265
Random effects models, 59-60
Reduced form
  parameters, 64
  relationship, 64
  unbiasedness, 31-34, see also Bias
Reference week, 313
Restricted data samples, 283
Retirement age dummies, 28-29, 86, 104-108
  coefficient estimates for men,

104-108, 114
  impacts on probability of and
      duration of unemployment of,
      347-348
  sample means for, 50, 331
Retirement effect, 153, 157, 193
Reverse regression, 66
RUG, 62

Schooling, see also Education
  systematic components of, 66
Scientific method, role of replication
    in, 6
Secondary
  workers, 158
  work force, 1-2
Selection bias, 3, 37, 60, 66, 81, 274
  in unemployment model, 319
Selection bias term
  coefficient estimates
    for Dummy, Split and Inertia
        Models, 209-210
    for men, 174-177
    ranked by employment rates,
        175-176
  conclusions for, 180
  definition of, in Inertia Model, 26
  Inertia model
    coefficient estimates for women,
        174-177
    impacts for hypothetical women,
        177-180
  total impacts of, 173-174
  Sensitivity of simulation results for
      Inertia Model, 294-312
    to changes
      in child status variables, 295-298
      in husband's income variables,
          296-298
    to marital status and changes in
        marital status, 298-306
    to race-specific differences in
        characteristics and estimated
        responses, 310-312
    to sex-specific differences in
        characteristics and estimated
        responses, 306-309
Shadow price of nonmarket time, see
    Asking wage
Signalling hypothesis, 12
Significance tests
  estimates of standard errors needed
      for, 40
  purpose of, 40
  use in this study of, 41, 84

Simulation checks, 34, 43-44
  with aggregate time series data, 34
  in-sample, 34-35, 43-44, 68, 198,
      275
  by macroeconomic model builders, 34
  out-of-sample, 34-35, 43-44, 68, 198,
      269-272, 275
  using
    distributional comparisons, 34
    predicted expected values, 35
  for subgroups, 253-269
Simulation comparisons
  for annual employment rate, 212-213
  for average
    annual hours, 213-214
    annual income, 214-215
    wage, 213
  based
    on annual averages, 212-217, 247
    on income cumulated over years,
        importance of, 212, 219
    on pooled distributions, 217-218,
        247-248
  for Dummy, Split and Inertia
      Models, 210-224
  for earnings histories, importance of,
      212, 219
  for income cumulated over 7 years,
      219-220, 250
  justification for, 210-211, 212
  for Models A, B, C and Inertia
      Model, 244-253
  for pooled distributions for annual
      hours, 217-218, 247-248
  for pooled distributions for annual
      income, 218, 248
  rankings
    based on average differences for
        actual and simulated annual
        averages, 215-217
    based on pseudo chi-square
        statistic, 220-223, 250-253
  sensitivity to extreme wage estimates
      of, 272-274
  for years
    of part-time or full-time work,
        218-219, 249-250
    of work over 7-year period, 218,
        248
Simulation comparisons for demographic
    subgroups, 253-269, see also
    Simulation comparisons for
    partitions
  reasons for, 254
  summary of results for, 268-269
Simulation comparisons for partitions

Subject Index   507

by age, 255-257
by child status, 255
by declines in husband's income, 259-261
by marital status, 257-259
by race, 261-265
Simulation data set, in-sample, 211
Simulation methods of specification analysis, 7, see also Simulation checks
using comparisons
for actual and simulated income cumulated over years, 219
for demographic subgroups, 253-254
Simulation methods, 18
Simulation population, 43, 211
in-sample, 211, 270
justification for removing individuals with extreme wage estimates from, 273-274
out-of-sample, 211, 270
Simulation procedure, 211-212
treatment of extreme wage estimates in, 198-199
Simulations results for partitions based on receipt of AFDC or Social Security benefits, 265-268
Social Security, see also Other income variables
auxiliary models for calculating financial flows for, 9, 13
dummy for receipt of benefits from, 29, 87
Specification error tests, 9, 33
Split Model, 200
data requirements for, 200, 210
definition of, 200
Standard Model, 17-18, 69-73, 119
data requirements for, 200, 210
definition of, 73
failure to capture continuity of work behavior of, 81-82
Stars on coefficient estimates, 41, 84
Starting hours
definition for, 56, 84
effects of wage change on, 183-186
sample means for, 56
Starting wage rates
definition, 56, 84
means for, 56
State average hourly wage rate in manufacturing, 194
State dependence, true, 291, 293
Structural
change, 32, 64, 254

parameters, 64, 66
relationship, 31, 64
unbiasedness, 31-34, 38, see also Bias
Substitution effects, 3, 180-181

Tastes and preferences, 17, 73
effects on work behavior of, 4
Tax laws
Canadian and U.S., 12, 19
treatment in this study of, 19
Time constraints, 69
Tobit-type specification, 16
Truncated normal distribution, 81

Unbiased estimator, see also Bias
analytic proofs of, 33
assumptions for, 30, 39
definitions of, 30, 64
meaning of, 31
Unbiased estimators of standard errors, problems of obtaining, 41, 67
Uncensored population, 79, see also Censored population; Censored sample
Uncompensated wage elasticity of hours of work, 87-88, 181-183, 189, 195-196
estimated
from Canadian data, 183
from experimental data, 181-182
from hours equations including or excluding variables for work experience, 290, 292-293
from nonexperimental data, 181-183, 189
for men, 181, 189, 196
sensitivity to estimation method of estimates for, 186-189, 196
for women, 181-183, 189
Unconditional labor supply function, 181
Underemployed, 313
Unemployed, definition of, 313-314
Unemployment
as choice state, 359
as distinguished from nonparticipation, 314
dynamic considerations in models of, 318
factors affecting probability or duration of, 318-319, 337-358
length of spells of, 318
mean weeks of, 321-324
multiple sample selection problems in

models of, 319
point estimates for probability of, 321
PSID data on, 313, 321
reservation wage models of, 358
as transient state, 359
voluntary nature of, 358
Unemployment behavior, 313-359
effects of unobservable factors on, 321
Unemployment benefit coverage, 314
limiting access of women to, 314
needs of unemployed women for, 336-337
Unemployment data base, 321
Unemployment rate variables, 193-194
national, 194
provincial, 194
state, 194
Unit time period, 171
advantages of annual, 171
problems in studies of unemployment with annual, 316
Unobservable factors, 20, 173
changes in, 19
correlated with observable factors, 19
embedded in lagged hours of work and wage variables, 18
fixed or persistent person-specific, 17-18, 25
Utility function, 69

Variable for number of weeks unemployed in previous year
definition of, 356
impacts on probability of and duration of unemployment in current year, 356-357

w, see Offered wage
w*, see Asking wage
w*(h), 315
w*(h,+), 317
w*(0), 315
w*(0,0), 317
w*(0,+), 320
Wage
cutoff, see Cutoff value
distribution, truncation of generated, 273
equation, justification for log-linear form of, 275
of unskilled labor, 194
Wage variable

advantages of linear versus log, 245-246
definition of, 71
deterministic portion of, 26
in difference version of Standard Model, 78, 80
Durbin rank instrument for, 61, 191
equation for log of, 71
errors-in-variable problems with, 37-38, 186
form of lagged, 60-61
in Inertia Model, 26
instrumental, 20, 28, 61, 62
residual portion of, 38
sensitivity to estimation method of coefficient estimates for, 186-189
in Standard Model, 72
Work, condition for, see Condition
Work behavior
ability of Standard Model to capture continuity of, 73
attachment to previous state of, 15
continuing, 4, 27, 61
continuity of, 4, 9, 11, 12, 18, 80-81, 198
earnings histories characterizing, 9
effects of person-specific unobservables on continuity of, 80
entering, see Work behavior, starting of men, 196
out-of-sample and in-sample characteristics of, 270
over life cycle, 5
starting, 4, 61
Work experience, 25, 192, 278-291
endogeneity of, 291
Heckman's variable for in-sample, 275
importance of collecting recall information for, 278-283, 292
as measured in PSID, 291
missing data in PSID on, 278
question
in 1970 U.S. Census questionnaire on, 276
in 1971 Census of Canada questionnaire on, 275-276
race-specific effects of, 311
variables for, 285, 290-291

Young child dummy, 28, 86
definition for, 62

Z, 24, 71, see also Age; Education variable; Macroeconomic variables; Race
  variables included in, 28
Z^*, 25, 69, see also Age; Child status variables; Marital status variables; Race
  variables included in, 28-29